ReFocus: The Films of Jocelyne Saab

ReFocus: The International Directors Series

Series Editors: Robert Singer, Stefanie Van de Peer and Gary D. Rhodes

Board of Advisors:
Lizelle Bisschoff (Glasgow University)
Stephanie Hemelryck Donald (University of Lincoln)
Anna Misiak (Falmouth University)
Des O'Rawe (Queen's University Belfast)

ReFocus is a series of contemporary methodological and theoretical approaches to the interdisciplinary analyses and interpretations of international film directors, from the celebrated to the ignored, in direct relationship to their respective culture – its myths, values, and historical precepts – and the broader parameters of international film history and theory. The series provides a forum for introducing a broad spectrum of directors, working in and establishing movements, trends, cycles and genres including those historical, currently popular, or emergent, and in need of critical assessment or reassessment. It ignores no director who created a historical space – either in or outside of the studio system – beginning with the origins of cinema and up to the present. ReFocus brings these film directors to a new audience of scholars and general readers of Film Studies.

Titles in the series include:

ReFocus: The Films of Susanne Bier
Edited by Missy Molloy, Mimi Nielsen, and Meryl Shriver-Rice

ReFocus: The Films of Francis Veber
Keith Corson

ReFocus: The Films of Jia Zhangke
Maureen Turim and Ying Xiao

ReFocus: The Films of Xavier Dolan
Edited by Andrée Lafontaine

ReFocus: The Films of Pedro Costa: Producing and Consuming Contemporary Art Cinema
Nuno Barradas Jorge

ReFocus: The Films of Sohrab Shahid Saless: Exile, Displacement and the Stateless Moving Image
Edited by Azadeh Fatehrad

ReFocus: The Films of Pablo Larraín
Edited by Laura Hatry

ReFocus: The Films of Michel Gondry
Edited by Marcelline Block and Jennifer Kirby

ReFocus: The Films of Rachid Bouchareb
Edited by Michael Gott and Leslie Kealhofer-Kemp

ReFocus: The Films of Andrei Tarkovsky
Edited by Sergey Toymentsev

ReFocus: The Films of Paul Leni
Edited by Erica Tortolani and Martin F. Norden

ReFocus: The Films of Rakhshan Banietemad
Edited by Maryam Ghorbankarimi

ReFocus: The Films of Jocelyn Saab: Films, Artworks and Cultural Events for the Arab World
Edited by Mathilde Rouxel and Stefanie Van de Peer

edinburghuniversitypress.com/series/refocint

ReFocus:
The Films of Jocelyne Saab

Films, Artworks and Cultural Events
for the Arab World

Edited by Mathilde Rouxel and
Stefanie Van de Peer

EDINBURGH
University Press

To Beirut

Edinburgh University Press is one of the leading university presses in the UK. We publish academic books and journals in our selected subject areas across the humanities and social sciences, combining cutting-edge scholarship with high editorial and production values to produce academic works of lasting importance. For more information visit our website: edinburghuniversitypress.com

© editorial matter and organisation Mathilde Rouxel and Stefanie Van de Peer, 2021, 2023
© the chapters their several authors, 2021, 2023
All images © Nessim Ricardou-Saab

Edinburgh University Press Ltd
The Tun – Holyrood Road
12 (2f) Jackson's Entry
Edinburgh EH8 8PJ

First published in hardback by Edinburgh University Press 2021

Typeset in 11/13 Ehrhardt MT by
IDSUK (DataConnection) Ltd

A CIP record for this book is available from the British Library

ISBN 978 1 4744 8041 3 (hardback)
ISBN 978 1 4744 8042 0 (paperback)
ISBN 978 1 4744 8043 7 (webready PDF)
ISBN 978 1 4744 8044 4 (epub)

The right of the contributors to be identified as authors of this work has been asserted in accordance with the Copyright, Designs and Patents Act 1988 and the Copyright and Related Rights Regulations 2003 (SI No. 2498).

Contents

List of Figures	vii
Notes on Contributors	ix
Acknowledgements	xiii

Introduction: A Synthesis and Testimony of Jocelyne Saab's Life and Work   1
Mathilde Rouxel and Stefanie Van de Peer

Part I Jocelyne Saab: Fifty Years of Creation in the Turmoil of Arab History

1. Telling the Tale of a World in Turmoil: Conversations with Jocelyne Saab   19
   Olivier Hadouchi
2. On Representing the War as Rupture: Jocelyne Saab and New Lebanese Cinema (1975–90)   37
   Ghada Sayegh
3. Jocelyne Saab's Hanging Gardens: A Multimedia Architecture through Stories and Time   51
   Joan Grandjean
4. A Filmmaker's Words: A Journey through the Archive of Jocelyne Saab's Unfinished Work   70
   Mathilde Rouxel

Part II Film as a Weapon against War and Oblivion

5. From Class Struggle to Sectarian Warfare: Jocelyne Saab's Beirut Trilogy   87
   Giovanni Vimercati

6   Beirut, There Was and There Was Not   97
    Mark R. Westmoreland
7   A Mother and Daughter Reunion: How Jocelyne Saab Shot
    her Last Documentary, *My Name is Mei Shigenobu*   112
    Yomota Inuhiko
8   Jocelyne Saab and CRIFFL: Dismantling Boundaries and
    Making New Routes for Asian Cinema in Lebanon   126
    Némésis Srour

Part III   Liberating the People, Freeing the Body

9   Guerrillas, Border Crossings and Internationalism: The Liberation
    of Non-Arabs in Jocelyne Saab's Early Documentaries   143
    Stefanie Van de Peer
10 'Talking about something much larger': Script Development and
    Creating Metaphor and Meaning in Jocelyne Saab's *Dunia*   159
    Margaret McVeigh
11 The Feminist Cinema of Jocelyne Saab: Women's Relationships
    and the Philosophy of Dance in Four Fiction Feature Films   174
    Maram Soboh
12 Exile, Gender and Empowerment in Jocelyne Saab's Films:
    Gender Café and *One Dollar a Day*   188
    Corinne Fortier
13 Twilight Reflections in Single Frames and Short Sequences   201
    Samirah Alkassim

Part IV   Advocating Poetry

14 *A Suspended Life*: A Cinematic Fall   221
    Marie Chebli
15 The City of Disasters and Dreams: Experiencing Beirut and its
    Urban Geography in Light of Jocelyne Saab's *Beirut, My City*
    and *A Suspended Life*   235
    Gregory Buchakjian
16 Fiction and Voyeurisms: For a Fantasmatic History   247
    Léa Polverini
17 Complete Catalogue of Jocelyne Saab's Artistic Output   262
    Mathilde Rouxel

Index   282

Figures

1.1	Jocelyne Saab and her DOP Olivier Guéneau filming in Western Sahara	9
1.1	Jocelyne Saab with a Sahraoui, playing with the camera	28
2.1	Still from *Beirut, Never Again*	42
2.2	Still from *A Suspended Life*	44
2.3	Still from *A Suspended Life*	46
3.1	Invitation cards for the exhibition openings of *Sense, Icons and Sensitivity* and *Sense, Icons and Sensitivity II*	55
3.2	Exhibition view, *Strange Games and Bridges*, Singapore National Museum	57
3.3	Poster of the first edition of the Biennale of Contemporary Art, Modern and Contemporary Art Museum, Alita	64
5.1	Abandoned chair on the shore, in *Beirut, Never Again*	88
5.2	Women in the siege, in *Beirut, My City*	94
6.1	Leila and Yasmine dwelling in the film set	99
6.2	Leila peruses Mr Farouk's film vault	107
7.1	Mei caressing Saab's hair in *My Name is Mei Shigenobu*	123
7.2	Original manuscript in Japanese of Fusako Shigenobu's 'Mei's Hide-and-Seek'	123
8.1	Poster of the second edition of the Cultural Resistance International Film Festival of Lebanon	137
9.1	Polisario fighters relaxing in the desert and talking to Saab	150
9.2	Young Iranian women discussing the hijab	152
10.1	The heart atop the taxi	164
10.2	*Dunia*, 'From here to there it's mine'	166
10.3	*Dunia*: the final dance	170

11.1	Khouloud wakes up in the book about her life	177
11.2	Leila and Yasmine dress up like actresses	178
12.1	Alexandre Paulikevitch sensually uses his hair while dancing	192
12.2	When an advertisement billboard becomes a home	196
12.3	Sacred images of Syrian child refugees in the port of Beirut	197
13.1	Alexandre Paulikevitch shatters gender codes of 'oriental dance', in *Gender Café*	211
13.2	Cafe goers and Syrian refugees inhabit the same space, one as an image the other does not see, in *One Dollar a Day*	213
13.3	Mei Shigenobu recalls her childhood in Lebanon, in *My Name is Mei Shigenobu*	215
14.1	Samar finds Karim's pink house and enters its inner courtyard	223
14.2	The first image of the film is a silent pan shot of a Beirut cemetery	226
14.3	Inside the pink house, Samar enters a new room with a grid on the floor and is compelled to cross it accordingly	228
15.1	*Abandoned Dwellings. Tableaux*	237
15.2	Still from *A Suspended Life*	240
15.3	Still from *Beirut, My City*	242
16.1	Abu Brahim and Oum Brahim indicate what used to stand in Tel al Zaatar before the bombings, in *Letter from Beirut*	251
16.2	The old lady reading Cavafy's poem 'I Went', in *The Ghosts of Alexandria*	254
16.3	The poet mends Khouloud's heart, in *What's Going On?*	256

Notes on Contributors

Samirah Alkassim is an experimental documentary filmmaker and Assistant Professor of Film at George Mason University. Her films include *What is Natural Contains Variety* (2006), *From Here to There* (2003), *Far From You* (1996), and *trip/ballade* (1993), among other experimental works. Her publications include the co-authored book *The Cinema of Muhammad Malas* (2018), and contributions to *Cinema of the Arab World: New Directions in Theory and Practice* (2020), *The Historical Dictionary of Middle East Cinema*, 2nd edition (forthcoming), *New Cinemas: Journal of Contemporary Film*, *Bidoun* and *Nebula*. She is also co-editor of the Palgrave Studies in Arab Cinema series.

Gregory Buchakjian is director of the School of Visual Arts at Académie Libanaise des Beaux-Arts-Alba. He is an art historian and interdisciplinary visual artist. His exploration of abandoned dwellings led to a PhD dissertation at Paris-Sorbonne (2016), solo exhibitions at Sursock Museum, Beirut (2018) and Villa Empain, Brussels (2019) and the publication *Abandoned Dwellings, A History of Beirut* (2018). He was part of the first Lebanese Pavilion at the 2018 Venice Architecture Biennale and in 2019, he co-organised the 2nd Alba Cinema Encounters 'Filming in Times of War, 1975–1990' for which he produced the installation *Where do Filmmakers go?*

Marie Chebli is Lebanese and living in France, where she studied cinema and is currently pursuing philosophy studies. She started a Deleuzian PhD project on Lebanese cinema under Giorgio Passerone (Lille3). She works as an art and photography teacher in an audio-visual DAT structure. She also contributes to cinema projects like *Little President* by Christophe Clavert, and photography projects like *Sur Mesure* by Danka Hojcusova. She has worked in cinemas in

Lille and was actively engaged in the NGO *Nouvelle Jungle*, which brought immigrants of the Calais Jungle into universities in Lille and promoted film and literature about the immigration experience.

Corinne Fortier is a cultural anthropologist and filmmaker. She is a researcher at the French National Centre of Scientific Research (CNRS), where she won the Bronze Medal 2005, and a member of the Social Anthropology Lab (LAS) (CNRS-EHESS-Collège de France-Universités PSL, Paris). Corinne conducts research in Mauritania and Egypt, as well as on Islamic scriptural sources related to gender, body and sexuality.

Joan Grandjean is a PhD candidate and Assistant at the Arabic Unit, University of Geneva. He started a PhD thesis in 2017, entitled 'What if? Imagining the History of Contemporary Art through Arab "Futurisms"', that studies the use of science fiction in the Arab contemporary art scene. He is a founding member of *Manazir* – Swiss Platform for the Study of Visual Arts, Architecture and Heritage in the MENA Region – and *Manazir Journal*'s editorial assistant. Joan is also a Research Fellow at the University of Geneva and is working with Prof. Silvia Naef on a project entitled 'Cultural Diplomacy at the Palace of Nations in Geneva. A Study of Donations and Gifts from MENA Member States' (Boninchi Foundation Research Grant, January–December 2020).

Olivier Hadouchi is a French independent film curator and researcher. He earned his Doctorate in Film from the Sorbonne Nouvelle University, Paris 3, in 2012. He co-curated the programme 'Jocelyne Saab, les astres de la guerre' with Nicole Brenez at the French Cinematheque, and co-edited the special issue about Jocelyne Saab in *La Furia Umana*, also with Nicole Brenez. He regularly works with international film festivals and has curated film programmes for international art centres and museums. He has published his work in magazines (such as *Third Text*, *CinémAction*, *Something We Africans Got*), and in edited collections such as *Chris Marker: l'homme-monde* (ed. Christine Van Assche, Raymond Bellour and Jean-Michel Frodon) and *Documentary in North Africa & Middle East* (ed. Viola Shafik).

Yomota Inuhiko is a film historian, cultural critic, poet and novelist, the author of dozens of books on a wide range of subjects including films, literature, manga, urbanism, drama and cooking. He taught film studies and comparative literature at Meiji Gakuin University (Tokyo) from 1981 until he retired in 2012. He has taught at Columbia University, Bologna University, Tel Aviv University, Universidade Federal Fluminense (Rio de Janeiro) and Chung Ang University (Seoul). He published *What is Japanese Cinema?* in English (2019) and translated work by Edward Said, Pier Paolo Pasolini and Mahmoud Darwish into Japanese.

Margaret McVeigh is Head of Screenwriting and Contextual Studies at Griffith Film School, Griffith University, Australia. Margaret has worked in the media in Australia and the UK, including as Commissioning Editor, John Wiley & Sons and as a Writer for the Australian Broadcasting Corporation's Online Education Portal, ABC Splash. She is co-editor of the book *Transcultural Screenwriting: Telling Stories for a Global World* (2017). Margaret has researched, collaborated internationally and presented at conferences in Asia, Europe, USA and South America on screenwriting, creativity and the creative process and is an Executive Member of the SRN (Screenwriting Research Network) International.

Léa Polverini is an alumnus of the École Normale Supérieure de Lyon. She currently teaches comparative and francophone literature at Toulouse 2 – Jean Jaurès University, while preparing a PhD about revolts and derision in contemporary Arabic literature. Her research deals with the undermining of reason and moral values in the context of societies in crisis, from the independence wars to the present day. Léa is also an independent journalist, specialising in Middle Eastern and Asian issues.

Mathilde Rouxel is a researcher and an independent curator, specialising in Arab cinema. Her PhD research deals with struggling cinema made by women in Egypt, Lebanon and Tunisia since 1967, as part of a general cinema history of Arab filmmaking. She published the first monograph on Jocelyne Saab (*Jocelyne Saab: la mémoire indomptée*, 2015) of whom she was a close collaborator during the last six years of her life. She worked with her on the CRIFFL and the BLICA, on all her last film projects, and on the editing of her book *Zones de guerre* (2018). Mathilde is currently in charge of Jocelyne Saab's artistic legacy, and founded, with Saab's son Nessim Ricardou-Saab, the Association of Jocelyne Saab's Friends, which works for the enhancement, restoration and dissemination of her artistic heritage.

Ghada Sayegh holds a PhD in Film Studies from Paris Nanterre University, and for several years was programme coordinator at the Institute of Scenic, Audio-visual and Cinematographic Studies, Saint Joseph University of Beirut, where she is currently a faculty member. Sayegh has also been a guest lecturer at several European Universities. Her research explores experimental Lebanese cinema and contemporary art, confronted with history. Her publications include *La trilogie autobiographique de Mohamed Soueid* (2017), 'Missing Images – The Hiatus' (in *Essays & Stories on Photography in Lebanon*, 2018) and *Between Images: Here and Elsewhere* (2018).

Maram Soboh is a script writer, film editor and filmmaker. She is also a freelance writer for film magazines in Egypt, a film trainer at the Princess Basma

Centre, an assistant director for TV productions, and a reporter for Palestinian TV (in the Amman office).

Némésis Srour holds a PhD in Anthropology from the École des Hautes Études et Sciences Sociales (EHESS, Paris). Her thesis focused on 'Bollywood Film Traffic. Circulations of Hindi films in the Middle East (1954–2014)'. She was part of CRIFFL in 2014 and 2015, as Curator for Indian films. Némésis is also co-founder of Contre-Courants, a curation and distribution platform.

Stefanie Van de Peer is Lecturer in Film and Media at Queen Margaret University in Edinburgh, Scotland. She specialises in Arab and African women's non-fiction cinema, and has a special interest in the historical absences and presences of women in cinema. She has published books on *The Pioneering Women of Arab Documentary* (Edinburgh University Press, 2017), *Animation in the Middle East* (2017) and *Women in African Cinema* (2020). Stefanie also regularly programmes film festivals and other film-related events throughout the UK and Europe.

Giovanni Vimercati is a scholar and critic whose work (often under the pseudonym Celluloid Liberation Front) has appeared in *Cinema Scope*, *The Guardian*, *Film Comment*, *Los Angeles Review of Books*, *Sight & Sound*, *Reverse Shot*, *New Statesman*, MUBI, *The Independent*, *Filmmaker Magazine* and others. He was the Sales & Acquisitions Manager at Camera CDI, Italy's leading distributor of current affairs and investigative journalism documentaries. He has a BA in Film Studies (London Metropolitan University) and an MA in Media Studies (American University of Beirut), and is currently working on a book about the political history of Lebanese cinema.

Mark R. Westmoreland coordinates the Visual Ethnography specialisation at Leiden University. He previously served as co-editor of *Visual Anthropology Review* before co-founding the *Writing with Light* journal for anthropological photo-essays. His work engages both scholarly and practice-based approaches at the intersection between art, ethnography and politics. Mark has written extensively on the interface between sensory embodiment and media aesthetics in ongoing legacies of contentious politics, including the crucial role experimental documentary practices play in addressing recurrent political violence in Lebanon and the activist mode of resistance-by-recording in mass street protests in Egypt.

Acknowledgements

This volume is the outcome of several intersecting friendships. Mathilde Rouxel's friendship with Jocelyne Saab was rooted in a fortuitous encounter, mentorship and long periods of collaboration. Stefanie Van de Peer's friendship with the filmmaker was based on fandom and a meeting during which we had to find shelter from a severe storm in Beirut. Mathilde and Stefanie became friends as we got to know one another through our writing about Jocelyne, a mutual admiration that resulted in shared grief when the filmmaker passed away in January 2019. The realisation that, apart from Mathilde's 2015 book *Jocelyne Saab: la mémoire indomptée*, there was not a single book dedicated to the filmmaker's work, came in that moment of sadness, alongside a sense of oversight that needed to be rectified. This book is the result. It is the first English-language book dedicated entirely to the work of Jocelyne Saab, the filmmaker, photographer, artist, cultural agitator and intellectual who impacted others through an all-encompassing friendship for the world beyond her home country, on all continents.

That international and internationalist approach to art, and the belief that culture can make the world a better place, brought the contributors to this volume together. In this book, we have authors from all five continents emphasising the global significance, not only of Saab's work but also of her persona and idealisms. In this book, scholars from Asia, Africa, Australia, Europe and America celebrate their encounters and friendships with Saab, often very deep and personal. We thank all the contributors for their flexibility, their openness and their rigour. We especially want to thank Olivier Hadouchi for letting us republish the interviews he has conducted with Jocelyne Saab over the years, and Yomota Inuhiko for his personal account of an intensive process researching Saab's last film. Stefanie wants to express her sincere gratitude to Mathilde, for carefully curating Jocelyne's legacy, to such an extent that she was able to share original content with this book's contributors for the first time. In return, Mathilde wants to take this opportunity to express great appreciation to Stefanie for her trust and support throughout the editing of this book, which was an inspiring and rewarding experience.

We want to thank Jocelyne Saab's son, Nessim Ricardou-Saab, for making available to us the films, images and recordings used in this book. We also want to acknowledge the Association des Amis de Jocelyne Saab/Association of Jocelyne Saab's Friends, working tirelessly to preserve Saab's oeuvre and make it widely accessible. Mathilde particularly wants to thank Jinane Mrad for her involvement in the Association; her intelligence, her hard work, her admiration for the work of Jocelyne Saab and her complete faith in the project assist in making Saab's work widely available. We also thank all the festivals, exhibitions and biennales that have, over the decades, given a platform to Saab's vision and voice. The many different voices at work in this book recognise in Jocelyne Saab an indomitable filmmaker, artist, and friend whom we all continue to love and admire.

At ReFocus and Edinburgh University Press we wish to thank Robert Singer and Gary D. Rhodes for being our 'amigos', supportive and encouraging beyond the call of duty, as well as Gillian Leslie and Richard Strachan, for ensuring the smooth and friendly process of acceptance and publication in times of the Covid-19 pandemic.

The English titles of Jocelyne Saab's work are used in the text and the French titles are also given in Chapter 17, 'Complete Catalogue of Jocelyne Saab's Artistic Output'. All translations in the text are the contributors' own unless otherwise stated.

Introduction: A Synthesis and Testimony of Jocelyne Saab's Life and Work[1]

Mathilde Rouxel and Stefanie Van de Peer

Jocelyne Saab's films, photography and artworks bear witness. From her early beginnings in television in the 1970s to her recent contemporary art installations, her oeuvre challenges its spectators. As a young woman with a great curiosity for the world, she began as a journalist and war-reporter at the start of the 1970s before going on to become a film director, photographer and artist.

Saab's training was not in filmmaking. In Beirut, and later in Paris, she studied political economy, and while this fulfilled her family's expectations rather than her own desires, she recognised the importance of that education in her work:

> When I was little I always wanted to work with images, but I wasn't allowed to. 'It's not a job for girls' . . . I'd spent my whole school life at the Dames de Nazareth, surrounded by girls. So I chose to go into the world of men. My father, who was a businessman and had travelled a lot, was a role model for me. I threw myself into studying political economy. I followed it through. It wasn't what I wanted to do, but I've since understood the important influence that this training had on my way of structuring my work and of seeing the world. By nature, I'm someone who's instinctive rather than reflective, but there's a certain rigour in my films that I inherited from the ways of thinking instilled in me while studying economy. (Rouxel 2015: 262)

Saab was born in Beirut on 30 April 1948. She grew up in a Christian family, in a huge mansion in a cosmopolitan area of West Beirut. She went to a Christian school in the east of the city. She started studying economics in Saint-Joseph University in Beirut and discovered political activism. Although she stayed away from the political groups, she did take part in meetings and humanitarian actions for the Palestinian refugee camps around the Lebanese capital.

It was in Paris that she was finally able to get closer to the image. After a few freelance jobs on Lebanese radio – where she presented a music programme called *Les Marsupilamis ont les yeux bleus* (*The Marsupilamis Have Blue Eyes*) – and on Lebanese television where she presented the news, she was hired by French television as a reporter. Daring and fearless, she covered the conflicts in Egypt, Libya and the Palestinian territories, to report on the political situation. Saab was one of the very few women working in the field, which, while it attracted the contempt of some, won her the trust of others. She was commissioned to report on Libya (*Gaddafi: The Green March*, 1973; *Portrait of Gaddafi, The Man Coming from the Desert*, 1973); in Egypt (*The October War*, 1973; *Middle East: Egypt*, 1973; *War in the Orient: Egypt*, 1973); in Syria (*Golan, On the Frontline*, 1973); in the Golan (*Middle East: Israel*, 1973); and in Iraq (*Iraq: War in Kurdistan*, 1973). She reported from Palestine (*Palestinians Keep Fighting*, 1973; *Palestinian Women*, 1974; and *The Rejection Front*, 1975) and was about to set off for Vietnam with a French team when war broke out in Lebanon. Prioritising the need to document this terrible upheaval, she decided to return to Beirut and report on the war as an independent journalist. Her reports were shown on three major public French television channels (TF1, Antenne 2 and France 3), throughout Europe (Canal+ in France, RAI in Italy, ZDF in Germany, TV Romande in Switzerland and in Sweden) and internationally (NBC in the US, NHK in Japan, RTA in Algeria and CBC in Canada). Her reports describe the development of the civil war and its deterioration over the years into a stalemate. She dedicated approximately fifteen documentaries to the subject: *New Crusader in the Orient*, 1975; *Lebanon in Turmoil*, 1975; *Children of War*, 1976; *South Lebanon, History of a Sieged Village*, 1976; *Beirut, Never Again*, 1976; *For a Few Lives*, 1976; *Letter From Beirut*, 1978; *Beirut, My City*, 1982; *The Lebanese, Hostages of their City*, 1982; *The Ship of Exile*, 1982; *Lebanon, State of Shock*, 1982; *The Woman Killer*, 1988; as well as one fiction film: *A Suspended Life*, 1985.

This war changed her relationship with the moving image. Fortified by the strong sense of independence that characterised her, both aesthetically and politically, from 1975 onwards Saab decided to escape the constraints of the journalistic format in order to develop her own language. The war, engulfing her country, inspired her to pick up the camera and create her images; but when she turned the focus away from the war and examined what had been 'the garden of her childhood', Beirut and Lebanon, her language became markedly more personal, the tone less militant and increasingly poetic. Overwhelmed by the horrors of the war, by the absurdity of a world that had become impossible to describe, she turned to other art forms, plastic and narrative, using them as different tools to bear witness: when it was no longer possible to show reality, fiction became the necessary tool of expression in an infernal war. Her first feature-length work of fiction, *Une Vie Suspendue* (*A Suspended Life*, selected at the Directors' Fortnight in Cannes in 1985 under the title *L'Adolescente sucre d'amour* [*Adolescent, Sugar of Love*]) was filmed in the middle of the war. This film was followed, after the war, by other feature-length fiction projects, two of which were set in Beirut and were about Lebanon (*Il était une fois, Beyrouth: Histoire d'une star* [*Once Upon a Time, Beirut: Story of a Star*], 1994; *What's Going On?*, 2009). More recently Saab turned to photography and video installations to depict her understanding of the world. *Strange Games and Bridges* (2007), a video installation presented in Singapore, portrays her thoughts about the renewed outbreak of war in Lebanon in 2006, shedding light on the severity of the wounds caused by the war and reopened by the resurging violence. Once again, to depict the unspeakable emotion engulfing her, she renewed her artistic practices of representation. With the videos exhibited in a specially designed space, she proposed a particularly creative alternative to fiction and documentary. In 2015 she turned to painting, colouring with gold, blue or green tints the black and white photographs she had taken in the Syrian refugee camps in Lebanon. These photos were printed in the *One Dollar a Day* project, in the format of billboards put up around Beirut to denounce Lebanon's 'new urbanism' which welcomed more than a million refugees who were then left to survive on less than $1 a day. In this work the colours and medium of paint emphasise hope, as the refugee children are depicted as gilded angels in a world in which value shifts multiple times: from the photographed jewels onto the billboard canvases displayed in the upmarket areas of Beirut, to those billboards being torn down and reused by homeless people to build shacks, allowing a protective environment to develop despite the circumstances: without cement to build with, the rocks holding down the canvas material of the billboards become precious stones in themselves.

Towards the end of her life, Jocelyne Saab was working on a feature-length film project dedicated to Mei, the daughter of Fusako Shigenobu, leader of the Japanese Red Army in Beirut in 1973. Mei Shigenobu was born in complete secrecy in the Lebanese Beqaa. Her father was a Palestinian fedayeen whose name was kept a secret; her mother was a militant internationalist activist who dedicated her life to the revolution. Telling their stories allowed Saab to talk about one of the most shocking experiences of her life, the Siege of Beirut in 1982, which forced Palestinian fighters to leave Lebanon. Fusako Shigenobu went with them, while Mei was raised by the Comrades and barely saw her mother before she was arrested in Osaka in 2000. After this date, Mei took back control of her identity. However, Saab was too ill by that point to finish this large-scale project, and instead she decided to create a very short film that emphasised Mei's story. *My Name is Mei Shigenobu* (2018) is not just a short extract of the film that she was aiming to make, but a testimony of her last political preoccupation in front of a world she was slowly leaving.

Beirut and Lebanon, though her preferred subjects, are not the only places that Saab turned her attention to from 1975 onwards. However, the aesthetic and emotional fracture that marks the evolution of her artistic work from the very beginning of the war merits attention. In order to understand the context within which she was reporting, it is useful to provide a brief overview of the events that stand out during the period of the civil war.

LEBANON AND CIVIL WAR(S)

Lebanon, because of its religious and cultural diversity, as well as its geographical position, has often found itself at the centre of regional ambitions and international geopolitics. An unstable recent history culminated in successive waves of Palestinian refugees and fighters arriving after the creation of the State of Israel in 1948. The interplay of these factors led to an increased communitarianism and polarisation within society, and the formation of pro- and anti-Palestinian militias, which led to the outbreak of war in 1975.

These are the events that led Jocelyne Saab to abandon her journey to Vietnam and return to Beirut to witness and record events. She filmed *Le Liban dans la tourmente* (*Lebanon in Turmoil*, 1975), reporting on a conflict in which everyone waged a war on everyone else, 'with a flower in the gun' – guns seized by more and more hands, as more and more people joined the militias; guns that men, women and children became experts in handling. Beirut was soon divided in two. The films Saab made on this subject (*Lettre de Beyrouth* [*Letter from Beirut*], 1978; *Beyrouth, ma ville* [*Beirut, My City*], 1982) are enlightening: despite the best efforts on the part of the militias to separate Christians and Muslims, the civil population was never really divided – not in the same way that the communities in former Yugoslavia were, for example.

One event led to another: assassinations, changing political alliances, and the involvement since 1976 of Syria and Israel in the Lebanese conflict. The fighting escalated and spread within each camp, until 1989, when the Taif Agreement was signed, reaffirming the independence of Lebanon and introducing major political reforms. As such, the war was interrupted by a general amnesty that demanded a ceasefire and national reconciliation. Saab filmed this war right up to the end of the siege of Beirut. With her feature-length fiction *Une Vie suspendue* (*A Suspended Life*, 1985) she proposed an entirely new way of looking at the war. In 1989 she investigated Jocelyne Khoueiry's radical turn from war to religion, but she could no longer film conflict. After 1991 Lebanon entered into a phase of reconstruction. In her own way, and well before others, Saab was an active agent in that reconstruction, as she laid the foundations for a Lebanese Film Library with her 1993 project *Beyrouth, Mille et une images* (*Beirut, a Thousand and One Images*) and the film, *Il était une fois, Beyrouth: Histoire d'une star* (*Once Upon a Time, Beirut: Story of a Star*, 1994) was born out of this project. This is a film that functions as heritage, a homage to pre-war Beirut, a record for future generations who had never known the Beirut of their parents – this so-called Switzerland of the Middle East where life had been sweet. A retrospective that was at once historical and cinematographic – the first of its kind – gave hope for a future.

She then turned her gaze away from Beirut until the bombing started again in 2006, when she filmed the bridges and motorways destroyed by the Israeli bombing campaign on the southern outskirts of the city and the south of the country. The wounds reopened; the pain was raw. Finally, in 2009 Saab made peace with her home city, and with Nasri Sayegh she went in search of its urban gardens in *What's Going On?*, a film in which the country takes on a mythological dimension, finding its strength and its beauty.

CINEMA, ARCHIVES AND HISTORY

Jocelyne Saab's position in this particular political context was personal. Her anguished interest in Lebanon was due to her experiences, her history, her identity as a Lebanese Christian woman who defended the Palestinian cause in a country strongly afflicted by sectarianism. Her position was delicate, dangerous even. She received death threats and was actively targeted after the release of her 1976 film *Les Enfants de la guerre* (*Children of War*). In the film she depicted the bloodthirsty nature of the Christian militias who massacred men, women and children in a Muslim neighbourhood in the north-east of Beirut, Quarantina. She refused to leave the country or stop recording what she was seeing. However, she did develop a new language to express herself. That traumatic period made her reflect on the meaning of images and their impact. Always open-minded, she left behind her explicit and militant rhetoric, which – while always characterised by a remarkable objectivity – had, up to then, motivated her reporting, in order to adopt a language that was increasingly poetic but remained politically engaged.

In 1991 the Lebanese parliament issued an amnesty law applicable to all war crimes committed between 1975 and 1990, thereby relegating immeasurable suffering of often profound trauma to individual memories, rather than developing a collective work of remembrance. It became impossible to look backwards. Yet in Beirut everything still points to a past that nobody wants to remember. With a film such as *What's Going On?* (2009), or her video installation *Strange Games and Bridges* (2007), Jocelyne Saab showed that she at least has not forgotten anything, and that she is determined to remind the Lebanese people and the wider world of what her country went through. The way in which she filmed what was left standing and not what had been rebuilt, what was and what can no longer be, referred to the issue of constructing a collective memory and conserving a heritage that bears witness to the history of a country.

At the start of the 1970s, Saab was part of what is now called the New Lebanese Cinema. The young Lebanese filmmakers working since the civil war in Lebanon wanted to propose a new form of cinema, while committing themselves to depicting as honestly as possible the political and social realities of their country. Many of these young filmmakers were trained journalists who had studied in Europe before returning home; their activism – in general left-wing and sympathetic to the Palestinian cause – gave their productions a distinct political colour. Besides Saab, one could mention Borhane Alaouié or Maroun Baghdadi, who share a similar concept of filmmaking as a form of resistance and protest. The artists and filmmakers who openly took sides or who were creatively active during the violence that shook Lebanon are few and far between. As such, because of their scarcity, the productions of these three filmmakers are precious documents.

In the ensemble of films about Beirut, it is clear that the historical fracture wrought by the war provoked a crisis in language and representation that would profoundly disrupt Saab's relationship with images. This is particularly clear if one looks beyond her films at her entire body of work. If prior to 1977 her work focused on Lebanon, after 1977 she reported from countries across the Arab world, touching on subjects that interested her: in 1977 she filmed *Le Sahara n'est pas à vendre* (*The Sahara is Not for Sale*), about the inhabitants of the desert forced into exile by the rivalry between Morocco and Algeria in El-Aouinet. That year she also returned to Egypt, whose culture and Arab identity she felt very close to, in order to report on the impact of globalisation and the modernisation of Cairo on poorer communities, and the mood in the City of the Dead, which she captured with an attentive and sympathetic gaze in *Égypte, la cité des morts* (*Egypt, The City of the Dead*, 1977). After briefly returning to Beirut to film her city and examine the Palestinian issue during the conflict, she went to Iran where she shot *Iran: l'utopie en marche* (*Iran: Utopia in Motion*, 1980), an analysis of the political and social situation in the country after the revolution that had ended the Shah's reign and brought Ayatollah Khomeini to power. Then it was back to Cairo for a series of reports on the source of Egypt's wealth: beginning with *L'Architecte de Louxor* (*The Architect of Luxor*, 1986) – a portrait of Olivier Sednaoui, the innovative architect who rejected modernism and concrete in favour of mud brick and majestic constructions of domes placed on square bases, thereby following in the path of the ancient master builders. This was followed by *Les Fantômes d'Alexandrie*

(*The Ghosts of Alexandria*), *La Croix des Pharaons* (*Copts: The Cross of the Pharaohs*) and *L'Amour d'Allah (L'intégrisme)* (*Love of Allah (Fundamentalism)*), all in 1986. The style of these documentaries was different from the commissioned reportage work at the beginning of her career. War, and the impossibility of its representation through traditional means, enabled her to develop a new language, entirely her own.

After the Lebanese civil war wound down, Saab refused to film conflict situations. Aside from her installation *Strange Games and Bridges*, for which she returned to Beirut to film the bridges destroyed by the Israeli bombing campaign during the 2006 war, she decided to dedicate herself to life instead. In 1989 she filmed a documentary about belly dancers in Egypt, *Les Almées* (*Al'Alma', Bellydancers*), shown on Canal+ in France. In 1991, in Bordeaux she made a documentary about the process of in vitro fertilisation in hospital, *Fécondation in video* (*Fertilisation in Video*). For this she used a medical probe equipped with a camera – the most advanced of its time – that allowed her to film the inside of a woman's body and biologically situate the origins of life. The following year she began the enormous task of recuperating films – both national and international productions – shot in Beirut before the war. This project, *Beyrouth, Mille et une images* (*Beirut, a Thousand and One Images*), was undertaken with the aim of building a heritage of Lebanese cinema and creating a film library in Beirut. It also facilitated the programming of a film festival at the Institut du Monde Arabe (Arab World Institute) in Paris. The archive materials that she gathered formed the basis for a new film, *Il était une fois, Beyrouth: Histoire d'une star* (*Once Upon a Time, Beirut: Story of a Star*, 1994) which, built around the plot of two young girls born during the war, used film extracts from a variety of genres and provenances to bring to light countless images of the city before the war.

In 1998 Jocelyne Saab returned to the documentary format with *La Dame de Saigon* (*The Lady of Saigon*), a portrait of a female doctor and activist working with minorities in Vietnam during the war. In some ways a mirror image of the director herself, the doctor became a politician at the end of the war, and still, today, despite her age, leads the battle against child malnutrition. One recognises, in the courage of a woman who committed herself to her country and its people, a reflection of the director herself, who – in her own time – committed herself to Beirut and its populations suffering around her.

In 2005 she made *Dunia* (*Kiss Me Not on the Eyes*), a feature film about a young woman studying poetry and Sufi dance in search of sensuality in a country where sexual pleasure is forbidden to women. A study conducted by the World Health Organization in 2000 showed that 97 per cent of young girls in Egypt still undergo female genital mutilation (Tag-Eldin et al. 2008). The film was censored in Egypt and Saab was issued with a *fatwa* by religious fundamentalists. The sanction was hard, and the repression against the film was traumatising for the director. In fact, the censorship only intensified awareness of the culture of repressed freedom that the film had itself denounced.

It was only in 2009 that Saab decided to return to Beirut, after the tragic episode of the 2006 war, which she had depicted in *Strange Games and Bridges* (2007), a video installation of twenty-two screens showing archive images of her old films as well as recent images of the bridges destroyed by the Israeli bombing. With her inimitable optimism and zest for life, Saab decided to arrange these images of conflict so as to invite the spectator to wander between them along the paths of a hanging garden. Indeed, throughout her childhood and in her memories, Beirut resembles a large garden that she has continually explored in her work. Her last feature-length film, *What's Going On?*, is testimony to this, as it tells the story of a young man, Nasri, looking for the gardens of Beirut and the rest of the world, which seem to have been lost but which the director unearths with boundless sensuality.

The relationship that the artist has with Beirut is unique and profoundly moving. However, the challenges that she faced when she attempted to define her Lebanese identity without referring to the suffering this entails encouraged her to extend her interest to the whole of the Middle East and the Mediterranean, where she searched for the foundations of her particular aesthetic tendencies and influences. If Egypt and its traditions (particularly the poetry, architecture and dance) occupy a place of privilege in the construction of her personality and the body of her work, the other Mediterranean countries and even further afield in Asia are no less significant. Many of these countries share the same traditions and have similar taboos, notably concerning the human body, as is evident in *Café du Genre* (*Gender Café*), her series of six short films produced in 2013 for MuCEM (Musée des civilisations de l'Europe et de la Méditerranée/Museum of European and Mediterranean Civilisations). Made up of six portraits of artists or thinkers critically engaged with issues of the body and gender in the Mediterranean, the films raise questions about liberty and the control of one's own being, questions that resonate with the rest of Saab's work.

So, despite being impressively multidisciplinary, Saab's work has a deep coherence. Through the gaze of the film camera, Saab explored with curiosity and tenderness every corner of her city, her country and the geographical zones that form its culture.

By creating a platform for those whose voices are normally not heard, she created portraits of places (Beirut, Cairo, the mountains of Kurdistan, the Bedouin camps in the Saharan desert, etc.) that are both unusual and poetic. She captures in these places something that is at the point of disappearing, of slipping away: the houses, the streets, the traditional buildings, the atmosphere of the Beirut of her childhood; in Cairo, the modesty of life, and the culture of dance and poetry; in Kurdistan, the potential and risks of independence; in

Figure I.1 Jocelyne Saab and her DOP Olivier Guéneau filming in Western Sahara

Bedouin culture, the possibilities of a peaceful life in the desert. She recorded what might soon be no more than a memory, and she fought against its obliteration. She constructed a heritage. At a retrospective dedicated to the director in March 2013, Olivier Hadouchi wrote about her cinema that it is 'a fight for life against everything that mutilates or tries to imprison or restrict it'; that it is 'a battle for the right to talk about and transmit something freely' (Brenez and Hadouchi 2013). Her strong foothold on reality provided her with the means to fight the disintegration that afflicts the culture and identity that she so valued. Always willing to listen to women and children, Saab's camera was, time and again, witness to earth-shattering events by which war, or a reactionary return to traditions, or increased globalisation, changed the daily lives of those we pay least attention to. Increasingly, the fracture imposed by war brought her to use her camera in the first person, to go in front of the camera and talk about what *she* saw and what *she* experienced.

Saab's engagement with others was total. She knew how to make the nuanced choices that lead to the construction of a collective memory. Her oeuvre is situated at the intersection of multiple narratives, at the crossroads of several civilisations, and it appeals to each of us, engaged in the construction of a world history, who are aware of the need to learn the lessons of the past.

Her political engagement and her cinematographic treatises propose alternative terms, methods and instruments for emancipation. 'Violent censorship inherently validates that which it is attacking' (Voltaire 1756: 34); the danger the director faced, throughout her professional life, whatever the format of her productions, is testament to her remarkably sincere ideology. She faced problems of censorship early on in her career: during the war, aside from the death threats she endured after the screening of her report *Les Enfants de la guerre* (*Children of War*, 1976) and nearly being kidnapped in 1982, she was, after the partition of Beirut in 1976, forbidden from crossing the city from east to west – where her family still lived – because of her political positions. *The Sahara is Not for Sale* (1977) earned her a life-long ban on entering Morocco; *Dunia* (*Kiss Me Not on the Eyes*) in 2005 angered the Egyptian Islamic fundamentalists, who pronounced a death sentence on her; and more recently some of her images from the *Sense, Icons and Sensitivity* (2007) photography exhibition in several Beirut galleries were censored as some of the subjects were considered indecent.

Jocelyne Saab's ideological coherence is just as profound in her aesthetic engagement. The most powerful lesson to be drawn from her work as an artist is without a doubt the idea that an image can be manipulated, shaped, constructed: if the militant discourse and raw images of her early reports have been toned down over the years into a poetic and dreamlike expression, of which *What's Going On?* is the most majestic example, it is because Saab understood that the image can also be a demagogue and that art, by virtue of its ability to confer meaning, has a power that surpasses discursive rhetoric. And as a result, she was profoundly aware of the importance of disassociating form and content.

It is interesting to highlight some of the forms that span this body of work and that stand out, independent of the era, the place, or the political situation in question. What gives meaning and unity to her work? What do these forms express concerning the engagement that motivates them? The sensitivity, full of hope and humanism, which makes Saab's images so touchingly unique, manifestly describes different constitutive elements of her identity. The question that drove her work for forty years is how, as Lebanese – and more broadly, Arab – and as a woman, one can situate oneself in this world. In the images that form the body of her work, the figure of a engaged woman is implicit, committed to life in a world torn to pieces, pointing out injustices and, using historically significant evidence, documenting remarkable situations with a poetic sensitivity clear in the language and the gaze that she adopts to confront the events of the world she lives in.

This engagement, marked by an active desire to better understand the world in order to better understand oneself, to denounce horror so as to assertively confirm the beauty of life and the importance of liberty, emerges as the heart of Jocelyne Saab's work and the discourse she constructed around aesthetic problematics that interest her intensely.

TRANSNATIONAL SCHOLARSHIP

The two editors of this volume, Mathilde Rouxel and Stefanie Van de Peer, were, like many women working on film and the arts in Lebanon, personally acquainted with Jocelyne Saab. We have experienced, first-hand, the strength, generosity and deep sincerity Saab put into her films, photographic projects, or monumental events. As young scholars of Arab cinema, we both reached out to her for interviews and became admiring friends.

Mathilde Rouxel worked closely together with Jocelyne Saab in the last six years of her life. At the time, Rouxel was studying for a Master's in film between Lyon and Beirut, and graduated with a dissertation on Saab's films, supervised by the director's close friend Nicole Brenez, who organised with Olivier Hadouchi the first retrospective of Jocelyne Saab's films in the French Cinematheque in March 2013. When Rouxel met Saab, the director was organising a film festival in Lebanon and needed an assistant. Rouxel worked on the three editions of the Cultural Resistance International Film Festival of Lebanon (CRIFFL), from 2013 to 2015, and later on the organisation of the Lebanese International Biennale for Cinema and the Arts (BLICA), which Saab launched in 2017. From 2013 onwards, Rouxel participated in all of Saab's projects, finished and unfinished. She mainly researched for and assisted Saab in the writing of her various film projects, and helped her in the making of her book of photograms and photographs *Zones de guerre* (2018), edited by Nicole Brenez. In 2015 Rouxel published her Master's dissertation on Saab's cinema, under the title *Jocelyne Saab: la mémoire indomptée*. On the occasion of this publication, Saab dug out her unreleased films (such as *For a Few Lives*, 1976) and decided to make her work available. Unable to contemplate the release of her films on DVD before finding the financial support to restore them, she decided to offer most of them on video on demand, despite the quality of the files. Rouxel also assisted Saab when she started the monumental task of archiving her work and life, and in the search for partnerships for the restoration of her films. Saab deposited the original materials of the films at the French Film Centre (CNC) in the 1990s while making *Once Upon a Time, Beirut: Story of a Star*. The conception of *Zones de guerre* was an opportunity for Saab to gather her positive reels that were, back then, stored between Beirut and Paris. Most of the images in the book were taken from these positive reels. Later, she decided to deposit the films at the French Cinematheque. This act was the second step in the preservation process. When Jocelyne Saab passed away in January 2019, Nessim Ricardou-Saab, her son, asked Mathilde Rouxel to continue this work. Together with other friends of the director they founded the Association of Jocelyne Saab's Friends,[2] which aims to archive and enhance her artistic heritage, and to find partners and funding to restore her twenty-three documentaries in 16 mm. One of the purposes of the association is to fulfil Saab's dream of releasing DVDs of her complete filmography (forty-seven films and videos).

Stefanie Van de Peer has written extensively on Saab's work, focusing on the documentaries, in her first monograph *Negotiating Dissidence: The Pioneering Women of Arab Documentary* (2017). She also screened many of Saab's films at international film festivals in Scotland, England and Belgium and hosted the director on a few occasions at events in Lebanon and the UK where she was an invited guest. Over the years, Rouxel and Van de Peer had been aware of one another's work, and indeed used it in their own publications, but they have still not had the opportunity to meet in person. The last time Van de Peer met Jocelyne Saab was in London in 2017, on the occasion of the Essay Film Festival, which screened a number of Saab's early documentaries. This also became the event to mark the publication of Van de Peer's book, and Saab's picture features prominently on the cover. Saab confided in Van de Peer that she was very ill and that she was really happy about the attention we were paying to her films at the event, as the anglophone world has overlooked her work for so long. At the time, Van de Peer was planning more screenings of her films, and Saab mentioned Rouxel's work. After screening *A Suspended Life* (1985), *Once Upon a Time, Beirut: Story of a Star* (1994) and *Dunia* (2005) in 2018, the news that Jocelyne Saab had passed away came as a shock. Van de Peer finally got in touch with Rouxel, and together they started planning this long overdue book, dedicated to Saab's memory and to her long, brave and very productive career.

The existing scholarship on Jocelyne Saab, while limited in quantity, is equally as broad ranging as Saab's output. Approaches to her work vary just as much as the work itself, but scholars often do their research in isolation. Individual chapters and journal articles have been published by French, English, Australian, American, Lebanese, Egyptian and other scholars. While Rouxel's book was the first anywhere to be entirely devoted to Saab's work, the present book is the first one in English. It brings together anglophone as well as several francophone authors, who are not used to writing or publishing in English. Most of the authors have known or worked with Jocelyne Saab – and so have some of the translators of the original texts by Mathilde Rouxel (Miriam Heard) or Ghada Rahal Sayegh (Abraham Zeitoun). As a pioneer of Arab cinema, Saab is often mentioned and praised, but a full picture of her work remained absent for a long time – just as the recognition Saab deserved for her contribution to Lebanese cinema has remained slow to emerge. The emphasis in scholarship seems to be either on her so-called Beirut Trilogy or on internationally successful fiction films like *Dunia*. It was perhaps the inclusion of a chapter on Saab by Dalia Said Mostafa in Josef Gugler's much-quoted collection *Ten Arab Filmmakers: Political Dissent and Social Critique* (2015) that brought her work to the foreground in anglophone Arab cinema studies. Nevertheless, the emphasis in publications on Saab's cinematography tends to focus entirely on the immediate national context in her Lebanese and Egyptian work, rather than opening up to the international nature of her oeuvre and significance. This may be a reflection of Arab cinema in general: historically, Lebanese and Egyptian cinemas have been the most successful in the region.

In contrast, with this book we emphasise the broad internationalist and emancipatory ideology central to Saab's oeuvre. From her earliest reportages for French television to her last, unfinished films, and from her experimental art installations and photography to her curatorial work for cinematheques and film festivals, this book covers a broader range of Saab's work than any previous publications. This book brings together international scholars and critics from across Lebanon, France, Jordan, the US, the UK, Australia, Switzerland and more, to reflect the transnational accomplishments of the director and artist. The multicultural nature of the book is its strength, and is reflected in the variety of approaches, which are highly poetic, testimonial and analytical. This provided us with the opportunity to paint a picture of an artist whose life was entirely dedicated to the visual arts, and whose curiosity, open-mindedness and idealism brought her to places and topics others may have feared to go to or address.

The book is divided into four main sections, which do not necessarily follow a chronological order. Instead, we focus on diverse themes and issues that were crucial to Jocelyne Saab's development as an artist and activist. In Part I, 'Jocelyne Saab: Fifty Years of Creation in the Turmoil of Arab History', this book offers four chapters in which the passing of time offers a way to find the past, both of the filmmaker and her films. Starting with an extended reflection on several in-depth interviews done over the years with Saab, Olivier Hadouchi's chapter provides space and time for Saab's own voice. She was an eloquent and engaging speaker. By putting this chapter at the start of the book, we enable the reader to engage with Jocelyne's voice first, before scholars from around the world and with diverse perspectives engage with her films, art installations and cultural events. Ghada Sayegh paints a revised picture of the Lebanese cinema of war through a reading of Saab's position as a Lebanese filmmaker of the so-called New Lebanese Cinema of the civil war. Joan Grandjean shows that Saab was more than a filmmaker. His work re-evaluates her as a cultural agent and a contributor to the global art world. Delving deep into Saab's archive, Mathilde Rouxel likewise testifies to Saab's very diverse oeuvre and sheds light on some of the final and unfinished work the artist had started just before her passing. As such, this first part of the book illustrates Saab's multidimensional artistic practice, the social and political significance of her work for Lebanese film history, and the importance of history as a philosophical and material subject for the study of her work.

Part II, 'Film as a Weapon Against War and Oblivion', contains four chapters focusing on the way memory functions as a narrative device while it also defines the changing style of Jocelyne's filmmaking practice and her involvement with CRIFFL, the Cultural Resistance International Film Festival of Lebanon, which she inaugurated. Giovanni Vimercati writes about the spectral quality of the Beirut memory across her documentaries and fiction films. He shows that, in the Beirut Trilogy, the Lebanese director tried to make sense of the civil war, while in *A Suspended Life* it is the choreography of time and space that portrays the senseless degeneration of an estranging conflict. Mark R. Westmoreland looks at the film from a material culture perspective, paying special attention to intertextual and architectural responses to the trauma of war and the way in which Saab's play with Beirut's representation and reality reveals a deconstructive vision of history. Yomota Inuhiko testifies about his own intense collaboration with Jocelyne Saab on her last film about Mei Shigenobu, and their attempt to revive and set right a forgotten piece of rebellious Japanese and Lebanese history, in Saab's effort to connect more visually the Asian continent. It is in Némésis Srour's chapter that this cinematic connection within the Asian continent really comes into its own, as she shows Saab's interest in the continent not only through her own films and artwork, but also in her efforts to bring to life a Lebanese past of Asian cinema through CRIFFL.

The five chapters in Part III, 'Liberating the People, Freeing the Body', delve deeper into the activist nature of all of Saab's work. First, we look at Saab's internationalism in films from the late seventies and early eighties, through an exploration of her allegiances with Kurdish, Sahrawi and Iranian citizens fighting the powers that oppress them, in Stefanie Van de Peer's chapter. Margaret McVeigh then delves deep into the script development and metaphorical representations in Saab's most well-known fiction film, *Dunia*, exploring the connections between women and family and these relationships' impact on women's bodies. Likewise, Maram Soboh's chapter looks at women's bodies and relationships across Saab's four fiction films, with an emphasis on the filmmaker's philosophy of dance and how physical self-expression leads to liberation of the feminist mind. Corinne Fortier's chapter then explores the concept of emancipation further, through the anthropological analysis of the male dancer in *Café du Genre* and the Syrian refugee women and children's lives and figurative depiction in Beirut's wealthy centre. Samirah Alkassim's chapter closes this part of the book with an examination of Saab's later artistic work in photography, video art and cultural curatorial practice. Exploring increasingly flexible formats of video art, photography and installation allowed the filmmaker a greater freedom of expression that continued her quest for emancipation of the oppressed and that simultaneously expanded her own and others' geographic borders.

Finally, Part IV, 'Advocating Poetry', contains three chapters of exceptional poetic power, in which the literary and poetic strengths of Saab's camera and voice are discussed in detail. Marie Chebli's chapter returns to Saab's enigmatic first fiction film, *A Suspended Life*, and explores the lyrical and narrative elements this film borrows from fairy tales. Through a Deleuzian reading, Chebli places emphasis on the mysterious identity of the young girl protagonist and the space and time she occupies in war-torn Beirut. Expanding on this preoccupation with urban spaces through a Deleuzian lens, Gregory Buchakjian discusses the destroyed architecture of Beirut through his own artistic practice, impacted by Saab's vision of Beirut in the eighties. Connecting Saab's films with the city's present, he asks how the present state of a city obliterated by external and internal power structures echoes the artist's philosophical preoccupation with art and its ability to reconstruct material and ideological memories. In light of the destruction of Beirut's harbour on 4 August 2020, his concluding point about the October 2019 revolution is more pertinent than ever. Likewise, Léa Polverini discusses Saab's cinema as an attempt to recompose vanishing worlds through fiction. The power of fiction to start to deal with the trauma of reality is read as an effort to restore an atmosphere or to recollect past events in order to preserve its memory. Finally, the book ends on a chapter by Mathilde Rouxel that provides a full catalogue of Saab's work, both finished and unfinished, which also highlights the efforts needed to restore and preserve her legacy for future generations. As Lebanon in 2020 undergoes another devastating financial, social and political crisis that is reviving its young population's disillusionment with their leaders, Saab's work is more important than ever.

NOTES

1. This Introduction is a translated (by Miriam Heard), abridged and edited version of the introduction (in French) to Mathilde Rouxel's 2015 monograph *Jocelyne Saab: la mémoire indomptée*, Beirut: Les Éditions Dar An-Nahar.
2. The website of the Association, https://jocelynesaabasso.com/, collects and makes widely available information on the legacy of Jocelyne Saab's life and work.

BIBLIOGRAPHY

Brenez, Nicole and Olivier Hadouchi (2013), 'Présentation du cycle Jocelyne Saab programmé à la Cinémathèque Française *Les Astres de la guerre*', <https://www.ressources.org/+cycle-jocelyne-saab-a-la-cinematheque-francaise-du-29-mars-au-24-mai-2013-paris,1048+.html> (last accessed 30 November 2020).
Mostafa, Dalia Said (2015), 'Jocelyne Saab: A Lifetime Journey in Search of Freedom and Beauty (Lebanon)', in Josef Gugler (ed.), *Ten Arab Filmmakers: Political Dissent and Social Critique*, Bloomington: Indiana University Press, pp. 34–50.
Rouxel, Mathilde (2015), *Jocelyne Saab: la mémoire indomptée*, Beirut: Éditions Dar An-Nahar.
Saab, Jocelyne (2018), *Zones de guerre*, ed. Nicole Brenez, Paris: Les Éditions de l'Œil.

Tag-Eldin, M. A., M. A. Gadallah, M. N. Al-Tayeb, M. Abdel-Aty, E. Mansour and M. Sallem (2008), 'Prevalence of Female Genital Cutting among Egyptian Girls', *Bulletin of the World Health Organization*, 86: 4, 269–74, <https://www.who.int/reproductivehealth/topics/fgm/fgm_prevalence_egypt/en/> (last accessed 30 November 2020).

Van de Peer, Stefanie (2017), *Negotiating Dissidence: The Pioneering Women of Arab Documentary*, Edinburgh: Edinburgh University Press.

Voltaire (1756), *Poèmes sur le désastre de Lisbonne*, Paris: Éditions Cramer.

PART I

Jocelyne Saab: Fifty Years of Creation in the Turmoil of Arab History

CHAPTER I

Telling the Tale of a World in Turmoil: Conversations with Jocelyne Saab[1]

Olivier Hadouchi

For Jocelyne, Nicole, Mathilde, Alaa, Nessim,
Rita, Aliette, Daniel and Yomota

It was through the documentary *Caméra arabe* (Férid Boughedir, 1987), screened at the Institut du Monde Arabe (Arab World Institute) in Paris in the late 1980s, that I learned about Jocelyne Saab. In that film, she appeared in action, at the heart of a chaotic battle in a Beirut that was still at war, and her lively and passionate temperament, her calm assurance, her courage and determination really impressed me. I had long wondered about how I could see her films, even though I did not really know what they represented. I did not know back then that I would get the opportunity to get to know her, and to become good friends, twenty years later. She really understood the importance and the art of friendship. She was always concerned with bringing people together. Whenever she spoke to someone, she would know how to put a person at ease from the start, whether it was a simple passer-by in the street, an artist, a child, an indignant civilian, a fearful or seasoned fighter, a future head of state (e.g. Yasser Arafat) or an established leader (e.g. Muammar Gaddafi).

On multiple occasions, I presented several of her films publicly and I really enjoyed organising and chairing events and meetings with her and an attentive and respectful audience: she dedicated herself to the game of questions and answers with great sincerity, naturalness and spontaneity. I also participated in two editions of a festival that she managed to create in Lebanon at a time when it was still jolted by sudden and devious blasts; a country struggling to recover from past wars and present conflicts. She had created this festival during the 2010s with very little material means, with the help of a small but very motivated team.

When I discovered her films – which were then very difficult to see because they were neither restored nor available on DVD or on file – I was immediately touched by documentaries like *Lebanon in Turmoil* (1975), *Beirut, Never Again* (1976) and *Beirut, My City* (1982). I wondered why her films were not shown or broadcast more often. Though *Dunia* (*Kiss Me Not on the Eyes*) (2005) had a small theatrical release in France, it was for a very short period. From the early 1970s onwards, Saab started to travel around the world as a war reporter, before her own country caught fire in the middle of the decade (after years of severe tensions). The city of her birth, childhood and adolescence, and even her own house, suffered terrible destruction, as she experienced the loss of people, of friends and acquaintances who lost their lives in this prolonged war. Even so, in her documentaries and her essays, we often find a strong, dreamlike narrative dimension. She knew how to tell a story with just a few shots, always accompanied by well-chosen words (both Etel Adnan and Roger Assaf wrote commentaries for important films by Jocelyne) or just with a few silent and very expressive images. She never lost sight of the poetic aspects of film and the relevance, the correctness of her gaze as a filmmaker.

Between 2010 and 2013, I conducted a series of interviews with Jocelyne Saab. They have been transcribed progressively, and she reread and sometimes supplemented or corrected them. Our discussions went on until her passing, and I still sometimes wonder what she would have thought of this or that event, she who had attended to so many dashed hopes and defeats, but who was always ready to start over again to support (peaceful) actions for change.

At the root of everything in Jocelyne's life and career, in her work as a film-maker, is childhood. Everything comes back to childhood, a childhood that was mistreated, abused by the wars and traditions of a society that boasted the appearance of modernity (a desire for unrestrained consumption, the Lebanon of tourist postcards), but which had mostly remained patriarchal and conservative. She was living in a society that at times felt alienating and suffocating for generations of women and men who aspired to a radical change, dancing to Lebanese or Egyptian music, or songs by English or North American pop groups from the 1960s and 1970s. She has always remained faithful to the child she was, with a capacity to marvel at and reinvent the world, another life; and – even at moments of intense crisis – to listen and to face the looks of children testifying for themselves and for generations to come. It all comes down to childhood. In *Children of War* (1976), which was screened during her funeral ceremony, she gave words, paper and pencils to young orphans who had survived the massacre of Quarantina. In her last works too, the series *One Dollar a Day* (2016), about Syrian refugee children in Lebanon, and the film she was looking to finish, *My Name is Mei Shigenobu*, childhood is the main concern.

The last time I saw Jocelyne was with a friend, Alaa, and another old friend of the director, a former Lebanon correspondent for the French newspaper

Libération. Despite her physical pain, she found the strength to smile as she told us anecdotes, like the one about the time when Arafat and members of the PLO had given her a pistol, which she immediately hid in her pocket; of about how she was invited by Abu Ammar[2] himself to join him on the boat of exile, after the siege of Beirut in the summer of 1982. Even at that last meeting, Jocelyne was wearing a red T-shirt with the image of Che, in a medical bed installed at her home in Paris. When we left, we knew this was probably the last time we would see her alive. Two or three weeks later, she passed away. Along with a large number of people who came to pay homage to her, we attended her funeral, and were sad to see her leave for the last time, to the sound of 'Dos gardenias', a Cuban song by Buena Vista Social Club, which she loved.

We will not forget her cinema, or the memory of her precious presence, or her elegance in every sense of the term, or her curiosity and her constant attention towards others and the world. Her cinema never ceases to assert and celebrate life against everything that mutilates, imprisons, stops women and men (of all ages) from flourishing. A cinema of resistance designed by a lucid, humanist and committed artist, who manages to claim the right and the possibility of telling, transmitting, with complete freedom, to generations to come, stories on a human scale and giving face, voice and presence to the anonymous people who do and undo History.

A SELF-TAUGHT DOCUMENTARY MAKER

Olivier Hadouchi: How did you begin your course of study as a filmmaker?
Jocelyn Saab: Actually, I did not study film or do any training to become a filmmaker. In my family, in the society of those days and the milieu in which I was living, cinema was not considered a serious vocation, in contrast to law school or economics, for example. I was studying economics when I realised that I was just biding my time, all the while readying myself to follow my desire, to orient myself towards journalism and film.

OH: What were your first films? These consisted of reportage, correct?
JS: Indeed, I began with shooting documentary stories, and I didn't come to fiction until much later. However, the frontier between the two is not all that well defined, and there are often documentary elements present in my fiction films and vice versa. Nonetheless, in that period there was a fabulous tradition of major documentary reportage, with film crews present in zones of conflict, who did not hesitate to take risks in order to bear witness, in order to bring back and report on images from these situations. The recourse to cinema, notably to documentary, with the intent to provoke or to accompany social changes, to denounce, or to provide the basis for action, all of that was very much present when I began. The effervescence of the sixties continued to energise a great

many young people in the world. Certainly, with the energy and no doubt the recklessness of youth, I found myself covering wars of very considerable consequence both on regional and global scales. Think of the October 1973 War, the Palestinian situation, when the Palestine Liberation Organization (PLO) had taken refuge in Lebanon after its problems in Jordan; or the Lebanese war, which blew up in 1975 and was to last many years; and I met political leaders, such as Yasser Arafat, Houari Boumediene and Colonel Gaddafi.

OH: The same Gaddafi who turned against his people?
JS: In those days he was viewed as a nationalist and progressive ruler, claiming the cause of Nasser and Arab unity; but also as a troublemaker – someone about whom one could not be sure, someone who already worried everybody.

OH: Among the films from this period, *Les Commandos suicide* (*The Suicide Commandos*) was going to be broadcast on television, under the title *Le Front du refus* (*The Front of Refusal*).
JS: In hindsight one may consider how the whole thing was put together in classic fashion, take a bunch of images, conduct an interview, then shoot some more images, then another interview . . . However, this project retains a certain relevance, even in hindsight, because it brought to light a reality that was destined to proliferate until the present day – that of the suicide commandos. Young men ready to die as martyrs for a cause, after having been recruited by the administrators of parties or movements . . . Leaders such as Nayef Hawatmeh (of the Popular Democratic Front for the Liberation of Palestine, the PDFLP) and Ahmad Jibril (of the Popular Front for the Liberation of Palestine – General Command, or PFLP-GC) were given the opportunity to speak at length, while being photographed from the back, without showing their faces. And we shot shock groups in training. But you'll notice I chose, in this context, to include a rather surprising and unexpected scene: one of the commandos is dancing, swaying rhythmically, his scarf tied around his waist. We must not forget how dance accompanies all the important acts of life. In those days I was made to promise that I would not reveal the location of this secret base. And this scoop caused a lot of jealousy on the part of my colleagues, together with reprimands and criticism from the more moderate branch of Fatah and the PLO.

OH: Journalists, intrigued, asked themselves how a young woman, new to the scene and relatively unknown, could manage to capture these images of the suicide commandos?
JS: And I can't begin to tell you the troubles I had when I came back to France because of this film. I was merely pursuing my work in journalism, in the process of trying to do my best. That's why I allowed those elements of the hardliners of the Palestinians, those who reunited under the wing of *The Front of Refusal*, to speak on their own behalf. That didn't mean that I would

support one or another of their positions. I was a journalist and I gave everyone a chance to speak.

OH: What were some of the criticisms raised by the members of the PLO?
JS: Members of Fatah reproached me for having collected the testimony of the hard line of the resistance movement – basically, for painting a bad image of the Palestinian struggle through showing the most radical fringe, the most violent. 'You don't see how they raise their hand – their gesture resembles a Nazi salute. In the West, once again those who struggle for a Palestinian state will make common cause with anti-Semites and proto-Nazis, or do you not think this is the case?' Were they, effectively, reviving the Nazi salute? In fact, in hindsight I don't think so, but, possibly, there may have been evil intent. In Lebanon, where I was raised, a truly cosmopolitan country, open to many religions, according rights to religious minorities, there was no anti-Semitism, not in that society. Following the various conflicts with the state of Israel, and all the bombings, criticism against that country was raised, often virulent criticism in view of the human and material damage; yet I believe that it is important to differentiate between the two and to recall the absence of a tradition of anti-Semitism in Lebanon and in the neighbouring countries. It is really something that I discovered in France, anti-Semitism, it wasn't part of my life in Lebanon.

In my work I presented and interviewed leaders from other currents, beginning with Yasser Arafat himself in 1973 – he wasn't giving a lot of interviews back then, so actually it was important – not forgetting the Palestinian population, the women, the inhabitants of the refugee camps in the south of Lebanon as well as at the gates of the capital. What I was trying to capture, in giving the floor to Yasser Arafat or to Fatah, in these documentaries, was not that I was adopting their point of view. The suicide commandos were something new in that period, the practice, alas, became much more ubiquitous in the Middle East and elsewhere. All those reprimands and discussions gave me the opportunity to mature artistically and to always reflect on what I was filming: why and for what struggle does one make an image? What should one show and present? Not for reasons of censorship, or self-censorship, nor for propaganda. All of this provoked, in me, a useful reflection – a necessity for cinema – on the significance of images and their reception.

OH: At the beginning of the war in Lebanon, in 1975, you returned to the country and decided to focus on what was happening there?
JS: The war correspondents were already stationed in numerous locations in Asia and the Near East. Eric Rouleau, Ania Francos, Jean Lacouture, Lucien Bodard – and I could cite many others – all passed through Beirut during the seventies, notably because the headquarters of the Palestinian Liberation Organization (PLO) were already established in Libya, because the conflict

in Cyprus had broken out, and because there was more freedom there than in other Arab countries. With the war, the press correspondents, the photographers and the reporters arrived in great numbers (Raymond Depardon; the American, Jonathan Randal). They inspired me, and I told myself that it would be necessary for me to understand what was going on in my country, since a very lively intuition told me that the war would not be of short duration, and that its consequences would be dramatic. I was very politicised all the same, sensitised by the 1969 demonstrations in Lebanon, 'Black September' which engulfed Jordan, the Vietnam War, the Palestinian question in general, and the division of Cyprus.

OH: What surprised me when I watched *Lebanon in Turmoil* is the distanced view it adopts relative to each of the protagonists. It is not dogmatic, even if one senses that it expresses, no doubt, more sympathy towards the left than towards the conservative right and the Phalangists, during an era in which the country enters the war, into the depths of radicalisation of discourses and approaches. Where does this detached approach come from?
JS: Perhaps it's thanks to my personal life experience (studies in Paris) and my partner in film, the Swiss journalist Jörg Stocklin, that I was able to acquire a certain distance and to benefit from a true perspective on my own country. Elsewhere, even when he was working in Beirut, in all instances Jörg maintained a view from the exterior, that of the stranger who often sees those things to which one does not pay attention when one is participating in such a society, when one evolves within the interior of a country. He was leftist, he supported the progressive camp during the conflict, but he always protected his own critical spirit, free of naivety. In short, when he would analyse the situation, he would possess a certain distance, and he was adamant that he wanted me to do the same. I should also mention my father, who never ceased to maintain a distance in the face of events, and never succumbed to the sirens of ideology of one camp or another, nor did he preach the exclusion of the other. The Phalangist discourse had no hold on him, he was sufficient unto himself, he would think for himself, and had no need for anyone to tell him what to do, what to think.

OH: In contrast to other leaders, Kamal Jumblatt is filmed alone in his palace.
JS: Back then I asked myself: why do you film all the political leaders or the religious and their partisans, except him? Kamal Jumblatt had the stature of a modern progressive leader. He was, after all, the one who assembled the left. He represented something important for us, and he was an open person as well. He'd often travel to India, to stay in ashrams and follow up with return visits. A great spirituality emanated from his person, and this gave us hope. One asks oneself: who is this man who goes to reflect on the state of the world? He represented something truly important. Although he did also have armed men

at his home, a militia like all the others, this was not the angle that interested me. For other political leaders I often gave directions, in choosing in which context I would want to question them, and to film them with their supporters. For example, I said to Pierre Gemayel, the head of the Phalangists, 'I want to film you at your common table, with your partisans.' As I was not in good graces with them and couldn't get permission, I made my father intervene in order to film them. Indeed, time and again I found myself face to face with a series of filming problems: a group of militant women questioned me bluntly and threatened me, they threatened to confiscate my camera and my shooting equipment, after having violently pulled my hair.

OH: The film had an impact in Algeria, which tried to play a role on the world stage, as an advocate for a new world order, more favourable to the interests of the South.

JS: In the mid-1970s, Algeria was very interested in what was happening in Lebanon, in particular because the PLO headquarters were in Beirut, and the Palestinian issue is a central concern for the Arab world. And I remember that some senior leaders of the National Liberation Front (NLF) began to wonder if a kind of civil war similar to the one that ignited Lebanon would come to pass in Algeria. I was invited by Boudjema Karèche and Yazid Khoja to present my documentary at the Cinematheque of Algiers, which was then a hotbed of global cinephilia, in front of a room full of Algerian officials; I think even the President of the Republic Houari Boumediene was present. The Algerian Institute of Film and Television bought several of my documentaries. I had interesting discussions with Algerian filmmakers, like Farouk Beloufa, who discovered Lebanon through my films. Shortly thereafter, he shot *Nahla*, a film that many Algerian critics consider one of the best films in their cinema – giving a role to Lina Tabbara, whom I filmed twice (in *For a Few Lives* and in *Letter from Beirut*). I gave him many personal contacts. Farouk was fascinated by the freedom of speech and movement and the proliferation of ideas of political parties in Lebanon in the seventies. He wrote his screenplay with Rachid Boudjedra, and he made use of my documentaries *Lebanon in Turmoil* and *Letter from Beirut* to research the Lebanese situation. In retrospect, it's interesting that the bureau of Algerian cinema acquired my film *Beirut, Never Again*, as shot in 16 mm. They decided to release it nationwide in 35 mm.

OH: In effect you understood fairly quickly that the left was in trouble, as well as the so-called progressive camp?

JS: When they assassinated Kamal Jumblatt in March 1977, everyone knew it was over. I left to go make a film in Egypt, then in the Western Sahara, that same year. But I continued to live in Lebanon, even when I had to set up camp elsewhere. When the Lebanese capital was put under siege by the Israelis in 1982, I was on location with my camera. I didn't leave Lebanon until 1985, when the saturation of violence became too much. Since then I've returned regularly.

OH: How did you come to work with Etel Adnan in *Beirut, Never Again*? This poet also appears in *Letter from Beirut*, shot two years later, if I am not mistaken?

JS: Etel is a talented poet and painter. She is also the author of a major text on the Lebanese war, a novel called *Sitt Marie Rose* (1978). I have read many books about the conflict, and hers is the best, I find, the most just. Moreover, I can go over the novel's characters one by one and give them their real names, since naturally she changed their names. The poetic texts in *Beirut, Never Again* and in *Letter from Beirut* are written from a single insight, she told me recently. She envisioned, in a single moment, all the images before her imagination, before she set about writing. I recently asked her how she recalled so much. Her response was, 'I love the images that come by instinct, I associate them with poetic text coming from the same source. You were the first person to come down into the street, to register these images in memory even though no one asked you for them. You knew how it was necessary to proceed, and you made them into something, you didn't hesitate a second. I could only follow you. For my part I understood instinctively what you were bringing to light. I was very sensitive to the children who understood, before any of us, that nothing and nobody could imagine a precedent for what was happening, that a whole period was coming to an end, and that we would never be the same. My strong sense was that I could only render homage to their lucidity.'

OH: And, a little while later you filmed another documentary, *Children of War*.

JS: After *Lebanon in Turmoil* I arranged for a camera and a car. In truth, I wasn't having financial problems, although I didn't have a lot of extra cash. And then I contacted my producer, I told him, 'Hey let's go!' I'd just spent the night in conversation with journalists returning from Quarantina (the refugee camp that had been taken over by the Phalangists), and I had seen the end of the massacre. When the slum was taken by storm, many of the adults were beaten in cold blood, and once the refugee camp was conquered, the assailants popped open the champagne bottles right next to the corpses. Children survived. When they emerged, at night, I had no light or anything, but I followed the children's pathways, to learn where they were, since they'd be unable to reach the slum, Quarantina, which had been obliterated, and their parents had been executed. I saw that they were staying at the cottages at the fancy beaches in the city, Saint Simon, Saint Michel – these became slums that still exist today. So, I went to buy paper, coloured pencils, and I went to meet them the next day. I took time to call my director of photography for TV, Hassan Naamani, who works with me; I told him, I'm coming to film Sunday, you show me your children's games. And they played war games on the beach, but it quickly became very violent, so much that I had to tell them to stop playing and I had to bring two of them to the hospital to get sewn up because they had been injured. Then I came back. And this is when I encountered the most powerful moment. They were a bit sheepish, as three of them were injured, but they emerged as if they were part of the violence they received – for it must not be forgotten that they came out of a massacre. I found them, between the chalets arranged as a fancy little village, and I suggested we continued filming. And there, wounded and traumatised as they were by what had happened, in order to liberate themselves from all of this, the children re-enacted the massacre. And I filmed. I carefully gathered my film canisters, and took the first plane to Paris to make television history. At that time, films would get developed for television in a secretive way. That was customary procedure, so that's what I did. This time I knew I had the right stuff, the real deal. I checked in with my editor (Jean-Marie Cavada) and I told him, 'Develop the 16 mm film, look at the pictures, and if you like it, I'll put together the film.' They developed it, without sending it back to me, and they put me in touch with an editor who did the montage TV-style. And little by little, journalists started hanging out in the editing lab and asked me if I had staged the children. The film was broadcast. Usually, at the time, one did not have a say in how it was edited. I was only asked to add text. Then, in due course, I made a name for myself. With *Beirut, Never Again*, I had gained the freedom to make the film entirely the way I wanted it. Thirty years later, I reused these images of *Children of War* for my installation in Singapore. I remounted the film by projecting onto three screens, accelerating certain passages so that the audience could find themselves immersed in the war itself. Once again, everything's in the approach. It is still the major question in documentary: how to reach people.

BEARING WITNESS WITH A CAMERA

OH: In 1977 you surveyed a new area of conflict in *Le Sahara n'est pas à vendre* (*The Sahara is Not for Sale*). Spain withdrew from its former colony and left it to Mauritania and Morocco. Morocco considered the Western Sahara to be a part of its southern territories, while the Polisario Front, supported by Algeria, claimed the independence of the territory.
JS: Several critics of the day emphasised the careful objectivity of the film, and so it was screened at the United Nations during a session on this issue. I genuinely had not tried to adhere to ideologies of Algerians or Moroccans concerning the Western Sahara. The funniest or most surprising thing is that the two countries indirectly contributed to the financing of the documentary. Both criticised me: Algerians did not appreciate that I showed archival footage of President Houari Boumediene. But I had bought these images and it seemed

28 OLIVIER HADOUCHI

Figure 1.1 Jocelyne Saab with a Sahraoui, playing with the camera

natural to include them, as Algerians were involved in the conflict and supported the Polisario Front. Morocco, on the other hand, preferred that I did not go too deeply into their views on the issue. Above all, it was the friendship with the Saharan desert dwellers that I appreciated the most. I have always been fascinated by the desert. I made the film for them, not as an account in favour of this or that state.

OH: You were assistant director on *Circle of Deceit* by Volker Schlöndorff. Was it an interesting experience?
JS: The film has been criticised a lot, and I must say I have mixed feelings towards it myself. However, I learned a lot from working on a fiction project with a large film crew, consisting of many people.

OH: On the set of *Circle of Deceit*, armed with your experience as a reporter, did you make interventions to influence the direction of the shoot, as it were?
JS: Volker Schlöndorff was at the height of his fame at the time – he won the Palme d'Or for *The Tin Drum* in 1979. And I was a young director with no experience working with fiction. In 1980, he filmed *Circle of Deceit* in Beirut. He opted for a classic plot that probably loses something in the thematic focus on the relationship between executioner and victim. The depiction of the conflict is successful aesthetically – despite a certain lack of awareness of its complexity – and inspired by a Camus-like vision. Today, the film is still an

important witness to the war. After all, to come and shoot in Beirut in wartime, is this not in itself an act of resistance against what is called 'war'?

OH: *Beirut, My City* is a very important film for you, isn't it?
JS: I do consider it one of the most important of my films, the one which I hold closest to my heart. In 1982, my house burned down. This was really something – it was a very old house. Here were one hundred and fifty years of history going up in flames and disappearing. Everything was suddenly annihilated. Our family's domicile, off the map, gone from the city, a mass of ruins.

OH: The war truly touched your family in a new way, at that moment?
JS: Oh yes, completely. I would go on to address this in a film in the aftermath, but only after six months, as I needed recovery time in order to find the strength to make it. Some would say to me, then, 'How can you offer the images of your burning house to a rival television channel (FR3)?' It was seen as simply a question of competition, whilst actually I felt it was necessary to come to terms with my experience first.

OH: In *Beirut, My City* scenes with emaciated children are really very hard to watch – scenes of total desolation.
JS: We knew that during the siege of Beirut, nobody had managed to reach a school for disabled children which was located near the Sabra and Chatila camps. The city was shelled constantly by the Israeli occupation army. We could not stop talking about the kids and were wondering if they were still alive. The area where they were was inaccessible – and it took the Red Cross several days to obtain a ceasefire, to stop the bombardments, so that they could access the school. It was on our minds every day, and we took it really seriously when we understood the symbolism of their survival. We said to ourselves, 'If the kids are alive, we will also continue to live,' and that gave us strength. When news of the children's evacuation came to us, it was as if we'd won a victory. When I found out that the children would be transferred to a school near my family home, which had already burned down – as can be seen early on in the film – I returned there with my camera, even though the zone was still dangerous. They were transferred by ambulance to the Armenian school, Honentmen. Every day we'd risk our lives during the siege of Beirut, as bombs covered the city non-stop. Strangely enough, this risk of death from the sky became abstract to us. I filmed the little ones, so thin and vulnerable, as living images of death coming towards me. At the same time, the act of capturing these images for me was equivalent to taming death. As if the process of witnessing and capturing the image could save me from my own death. When I was filming and my eye was one with the lens, I believed I was invincible.

OH: What was your usual pattern during the day-by-day bombings during the siege in 1982?

JS: To go out to film, to witness, as soon as the planes had passed over. To buy boxes of cheese like 'Laughing Cow', to find gasoline, and water. To go get dinner from the two or three restaurants that were open. It was like we were telling ourselves a story. We created for ourselves the illusion that we were continuing to live a 'normal' life. To save people, to film, to find what remained, to find out what was going on, to assure ourselves that others were still alive. I had my car and I would spend every day at the headquarters of the PLO to stay informed about the situation. In the city there was hardly enough to eat, the misery of extreme poverty and hunger was pervasive. Among our group, there were about fifty artists and intellectuals. One of us was assassinated. As we were leaving a restaurant, a car went into a fishtail spin, some guys came out and started shooting – our friend was killed in a barrage of machine gun fire because he had been distributing water to the entire city under siege.

OH: Despite the incessant bombings during the siege, you went out all the same?
JS: We went out in the evenings. We were crazy. We went to one of the restaurants or to the Commodore Hotel, where journalists hung out. During the day, I got around on a moped. The Palestinian resistance made arrangements so that we could work and continue to witness as journalists. They knew who was who, and we were essential to them, so we were able to stay on the move. I went to get gas every day. We moved house four times during the siege. The Israeli army wanted to assassinate Arafat, thinking that they could get to him if they went on destroying entire buildings. Often, dozens of dead and wounded would turn up but there was no trace of the PLO leader. On one occasion an entire building was destroyed by a bomb, right next to ours.

OH: What an extraordinary period for you and your friends.
JS: If you ask people who lived through the siege, they'll all tell you that this was the most beautiful period of their lives. At that moment, reasons to live multiplied a thousand times over, because if you'd chosen to be there, to stay put, you believed in your own fight for the cause. This was an act of resistance. 'By what right do you come and occupy Beirut and Lebanon?' This was the question that we were posing, to the entire world. By staying on site, one bears witness to, and one is together with those who are being attacked and bombed. Everything was intensely difficult. As destructive as it was, it was an exceptional moment. Whenever I am confronted by a film that evokes war without sincerity, I experience immediate indignation: there's no truth in it. You can't get away with this. Authenticity matters. When you're this deep into it, with real sincerity, you need to hold artistic production and journalism to a very high standard of excellence.

OH: After the siege, in your next film, you immortalised the departure of Yasser Arafat and the PLO fighters with *Le Bateau de l'exil* (*The Ship of Exile*).

They left Beirut and moved into a place and a future that seemed all the more uncertain.

JS: When I filmed these images, definitely, I sensed that I was living in and through a historic moment. I didn't want to leave the city and I hesitated before getting on board the ship. However, I was curious about the idea behind those people who arranged the embarkation for Arafat and his group naming the boat *Atlantis*. The ship's name concentrates the main thrust of the filming. I was the only journalist allowed onto the ship, and I've never known who gave permission for me to get on. People have implied that it was Arafat himself. And now, this film plays a part in Palestinian history – I've given them a copy – it's dedicated to them.

FICTIONAL STORYTELLING

OH: How did the filming of *A Suspended Life* go?
JS: Omar Sharif was originally going to play the main character, but he didn't want to work in Beirut, the natural setting for the film. Most of all he was afraid of the Lebanese war, as it was still raging. So instead of Sharif, my producer suggested Jacques Weber, and Selim Nassib wrote a lovely article in *Libération* (the newspaper) concerning the film.

OH: In the film, Jacques Weber speaks Arabic, was he dubbed?
JS: No, that's his voice in the film. He took a lot of conversation classes with excellent teachers, and I'm quite pleased with the result. What's more, he told me that the fact that he had to speak in a language he didn't fully grasp gave him a certain distance, and gave him more room to develop the character in a better way. As for me, I'd never filmed a work of fiction, and I must say I was a little scared.

OH: You were filming in the depths of war. How did that go?
JS: It all began with a big fracas that very nearly precipitated an attack on my principal actor. We were in the streets parallel to Hamra Street, and the fighters followed us. When the militias saw this big guy with a foreign air, they immediately thought that he was an Israeli or European spy. They positioned themselves in front of us and proceeded to aim their machine guns at him. I cried out, 'You have no shame! I am your mother, you're going to kill your mother?' As soon as they heard the word 'mother', they lost their edge. They understood they'd made a mistake. They let us pass on through. I feared that he'd refuse to continue filming. He could have taken the first plane back to Paris. But he figured I'd saved his life, so he accepted the challenge to continue, to bring the project to conclusion. His wife, Christine, summed things up well when she noted that the film had a strong start!

EGYPT TAKES CENTRE STAGE

OH: In your films you are often in dialogue with Egypt. One could even speak of a long relationship dating back to the seventies.
JS: In the sixties and seventies, Egypt was the centre of the Arab world. In 1967, I shared the humiliation of Arabs listening to the radio, hearing about the Defeat against Israel. At least when Nasser lost the 1967 war over the course of a couple of days, he announced his desire to step down. Yet it was the people who insisted that he stay on. Whole crowds assembled to urge him to continue. In 1973, I covered the October War. Following that period, I became acquainted with several members of the Egyptian Left and we stayed in contact. From the beginning I was intrigued by the nationalist sentiment. I entered into dialogue with men like Mohamed Sid Ahmed, someone with a real political consciousness. He offered his point of view concerning anti-imperialism, the will of the Egyptian people to live freely without external interference, to make use of their rich natural resources.

OH: You filmed *Egypt, The City of the Dead* in 1977.
JS: I still ask myself how I could mesh surrealism with social realism in this film. The great poet Ahmed Fouad Negm was still in prison, since his protest texts had displeased the regime at that time. You could be put in prison for practically nothing, at the drop of a hat. So, accompanying his partner Azza to a spot under his prison window, I retrieved the poems he threw through the bars of his cell. Sheik Imam sang his poems to the revolutionary students who gathered in the City of the Dead. We still believed we could change the world. I'd discovered Egypt in 1970. Back then miniskirts were as common as gallabiyahs on the streets of Cairo. And I was grateful for the Egyptian Left, we really got along well. I was in touch with everybody, leaders, artists, but also the Egyptian people, whom I adore. My close observation of these people comes from that love. In real life I could always search out and find characters that were so much like the literary creations of Naguib Mahfouz and Ihsan Abdel Kouddous. They taught me so much.

After I finished *Egypt, The City of the Dead* I was barred from travelling to the country for seven years because I had delivered an account of the impoverishment of the general population, and because, just like the rest of the press, I was critical of and involved in exposing the so-called politics of inclusion. That concept was in fact the establishment of an economically savage liberalism, based in corruption, repression and back-tracking. As soon as I could manage it, after those seven years, I returned to Cairo. For a while I did not understand one of the reasons for the interdiction. I had touched on a taboo subject: the City of the Dead is considered a sacred site for Egyptians, as many Islamic religious figures are interred there, including close associates and family of the Prophet. I did not know that when I shot the film.

OH: You also met and got to know other directors such as Tawfik Saleh, Shadi Abdel Salam and Youssef Chahine during various trips to Egypt?
JS: Chahine always had success finding financing for his films. He was somebody who was always sympathetic to me and gave me advice on several occasions. Tawfik Saleh was well known for his film *The Dupes* (1972). At one point he became seduced by the opportunity to make a lot of money on a certain project: he shot a hagiographic portrait of Saddam Hussein in the seventies. After that he was marginalised as a filmmaker in Egypt, but he could still teach at the university. It's a shame that he did not make more films, because he was so talented. Shadi Abdel Salam directed a masterpiece recognised worldwide, *The Night of Counting the Years* (*The Mummy*, 1969). He had a great quality of presence, and true elegance. We would regularly run into each other on the train to Upper Egypt. He worked in the Cairo Museum to restore the chair of Tutankhamun. He dedicated a film to the subject of the restoration. Shadi had beautiful hands; he'd often place them on the table in the manner of a pharaoh. One day, I was explaining to Gérard Brach, my writer for *A Suspended Life*, the notion of time in the East. I decided to introduce him to Shadi Abdel Salam. The visit to Shadi saved me a lot of speeches. Gérard Brach said then, 'I never would have thought that in this life I'd one day meet a pharaoh.'

OH: In 2005, *Dunia* was released, after many obstacles: intimidation, threats and death threats.
JS: Yes, the project took a long time to fall into place, and I underwent a great deal of pressure, but I stood my ground.

OH: Can you speak of your work directing the actors in *Dunia*?
JS: When I showed the film to the actors, they told me, 'You've directed us as if we were strangers' (meaning Westerners). In my direction, I searched for a certain gravity of tone and method, I was trying to avoid at all costs the over-acting that one notices in numerous Egyptian productions. At the same time, I also wanted to pay tribute to the energy of these women, and not to betray Egyptian culture, since the norms and criteria of beauty, for example, can vary depending on the country. For the dance scenes in *Dunia* I worked with a professor of dance, a very talented man, who in a certain sense played himself, Walid Aouni. He was director of the contemporary dance ensemble at the Cairo Opera, and was an early pupil of Maurice Béjart. As for Mohamed Mounir, he was a superstar in Egypt. However, to convince the principal actress, Hanan Turk, to play her role, I was obliged to resort to patience and a lot of conviction in order to bring her around. She was a very professional actor, and at the same time very intuitive. I was very disappointed when she was drawn into fundamentalist circles, later. She did not defend the film.

OH: Feminine characters wearing intense colours, and the use of pure red, often reminds me of the work of Almodóvar. Might there also be a Mediterranean sensibility involved here in a certain way, although your own world is unique, just as his is?

JS: I'm charmed by your analogies. You're not the first to have made the connection. You are thinking of Almodóvar's *High Heels* (1991), for example, working with the colour red and its effect. You know, I played around a lot with colour, working with my director of photography. Red is very important, very charged with emotions and meanings. Spanish audiences generally perceive and grasp the sense of *Dunia* very well. I am reminded of this every time I get involved in a film production in Spain.

TRANSNATIONAL PROJECTS

OH: In your work, one senses an interest to really follow life into the very heart of war and chaos. In this way your documentary *Fécondation in video* (*Fertilisation in Video*, 1991) involves the question of life itself. Was it a commissioned film, or did it correspond more closely to a personal preoccupation?

JS: The initiative could not have been more personal. At the time I was discovering the effects of the war on my body, as they slowly became apparent. I was spending a lot of time at the hospital. On top of all that, my doctor diagnosed me as suffering from intense anxiety. Then he came up with the idea that I might study in vitro fertilisation, which then came into being as a practice, thinking this might give me some ideas. So, I did research in the hospital for a while. The adventure lasted six months, not counting the time I spent finding medical sponsorship. The broadcaster France 2 entered into the production of a documentary, thanks to Roland Paringaux MK2/Le Monde. It became a very personal film. It won awards and touched a large public and went to broadcast television. It was a very personal project, which without a doubt gave me the energy to continue.

OH: In *La Dame de Saïgon* (*The Lady of Saigon*, 1998), you set about filming a very elderly and honourable Vietnamese communist, whose origins were in the bourgeoisie, who was bringing necessary medical assistance to the poor in remote parts of the countryside after the Vietnam war. Who was this grand dame of Saigon?

JS: Madame Hoa was a doctor. She undertook a daunting humanitarian task. She came from a family of wealthy merchants, of literate Chinese origin, yet she supported the communist liberation movement, and even spent seven years with the resistance in the forest. After having taken on various high-level functions during the Vietnam War, she became Minister of Health in the Provisional Government of South Vietnam. Then she decided to pursue an independent path, and stay at a distance from power, in order to dedicate her life to health care among the rural population, setting out to help people of modest families, even in the most distant and least accessible locales. She remained in her country, to take care of the population, and to instruct them to participate in reconstruction, and that really impressed me. Some people told me she was authoritarian, directing her dispensaries with a lot of energy while at the same time being dictatorial. Everyone has their faults, and that is the complexity of human nature. I was really taken with her, and at that moment in my life, as with a lot of people involved in my other projects, I believe that she saved me.

OH: Were you under scrutiny from the Vietnamese authorities during the filming?
JS: Madame Hoa and her husband were constantly under surveillance, so we transported the film canisters to France while making it possible for them to leave the country under clandestine circumstances.

OH: After this film, there was nearly another film set in Asia, and then there were your two major fiction films *Dunia* (2005) and *What's Going On?* (2009).
JS: That's the case with so many of my films. Lurking behind each one is another. As for *Dunia*, someone should write a book about the film, and all that it entailed, to really do it justice. I would love for someone to take that on.

OH: I know that you carefully follow current world events, especially those that concern the Middle East – the Iraq wars, the wars in Afghanistan, not to mention the movements for change that have developed in several Arab countries, the Arab Spring – has it inspired you in some way?
JS: My experience as filmmaker and as a reporter-journalist, my experience of the Lebanon War and other conflicts, brings me to say that the problems in Afghanistan and Iraq are not over yet. These conflicts are going to continue for a long time, without a doubt. For the countries in question, there will be heavy consequences. Those who start wars don't always have control over the course of war, nor the outcomes of it. And I support the Arab Spring. I hope it will yield great results in all the Arab countries that need real social and democratic reform. But I also know that this is a very long and slow process and requires hard work. I am against exterior interventions and military incursions that are not in the interest of the people.

NOTES

1. The interviews upon which this chapter is based were translated by Christina McPhee. They were originally published online on 25 June 2013 at <https://www.criticalsecret.net/> (last accessed 1 December 2020).
2. Abu Ammar is Yasser Arafat's *nom de guerre*.

BIBLIOGRAPHY

Adnan, Etel [1978] (2011), *Sitt Marie Rose*, Sausalito, CA: Post Apollo Press.
Association of Jocelyne Saab's Friends, <https://jocelynesaabasso.com/>.
Brenez, Nicole (2013), 'Cycles Les astres de la guerre et Contre-culture générale', 29 March–24 May, Cinémathèque Française.
Eilmes, Élena (2012), 'Interview with the Lebanese Filmmaker Jocelyne Saab: "My Country Was a Beautiful Garden"', *Qantara.de*, 17 August, <https://en.qantara.de/content/interview-with-the-lebanese-filmmaker-jocelyne-saab-my-country-was-a-beautiful-garden> (last accessed 1 December 2020).
Fawaz, Ghassan (1996), *Les Moi volatils des guerres perdues*, Paris: Seuil.
Fawaz, Ghassan (1998), *Sous le ciel d'Occident*, Paris: Seuil.
Hillauer, Rebecca (2005), 'Jocelyne Saab', in Rebecca Hillauer, *Encyclopedia of Arab Women Filmmakers*, Cairo: American University in Cairo Press.
Sanbar, Elias (2000), *Dictionnaire amoureux de la Palestine*, Paris: Plon.
Traboulsi, Fawwaz (2007), *A History of Modern Lebanon*, London: Pluto Press.

CHAPTER 2

On Representing the War as Rupture: Jocelyne Saab and New Lebanese Cinema (1975–90)

Ghada Sayegh

VISIBILITY OF FILMS ON THE LEBANESE CIVIL WAR

How does one film the war? What do these images that arise from history, as fragments of multiple narratives and temporalities, represent to us today? What is their relationship to the event and to the Real? The task of a film historian is complex, as we work with an incomplete corpus of cinematographic works that includes the invisible. That which is not there is concrete matter, both where it concerns the archive and because the cinematographic enterprise of filming war is linked to the confused, evanescent and traumatic topic it covers. It would thus be interesting to question a revealing aspect concerning the circulation of Lebanese films, as well as the state of the copies that remain today. From *The Adventures of Elias Mabrouk* (*Mughamarat Elias Mabrouk*, 1929) – the first Lebanese film, directed by the Italian Giordano Pidutti – up until the present day, the history of Lebanese cinema has been characterised by a lack of visibility and, in some cases indeed, the complete disappearance of certain films which thereby 'acquired the status of urban myths in Lebanon, talked about but never encountered'.[1] The main causes of the disappearance of films are a combination of circumstances surrounding the successive wars in Lebanon, the lack of infrastructure or political will to safeguard the national cinematographic heritage, but also the lack of support for production and distribution of Lebanese films, most of which have not benefited from a DVD release. The absence of efficient national structures thus compels filmmakers or their rights-holders to cater for this heritage themselves, which – without substantial funding – makes the success and sustainability of their work entirely precarious. Especially when it comes to films made during the civil war (1975–90), the economic and security situation of the country in that period did not allow directors to produce or archive their films in conditions that safeguarded their ultimate preservation. Some have disappeared or been destroyed, while those that survived are only available in copies of poor quality.

This observation should, however, be put back in perspective, in a country with a rich and dynamic film heritage that has not lacked in diverse initiatives despite the lack of means and the vagaries of history to try to safeguard this heritage. In fact, the first project for a cinematheque in Lebanon was created in 1969 by Maurice Akl, founder of the Beirut film club, at a time when 'the Lebanese were perceived as the cinephiles of the Arab world' (Rouxel 2018: 111), but it was destroyed by heavy shelling in the first fires of 1975 with the outbreak of the civil war. Rouxel returns to this cinematic effervescence of the 1950s and 1960s, recounting the numerous cinemas of the country and of Beirut in particular, devotedly screening both international films and films from the Arab world (see Soueid 1996). It was thus through cinephilia that Jocelyne Saab's desire for images was born, with *A Suspended Life* (1985) and *Once Upon a Time, Beirut: Story of a Star* (1994) especially steeped in multiple filmic influences. The filmmaker was also at the origin of the foundation of the Lebanese Cinematheque in 1999,[2] following the titanic research carried out for the realisation of *Once Upon a Time, Beirut*, which gathered no fewer than 400 films about or that were shot in Beirut, twenty-five of which have been restored and placed in the Lebanese Ministry of Culture – to which the cinematheque is attached – thus forming its foundation. Since then, several individual or private initiatives have emerged with a main mission to collect, preserve and disseminate Lebanese cinematographic heritage.[3] In June 2018 the Cinematheque Beirut project led by the Metropolis Association was inaugurated, placing itself at the crossroads of these multiple initiatives, with a digital platform forming a database listing Lebanese films in all genres and formats, whether classic or contemporary, and creating a new dynamic to the preservation and dissemination of the national cinematographic heritage. However, the financial and material difficulties, recently exacerbated by the unprecedented economic crisis that the country is experiencing, have postponed the prospect of establishing a cinematheque – in the short or long term – that would centralise the physical archives while allowing for accessibility, consultation and dissemination. With these considerations in mind, looking at Lebanese films, and more specifically those made during the Lebanese civil war, reveals problems with their visibility, as well as their potential – but problematic – resurrection.

These questions orient us towards film as an object or format that enters, so to speak, the archive from birth. It is perpetually threatened with disappearance, whether through the chemical fragility of the filmstrip, or as an image format that carries its own technical limitations. Film is thus inherently characterised 'by its gaps, its losses, its risks of disappearance' (Habib 2005a). André Habib, who is particularly interested in the imaginary of 'ruin' in cinema as a motive, but also through the 'ruin' of the film itself and that of the film stock, underlines the presence of 'the memory of a time', which remains available in the marks, traces, and the decomposition of the film. Time, according to Habib,

> would be all the more *visible* when it is *read* in the voids and marks that fragment or eat away at the film, and which make the film archive an ambiguous tomb, characterized by its shortcomings, and which decomposes slowly. (Habib 2005a; original emphasis)

The films of the Lebanese civil war today offer a reading that opens a breach in time through their (non-)visibility, as well as their technical and aesthetic failures. They offer filmic, aesthetic and narrative elements that trace the time and space of disaster from their actual content, quality of form and support.

THE SPACE–TIME OF WAR, BETWEEN DOCUMENTARY AND FICTION: A SHATTERED REALITY

The young filmmakers and founding figures of the New Lebanese Cinema – Borhane Alaouié, Maroun Bagdadi and Jocelyne Saab – were aware of the need for a radical change in the fields of art and cinema and therefore positioned themselves against a cinema devoid of links to the country's social reality. The directors were confronted with a context of violence that quickly generated a caesural crisis in representation. Through documentary and fiction, they initially created a cinema that sought to witness history: documenting the present was an emergency for these filmmakers who were caught in the whirlwind of the event, whose shock imposed the need to understand and to attempt to testify. However, faced with the shock of the event, this impulse, which was situated in a desire for political and social engagement, was instilled into a double movement. The necessity that saw its birth subsequently oriented its gaze towards an elusive reality: attempting to apprehend the Real resulted in an embrace of its ethereal fragility. While documenting the historical events they undergo, these filmmakers adopted a distanced posture, between the double necessity to both *be implicated* and *to step aside*.

The New Lebanese Cinema directors' quest for the image engaged them in directing their camera towards a reality in turmoil, which required testing the sharpness of their gaze as well as taking a stand. Rendering an image of reality amounted to questioning it. Violence and war impacted any relationship between objectivity and subjectivity, reality and imagination, person and world. Documentary and narrative (fiction) cinema coexisted, participating in the quest for a cinematographic language beyond any delimitation of genres.

But is documentary cinema as a 'direct imprint of reality' (Niney 2002: 13) possible in a country at war? And does narrative cinema as an imaginary construction with a dramatic or romantic structure generate the blips of history? If the boundaries between documentary and fiction have been blurred, the documentary and fictional works of the directors of New Lebanese Cinema show a sensitivity that challenges genre codes, which implies taking a position.

The events of 1975 marked a turning point in the career of journalist and war reporter Jocelyne Saab. Henceforth, the filmmaker no longer filmed the war of others but that of her own country, as the urge to understand and analyse came into being. In her first documentary film on the war, *Lebanon in Turmoil* (1975), the Real still appeared to fall under the regiment of signification, and the documentary in an objective restitution of reality. Scrupulously tracing the origins of the Lebanese conflict, the filmmaker travelled the length of the country and interrogated the leaders of the different political parties with one main question: why are you armed? With ironic distance, the director drew up a political assessment only a few months into the outbreak of the war, reflecting on the motivations and ideologies of the different parties, while immediately grasping the dramatic and human impact of the escalation of violence. If *Lebanon in Turmoil* attempted to 'objectively reconstruct a certain reality through film' (Niney 2002: 13), with voice-over commentary, the presence of the author was marked by the confrontation and multiplication of points of view, whether through the images or the diversity of testimonies. As such, this film is situated at the crossroads of a cinema that undertakes the task to document history, while being permeable to the enduring catastrophe, anticipating and surpassing it, and marking a temporal and historical discontinuity. The interviews and commentary that punctuate *Lebanon in Turmoil*, although carried by a critical outlook, gave way to the poetic text of Etel Adnan in Saab's next film, *Beirut, Never Again* (1976), which captured the gap between words and things.

TIME-ZERO

This need to search for new forms of representation seems to have been at the heart of a cinema that tries, despite everything and in times of war, to represent a reality; a present that eluded it. Filmed a few months after *Lebanon in Turmoil*, Saab's next film, *Beirut, Never Again*, marked another rupture and fracture in her work. Although the film was labelled a 'reportage' in the credits, here we will allow ourselves to analyse it as a documentary. Beyond targeting immediacy, information and so-called objectivity, the film explored a cinematic language and staging that tested reality. Saab no longer questioned politicians and no longer sought explanations or analyses, but rather testified – through a commentary by Lebanese poet and artist Etel Adnan – to the shock felt at the disappearance of Beirut. Unlike the analytical commentary of *Lebanon in Turmoil*, the voice-over here conjured up the stupefaction felt when faced with an apocalyptic reality.

Beirut, Never Again thus moved away from the descriptive and informative documentary images of *Lebanon in Turmoil* towards more disturbing and trembling images of apocalypse, taking the measure of both past and future violence, with the commentary infusing a poetic gap, incorporating the historical divide. 'Beirut no longer exists!' says the voice-over – a bitter observation expressed immediately before showing images of the city centre – where only a year earlier alleys still teemed with people. The city centre's many souks, shops and bars became a heap of ruins and a ghost town in the space of merely a few months. 'The unusual has destroyed the order of things', whether 'shops have spit out their old merchandise', or at times people have become corpses that no one ventures to recover, 'all laws having disappeared'. 'War imposes new rhythms on cities, and unexpected situations to say the least. The fighters read *Tintin*.' Slumped on their chairs and spinning around, they rest from the previous day's battles while awaiting the next. 'We demolished everything, both beings and objects. [. . .] But nothing completely disappears. The street signs regard us as a temptation whose power has not yet disappeared. They are the milestones of memory', traces of a past, objects of disappearance. Saab emphasised the before and after of the event, 'the most terrible catastrophe of the century' having transformed these objects into vestiges of the past. The ruins of the Hajj Daoud cafe, one of the oldest in Beirut, which was frequented by the characters of Maroun Bagdadi's first feature film, *Beirut, Oh Beirut* (1975), are enfolded between two waves on the coast in Saab's documentary. Despite the 'mornings without memories', the objects and details – a destroyed typewriter, a vinyl record lying around – form traces of a forever-modified life and city. They are recovered by children (whose playground is now a field of ruins where they loot and recycle these unusual objects); looting is seen as 'an instinct for life, a faith in the future'. Following the temporal rupture caused by the disaster, Saab thus explores the possible links between the past and the future, and the traces of Beirut's disappearance, which can paradoxically shape these links. 'The gestures of normal life are slow to die.' Just like the scenes of women in the Palestinian camps who bake their own bread, 'it is through such images that a population is reassured that their links with the past are somewhat maintained'.

But those moments of respite between emergencies and shrapnel are fleeting *time-zero*, between the before and the after, doomed to repeat themselves, and painfully reminding us that the worst is yet to come. The wanderings of children pillaging the ruins of Beirut resonate with those of Roberto Rossellini's children in *Germany Year Zero* (1948). As child soldiers, one of whom testifies to the pain of a society doomed to a fratricidal war, they haunt alleys

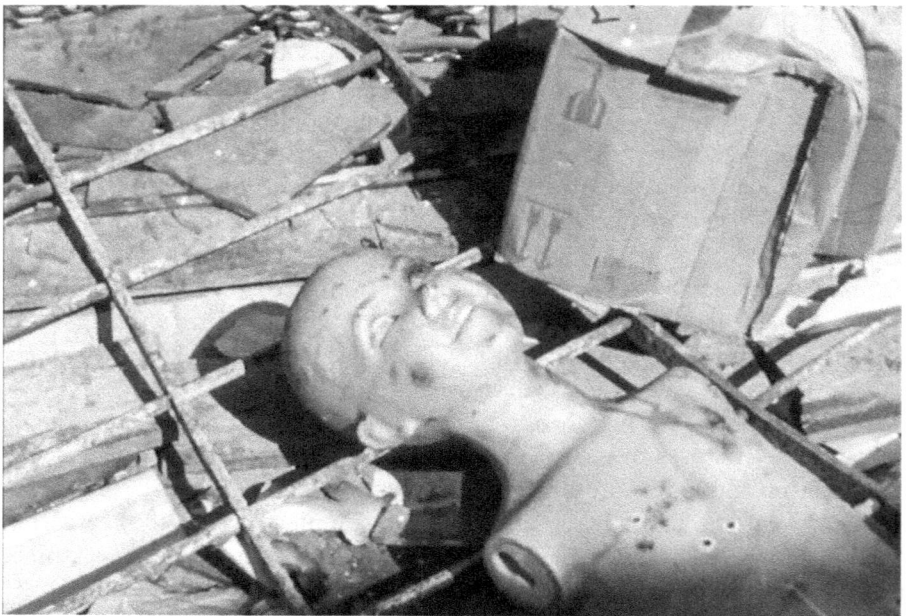

Figure 2.1 Still from *Beirut, Never Again*

covered in rubble, like young Edmund wandering through the ruins of Berlin. The ruins being,

> in the strictest sense, a montage of heterogeneous blocks of time. They are a past present, a present past, and yet also harbour a past future. The ruins, in other words, mobilize and combine the times, and they allow us to catch a glimpse of certain beats in history. (Habib 2007: 97)

The ruins of Beirut filmed by Jocelyne Saab in 1976 appear to us today as 'the place of a fracture or a resetting of the dials of history' (Habib 2007: 92),[4] allowing an anachronistic return to the ruins of the Berlin of year zero, in 1945, and a 'historical projection' (Habib 2007: 95)[5] on the ruins of Beirut. The ruins are doomed to infinite destruction and metamorphosis,[6] something that will haunt many works in times of war and its aftermath.

MEANING IN QUESTION

The ideals that fuelled the first years of war were succeeded by an increasingly violent and absurd conflict in the early 1980s. As the war turned into a war of militias, sects and clans, the need to understand and analyse the events in more detail lent itself to a type of observation that gave way to expressions of dismay in the absence of meaning. The Real was no longer comprehensible, nor explicable. The aesthetic fracture became immense. War was now a 'traumatic past-present' that imposed a 'new regime of images [introduced] *by force* into cinema' (Habib 2005b: 62; original emphasis), similar to the 'new type of image' that Italian neo-realism invented at the end and the aftermath of World War II.

The filmmakers of the New Lebanese Cinema would thus be faced with new modes of narration and representation, imposed by the loss of meaning. Although this new form of filmmaking did not create a realistic cinema with which a rupture would be imposed, the crisis was all the more marked as it accompanied the films since their inception. Consequently, the characters could only embody a phase shift between man and the world, unable to react in the face of 'a dispersive and incomplete reality' (Deleuze 1983: 285), wandering in empty disconnected spaces, and along trajectories that could not intersect as they were condemned to wander in a labyrinthine space–time. They could neither integrate fiction nor become part of an impossible narrative. The filmmakers of the New Lebanese Cinema thus found themselves unable to construct 'a linear, vectorised path that leads to a real or imaginary destination [. . .] whether through documentary or fictional means' (Frodon 2011: 367).

As the war made it impossible for the filmmaker to grasp, transmit or represent the Real by means of realism or documentary, Saab moved towards fiction, declaring 'the death of her lens as a documentary filmmaker'.[7] With *A Suspended Life* (1985), she questioned the representation of this state of being a stranger to oneself, this absence of meaning, this discrepancy between people and the world, in places crossed by characters who cannot inhabit them. Samar, a teenager who grew up among the fighters, squats with her brother and parents in an old house alongside other families who have fled the south of the country. Displacement and exile on one's own land seemed to be the fate of many Lebanese who resided in places of transit without truly living there. These were deserted if not derelict places, and therefore already in ruin, as expressed in the words of Jalal Toufic:

> I along with my two siblings and my mother deserted the family apartment during the 1982 Israeli invasion of Lebanon. Did this make the apartment a ruin? Yes, and not because it was severely damaged and burned during the last days of the offensive: even after it was restored, it remained a ruin. [. . .] Maybe the refusal of the Bustrus family to sell their house (Jennifer Fox's *Beirut, the Last Home Movie*) was due less to their obstinate nostalgia to never part with it, and much more to an apprehension that were they to sell it, it may be more readily deserted in a situation of intensive bombing by those who bought it, this ushering

and completing its becoming a ruin. Will we one day learn how to live in a place without dwelling in it, so that the act of deserting it would not turn it into a ruin? [. . .] Ruins: places haunted by the living who inhabit them. (Toufic 2006: 7–8)

Samar lives in a large house, in which the particular function of various rooms does not make it possible to distinguish between living room, bedroom, interior or exterior courtyard. She and her family sleep on mattresses on the floor, in different rooms depending on the days, and they are surrounded by merchandise that was once displayed in a shop that no longer exists. She falls in love with Karim, a painter who lives in a large, typically Lebanese house, with its arcades across the facade, a spacious interior and a high ceiling. This house takes a central place in the film, and we learn from the very beginning that Samar has dreamed of having gone there three times. We also know that she must fulfil this dream, seeing as it is bad luck not to do so. When she breaks into the house, she discovers a place that seems abandoned, where old objects and furniture are piled up, as well as an old pendulum clock, which she opens and tries to stop from ticking. She also finds an album containing postcards of pre-war Beirut and its traditional houses with tiled roofs by the sea. These are old houses threatened by disappearance, decimated by war. As we know, this is also the case for the filmmaker's own home, which she shows,

Figure 2.2 Still from *Une Vie Suspendue* (*A Suspended Life*)

totally destroyed, at the start of her documentary *Beirut, My City* (1982). When Samar visits Karim for the first time, he tells her that the house is not his, and that he is only renting a studio space there. He lives in a place abandoned by its inhabitants, and the old objects and furniture he uses belong to others. This accumulation of non-places, anonymous spaces, and 'ruins [are] places haunted by the living who inhabit them' (Toufic 2006: 8), without the possibility of dwelling there. And so 'if a place can be defined as relational, historical and concerned with identity, then a space which cannot be defined as relational, or historical, or concerned with identity, will be a non-place' (Augé 1995: 77–8).

Marc Augé's hypothesis is that the non-places produced by supermodernity are 'spaces which are not themselves anthropological places', which do not 'integrate the earlier places', and whose link with the past and the future would be ruptured; 'A world thus surrendered to solitary individuality, to the fleeting, the temporary and ephemeral [. . .]', a space that man cannot appropriate, condemned to become anonymous (1995: 78). Like the non-places of supermodernity ('transit points [. . .,] hotel chains and squats, holiday clubs and refugee camps, shantytowns threatened with demolition or doomed to festering longevity' [Augé 1995: 78]), the buildings damaged by war and those deserted intact houses embody 'the torn weft of time' (Habib 2011: 45). Both are in fact non-places in that a person cannot live in them, and in that they crystallise the impossibility of 'being-in-the-world':

> [In the German language] 'I am' also means 'I live'. I live in a world, as it is familiar to me. To be, as the infinitive verb of 'I am', means 'to live near', to be familiar with this habitat that is habit and familiarity. In short, these filiations in the German language between 'I am' and 'I live' press Heidegger to state that to be in the world means to live.
>
> From this perspective, exile – not as an opening to the diversity of the world, but as an imposed wandering – is a calamity, because it excludes the individual from his house and the little everyday things that usually govern his life. Exile drives out the individual and cuts him off from a known self in favour of a reality imposed on the self by contingencies, with hazards occurring along the way. Exile, in this sense, is the antithesis of the dwelling. It is alienation [in the sense of being foreign to ourselves] because it breaks with the state of harmony that the house symbolizes. (Martinez 1999)

An absence from the world equates to an absence from oneself, symbolises a gap between a person and the world, with 'characters [. . .] unconcerned, even with what happens to them [. . .]' (Deleuze 1985: 19). It is in such a spirit that Samar wanders from one street to another, from a ruined staircase to another one, idle, dreaming of love and of another place. Carrying a jar of water on her head, she visits Karim, or a sniper friend, in a deserted and crumbling cinema. She appears to be a very small being that moves in nondescript spaces that are empty and disconnected. This interest in places and spaces begs a question about the significance of the scene in which Samar speaks with her friend about her infatuation with Karim, in the surreal setting of the destroyed Beirut municipal stadium. How can these two young adolescent girls speak of love in a landscape of nuclear cataclysm, and how can these elements, whose ontological gap gives shape to the divide between a person and the world, be united in the same shot? A gap manifests itself as an absence of meaning: a gap between gestures and words, action and reaction, and an impossibility of 'reacting to situations' (Deleuze 1990: 74). At several instances in the film, Samar glares at the sniper opposite her, without even blinking when he shoots. When a local militiaman amuses himself by shooting birds as he would a passer-by, Samar turns around calmly with the jar steady on her head, and then continues on her way as though nothing had happened, while the children around her run. When her younger brother announces that their parents have been killed, a glimmer of emotion emerges from the young adolescent, but she continues on her path, in the same way as she does in the last scene of the film, where she defies the gaze of a sniper who has just shot Karim.

Figure 2.3 Still from *Une Vie Suspendue* (*A Suspended Life*)

RUPTURE OF LANGUAGE

A Suspended Life (1985) follows the wanderings of a teenage girl who falls in love with a forty-something-year-old artist in the midst of a civil war. As soon as she speaks of love, Samar mostly expresses herself as would the characters of the Egyptian films ever present on television, as if to mark her share of a dream in a world that has deprived her of it. As Tony Chakar describes it:

> But how will she find the language to talk about love in these ruins? She cannot because that language has withdrawn. So after circling around the subject, she starts borrowing another language, the language of love as it is spoken in popular Egyptian movies, fragments and semi-sentences that have become extremely popular over the years: 'Say hello to the aubergines' or 'The honour of a girl is like a matchstick, it can only be lit once.' (Chakar 2010: 76)

At the same time, the French actor Jacques Weber, who portrays Karim, learned his dialogues in Arabic phonetically as words he speaks without understanding, similarly to the Japanese actor in *Hiroshima mon amour* by Alain Resnais (1959), who did not speak a word of French. Samar's description of the Arabic calligraphies that Karim draws, which she cannot decipher, turns into a destruction of language, and reinvention of words, letters, shapes and colours:

> I don't know what he draws, they're incomprehensible shapes that shine like gold. This is what we see when we close our eyes after having fixated on the sun: stars of all colours, red, yellow, and green, and butterflies of fire!

She also claims to have seen the area of Nabaa (a popular district in the suburbs of Beirut) at the time she left it after the bombardments, with its 'black roads like ink, the smoke of chimneys like ghosts which blackened the sky, and bloody sabres', the description of the roads and smoke reminding us of the calligraphic shapes in 'black ink'. These calligraphies that she cannot decipher are letters that she cannot write. After all, because of the rupture of language, 'it's perhaps better not to be able to read or write', as Karim says. When Samar writes her name backwards, Karim tries in vain to teach her to write the right way. The only success comes when Samar learns to write the word 'the South' in Arabic, from right to left. This is the loss of meaning, of landmarks, as incomprehensible forms that manifest destruction, but also love. Karim draws the sun and the earth for Samar, using a compass and a set square; reinventing the language of love and of life, through clairvoyant and visionary characters, aware of the discrepancy between words and their meanings, and of time that comes to a standstill. 'I know the moon will stop being beautiful, because I'm not going to see you any more. There are things you know but you can't say', says Samar. Soon after this encounter and the prediction, Karim is killed by a sniper.

And so, it becomes clear that the film is a fable of a suspended life, of an adolescent love, described by Saab herself as a *Sugar of Love*[8] in the opening credits to the film. It is a film about a girl and a city that both have no age. Indeed, from the top of the Beirut lighthouse Samar says, 'I am 4,000 years old. I'm 5,000 years old. I am the city. I'm Beirut, a sponge in my hand, and a piece of chalk in the other. With one hand I write children's stories, build avenues and palaces, and with the other, I erase children, avenues, and palaces' – tabula rasa.

A film made at the same time as *A Suspended Life*, *Beirut the Encounter* (1981) by Borhane Alaouié tells the story of an unsuccessful encounter between Zeina, who lives in East Beirut, and Haïdar in the West, separated by a fragmented city. Twice in this film, they arrive either too early or too late for the encounter. Neither their bodies, their gazes, nor their voices are able to cross paths in the city of Beirut, as it is a set of closed spaces that mark the separation or disintegration of all the elements of the city: atomisation of the city, of stone, bodies, voices, words and their meanings. Sent back to their confined spaces, they resign themselves to an attempt to hear one another, sending each other words through cassette tapes. Aware of their crumbling, collapse, and the destruction of language, Haïdar begins his message:

> Do you think we can still talk like before? [. . .] The dictionary has changed. Whoever used a word three years ago would give it a different meaning today. Some words now mean 'ruins and 60,000 dead . . .' Who would have thought that? At least I have many reasons to see that between you and I, I don't mean that there are 60,000 dead, but between you and I, or between two beings who are looking for each other in Beirut, there is a quarter of a million cars, 2,000 mountains of garbage, a million words written on the walls, bullets, bodies, voices . . . When I speak to you, the word passes through all these beings and these things, and I wonder what you understand . . . Today, I went to meet you in the flesh. I went through things and beings without reaching you. Like two balls thrown towards each other, but the stones, the earth and the wind carry one to the left, the other to the right.

It is an 'ontological rupture between oneself, language, and the world, [. . .] a collapse of language and narrative' (Habib 2005b: 75), and of the possibility to register in a temporal continuity of transmission and of heritage, directly linked to a crisis of thinkable and communicable experiences that define the condition of the modern regime of historicity.

'This much is clear', wrote Walter Benjamin in 1933:

> experience's stock has fallen and did so for a generation that underwent, from 1914 to 1918, one of the most horrific experiences in world history. [. . .] Was the observation not made at the time that people returned mute from the battlefield? They did not come back richer in experiences they could impart, but poorer. (Benjamin 2000: 365)

As such, how can the artist represent and give image to the impossibility of saying and seeing? Filmmakers and characters reinvent a language, while taking the measure of its collapse. New Lebanese Cinema films – made during the Lebanese civil war – and specifically those by Jocelyne Saab discussed in this chapter, asked difficult existential questions about how one may continue to regard reality, during times of war and death, without integrating the imposed aesthetic and spatiotemporal fractures that they engaged with on a deep level and that call for a redefinition of the artistic and filmic language to better rearm their eyes, and ours.

NOTES

1. Lina Khatib recounts the course she had to follow in order to collect Lebanese films and press articles useful for her research, a path similar to that of any researcher in Lebanon who is interested in the national cinematographic heritage. For more information, see Khatib 2008: 48–50.
2. The Lebanese Cinematheque was founded thanks to an initiative by Jocelyne Saab, Randa Chahal Sabbag, Hares Bassil, Sami Koronfol and Souraya Bagdadi.
3. We mainly note Beirut DC, Né à Beyrouth, Metropolis, Nadi Lekol Nas (NNK), UMAM, or the Lebanese Cinema Foundation, as well as individual initiatives by, for example, Abboudi Abou Jaoudé, a fervent collector of cinematographic posters.
4. The year zero, which represents temporality after the catastrophe in *Germany Year Zero* (1948) by Roberto Rossellini, or *Germany Year 90 Nine Zero* (1990) by Jean-Luc Godard, could be considered in *Beirut, Never Again* (1976) by Jocelyne Saab, as a time-zero. The fractures of historical time caused by conflict would generate repeated time-zeros, breaking all temporal linearity in the space–time of the catastrophe.
5. See André Habib's analysis of 'the historical projection of Godard, what is commonly called anachronism. [. . .] Godard essentially tells us that a cinematographic image always projects more than an image of its own present: it always projects into the future from the past. This projection and the montage of time that it allows to build are what allow us through cinema to see history by redeploying the "memory of a future [. . .]"' (2007: 95–7).
6. The Lebanese civil war lasted from 1975 until 1990. The destruction of Beirut for over fifteen years, a city already seven times destroyed, and seven times rebuilt following the cataclysms which it has endured throughout its history (earthquakes, tidal waves, tsunamis . . .), is seen at the end of the war disfigured by the destruction of the ruins and the reconstruction of the city centre.

7. Jocelyne Saab, in an interview with the author, July 2009.
8. The film has two titles, *Une Vie Suspendue – L'adolescente Sucre D'amour* and *A Suspended Life*.

BIBLIOGRAPHY

Augé, Marc (1995), *Non-Places: Introduction to an Anthropology of Supermodernity*, trans. John Howe, London: Verso. First published as *Non-lieux: introduction à une anthropologie de la surmodernité*, France: Paris: Seuil, 1992.

Benjamin, Walter (2000), 'Expérience et pauvreté', in Walter Benjamin, *Œuvres, Tome II*, Paris: Gallimard.

Chakar, Tony (2010), 'The Eighth Day: God Created the World in Seven Days. This is the Eighth Day', *Architectural Design*, 80: 5, 74–7.

Deleuze, Gilles (1983), *Cinéma 1: l'image-mouvement*, Paris: Éditions de Minuit.

Deleuze, Gilles (1985), *Cinéma 2: l'image-temps*, Paris: Éditions de Minuit.

Deleuze, Gilles (1990), *Pourparlers (1972–1990)*, Paris: Éditions de Minuit.

Frodon, Jean-Michel (2011), 'Les guerres du Moyen-Orient et le cinéma: le récit impossible', in David Lescot and Laurent Véray (eds), *Les Mises en scène de la guerre au XXe siècle, théâtre et cinéma*, Paris: Nouveau Monde Éditions, pp. 367–76.

Habib, André (2005a), 'À propos de *Lyrical Nitrate* de Peter Delpeut, Ruines et Temps du Cinéma', *Hors Champ*, 26 November, <https://www.horschamp.qc.ca/spip.php?article197> (last accessed 2 December 2020).

Habib, André (2005b), 'Survivances du *Voyage en Italie*', *Intermédialités*, 5, 61–80.

Habib, André (2007), 'Le temps des ruines: histoire et mémoire de l'année zéro, de Rossellini à Godard', in Philippe Despoix and Christine Bernier (eds), *Colloque international Max et Iris Stern: arts de mémoire. Matériaux, médias, mythologies*, Montreal: Montreal Museum of Fine Arts.

Habib, André (2011), *L'Attrait des ruines*, Crisnée: Éditions Yellow Now.

Khatib, Lina (2008), *Lebanese Cinema: Imagining the Civil War and Beyond*, London: I. B. Tauris.

Martinez, Annick (1999), 'Habiter: être-au-monde', 3rd International Phenomenological Humanist Seminar in Montréal: *Habitation et symbolisation*, <http://www.annickmartinez.com/pdfs/amae_textes_4.pdf> (last accessed 29 October 2012).

Niney, François (2002), *L'Épreuve du réel à l'écran: Essai sur le principe de réalité documentaire*, 2nd edn, Brussels: De Boeck University.

Rouxel, Mathilde (2018), 'Jocelyne Saab, cinéaste témoin de la cinéphilie libanaise', in Jean-Paul Aubert, Cyril Laverger and Christel Taillibert (eds), *Les Représentations de la cinéphilie*, *Cycnos*, 34: 1, 111–27.

Soueid, Mohammed (1996), *Ya Fouadi: A Chronicle of Beirut's Late Movie Theaters*, Beirut: Dar An-Nahar.

Toufic, Jalal (2006), 'Ruins', in *We Can Make Rain but No One Came to Ask: Documents from the Atlas Group Archive*, ed. Michèle Thériault, Montreal: Leonard & Bina Ellen Art Gallery, Concordia University, pp. 7–15.

CHAPTER 3

Jocelyne Saab's Hanging Gardens: A Multimedia Architecture through Stories and Time

Joan Grandjean

THE CONSTRUCTION OF AN IMAGE

Jocelyne Saab (1948–2019) has worn more than one hat in her life. She has not been just a pioneer of the New Lebanese Cinema. It is as an inherent part of the global art world that her entire photographic and cinematographic oeuvre as well as her work as a cultural agent and her new media artistic creation must be reflected upon. Saab adopts an approach that favours the construction of an image, where testimony and discourse can be revealed, at the crossroads of territories and disciplines.

An attitude towards representation of the event, the official history and the archive has dominated the Western contemporary arts discipline at the end of the twentieth century and the beginning of the twenty-first century. Commonly known as the 'artist as historian' (Godfrey 2007), this attitude refers to artists whose practices examine historical documents or subjects that have been overlooked, or who have undertaken archival research, using installation, film, video or photography to shape their investigations. Saab adopted this working method from her first reports in the 1970s, before it permeated her multimedia artistic production in the 2000s. Her whole production has been characterised by the development of an artistic and multimedia approach to the documentary genre. In this sense, she is considered to be a leading figure in Lebanon and in the Arab world. It should be emphasised how much this attitude influenced the development of Lebanese post-war artworks made by a generation of artists, such as Walid Raad, Akram Zaatari, Jayce Salloum, Lamia Joreige, Joana Hadjithomas and Khalil Joreige, who have put memory and the public act of remembrance at the heart of their concerns (Chabrol 2010; Elias 2018), while at the same time working to '(re)contextualise' (Berndt 2018) the historical sources and subjects of the narrative. Photography, video and film constitute privileged fields of this aesthetic because of their ontological and editing process. Furthermore, the interest in social policies, research and their integration into the creative process pushes Saab to raise other questions about creation, to attempt another materialisation of thoughts in order to cultivate the artistic fabric of personal and collective memory.

I have been granted access to the artist's digital archives composed of image files of her artworks, texts and PDF documents (drafts, grant application letters, memoranda of intent, press releases and articles, exchanges with institutions, invoices, artwork presentations, etc.). After she passed, Saab's son Nessim Ricardou-Saab had to deal with all the archive material. To this end, he co-created the Association of Jocelyne Saab's Friends in order to preserve and to make accessible her works and this material. Therefore, this study is based on Saab's archives, numerous publications and research on Saab's film and documentary production. From this material, this study describes under which circumstances Saab's contemporary art and her work as a cultural agent were activities she developed at the end of her life. In addition, it highlights the construction and continuum of Saab's image in her contemporary artistic creation when she operated a media transition.

This study begins by describing Saab's first detour in contemporary art as an alternative way of constructing an image and its context of creation with her art installation *Strange Games and Bridges* (2007) and the photographic series *Sense, Icons and Sensitivity* (2007). Then I will get into the latter part of her life, when she favoured the video medium (documentary video series *Gender Café*, 2013; video *Imaginary Postcard*, 2016; and multimedia art installation *One Dollar a Day*, 2016), a time when she was an active cultural agent too, and created the Cultural Resistance International Film Festival of Lebanon (CRIFFL) and the Lebanese International Biennale for Cinema and the Arts (BLICA). Although this study adopts a chronological framework, its aim is to understand the latter part of Saab's life and to analyse her construction of images as a creator and a cultural agent.

ALTERNATIVE REPRESENTATIONS IN CONTEMPORARY ART

Besides the representational system, the role of contemporary art aesthetic experience and works of art in society differs from that of the cinematographic field in terms of creation, funding, interactionism and reception (Shapiro and Heinich 2012). This materialistic vision of contemporary art reflects the creative process needed to understand what Saab did, how she achieved it, the materials she used, the places she went, the people she interacted with, and her artist's statement:

> I think that for an Arab film director, contemporary art today represents an alternative seductive language of expression, whether through photography or installation, that cinema is not anymore capable of providing because of censorship and the difficulty to raise funds for production. It's another way to explode images and explore new means of editing. (Saab 2009)

This statement, in which Saab explained her media transition, comes from a memorandum of intent, classified in the 'Sense, Icons & Sensitivity' archive collection. This is one of the first manifestations of contemporary art in Saab's work.

The dual series *Sense, Icons and Sensitivity* (2007) is composed of 100 photographs and is organised into two themes: a figurative series entitled *The Opposite of Occidentalism* followed by an abstract one, *Soft Architecture*. Saab adopted the photographic medium right after the release of her feature film *Dunia (Kiss Me Not on the Eyes,* 2005), celebrated in major international festivals (Sundance, Toronto, Asia Pacific Screen Awards, etc.) but banned in Egypt. Although the film encountered many complications in its making, its Egyptian release was fraught with problems (Hillauer 2005: 182). After a seven-year shooting and editing process in very precarious conditions, which cost Saab a lot of money and energy, the first screening of *Dunia* at the Cairo International Film Festival in 2005 subsequently led to a ban on screening the film (Mostafa 2015: 45–7). This decision was in part due to its stance against female genital mutilation and the way in which it addressed female desire as well as freedom of being and thinking. Being rejected and receiving threats and a death sentence from the fundamentalists, Saab was so traumatised that she suffered an ischemic stroke. Afterwards, she could not make another film because of her financial and health conditions, but at the same time it was impossible for her to stop the work she had started with *Dunia*. When she made the photographic series *Sense, Icons and Sensitivity*, she wanted to revisit the sense of the subjects' issues in the film *Dunia* and the cinematographic medium (representations of women, desire, sensuality, liberty and philosophy), using icons and kitsch concepts to reveal the sensitivity of discourses and construction of images in an alternative medium as well as in a different network.

Both parts of *Sense, Icons and Sensitivity* propose different gazes to question the relationship between Arabs and Westerners, both of which invite us to decipher the way Arabs look at themselves and explore the mechanisms of rejection and fascination of the Arab imagination. *The Opposite of Occidentalism* features fashion dolls, pursuing Saab's representation of the

Arab imagination towards the West. Saab went from Cairo to Beirut and Parisian flea markets to collect fashion dolls, sometimes headless and generally armless, mostly naked or randomly covered with dust and finely chopped rags. She staged the dolls to embody subjects of history, mythology and genre such as Zeus, Saddam Hussein and Barbie as an allegory for *lambda* women or the personification of the USA and Europe.[1] In addition to the dolls, she mixed posters and objects featuring other icons of the last century, such as the late American actress Marilyn Monroe, the late Egyptian president Gamal Abdel Nasser and the Coca-Cola brand. The whole set-up was based on Edward W. Said's essay (1978) on a reversal of what he called 'orientalism' – defined as the West's patronising representations of 'The East' – into *occidentalism* – clichés of 'The West'. According to Saab, the series features privileged icons to symbolise the cliché of Western women, at the heart of an Arab world dominated by religion and a conservative policy that is dangerous for the freedom of bodies.

In the same year, Saab realised her abstract series *Soft Architecture* in the Egyptian desert. More than photographing Sahrawi people, she did close-ups of fabrics of the Bedouin tents at different times of the day. The soft architecture of Bedouin tents was intended to reflect the sensuality of the Orient, although repressed and often forgotten. The titles of the photographs also emphasise this approach by suggesting carnal representations, romantic landscapes or genre scenes, for example 'Discussions Before Love', 'Sunset' or 'Tricks and Intrigues'. Through the interweaving and the ruptures of the fabric's threads, Saab saw some representations and subjects that are materialised through the titles she gave them. According to her, the one entitled 'Dual Look' is the most representative of the series:

> This iconic picture, 'the dual look,' defines the beginning of it all. I was invited to give a talk in Berlin about the power of the image and migration at the European film academy. I wanted to explain using this photo, so I went back to the Arabic tongue: 'the eye,' the image, which also means reflective springwater [sic]. I began questioning how we look at each other, and ourselves, especially after September 11. (Saab 2008a)

Sense, Icons and Sensitivity draws its inspiration from this dual gaze and its evolution over time. At first glance, it is difficult not to wonder whether Saab has an orientalist approach in her representations (the desert, women, shadows and light, Islamic philosophy and sensuality), or if this approach is intentional as an intermediary in the role reversal she proposes. Furthermore, in her personal archives, there are two letters addressed to the Gaddafi Foundation in Libya, part of an unfinished project to build a material collection of orientalist artworks in order to create a museum of orientalism and national identity in Lebanon (Saab 2010, 2011). The question of orientalism was a concern that

Figure 3.1 (left) Invitation card for the exhibition opening of *Sense, Icons and Sensitivity*, Planet Discovery, Beirut, 4 November 2008; (right) Invitation card for the exhibition opening of *Sense, Icons and Sensitivity II*, Agial Gallery, Beirut, 6 November 2008.

she wanted to explore. However, her fascination with images and the creation of 100 photographs that favour a double vision of the cultural imaginations of East and West question Saab's own imagination.

The circulation of *Sense, Icons and Sensitivity* addresses another aspect of Saab's orientalism or occidentalism. During its iteration, the series went to different venues and institutions in the United Arab Emirates, France, Italy, Libya and Lebanon. Each time, the titles of the photographs were adapted depending on the location of exposure in order to fit in with a particular event or to thwart censorship. It was not possible to show the series in the Arab world the way it was shown in Europe and vice versa – Saab modified titles, selected photographs, adapted the scenography, exhibited one series and not both. For example, in 2008 she exhibited a selection of *The Opposite of Occidentalism*, entitled 'Marilyn and the Arabs', at the Art Paris international art fair, at the Grand Palais, whereas she exhibited the *Soft Architecture* series for the same event at the Emirates Palace in Dubai. According to Victoria Ambrosini, who specialises in the appropriation and representation of popular culture in contemporary Arab art, the aim of the kitsch aesthetic was

> to produce a visual escalation that carried ambivalence and a wavering sense of meaning. The representation of cultural identity was thus given to ostentation, introducing distance and nuance through which the

artists could assert their belonging, provide an answer to the orders of the local and international markets, and inject an element of irony. (Ambrosini 2015: 6)

The adaptations of the *Sense, Icons and Sensitivity* dual series highlighted a specific discourse regarding the place of exhibition as well as the reception of the public, something that is difficult to produce in the cinematographic world. Saab explained:

My status as a transnational citizen living in a global world between East and West gives me the liberty and the distance to play with different concepts and ideas. As much as I need to reinvent my loyalty to the different countries I belong to, I feel free in my creation. (Saab 2009)

Despite her wish to establish a dialogue between the Middle East and the West, the modification is intended to materialise other scenes from the same picture to play on the polysemy of Arabic words. In the abstraction series *Soft Architecture*, titles give an intense representation, whereas the series of modern icons from the last century, *The Opposite of Occidentalism*, plays with a scramble of the codification of genre and the 'identity posture' (Dakhlia 2006: 55) from both regions. Symbolism generated in the whole series, between politics and popular culture; it is part of a double 'exoticization process' (Ambrosini 2015: 94) inherent to the perception of difference.

Saab adapted the notion of kitsch to recreate experiences that exist only as memory or fantasy (Saab 2008). As Ambrosini explains, 'Kitsch art becomes a privileged medium for integrating the artistic heritage of orientalism, and kitsch theory renews the interpretation of the representation of cultural identity' (2015: 102). Through visual overkill, kitsch creates a tension between representation and aesthetics. This is what characterises much of Saab's work. For example, in *Once Upon a Time, Beirut: Story of a Star* (1994) she collected old films with a Beirut setting or location, gathered together and narrated by two young actresses. She set out to create images from fragments of truth in order to represent the city in all its complexities. *Once Upon a Time, Beirut* deconstructed the memory and the fantasy of Beirut perceived as 'the Switzerland of the Middle East' before the civil war. With *Sense, Icons and Sensitivity*, she returned to the fascination that Arabs have with Westerners and vice versa through a kitsch aesthetic to question this new episteme between the two cultures after 9/11. Both works produce a new level of reading the ruins of modernity as well as the confused final stage of globalisation penetrating the world and creation. As such, in *Sense, Icons and Sensitivity* Saab reproduced the Arab perception of philosophy and sensuality suggested in *Dunia* from another perspective in her dual series. A kitsch aesthetic aims to produce a visual outbidding that conveys ambivalence and makes the meaning of the work float. If the origin of the photographic project was to challenge and denounce Egyptian hypocrisy, it opened itself up wide to a critique of both the contemporary Arab and Western geocultural areas.

This painful aesthetic shift in Saab's career was not only the result of censorship and rejection. As a matter of fact, the year she was threatened by the fundamentalists in Egypt, violence and war resurfaced in Lebanon with the 2006 July War. Since Saab was not in Lebanon when Beirut was bombed by Israeli forces, she carried out a mixed-media installation in Paris to react to it and testify, revisiting her previous films with new readings and contexts of the war, and representing the subjects of garden, memory and architecture.

After discovering Saab's work through a screening of *Dunia* at the Singapore International Film Festival in 2006, the Singapore National Museum was the first institution to invite her to exhibit *Strange Games and Bridges* (21 March–22 April 2007). The mixed-media installation was designed by garden landscaper Laurence Rasse. It is composed of a 42 metre-long raised bridge platform in a U-shape formation. The whole consisted of a layered garden-city landscape in which Saab's videos were suspended and projected. The visitor was invited to walk downstairs and upstairs where twenty-two televisions and projectors broadcasted archives and rushes of her previous documentaries – those that testified to the destruction of Beirut during the multifaceted

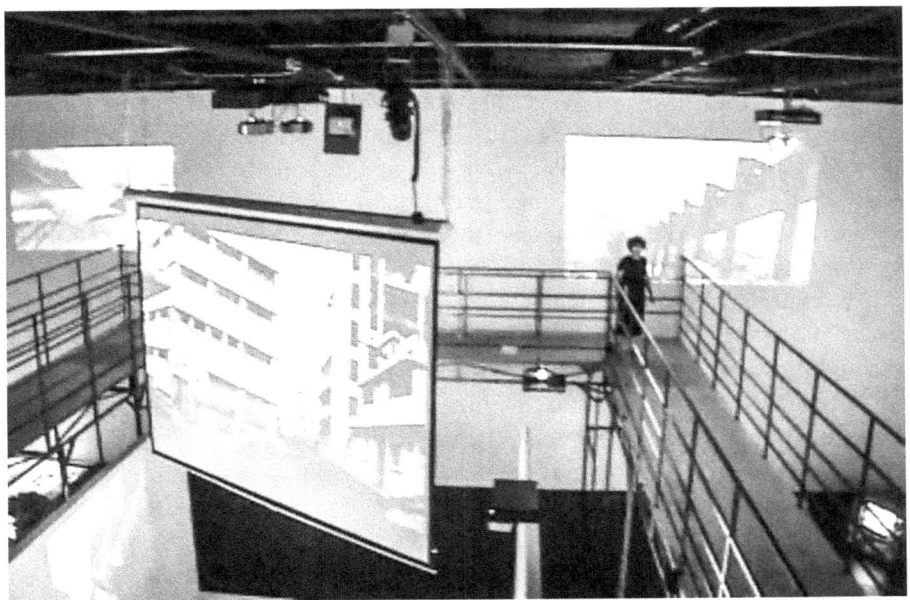

Figure 3.2 Exhibition view, *Strange Games and Bridges*, Singapore National Museum, 2008

Lebanese civil war (1975-90) – in parallel with more recent images of infrastructure destruction she shot just after the July War. These cinematographic images, whose diffusion speed was stretched and accelerated, were turned into video art. This media transformation leads the public to transform its perception of time – a 'suspended time', Roger Assaf commented in *Beirut, My City* (1982) – to the new discourse Saab wants to convey through her pictures to question the resurgence of war thanks to a suspended garden.

In addition to mixing the media, the appearance of the garden through the architecture of the installation was coupled with the image of the war Saab had been cultivating in her previous films. In her artist's statement Saab explained that she was inspired by urban planning reconstruction and excavation:

> In the 1990s, a developer cleared areas of central Beirut in a large-scale reconstruction project. The bulldozers shifted the ruins of war, and archaeologists opened the entrails of the city. The inhabitants of the city were able to walk along the Phoenician, the Greek and the Roman streets, before they were buried again under asphalt and concrete. I do with STRANGE GAMES AND BRIDGES what archaeologists did with the city of Beirut, allowing a passage through layers of experience, creating a garden in suspension. (Strange Games Bridges 2007)

The creation of a 'garden in suspension' immediately refers to the Hanging Gardens of Babylon. Following the example of Nebuchadnezzar II who built the Hanging Gardens of Babylon to remind his wife, Amytis of Media, of the wooded mountains of her native land, Saab built a hanging garden of memory in the form of an artistic installation in order to remind the Lebanese of their native land. Saab excavates a garden of memory using several layers of history: the official history; revisitations of the suspended time she had previously captured in her films to offer new readings and contexts; and the new images created for the occasion insisting on the demolition of bridges and the need to rebuild them. Saab evaded historical representation to represent historical experience through memory, a memory that was obscured, sometimes destroyed along with the landscape, and some parts of which can only exist through the archive, hers.

After more than thirty years of filming documentaries and feature-length films, Saab revisited all her work done in the urgency of the war and recreated a mixed-media art installation renouncing war by setting out to rebuild bridges. Saab's installation interrogates the resurgence of war with the architecture of an urban garden. She thus compares the literal disappearance of gardens to the oblivion of memory in Lebanon. Both are a maze where the author has written every possible option of the history – as Jorge Luis Borges did in *The Garden of Forking Paths*, a 1941 short story. Whenever various possibilities arise in all the possible fictions of memory proposed by Saab, the public can adopt one and eliminate the others; Saab adopts them all simultaneously. In this way, she created various futures, various times that also proliferate and branch off. From there, the contradictions of her installation went beyond the suspended time she had previously created and moved towards a suspended garden in order to create a living archive. Lebanese-Canadian artist Jayce Salloum explains that using video makes it possible to generate a kind of 'living archive' (Salloum 2006). Different screens allow the artist and the public/spectator to explore interstitial spaces. Finally, in a subjective, political or geographical vein, these spaces articulate the conditions of displacement and orient them between borders, ideologies, nations, cultural polarities, geography and history. As Foucault explained, the history of ideas characterises elements of discontinuity between broadly defined approaches of knowledge, but believing that those approaches exist as an aggregate fails to do justice to the complexities of discourse. Thanks to her suspended garden, Saab employed archaeology as a discipline and a theory to offer visitors a journey through the times of the Lebanese natural and belligerent catastrophes so that they themselves could reconnect the different layers of history they preferred. This art installation furthermore aimed to capture the event of the July War to overcome what happened when the amnesty law for war crimes committed between 1975 and 1990 was passed by the Lebanese parliament in 1991. She made this contribution to the edifice of the Lebanese collective memory, whose foundations are still fragile nowadays, in order to reconnect its scattered history right away.

In 2009 Saab regained the strength to make another fiction film entitled *What's Going On?*, an experimental work continuing the development of images and creation she was experimenting with in *Sense, Icons and Sensitivity* and *Strange Games and Bridges*. The synopsis tells the contemporary story of Beirut through a young man, Nasri, in search of the gardens of the city and the remnants of a world that seems to have disappeared, but whose roots the director exhumes with sensuality. Since her aesthetic shift, Saab started to think about images differently, as a new way of looking at the world, combining themes, conferring on the evolution of her art a profound coherence despite its multidisciplinary nature and subjects. For example, a few minutes before the end of *What's Going On?* the writer crosses the path of a woman who tells him about her life during a night walk. Before separating, she gives him her purse and says, '[in North Levantine Arabic:] Here, you have all my life in this purse. Let me see what you'll do with it. [in French:] You can even make an installation out of it!' While Nasri's search for gardens echoes *Strange Games and Bridges*, with her purse the woman refers directly to the medium of art installation, thus resonating with the approach of the artist. Throughout Saab's career, this approach has endeavoured to build what Mathilde Rouxel calls an 'untamed memory' (Rouxel 2019).

Sense, Icons and Sensitivity and *Strange Games and Bridges* testify to a medium shift in Saab's practice. This phenomenon appeared when her health was deteriorating and responded to a need to engage in creation. The artist's work turned towards the paradigm of contemporary art, in which she found an alternative way of creating. She collaborated with the gallerist Saleh Barakat who had represented her at the Agial Art Gallery in Beirut, one of the leading galleries for the dissemination of modern and contemporary art from Lebanon and the Arab World since 1991. Thanks to this new collaboration, Saab exhibited all over the world in the framework of international contemporary art fairs (Art Dubai, Abu Dhabi Art, Art Paris), galleries (Agial, Regard Sud), museums and cultural institutions (Singapore National Museum, Les Halles de Schaerbeek, National Museum of Tripoli, Institut Français, Katzen Arts Center), as well as at film festivals (Vesoul International Film Festival of Asian Cinema; Festival Internazionale di Cinema e Donne, organised by Laboratorio Immagine Donna).

CONTEMPORARY ART VIDEOS AND ART FESTIVALS

From 2009, Saab embarked on projects that remained unfinished business. Her search for truth through other forms of representation did not stop with the series *Sense, Icons and Sensitivity*. In 2008 she made another one entitled *Masks*, continuing her research on icons through a poetic series of portraits of Nubians from Egypt, whose faces are coated with clay, which she never managed to exhibit. Later, in 2013, she tried to set up an exhibition of Egyptian and Lebanese cinema posters, entitled *This Floating Object of Desire*, which remains on hold. The project that brought her back to the forefront was a video series entitled *Gender Café* (2013).

For its inaugural exhibition, the Marseilles-based MuCEM organised an exhibition devoted to the many ways of being a man or a woman in the Mediterranean region. Entitled *Bazar du genre* (7 June 2013–6 January 2014), the show featured artists from the Mediterranean region and as such gathered a very eclectic collection of artworks, videos and objects in order to question gender theories in different Mediterranean countries (Fabre and Portevin 2013). The final section of the exhibition, entitled 'To Each His Own Gender!' ('À chacun son genre!'), focused on the increased opportunity for individuals to play with codes and reversals of sexual and gender roles. Saab's *Gender Café* videos were exhibited in a small unit which allowed the audience to access the intimate dimensions induced by a concept such as gender. Each video corresponded to a table where the visitor was invited to sit and listen to the little-known adventures of gender theories and activism in the Mediterranean world, a short time after the popular uprisings re-evaluated political and social freedom. The audience was invited to listen, through headphones, to the often disturbing and moving testimonies of contemporary intellectuals, activists and artists from Algeria, Egypt, Turkey and Lebanon.

At the first table, *The Table of Walid Aouni, the Green Mad Man*, one could listen to the journey of Walid Aouni, 'the Green Madman'. The title of *The Green Madman* carries echoes of the painting *The Green Fool* (1951) by Egyptian artist Abdel Hadi Al-Gazzar. Walid Aouni, the Lebanese choreographer and former student of Maurice Béjart, who became instrumental in the development of the Cairo Opera House, adapted it for his dance performance, to celebrate the richness of Egyptian modernity. After more than twenty-five years at the Cairo Opera House, and inspiring generations of Arab artists like Jocelyne Saab (Rouxel, in this volume), Aouni was forced by the current regime to step down from his role after the 2011 Revolution.

The Table of the Painter of the Pharaohs and the Dancers took the spectator to the studio of the Egyptian artist Adel Siwi in Tahrir Square. After he showed the diversity of his paintings celebrating Pharaohism and dancers, a text indicated the importance he attached to exhibiting in his country, despite the hostility current politics may have harboured regarding his paintings.

The next one, *The Table of the Magazine on the Body*, was a terrace in the Beirut souks. *Jasad*, a magazine on the body, was lying on the table, covered with a leather binder. Its editor Joumana Haddad, a feminist, a writer and the actress playing Lilith in *What's Going On?*, opened the magazine. She described it and explained the role of the Arabic-language cultural magazine specialising in the literature, art and science of the body, based in Beirut and broadcasted all over the Arab geocultural area.

The Table of the Golden Okra took place in Istanbul and introduced Cuneyt Cebenoyan and Melek Ozman, the founders of the Golden Okra Award in Turkey, that rewards films considered the most macho of the year.

The Table of Dance and Pride led the audience to Lebanon a second time, to listen to *baladi* contemporary dancer and activist Alexandre Paulikevitch who danced the mutations of a society attached to its culture and aspiring to change.

Finally, *The Table of Exigency* concluded with the words of Wassyla Tamzali, an Algerian writer, lawyer and feminist, who evoked her intellectual and activist path. Saab brought together interviews with men and women of different generations and artistic and intellectual backgrounds who all advocated a sense of reunification and peaceful resistance to contemporary political oppression. They testified to her will to develop what she experimented with in her previous work on activism, femininity, sexuality, gender minorities and the body, while also updating these themes.

Saab's participation in this exhibition made her rethink the documentary format to which she was accustomed, by producing a series of short video documentaries broadcasted on six screens at the same time. As she had already experimented with the exhibitions of her photographic series *Sense, Icons and Sensitivity* and art installation *Strange Games and Bridges*, the dissemination of her work outside of spaces devoted to cinema is not insignificant. Image and digital technology raise new questions about the media reflexivity of the event in contemporary art – as Mark Godfrey explains in 'The Artist as Historian' (2007) – along with the public reception in museums. New media culture permeated museums as well as museology, and encouraged documentary filmmakers, as well as artists interested in documentary, to think differently about the dissemination of their work. Apart from the fact that video productions are more often financed by cultural institutions, because they are not expensive, they fit with public expectations regarding moving images, and do not require too much management; the video format must be adapted to a scenography when displayed in a museum. Saab was sponsored to produce an audiovisual production by Marseille-Provence 2013, whose general manager Bernard Latarjet wanted to highlight the 'Euro-Mediterranean' space as well as the documentary production (Latarjet 2010). This observation gives rise to another relationship with the medium in an exhibition situation (management of duration, multiplication of projection surfaces, reception by a mobile spectator).

After *Gender Café*, Saab wanted to make feature films again. In 2015 she obtained a development fund from the Arab Fund for Arts and Culture (AFAC) to direct a biopic of the Lebanese-Egyptian actress and producer Assia Dagher and the Egyptian actress Faten Hamama (see Rouxel, in this volume). Unfortunately, the project had to be halted because Hamama died and Saab herself was diagnosed with cancer at the same time. She was no longer in a position to carry out projects on too large a scale. So, she returned to her role as a cultural agent, to continue working and remain an influential personality in the world of art and culture.

Before she became a newsreader and a war reporter, Saab collaborated with several media to promote contemporary culture. In the early 1970s she hosted a pop music programme on the national Lebanese radio called *The Marsupilamis Have Blue Eyes* (*Les Marsupilamis ont les yeux bleus*). In 1972–3 she collaborated with Etel Adnan, an American-Lebanese poet and painter, for *Al-Safa* newspaper cultural pages in which she reviewed pop music. After she became the pioneer of New Lebanese Cinema, Saab organised several large-scale events. For example, in 1992 she committed herself to the reconstitution of the Lebanese Cinematheque. She carried out archival work and catalogued more than 250 films that evoke Beirut and Lebanon before and during the Lebanese civil war. From these archives, she organised in 1993 the screening cycle *Beirut, a Thousand and One Images* at the Institut du Monde Arabe (Arab World Institute) in Paris, the Carthage Film Days in Tunis, and the Casino du Liban in Tabarja, presenting the Arab films selected for the reconstruction of the Lebanese Cinematheque. Following the handing over of about fifteen restored films to the Lebanese Ministry of Culture, she was awarded the title of Knight of the Order of Arts and Letters (Chevalier de l'Ordre des Arts et des Lettres) in 1995 for this monumental work. Even if the Lebanese Cinematheque never saw the light of the day, she kept a record of it in the film *Once Upon a Time, Beirut: Story of a Star* (1994) (Rouxel 2018b). In parallel to her activity as a filmmaker and artist, she also conducted workshops and taught at higher education institutions, including the Institute of Scenic, Audio-Visual and Cinematographic Studies at Saint Joseph University in 2013.

Also in 2013, Saab founded CRIFFL through her Cultural Resistance Association. The inception of this festival stemmed from the success of her film *Dunia* in Asian countries, which allowed Saab to join the Network for the Promotion of Asian Cinema (NETPAC). After joining NETPAC, Saab wanted to find a way to insert it in one of Lebanon's film festivals. As she could not find anyone willing to promote Asian cinema in her country, she decided to do it on her own. As such, CRIFFL showcased films from Asian and Mediterranean cultures that question the history and situation of contemporary Lebanon through similar topics such as war, memory, women, youth and heritage. Throughout its three editions (2013–15), the festival promoted reflection on the possibility of peace and inter-community respect, as well as the decentralisation of culture, by extending itself throughout the Lebanese territory in the cities of Beirut, Tripoli, Sidon, Tyre and Zahle. It also brought to the event all major Lebanese universities, organising seminars with leading essayists, critics and film teachers from around the world such as Nicole Brenez, Wassyla Tamzali, Daniel Guibert, Aruna Vasudev, Sam Ho and Phillip Chea. Moreover, it organised a Critical Writing Competition for young people on the basis of films screened at the festival. The team introduced original screenings from different Asian countries, that had never been shown in Lebanon before. The challenge of this approach lies in the fact that it wished to decentralise the Lebanese audience's viewpoint by not promoting Western cinema and to show them another cultural facet made on the same continent.

In 2017 the association that ran Cultural Resistance returned to programme the first edition of BLICA at the Modern and Contemporary Art Museum (MACAM, Alita, 16 September–30 December 2017). The year before, Saab conceived and initiated with film historian Mickaël Robert-Gonçalves, philosopher Andrés Claro, and architect Daniel Guibert, the Oscar Niemeyer Competition in order to select artists under the theme 'Rupture in the Representation of the Real'. The competition took place in Tripoli and was inspired by the phenomenal but unfinished architectural structures at the Tripoli International Fairgrounds (1967–74) by the Brazilian architect Oscar Niemeyer, whose work had to stop with the outbreak of the Lebanese civil war. Faithful to her aesthetic, she conceived of the idea to give life to the theme by choosing this unfinished modern architectural monument to refer once again

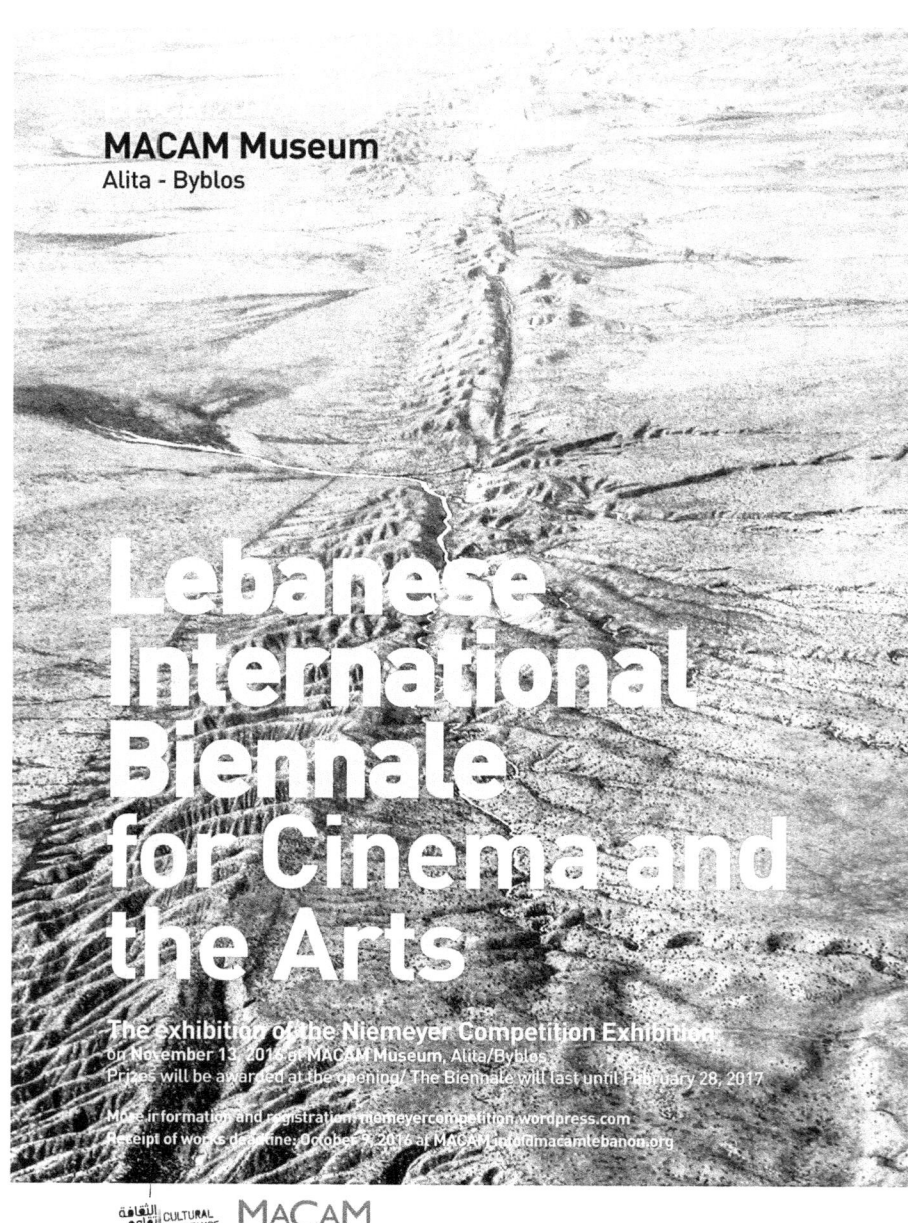

Figure 3.3 Poster of the first edition of the Biennale of Contemporary Art, Modern and Contemporary Art Museum, Alita, 16 September–30 December 2017

to a Lebanese memory under construction. Named after the architect, the competition brought a selection of forty-five global artists from twenty-four countries to Lebanon to participate in BLICA. The multidisciplinary exhibition showcased film, installation art, painting, photography and text.

In parallel with her activity as a cultural agent, Saab created some new work, screened and exhibited in the margins of BLICA. In 2015 Saab returned to her camera when she was invited by the Boğaziçi Üniversitesi (University of Bosporus) in Turkey to take part in the Boğaziçi Chronicles residency programme at Tubini House. She directed a video chronicle on the university campus in Bebek and views of the 15 July Martyrs Bridge, crossing the Bosporus, connecting Europe and Asia. She explains her approach in an interview:

> In my imagination, I think [the bridge] is a metaphor of this tension between East and West and I thought I might choose this to tell a story. As a filmmaker, I was looking for a story to tell it, which is not easy. The second point is I find this sort of magnetism, let's say attraction, being at this point of the university. I find that there is a pole of attraction as if it were a magnetism in the land. So, I go to look for it, what makes it like this. So, it is in the environment and also in what the university represents. (Boğaziçi Üniversitesi 2015)

During this residency programme, Saab had carte blanche and decided to play on her imagination and fantasy. The image of the bridge is being used yet again to recall the connection between the two continents and the consequences it has had in history and geography. The video took the form of an imaginary postcard written to Turkish author Orhan Pamuk, in which she wrote about her illness, about the fragility of her body, and the situation in the Middle East ravaged by war.

The same year she directed another short video, entitled *One Dollar a Day*, which marked another collaboration with her friend Etel Adnan, who wrote a text for the occasion. Saab's video shows the experiences of the Syrian refugees in the Bekaa Valley, close to the border. There, she photographed dozens of Syrian refugees, documenting how they built a temporary life for themselves for one dollar a day, their daily allowance. Thanks to the United Nations High Commissioner for Refugees (UNHCR) aid, they have a temporary circulation permit that also entitles families to daily ration cards, worth one dollar, which enable them to obtain daily supplies of basic necessities. The video denounces the living conditions of these families, which Lebanese society strives not to see. Saab included shots of urban areas of Beirut. In addition to the video, for one week in November 2015, she took over the city centre by displaying a black poster on a billboard with large white capital letters: 'HOW TO LIVE WITH ONE DOLLAR A DAY' Another billboard displayed excerpts of her video staging Syrian refugees showing their certificate issued by the UNHCR, which is the only document that proves their existence. Finally, on the cranes in the harbour she suspended large posters representing a selection of the photographs from the Bekaa Valley. She decorated the posters and photographs with gold leaf, to highlight the children's faces and landscapes. In an interview she explained:

> I thought of these panels as a triptych torn from the land of the Bekaa. I wanted to give a biblical, iconic dimension to these children to remind us of what's at stake here: the consequences of the war, the future, without provoking pity, but to make us take these images in our faces. (Agenda Culturel 2017)

In her multimedia installation, Saab primarily directs her camera to depict some of her iconic subjects – war, displacement, women and children – coupled with makeshift tents, made out of advertising tarpaulins showing female models promoting different brands encouraging and representing consumption. When she used video billboards to show how the icons of luxury covered the refugees' tents, Saab reversed the system of representation by broadcasting these icons onto where they belong, without hiding their use (Saab 2019). The whole artistic project was in stark contrast to the consumerism that reigns in the business and shopping districts of Beirut. However, there was absolutely no reaction to the installation of the triptych in the city, no public response or media attention. In 2017 the video, the series of photographs and advertising tarpaulins were exhibited at the Depo İstanbul Art Centre (15 April–14 May 2017) in Turkey and then at the Beirut Institut Français Gallery (1–27 June 2017) in Lebanon.

After being awarded the title of Officer of the Order of Arts and Letters (Officier de l'Ordre des Arts et des Lettres) by the French ambassador, Saab also received a medal in Lebanon. This award testified to Saab's dedication to arts during her entire life but also her involvement in the cultural diplomatic system, while maintaining a vibrant artistic network.

CONCLUSION

Despite the ups and downs in her personal history and in the official one, Saab's itinerary led her to multiple mediums, subjects and genres, with the imperative that she remain true to herself and with the credo that she would be completely independent in her creative endeavour. Saab's construction of images in contemporary art is a continuum of her cinematographic and documentary production, addressing topical issues such as democracy, the status of women and freedom. These themes were represented through three recurring concepts in her artworks. First, *Sense, Icons and Sensitivity* used icons and kitsch as a reference to popular culture, in order to create a tension in representation. Second, *Strange Games and Bridges* is a synthesis of reports, documentaries and films produced about Lebanon and the war. Here, the image of the garden is central as it symbolises memory, which tends to disappear from an urban planning point of view – an enclosed garden common to Islamic culture (*ar-riyāḍ*). Third, the theme of architecture echoes the reconstruction of the landscape after a time of war. It also reminds us of the excavation, experimentation and construction of images as discourses, as an analytical method to determine the conditions of knowledge and thought. This experimentation through the medium of installation art allowed Saab to revisit her previous works and construct them alongside new videos, creating a 'living archive' for the next generation. This experiment with image and installation influenced *What's Going On?* Experimental in nature, the film develops the work started in *Strange Games and Bridges* by questioning the possibility of straightforward representation. This is also echoed in *Imaginary Postcard* and *One Dollar a Day*. The kitsch of popular culture, the trauma of the Lebanese war and the promise of reconstruction and experimentation are three concepts that are brought together in *Gender Café*. These three concepts echo each other in the entirety of Saab's creation and occupy a predominant place in her contemporary art production.

Despite the numerous exhibitions she participated in all over the world between 2007 and 2018, it was not until Mathilde Rouxel brought Saab's fragmented visual art together in *Jocelyne Saab Against the Tide*, at MACAM (9 June–14 September 2018), that a retrospective was curated of her work. This first retrospective exhibition of the Lebanese artist highlighted the aesthetic turn Saab went through in the second half of the 2000s, when she started to create art installations, videos and photographs. The show put forward the Lebanese artist's multidimensional oeuvre by highlighting her important contributions as a 'plastic artist' (Rouxel 2018a). In December 2018 Saab knew she was nearing the end of her life and so she published, under the supervision of Nicole Brenez and with the support of Jean-Luc Godard, a collection of photographs and photograms entitled *War Zones* (*Zones de guerre*) as a final statement. This book was a photographic panorama of all of Saab's realised and unrealised projects. For over forty years of creation, it testifies to the diversity of her work as a cinematographer, photographer, artist and cultural agent, also including two texts by intellectual, cultural and artistic figures of Saab's generation that form part of her rich and diverse artistic interactionism, Etel Adnan and Elias Sanbar. Saab's life was as fragmented as her work is. In her later work, she reviewed the work she accomplished by *architecturing* fragments of a memory fabric, including her own two sides: her films and her 'installed' images, most of them recycled, to make something more than a representation of reality. In order to understand her work more thoroughly, it has to be studied as a whole. Saab's approach challenged the creation of images, whether these were by herself or by other image-makers.

NOTE

1. The *lambda* is a Greek letter that has come to symbolise progressive Western subcultures.

BIBLIOGRAPHY

Agenda Culturel (2017), 'Les réfugiés de la Bekaa dans le viseur de Jocelyne Saab', <https://www.agendaculturel.com/article/Art_Les_refugies_de_la_Bekaa_dans_le_viseur_de_Jocelyne+Saab> (last accessed 30 May 2020).

Ambrosini, Victoria (2015), 'Art populaire, art contemporain et pratiques politiques au Moyen-Orient: entre orientalisme et Révolution égyptienne, 2000–2014', PhD dissertation, Paris: École des Hautes Étude Sciences Sociales.

Berndt, Daniel (2018), *Wiederholung als Widerstand? Zur künstlerischen (Re-)Kontextualisierung historischer Fotografien in Auseinandersetzung mit der Geschichte Palästinas*, Berlin: Transcript.

Boğaziçi Üniversitesi (2015), 'Jocelyne Saab ile Güney Kampüs'te Bir Gün | BU+ Boğaziçi Chronicles', video, YouTube, 24 November, <https://www.youtube.com/watch?v=OB5SXsFQ4FE> (last accessed 2 December 2020).

Borges, Jorge Luis (1941), *El jardín de senderos que se bifurcan*, Buenos Aires: Sur.

Chabrol, Arnaud (2010), 'La fabrique artistique de la mémoire: effet de génération et entreprises artistiques dans le Liban contemporain', in Franck Mermier and Christophe Varin (eds), *Mémoires de guerres au Liban (1975–1990)*, Paris: Sindbad/Ifpo and Arles: Actes Sud, pp. 485–509.

Dakhlia, Jocelyne (2006), 'Pleinement contemporains', in Jocelyne Dakhlia et al. (eds), *Créations artistiques contemporaines en pays d'Islam: des arts en tension*, Paris: Éditions Kimé, pp. 11–67.

Elias, Chad (2018), *Posthumous Images: Contemporary Art and Memory Politics in Post-Civil War Lebanon*, Durham, NC: Duke University Press.

Fabre, Thierry and Catherine Portevin (eds) (2013), *Au bazar du genre: féminin/masculin en Méditerranée*, exhibition catalogue (Marseilles, MuCEM, 7 June 2013–6 January 2014), Paris: Textuel.

Foucault, Michel (2002), *Archaeology of Knowledge*, trans. A. M. Sheridan Smith (London and New York: Routledge).

Godfrey, Mark (2007), 'The Artist as Historian', *October*, 120, 140–72.

Hillauer, Rebecca (2005), 'Saab, Jocelyne (1948–)', *Encyclopedia of Arab Women Filmmakers*, Cairo: American University in Cairo Press, pp. 173–82.

Latarjet, Bernard (2010), 'lettre recommandation marseille.pdf', *Café du Genre* collection, Adobe PDF document, created 28 August 2019. The artist's personal archives.

Mostafa, Dalia Said (2015), 'Jocelyne Saab: A Lifetime Journey in Search of Freedom and Beauty (Lebanon)', in Josef Gugler (ed.), *Ten Arab Filmmakers: Political Dissent and Social Critique*, Bloomington: Indiana University Press, pp. 34–50.

Rouxel, Mathilde (2018a), 'Jocelyne Saab', in *Jocelyne Saab Against the Tide*, exhibition booklet (Alita, MACAM, 9 June–14 September 2018), Alita: MACAM.

Rouxel, Mathilde (2018b), 'Jocelyne Saab, cinéaste témoin de la cinéphilie libanaise', in Jean-Paul Aubert, Cyril Laverger and Christel Taillibert (eds), *Les Représentations de la cinéphilie*, 34: 1, 111–27.

Rouxel, Mathilde (2019), *Jocelyne Saab: la mémoire indomptée (1970–2019)*, Tunis: Éditions Nadhar.

Saab, Jocelyne (2008a), 'citations for selected pictures', *Sense, Icons and Sensitivity* collection, Microsoft Word 97 document, created 18 October 2008. The artist's personal archives.

Saab, Jocelyne (2008b), 'COM PRESS NASRI FR', *BARBIES DOCUMENTATIONS* collection, Microsoft Word 97 document, created 22 October 2008. The artist's personal archives.

Saab, Jocelyne (2009), '1 essai presentation expo', *BARBIES DOCUMENTATIONS* collection, Microsoft Word 97 document, created 17 February 2009. The artist's personal archives.

Saab, Jocelyne (2010), 'lettre brouillonlybie a l'ingenieur 05 10 10.doc', *DIVERS DOCS DE PRESENTATION* collection, Microsoft Word 97 document, created 29 August 2019. The artist's personal archives.

Saab, Jocelyne (2011), 'lettre El akhder Lybie definitive.doc', *DIVERS DOCS DE PRESENTATION* collection, Microsoft Word 97 document, created 28 August 2019. The artist's personal archives.

Saab, Jocelyne (2019), 'Projet à l'origine – UN DOLLAR PAR JOUR', *ONE DOLLAR A DAY DOCUMENTATION* collection, Microsoft Word 97 document, created 28 August 2019. The artist's personal archives.

Said, Edward W. (1978), *Orientalism*, New York: Pantheon Books.

Salloum, Jayce (2006), 'Sans titre/Untitled. The Video Installation as an Active Archive', in Charles Merewether (ed.), *The Archive*, London: Whitechapel and Cambridge, MA: MIT Press, pp. 190–3.

Shapiro, Roberta and Nathalie Heinich (2012), 'When is Artification?', *Contemporary Aesthetics*, 4, <http://hdl.handle.net/2027/spo.7523862.spec.409> (last accessed 2 December 2020).

Strange Games Bridges, 'The Work' (2007), 28 June, <http://strangegamesbridges.free.fr/EXPOstrange/pages%20english%20ok/creation.html> (last accessed 2 December 2020).

CHAPTER 4

A Filmmaker's Words: A Journey through the Archive of Jocelyne Saab's Unfinished Work

Mathilde Rouxel

'I was born in 1948, the year of the *Nakba*, in a house full of secret alcoves, on Emir Abdel Kader Street.' On the second page of an unfinished book of memoirs called *Témoignage* (*Testimony*, uncompleted, 2010–18), Jocelyne Saab establishes who she is. The house she is talking about was a mansion full of old works of art, bedecked with Ottoman Empire rugs. Her maternal grandfather was a collector and the house held '150 years of history'. This is explained in Saab's film *Beyrouth, ma ville* (*Beirut, My City*, 1982), as she stands amid the ruins of the past, the ruins of her own family history and those of an entire country: everything the house had witnessed had gone up in smoke, one night, after a conflict:

> My grandfather, sitting next to the large oak radio set that stood in the corner of the living room, listened to the news that announced the partition of Palestine. It was a war. Palestinians were being chased off their lands. Every evening, sitting on his lap, I listened to the BBC, to 'The Voice of the Arabs', and 'The Voice of America'. Words, dates, phrases that still resonate with me today: 'Karameh', 'Deir Yassine', '1956: the triple aggression of Israel, France and England allied against Egypt . . .' (Saab, *Témoignage*)

Jocelyne Saab was born at a moment when the Arab world as an ideological creation was beginning to crumble. She was a daughter of revolution, of the left-wing independence movement which she, profoundly impacted by the many wars that ravaged the lands she lived and worked in, spent her life trying to (re-)define. When she died, Saab left behind several boxes containing the research for films she was preparing. Most of the projects were left unfinished, as was the book of memoirs that she never really had the heart to complete.

Taken together, these archives show us another Jocelyne, and reveal many more layers of her. A daughter of the *Nakba*, an anti-imperialist, Arab and proud of it, Saab was also fascinated with Asia, to which she felt a strong affiliation. Geographically, Lebanon is part of the Asiatic continent, and to place its historical roots within that context allows one to rethink the country outside of the frame of its endless comparisons to the West, as 'the Pearl of the East' as Yasmine quotes in *Il était une fois, Beyrouth: Histoire d'une star* (*Once Upon a Time, Beirut: Story of a Star*, 1994). This chapter offers a new portrait of Jocelyne Saab, as seen through the work she never had the opportunity to finish. Her own words, quoted from her book of memoirs, will be central to clarifying how she developed her unique creative world.

JOCELYNE SAAB: AN ARAB WOMAN IN THE EYE OF THE STORM

In a project she called *La Mère du monde* (*The Mother of the World*), written around the year 2000, but never developed beyond initial sketches, Saab underlines the contradictions that tear her apart when she reflects on the Middle East:

> In 1970 we were living in Beirut, and it was the golden years, the 'dolce vita' just before war broke out in 1975. My mother was 40, and she secretly bought one of the costumes of Nadia Gamal, a very popular belly dancer in the Middle East, to wear to the bourgeois parties. My mother had learnt to dance in secret and when she did her number it was quite a success among her friends. This whim of hers surprised me because it didn't fit in with the usual behaviour in the Christian, very westernised, and fairly conservative part of Beirut society. Lebanon is different today, and the regressive spirit that dominates in the Arab world hasn't spared the country; my mother has aged and forgotten the audacity of her youth, and she's become an iconoclast. She reproaches me for speaking out, for looking at the world through my camera, for having ignored the traditional choices that are imposed on an Oriental woman.
>
> This film project is born precisely out of my desire to reconcile myself to the Oriental woman that I am and that I've always refused to be.
>
> In *Le Dernier métro* Gérard Départdieu tries to seduce Catherine Deneuve by saying to her 'there are two women in you'. It's with the same duality that the West is fascinated with the Oriental woman, who is either the veiled and subdued woman, or the public woman who dances and discovers her body through the gaze of men.

But in the Orient these two women are not always separated; sometimes it is the same woman who's veiled, who dances, and who passes on to her daughters the gestures of the dance in family celebrations. Dancing is experienced as a foundational act, a personal initiation that reproduces the movements of childbirth. Daily chores are also reminiscent of the oriental dance, the rolling strides of the women bringing water back to the house, the washerwomen beating the linen on the banks of the Nile, the young women arguing at the marketplace, a child hanging off one hip. (Saab, Director's statement for *The Mother of the World*, undated, 2000s)

She almost certainly decided to film this after she had finished work on *Dunia* (*Kiss Me Not on the Eyes*, 2005), which revealed the two conflicting sides of its leading actress, who had been torn between her desire to act and the moral rules of religion, and who eventually married a Saudi sheikh after the film release. These notes are perhaps a rough outline for *Être femme en Méditerranée* (*Being a Woman in the Mediterranean*, 2011–12) and the origins of her project *Café du Genre* (*Gender Café*, 2013) that paid homage to Walid Aouni and Alexandre Paulikevitch, two contemporary male Arab dancers who revived oriental dance and made it socially acceptable once again. In 2011 she had started more specific research into these men, who had become the guardians of a culture that was perceived as degrading by the increasingly conservative Arab societies.

Despite the dual identity that she claims to have rejected throughout her life, Saab's fascination with Egypt is evident in her work. In *Égypte, la cité des morts* (*Egypt, The City of the Dead*, 1978) she roams around Cairo with the eyes of a besotted lover. In *Les Fantômes d'Alexandrie* (*The Ghosts of Alexandria*, 1986) she films the walls of Alexandria with amazement, while worrying about the political and social situation in her own country. *Dunia* (2005) is perhaps the clearest example. In fact, the problems Saab experienced when the film came out had more to do with her nationality than with the film's themes: a foreigner – even a Lebanese – had no right to criticise the way Egyptians lived in Egypt. But Saab was not bound by frontiers, as she also showed in *Le Sahara n'est pas à vendre* (*The Sahara is Not for Sale*, 1977), which she filmed in four conflict zones: Western Sahara, Morocco, Mauritania and Algeria. With both films the reaction was brutal: Saab was banished from Egypt for seven years after *Egypt, The City of the Dead* came out, and in 1978 she was banished for life from Morocco for *The Sahara is Not for Sale*. In 2005, when *Dunia* came out, it was no longer the governments but rather the religious fundamentalists who condemned her.

At the start of the 2000s, Jocelyne Saab was developing *Dunia* as well as several documentary films with Catherine Dussart Productions (CDP). One of these was a documentary-fiction about Ramses II and Nefertari in Abu Simbel, entitled *Abu Simbel. La Nuit du solstice d'été ou Le Rayon d'amour* (*Abu Simbel. The Night of the Summer Solstice or The Ray of Love*, undated, 2000s), written by Saab and rewritten by Catherine Arnaud.

The difficulties she encountered with *Dunia* did not discourage Saab from thinking about other projects to film in Egypt. After she produced the series of photographs *Sense, Icons and Sensitivity*, she went to the south of Egypt, to Luxor, where she shot another series of photos, which are still unedited. Called *Les Masques* (*Masks*), this was a series of portraits of the Egyptian Nubians whose faces had been coated in clay that then dried and cracked in the sun. In 2011 she was inspired by the story of the Egyptian singer Asmahan, her brother Farid Al-Atrache and the fate of the Lebanese Druze academic Nazirah Zeineddine who was twenty years older than them. She decided to develop a film about them, a fictional romance set in the context of the 1940s, during Egypt's royal era under King Farouk. The project is unfinished and does not have a title. In 2013 she shot again in Egypt when she was making *Gender Café*, to film Adel Siwi and Walid Aouni. At the same time, she launched an ambitious project of Egyptian film posters called *Cet objet flottant du désir* (*This Floating Object of Desire*, 2013) which, although Islamists were taking power in Egypt, hoped to depict

> history in the making [. . .], the process of closing down and suffocating the freedom of bodies. [. . .] The spectators, discovering the Arab world at a time when bodies were freer, could ask themselves 'what connection is there still between the women of these posters and the women of today?' (Director's statement for *This Floating Object of Desire*, 2013)

That same year she taught a course at the Institut d'études scéniques, audiovisuelles et cinématographiques de Beyrouth (IESAV) on the cinema of Henry Barakat, setting her students a project on the Egyptian filmmaker and his work. Plunging into the so-called Golden Age of Egyptian cinema, Saab became fascinated by Assia Dagher, about whom she hoped to make a biopic (*L'Honneur de Faten Hamama/The Honour of Faten Hamama*, 2014).

Assia Dagher was an important film producer in Egypt during the 1930s and 1940s. Born in Tannourine in Lebanon, illiterate and married off at a young age, she ran away from Lebanon to Egypt, leaving behind her young daughter. In Cairo she tried her luck as an actress and worked on several silent films. Slowly she established herself, and then opened a production company called Lotus. She was surrounded by entrepreneurial Lebanese women such as Badia Massabni, owner of the chicest cabaret in Cairo, and Rose El Youssef, who published a hugely popular Cairo newspaper that carried her name: *Rosa El Youssef*. At first Saab conceived of the project as a classic biopic, chronologically tracing the life story of Assia Dagher from her childhood in Lebanon to the last big films she produced in Nasser's Egypt. The project was well received, and Saab obtained development funding from the Arab Fund for Arts and Culture (AFAC) in Lebanon. But she also still owned other materials that she felt she should use: footage she had shot when the American University of Beirut had conferred an honorary doctorate on Egyptian actress Faten Hamama, another star of this era of Egyptian cinema.

Fully intending to use this material, Saab developed the project into a documentary with the idea of asking Faten Hamama – who had acted in several films produced by Assia Dagher, and who to some extent owed her success to the producer – to narrate the film. Saab met with Hamama in Egypt and, although the actress had not been filmed for many years, she liked the plans. But before another meeting could be set up to start work on the project, Faten Hamama passed away. It was a blow for Saab, but she did not stop developing the project. It was adapted into an Egyptian-style musical, telling the story of three women, all trailblazers on the cultural scene of Cairo for two decades. She was thinking of asking Salma Hayek for the main role, and the Lebanese *baladi* dancer Alexandre Paulikevitch to play Badia Massabni who – aside from being a successful businesswoman – was also a dancer, singer and actress. Saab was already discussing the choreography of the film with Walid Aouni, with whom she had worked on *Dunia*.

But Egypt was not the only country to hold a fascination for her. Her connections with the southern Mediterranean remained clear until the end of her life. In *Témoignage* she wrote:

> My maternal grandparents were from the Greek Catholic community. But I was born Maronite into my father's tradition. Those who've traced the genealogy of our family tree say that we were originally part of a Bedouin tribe that came from Yemen and adopted the customs and the religion of wherever they settled. The name Saab is found among the three main Lebanese communities: the Druze, the Christians and the Muslims. (Saab, *Témoignage*)

As all of Jocelyne Saab's work seems anchored in a family history that she fights to keep alive despite the way the war damaged the close personal relationships in her family, it is possible that knowing about this distant Yemeni past awoke her particular interest in the country. In 2015 she was considering adapting for television the novel *The Hostage* (1984) by the Yemeni Zayd Mutee' Dammaj. The story, set in the 1940s, is about a twelve-year-old *duwaydar* (a child taken from their family to be put to work in the Governor's palace), who decides to find out about his past. In his search he meets a man who initiates him in pleasure, without managing to subjugate him. It is a story not only about the last defence of the common people against the powerful, but also about the vital physical passion that interests Saab in this astonishing story. These are vibrant bodies who derive all their humanity from the right to experience pleasure. The project was never developed, but it speaks of Saab's attachment to the condition of the Arab people, which she was never afraid of addressing despite the fact that she was living her day-to-day life in Paris.

Saab travelled extensively, and her life was mostly spent in Paris and Beirut. And the eternal subject of the films she longed to make was, of course, Lebanon:

> My first friends in the neighbourhood were called Issam, Christian, Ghada, Gisèle, Alain, Henri, Ahmed, Vahé, and Sélim. They were Muslims, Christians, Armenians, or Jews. So, I grew up without making any difference between us.
> One day my mother flew into a rage because my younger brother had fallen in love with a young Muslim girl. I couldn't understand why she was so angry. I was incredibly upset with her. I found it unfair that my younger brother couldn't be in love with the beautiful Hala, who lived a few streets away on the Basta hill, just because her parents were Muslim.
> Inter-communitarian marriages are still rare, and the civil war didn't help things. Religion is an identity, not a belief. So, you can understand why I never wanted to be part of one camp or the other, in which only one religion is accepted. You can also understand why I could never accept the holy war. You can understand why since the beginning of the war I consistently defended tolerance and human rights. (Saab, *Témoignage*)

During the civil war all Saab's projects focused on Lebanon. In the first years of the war she had prepared, with Jonathan Randal, a series of four documentaries for television, under the title *Les Amours contrariés de l'Orient et de l'Occident* (*The Thwarted Loves of the East and the West*, undated, 1980s), which was meant to retrace the history of the Middle East since the Ottoman Empire. But she was also already interested in fiction, and at the end of the 1980s she wrote the screenplay for a feature film, *L'Arrière-quartier* (*The Backstreets*, undated, 1980s) set in Beirut, with Sélim Turquie. The story depicted the animosity between the communities, even in places and among people who believed in mixed communities. At the end of the war, in 1989, she developed *Le Temple de la tortue* (*The Temple of the Tortoise*, 1989) out of the following synopsis:

> Equinox. The city that has been at war for 15 years has been evacuated after suffering deadly radiation. Only a handful of orphan children are hidden away in their underground kingdom, the Temple of the Tortoise. They're determined to stay in the city: it's all they have. They dream of their future and that of their city, telling their fortunes by looking at the shells of tortoises. The outside, adult world, can't bear

the threat of the radioactive city and decides that the children have to leave Equinox within 72 hours so that the city can be flooded. They use every trick in the book to 'save the children': temptations, threats and violence. These children of war, used to violence and death, play games to calm their fears, re-writing the rules for the 72 hours they have left in Equinox. The flood will have no mercy. (Synopsis of *The Temple of the Tortoise*, 1989)

In this script Saab shows how worried she was for the children growing up after the civil war. She was a mother herself at this point, and she was particularly concerned about the children who had seen conflict, who had experienced bereavement or been orphaned. It is clear from her casting proposals that she was thinking of working with the children of her closest friends:

At the heart of the film is not the perpetual confrontation between the adult world and the child's world but rather the experience of childhood that survives despite the war raging in everyone. The screenplay and the concept of the characters was read to groups of children, traumatised by the war, in therapy sessions in Beirut. Their reactions and commentaries were included in the dialogue. (Director's statement for *The Temple of the Tortoise*, 1989)

A few years later, she again wanted to work with some of these children. At the start of the 2000s, Saab became interested in the story of a woman, Joumana, who had been injured in an attack that had killed her husband. She had been in a coma and lost all memories of several years of her life. In the documentary she developed, Saab introduced a young man, Kamal, whom she had wanted to cast as the head of the gang of children in *The Temple of the Tortoise*. In the screenplay of the documentary she constructs the revelation of the amnesia and Joumana's tragic past in the interaction with four young adults in their twenties who interrogate her. Joumana was the wife of an ambassador who had, at the outset of the Lebanese civil war, been involved with the extreme right-wing militia groups. He had been assassinated in Spain by a bomb attack on the embassy building where they were living. A large scar on Joumana's neck is a physical reminder of the attack. This film, which Saab was developing with France Saint-Léger, was meant to become a film about the difficulty of writing down memories.

After the war, Saab still felt a strong need to address this topic of memories and remembering, to depict and discuss it meaningfully on screen. In 1996 she thought about adapting the novel *L'Homme de parole* (*A Man of His Word*, 1996) by Nazir Hamad, and with Randall Holden she wrote a screenplay in which she wanted to 'tell a story with great simplicity about honour and dignity after the fire and blood of war', as though to exorcise the civil war (Director's statement for *A Man of His Word*, 1996). And yet Saab had for many years not focused on Beirut. After she made *Once Upon a Time, Beirut: Story of a Star* (1994), she left her country and only rarely went back with her camera in hand. Her last feature film, *What's Going On?* (2009), was filmed in Beirut amidst the ruins of a reconstructed city that Saab barely recognised.

In parallel to the filming of *What's Going On?* Saab shot some scenes for another film with the working title *Le Rouge et le blanc* (*The Red and the White*, 2009). It was to be an unusual love story between two people, which takes place in a car park – the car park that stands on the land where Jocelyne Saab's house, burnt down in 1982, had once stood. 'The car park where the action between Ishtar and Simon takes place, is a subtle mirror of their mental universe; the life of the car park is choreographed', she wrote in the notes she put together with Ishtar Yasin, who had already acted in *What's Going On?* (Director's statement for *The Red and the White*, 2009). It was an implicit portrait of what Beirut had become after the reconstruction.

Two years later, in 2011, again with Ishtar Yasin, she wrote a screenplay conceived as a love letter to her two favourite cities: Cairo and Beirut, which she wanted to portray in a project called *Landscape from Beirut and Cairo to Romeo and Juliet's Town: My Architectural Cities' Love*. Of particular interest to her in this project was the architecture of the cities: each would be assigned a character: Ishtar in Beirut and Dunia in Cairo. 'To be a filmmaker and a photographer is also to be an architect, to build with light and create a visual pleasure just as you give pleasure though urban planning' (Director's statement for *Landscape*, 2011).

EXILE IN FRANCE

During and after the civil war Saab lived alternately in Beirut and in Paris. The French capital held little charm for her. Only the hospital rooms really attracted her attention. She started observing them after the war, when she was hospitalised for an ulcer. After the war, when she had already filmed *Fécondation in video* (*Fertilisation in Video*, 1991), which was a great success, Saab was inspired by the technical advances in medicine. In 1994 she underwent an operation for myopia – both eyes at the same time, which was very risky, as she herself admitted – and the procedure amazed her. She wrote the screenplay for a documentary called *L'Oeil et le miracle du laser* (*The Eye and the Miracle of the Laser*, 1994) that she sent to her doctor. The film was never made, but the screenplay shows how avidly Saab was inspired by anything and everything in life.

In 1992 Saab fell into the Canal de l'Ourq in Paris due to a stroke. It was her first stroke. This accident gave rise to a project that she developed with Francis

Lacloche, which nearly made it to the production stage (a trailer was created) and which was entitled *Paris amoureux* (*Paris in Love*, 2002). Conceived of as four short films, it was to be a poetic and phantasmagorical meander around Paris as she rediscovered the city after her stroke. These are the only two unfinished projects that evoke her life in Paris.

AN ASIAN IDENTITY

> My grandmother was originally from Deir El Kamar, that is, 'the convent of the moon', the capital of Mount-Lebanon at the beginning of the 17th century under the reign of the Druze Emir Fakhr-al-Din II until his death in 1635. It used to be called DAR EL KAMAR, which means 'the residence of the moon'. I concluded that her silences and her reserved manner were linked to her origins: she was in the moon, and like her I often withdrew into myself as well. I've never fallen out of this pleasant habit. I can still remember her faraway gaze while she described to me the pig celebration, or while at mealtimes she regaled us with anecdotes about the emirs so as to teach us a bit about Lebanese history. Then she'd lose the thread of her story as she talked about Bashir the Great and Fakhreddine II. (Saab, *Témoignage*)

Jocelyne Saab's fascination with the Ottoman Empire and its aftermath was born out of the countless tales her grandmother, grandfather and her father told her about the history of Lebanon. It is the nostalgia for a world and a region rich with intellectual fervour and vision that she would carry with her throughout her life, as numerous Lebanese or Arab citizens did. Her fascination with the Egyptian president Gamal Abdel Nasser, an Arab nationalist who took power and settled a socialist revolution in Egypt in 1952, and his pan-Arab way of considering politics is indicative: the idea of restoring an Orient that is proud of its culture and civilisation is very present in Saab's work, and is perhaps at the origin of her desire to develop a project around Mustafa Kemal and his vision for a modern Turkey. In 1997 Jocelyne developed a portrait of the Turkish head of state known as Atatürk for the production company that had produced *La Dame de Saïgon* (*The Lady of Saigon*, 1998). She was intensifying her research into this Middle Eastern statesman who had been, in her eyes, capable of singlehandedly taking his country into the modern era. A director's statement that she wrote about the project testifies to her interest:

> Why make a film about Atatürk? [. . .] Mainly because Mustafa Kemal was a formidable statesman in an Islamic environment; and Islam – from Morocco to Pakistan – has never encouraged the emergence of

statesmen, that is, men who govern and think about the needs and the future of a nation, rising above the vested interests of clans – whether corporations or families – that is so typical of the sociology of the Muslim world. The modern state that founded a new connection of solidarity – citizenship – is above communitarian or religious connections. [. . .] Seen this way, the foundational example of Turkey that has been a reference for several nationalist movements in the Arab world, seems to be a particularly interesting subject to analyse. (Director's statement for *Mustafa Kemal*, 1997)

The documentary was never made because of a disagreement between Saab and the person at ADR Productions with whom she was writing the script. A year's worth of work was lost, but the extremely detailed research material that she kept shows her fascination with this man whom she felt had established 'the first nation state in Islamic lands'. She had been developing this project to coincide with the celebrations for the seventy-fifth anniversary of the Turkish republic. In her director's statement she wrote:

It is during this period that Turkey develops a film industry, specifically at the instigation of Kemal who loves cinema and artists. In fact, Kemal appears as himself several times in the triptych by Muhsen Urtugrul about the war of independence. (Director's statement for *Mustafa Kemal*, 1997)

Jocelyne Saab chose Atatürk because he loved cameras. He was an excellent character for a film, complex and strategic, a real film hero:

What is seductive about Mustafa Kemal is also his strategy for coming to power. The Kemalian saga from 1919 to 1923 perfectly illustrates one of the recommendations developed by Machiavelli in *The Prince*. Mustafa Kemal knew how to make the most of an opportunity to exercise his nationalist vision, to impose it on his opponents because of his military talent, to found new republican and authoritarian institutions and to stay at the head of the country until his death. (Director's statement for *Mustafa Kemal*, 1997)

As well as books on the subject, innumerable press cuttings and lists of archive film material that could potentially be used in the documentary, her archives also contain transcriptions of interviews with specialists on the subject, and proposals for editing.

For another film project set in Turkey, in Antioch, there is very little written information in her archive, but she had already filmed a significant amount of material. She began this project much later, in 2011. She had started to follow Meltem, an Alawite Syrian by birth, with both Turkish and Dutch nationality, who had returned to the region she came from in search of her identity. With Meltem, Saab was investigating how traces of the borders had been established in the maelstrom of the years between the two world wars – a theme that had been central to Saab's work since the first images she shot. In the same year, 2011, she wrote a fiction: *Salwa la Turque* (*Salwa the Turk*, 2011) which tells the story of the emigration of a Turkish family to Colombia after the fall of the Ottoman Empire. Fascinated by this monumental civilisation, Jocelyne Saab always rooted her Arab identity in Asian soil and focused her interests beyond the borders of the so-called Arab world.

The admiration Saab felt for her father, who died too young – before he could shatter the myth that she had built up in her childhood and then as a young woman – directly led to her exploration of the Asian continent:

> My father's journeys took him to India and China. An autodidact, he had taught himself more than ten Chinese dialects, as well as Hindi, Malay and Laotian . . . In Li Chou in Laos he had owned a gold mine that had been abandoned by the English. I went at least five times with my nanny, in secret, to the Empire Cinema in Beirut to watch Marilyn Monroe and Robert Mitchum in *River of No Return*. I imagined my father going down the river on a makeshift raft to take the cargo of gold to the town. I saw him battling the rapids and cascades while fighting off the attacks of all kinds of brigands. I returned to Laos when my son was five years old, to look for the Li Chou goldmine. Unfortunately, I never managed to find it. (Saab, *Témoignage*)

Saab also went to Vietnam, as though to satisfy an age-old curiosity. In 1975, as the extreme right-wing Christian Phalangists were shooting at a bus transporting Palestinians through Ain el-Mreisse in Beirut, she was preparing for a journey to Vietnam to document the liberation of the country. The journalist friends with whom she was meant to travel had disappeared or been killed. She chose to stay in Beirut; but the curiosity always remained. The years of research that Saab had dedicated to *The Lady of Saigon* (1998) inspired her to develop several different projects in Asia, both in Vietnam and in India, where she had even considered moving to. With the novelist Philippe Franchini she wrote *Vietnam, notre amour* (*Vietnam, Our Love*, undated, second half of the 1990s), a fictionalised version of the story of Dr Hoa, whom she had portrayed in her 1998 documentary. With the producer Catherine Dussart she researched and wrote *Portrait d'Hanoi, ou Comment inventer la modernité* (*Portrait of Hanoi, or How to Invent Modernity*, undated, second half of the 1990s), spending several weeks in the city looking for locations for this project that she was, in the end, unable to produce. Her approach to the city was, naturally, informed by her personal experiences:

> After decades of war, the population continues to live with a spirit of survival: the Vietnamese live in the present, in the here-and-now. There's no sense of a project. Yet the city is changing daily and it has to negotiate its move into modernity. Is the population aware of its urban heritage in order to accompany it in this new and delicate evolution? It's up to those who live in and use the city that have to make it theirs. (Director's statement for *Portrait of Hanoi, or How to Invent Modernity*, undated, second half of the 1990s)

She developed this project six years after the ceasefire in Lebanon. The questions that she asked here are already present at the heart of *Once Upon a Time, Beirut: Story of a Star*, which deals with Beirut's ability to rebuild itself after the disasters of war. With *Portrait of Hanoi* she intended to show the experience of a city and its citizens in the process of reconstruction – urban reconstruction but also a social and psychological regeneration.

Saab was also fascinated with India. Surprisingly enough, she never wrote about the subcontinent. In her archives all there is, is material written by Rose Vincent for a fiction-documentary about the history of the city Fatehpur-Sikri in the Indian state of Uttar Pradesh:

> When I was a bit older, my father often spoke to me about Ghandi. During the time he was working on Indian construction sites, he'd often walked for kilometres to listen to this man whom he greatly admired. It was also a way of having a little break from the pythons whom, he said, circled his bed at night. Because he slept in the open air on the construction sites, and only survived because he kept his feet in bowls of water overnight.
> My father was my first hero.
> Ghandi was my second hero. (Saab, *Témoignage*)

A LOOK BACK AT A PAST THAT IS DISAPPEARING

Towards the end of her life, Jocelyne Saab was able to bring together two sides of her life, what she made in the Arab world and her experiences in Asia. She did this both with the project of the Cultural Resistance International Film Festival in Lebanon, where the programming focused on films from Asia and the Mediterranean, and with her last feature film project. This last project was based on the story of Mei Shigenobu, the daughter of Fusako Shigenobu, (female) founder of the Japanese Red Army (JRA) in Lebanon. Collaborating with the PLO, the JRA fought for the Palestinian cause. Mei was born in 1973, in secret, and her father's identity was never revealed – he was a Palestinian leader. Mei's safety was constantly under threat from the Israeli Secret Services, and she grew up in Lebanon as though she were a mini-secret agent, regularly changing her identity and school until the Palestinians were forced out of Lebanon in 1982. Her mother had to flee, and Mei also had to leave Beirut. When she returned on later occasions, it was always under an assumed name. The day her mother was arrested in Osaka in 2000 was also the day of Mei's liberation: she could finally start the process of getting back her true identity and, for the first time in her life, had a real passport.

Saab was inspired by this woman's story and how it allowed her to tell one last time, before her death, the story of the siege of Beirut. With the feeling that she was reaching the end of her life, at a time when it seemed that the world had lost the capacity for engaging with ideals, Mei Shigenobu's story also allowed Saab to revisit the principles she had fought for her entire life. Right up to the end, she argued for the need for a revolution, and the large-scale pan-Arab ideals never left her. This planned film gave her the chance to express her outrage, while at the same time focusing on a generation that had suffered because of their parents' militant engagement, and who today absolutely refuse to commit themselves to a cause. Saab understood that generation: she lost many friends who died because of their political militancy. So her project was uniquely sensitive: what she wanted to show of Japan were the myths with which Fusako, the mother, had nourished her daughter Mei during those years hidden in the mountains of Lebanon – the samurais from the past, the rice cakes of her mother and the cherry blossoms in spring.

Shigenobu, mère et fille (*Shigenobu: Mother and Daughter*, uncompleted, 2018), would be a documentary about childhood and motherhood. To retrace Mei's early years Saab turned to a graphic novel that Fusako had written in prison, and that detailed her life with Mei in Lebanon between 1973 and 1982. Saab's idea was to use animation to tell the story of Mei's past. Initially, she considered using manga, but then decided to use Fusako's drawings – they are simple, easy to animate and have a naivety that inherently captures the childlike nature of the world she is depicting. As such, the documentary would give her the opportunity to tell a story of Beirut in 1982 without telling the story of the civil war once again. Among the JRA guerrillas were a number of excellent filmmakers: Masao Adachi and Koji Wakamatsu had come to support the Palestinian cause in Lebanon. Adachi had set up home in Lebanon and was close to Mei throughout his life. Wakamatsu financed the resistance from a distance. It was he who organised Mei's 'coming out': arriving in Lebanon with an entire film crew, he filmed the young woman and sent the material to all the Japanese TV channels. It was a sort of second birth for her. Wakamatsu's creative universe interested Saab tremendously, and she decided to use extracts from his films from the *pinku eiga* era of his work in the 1960s, to express the violence of the times. The development of this ambitious film began not long after her diagnosis and occupied the last three years of her life. She planned for the film to be an edit of found material, as she was fully aware of the fragility of her health.

CONCLUSION

Jocelyne Saab's catalogue is extensive: forty-seven films, as well as various collections of photographs and installations. On top of that, her unfinished work reveals numerous unknown facets of this filmmaker who was so deeply engaged in the story of the Middle East. A traveller like her father, she went far and wide. Her imagination was carried by the rivers of Asia in an incessant ebb and flow, while she constantly felt the need to record the story of her own damaged country.

As her body of work is brought together in this book and in forthcoming events dedicated to her work, the archives described here reveal an artist who never stopped reinventing herself. Everyone with whom she collaborated became part of a process that made her work curious and diverse, embracing science fiction, historical re-enaction, classical documentary-making and experimental montage film. The only thing that these various elements of her extraordinarily varied body of work share is a deep desire to defend social justice, and an irrepressible need for poetry. This is a need that underpins her work as though to shield her from a tragic and burdensome family history which, as much of the material examined here reveals, haunted her right to the end of her life.

PART II

Film as a Weapon against War and Oblivion

CHAPTER 5

From Class Struggle to Sectarian Warfare: Jocelyne Saab's Beirut Trilogy

Giovanni Vimercati

> The poor man lacks only what the rich man has.
> – Ali Bin Abi Talib

> If it were again a question of the liberal economy in which the strong oppresses and exploits the weak, if it were the case of the prosperity of the tiny capitalist minority and of bourgeois society, if the Lebanese Miracle should continue to express itself in terms of improvisation, approximation, lack of foresight, invisible revenues and non-taxable returns, if it were finally the case of the Lebanon of the privileged few, we shall quickly see the positive security of the majority threatened by the gravest of dangers and face a catastrophe from which Lebanon will not stand up again.
> – Grégoire Haddad, Greek Catholic Bishop of Beirut, 1975

'When anger is imprisoned, it bursts into flames', the voice-over in Jocelyne Saab's *Beirut, Never Again* (1976) observes, stupefied. Yet it is not the flames nor the conflagration before them that the documentary is concerned with. While in her previous documentary, *Lebanon in Turmoil* (1975), the Lebanese director, armed with empathic journalistic rigour, had pieced together the causes of the imminent explosion, in *Beirut, Never Again* she captured the dislocation that followed it. The cognitive displacement of civil war, and its fumbling around, impacted Saab's filmmaking directly, narratively as well as aesthetically. Gone is the analytical acumen with which she had investigated the complexity of causes fuelling the impending conflict in *Lebanon in Turmoil*, replaced by a metaphysical impressionism that – without forgetting the reasons for war – focuses on its unreason. For the Lebanese director and her colleagues, the beginning of the civil war coincided with the beginning of their careers. Jocelyne Saab belonged in fact to that generation of Lebanese filmmakers that started making films during or right before the war – people like Maroun Baghdadi, Randa Chahal, Jean Chamoun and Borhane Alaouié whose films 'about Lebanon were rarely screened in Lebanon' (Zaccak 1997: 116). Arguably, *Beirut, Never Again* marks Jocelyne Saab's passage from journalism to cinema, that is to say, from the chronicling of reality to its artistic sublimation.

Not that war was new to her. As a journalist she had documented the 1973 Arab–Israeli War, visited Palestinian camps, documented Gaddafi's 'Green Revolution' and exposed the persecution of Kurds in Iraq, but the fratricidal fighting that torn apart her native Lebanon was different. It was personal, and painfully so. 'Every civil war has something absurd about it, it's crueller and more saddening than other wars', remarks the voice-over, written by the American-Lebanese poet Etel Adnan. The narrative and aesthetic shift occasioned by war is not a mere stylistic choice but the emotional reaction to a wound that is also her own. As Mathilde Rouxel (2019) has observed, militancy made way for poetry in Saab's filmmaking, perhaps to account for the intimate agony that civil wars as a matter of historical course imply. When the slain enemy is no longer a faceless golem but your neighbour, (former) lover, colleague or even a relative, it becomes impossible to keep the demons

Figure 5.1 Abandoned chair on the shore, in *Beirut, Never Again*

of carnage at bay. When the killing is fratricidal, the pain inflicted on others is also your own – mourning becomes a constant, which might account for the director's sensitive ability to empathise with everything and everyone in front of her camera. Filming children roaming the devastated streets of Beirut the filmmaker ponders, 'They see in one day what others elsewhere never see in their whole lives.' The focus is no longer on the subject of the gaze, but on the immoral injustice of having to see at all. In the eyes of Saab, the horror and the insanity of war could not be told through the protocols of journalism, however impeccably she had practised it up to then.

The civil war, as the title that inaugurated her 'Beirut Trilogy' suggests, was to radically change the very face of the Lebanese capital beyond recognition. As Lina Khatib has opined, 'the Civil War left its mark on the physical appearance of the city, and on the cinematic imagination of Beirut' (2008: 57) itself. *Beirut, Never Again* is in fact a morphological reconnaissance of a city dismembered by war, in the guise of an audio-visual poem. The director focuses on the metaphysical improbability of the new landscape designed by the cruelty and inadvertent creativity of firearms. Images of maimed mannequins on the barricades are thus accompanied by Adnan's lyrical musings:

> frustrations work themselves out on dummies. These human shapes paid their tribute to terror, these copies of life tell what real bodies have suffered. They have been torn to pieces, submitted to profanation as if even abstract matter has been subjected to suffering.

Poetic contemplation is never gratuitous; quite the contrary, it stems from the despondency of reality to investigate its dark philosophical matter. The images of a city in ruins are not aestheticised for their own sake, but are instead traced back to their painful signifiers. When looking at the cubes of cement strewn along the road, Saab laments how they 'choke the streets the same way the political horizon is also choked'. Images are no longer used to build an argument or a journalistic narrative; meaning is deduced from them rather than imposed on them. The image takes centre stage simply because rational explanations no longer suffice to account for the madness of warfare. It is the latter's visual reverberations onto reality that the director follows.

Renouncing the journalistic exactitude of her previous TV work does not mean for Saab to overlook the social roots of the conflict. A single image can in fact tell us more than any reportage ever could. Even the playful looting of children in the ruins of downtown Beirut, as examined by her keen eye, serves to debunk the simplistic narrative of a war between Christian and Muslim sects. 'The foreign goods that the Orient always finds amazing' are now lying in the streets, the windows that once guarded them shattered by bullets. 'This amazement the children of the poor are also discovering with a sort of reverence', her voice-over states as images of kids scavenging the shopping district of Beirut go by. 'All the elements of a world so far forbidden are suddenly within their reach', the director remarks matter-of-factly, pondering on the momentary ransom of the have-nots. 'It took the hardest of the catastrophes of this century for the children and adolescents to take into their hands the luxurious objects that Beirutis used to import carelessly', she concludes. Contained in these brief yet piercing remarks is the director's awareness of the material, rather than religious, root causes behind the raging conflict.

Though routinely and simplistically reduced to a religious conflict between Christians and Muslims, the civil war that ravaged Lebanon from 1975 to 1990 stemmed from more complex social causes. The late 1960s in Lebanon, like elsewhere, were a time of social and political turmoil. The increasing prominence of the banking sector at the expense of other productive sectors of the Lebanese economy resulted in deepening class differences and, consequently, conflict (Nasr 1978). The year 1968 witnessed a major agrarian movement in the Akkar plain where peasants revolted against the semi-feudal conditions they were working and living in. The industrial sector too was overrun by a wave of strikes and mobilisations. In November 1972 workers at the Ghandour biscuit and chocolate factory went on strike to 'demand a wage increase, equal pay for men and women workers, the recognition of the shopfloor committee and their right to trade union organisation' (Traboulsi 2012: 168).

While none of these labour movements was organised along sectarian lines or brought religion to the fore of their demands, the demographic make-up of the lower classes of Lebanese society was by no means devoid of sectarian connotations. In his 1962 study on Lebanese business, *Entrepreneurs of Lebanon*, Yusif Sayigh noted how 'a larger proportion of [Lebanon's] business leaders are of the Christian faith' (1962: 65). Out of 207 business leaders at the time, 'four fifths are of the Christian faith, though only half of the population is. On the other hand, the Moslems constitute about one sixth of the entrepreneurial group, but 44 per cent of the population' (Sayigh 1962: 69). Ten years later, the situation had not changed much, as Boutros Labaki showed in his 1973 study 'L'économie politique du Liban indépendant'. 'Conversely, among the industrial working class, 75% of the workers were Muslims, Shi'a in particular, against 25% Christians' (Traboulsi 2012: 163). It is within this demographic and economic scenario that the conflation of class and sect, if not inevitable, appears to be retrospectively understandable at least (though it turned out to be fatal in political terms for some of the leftist formations that championed it).

Religious leaders like Musa al-Sadr (founder of the Shi'a Movement of the Dispossessed, Amal's precursor) were not alone in conflating class and sect in Lebanon; some Marxists too adopted a symmetrical viewpoint. At the outset of the civil war, confessional disparity coupled with the weaponisation of conflict gave rise to the concept of 'community class' or 'class-sect'. As Joseph Daher explains, 'according to this theory the predominant weight of Christians in Lebanon's business elite meant that Christians could be understood as constituting the bourgeoisie, while Muslims (particularly Shi'a) made up the vast majority of the working class and poor' (2016: 22). Classes and sects were thus made to coincide to a significant and problematic extent. However indirectly, these issues are disentangled in Saab's Beirut Trilogy, which in fact rejects the narrative of a 'religious war' to investigate the contradictions of a conflict rooted in socio-economic inequality. It should be noted in this regard that the director had studied political economy and that, according to her own testimony, this course of study had a profound impact on her understanding of politics and injustice. She once stated, 'It was a course on Middle East finance that opened my eyes; economy made me aware of political realities, of the concrete forces at play, it provided me with an analytical structure and rectitude that is always with me' (Rouxel 2019: 35). Though devoid of political elaborations, her documentaries on the civil war are visibly informed by this awareness – identity and its ostensible politics are never adduced as the cause of conflict.

Another myth that the Lebanese director obliquely dismantles, however retroactively, is that of Lebanon being the 'Switzerland of the Middle East' and the 'Paris of the Orient', iconographic legends that cinema too contributed to foster and propagate (as she would show in her 1994 feature film *Once Upon a Time, Beirut: Story of a Star*). If armed conflict put an abrupt end to this delusional idyll, the socio-economic contradictions that led to its dissolution had been brewing for a long time. The 'Paris of the Orient' was in fact a private-membership club from which the majority of Lebanese were excluded. It was not war that brought misery to Lebanon, but the other way around. When Saab's camera ventures into the abandoned places of pleasure and luxury, the ghosts of the dispossessed are let loose. 'The feast is over, or it has been replaced by a bloody one', she announces in *Beirut, Never Again* while panning over the dilapidated remains of nightclubs, five-star hotels and brothels as music echoes in the background like a spectral presence. With the illusion of wealth carbonised along with its elitist ostentation, 'fate has decided that the hotels' balconies reserved for the tourists become now shooting posts'. The bare skeletons of these former temples of luxury are lapidary reminders of an unsustainable economic model that war both exposed and preserved. It took the fury of armed conflict to demystify the fallacy of the 'Switzerland of the Middle East' or the 'Paris of the Orient' and their orientalist clichés. But it was the very same war that would repurpose their economic foundations for the neo-liberal age of reconstruction. Yet recrimination, not even of the political kind, has no place in Saab's documentary. It is as if the distress of war was too excruciating to even look for a culprit. Surrounded by death, the very lives of survivors become the only element of vital if spectral importance. An old man talks about the dreary surprise of meeting people in the devastated streets of Beirut, confiding how he cries whenever he meets an old acquaintance by chance: 'Every time you meet someone it's like they've resuscitated, you can't believe they're still alive.'

Possibly due to the time passed (three years into the war) or because of its epistolary nature, *Letter from Beirut* (1978) possesses a more probing quality. There is an attempt to make sense out of senselessness, to record the many, ineluctable ways in which life keeps going on despite the devastation of war. In the second instalment of her Beirut Trilogy the director boards a bus to gauge the daily strategies of survival adopted by common men and women. Ordinary reality is haunted by a conflict that has redrawn the coordinates of the everyday, has restricted freedom of movement and inflicted on the general population a sense of permanent indeterminacy. The bus lends itself as the perfect sampler of societal attitudes and coping mechanisms. To a woman who complains about having lost her ability to sleep since the war began, a passenger sarcastically replies, 'That's good for the sale of sleeping pills', adding 'Businessmen have to make money, that's what political parties want.' Once again, the material interests behind the conflict, rather than their supposed religious causes, are known to the man in the street more than they were to many (foreign) journalists and commentators. Popular wisdom, imbued in the cynicism of war, is on display everywhere on the bus. This dialogue between a passenger and the ticket inspector about the hike in bus fares epitomises the spiteful and surreal coexistence of life with death:

> Passenger: 'Everything has been revalued except human life.'
> Ticket inspector: 'Everything is valuable except death.'

As far as the conflict itself was concerned, the involvement of foreign powers and the Israeli invasion had added a layer of political complexity and ambiguity to the civil war. Israel stormed into the country from the south, creating 'a frontier zone under the control of Saad Haddad's Army of Free Lebanon' which was 'financed, armed and officered by the Israeli army' (Traboulsi 2012: 212). Following the Israeli aggression, an increasing number of internally displaced people found themselves homeless; in the case of Palestinian refugees, for the second time around. As the director moves out of Beirut to explore the political topography of a country that was being violently reconfigured, the spectator gets a glimpse of what was perhaps becoming the first global civil war. 'My itinerary also belongs to science-fiction: can you imagine yourself visiting ten countries in less than five hours?' ponders Jocelyne Saab as she meets UNIFIL troops from Nigeria, Fiji Islands, Norway, Nepal and Senegal. In war, as it had been in peace, Lebanon served in fact as 'one of the principal entry points for the economic penetration of the Arab East' (Nasr 1978: 7) by Western powers and their economic interests but also by regional actors. Since armed conflict is always good business, for warlords as well as arms dealers, the Lebanese civil war attracted a disproportionate amount of foreign and regional actors. As the late Lebanese journalist and commentator Samir Kassir remarked, 'nationals of almost three dozen countries participated in the hostilities' (2010: 18) during the Lebanese civil war. Some came in solidarity (with the Palestinian cause), some for strategic or geopolitical interests, some others on mercenary duty. Superpowers deployed peace-keeping forces as 'a way to appease their conscience' as the director aptly puts it. Even 'the French are back' she notes, 'but under a new flag'. Political reformism, anti-Zionism and revolutionary impulses would by the end of the war decompose into ethno-religious nationalism, militia-capitalism and political opportunism of the most nihilistic kind. The war in *Letter from Beirut* is in fact already exceeding the grasp of its participants, not to mention that of its victims.

'It was a land of refuge, it has become a land of refugees', Saab reflects as she follows Palestinian refugees around a country that had ratified their right to armed self-determination from Lebanese soil with the Cairo Agreement of 1969. The accord, brokered by the Egyptian president Gamal Abdel Nasser, validated the armed presence of Palestinian guerrillas in south-east Lebanon whose actions against the Zionist enemy were to be tolerated by Lebanese authorities. The civil war, and Israel's involvement most notably, were to effectively invalidate this agreement and condemn the Palestinians to an exile that lasts to this very day. Speaking about refugees, Saab declares, 'It's a new form of nomadic life, unsolicited, typical of our century.'

Specular to the figure of the refugee is that of the fedayeen, the resistance fighter whose hopeless life in the camps has been destigmatised by armed struggle. The eyes of the director convey the thrust of internationalist solidarity that a whole section of Lebanese society had expressed towards the Palestinian cause. Her profound, crystalline empathy is alternated by continuous attempts to, if not explain, at least understand the ongoing conflict. A discussion among intellectuals (we will learn about the death of one of them, Kareem, in *Beirut, My City*) sheds some light on the political dynamics of the civil war, with one highlighting how 'internal conflicts prevailing among communities' led to the retreat into one's own community 'to find an answer'. Another one adds, 'What's interesting is that this relapse into communitarian bonds simultaneously resorts to outside forces such as UNIFIL or the Arab Deterrent Force in the attempt to solve these problems. [. . .] But these "solutions" became problems themselves.' He concludes bitterly, 'those who came to Lebanon trying to find solutions, became additional problems rather than solutions.' Suspended between stupefaction and indignation, between the irrational onslaught of warfare and the need to make sense of it, *Letter from Beirut* seems to presage the lethal wound that was soon to be inflicted on the Lebanese capital by Israel's air force and army.

'One of the most striking events of her life' (Rouxel 2019: 16), the 1982 siege of Beirut was to leave a permanent mark on the director's memory and that of

Figure 5.2 Women in the siege, in *Beirut, My City*

her city. *Beirut, My City* (1982), possibly Saab's highest artistic achievement, begins with the director in front of the camera surveying the destruction of her own family house at the hands of the Israeli air force. The house is, in her own words, the house of every Lebanese person who has lost one, whose memory now lies in carbonised ruins. The last instalment of Jocelyne Saab's Beirut Trilogy delivers itself from any analytical entrapment and plunges into the feverish depths of West Beirut under siege. Neither fiction nor documentary, intimist but never onanistic, *Beirut, My City* is an essay film *avant la lettre*, an expressionist ethnography of an urban microcosm where utopia and dystopia were forcibly made to coincide. The Palestinian struggle evacuated by the colonial arrogance of the Israeli army left the inhabitants of West Beirut indefinitely detained for having shown solidarity with the resistance. Time in *Beirut, My City* seems to have stopped or, as the voice-over written by the Lebanese playwright Roger Assaf declares, 'Time has taken its time, or rather, war has taken our time.' There is a sense of febrile immediacy that scorches every single frame of this film, something that the spectator feels rather than sees. Narrative is replaced by an aesthetic convulsion where the different elements of the audio-visual experience collapse into each other. More than a vision, *Beirut, My City* is the rendition of a collective delirium. Reality and its surreal doppelganger are no longer distinguishable. A sequence showing disabled, abandoned children in the Beirut Stadium, an open-air structure, is as haunting as an image can get. Unexplained, unwarranted, it exposes the atrocity of war in all its meaningless folly. It is a funereal scene sound-tracked by the lacerating melancholy of a saxophone and the electronic glitches of a lone synthesiser.

The surreal desolation of the western sector of the city is illuminated by its dignity, 'the pride of being from West Beirut, of having forced the Israeli army to show all its strength and having thus exposed its impotence', Roger Assaf's voice-over sombrely enthuses. An old man watering a flower bed by the sidewalk, what appears to be a father with his son carrying a cross, each, literally and allegorically, his own. *Beirut, My City* is replete with sequences and images of a city caught in a state of agonising transcendence, one where it is hard to tell the director's point of view apart from one's own reaction. It is a film that involves the spectator sensorially, if not physically. The transport with which West Beirutis bid farewell to the fedayeen, forced out of the city and Lebanon by the invader, is so vehement that images glow with it. The siege of Beirut stifled a dream, a possibility, and depoliticised a conflict. From then on it would be war for war's sake; militia-capitalism and intra-sectarian infighting would pretty much be the only features of the civil war. For a few weeks, in the summer of 1982, West Beirut was something else. Assaf's words sound and read like an epitaph; he declares with rapture:

> We say I'm from West Beirut and for once we behave in ways that transcend the rules of the petty community: we can be Shi'as or Christians, Jews or Sunnis, Lebanese or Palestinian, and being at the same time in the same space someone from West Beirut, following the forms of a possible society, that of a certain Arab dream. [. . .] To be Arab and Lebanese was possible, Jew and Palestinian it existed, Muslim and progressive, woman and in charge, anarchist and organised. But utopia is expensive and we didn't know that the bill would have cost us twice as much.

Beirut, My City is both political elegy and requiem, as well as a hallucinatory reminder of the historical weight of images.

It is precisely these images, impressed on the spectator's mind with the force of trauma, that Jocelyne Saab has delivered from oblivion. Her Beirut Trilogy, in a country where there still is no unified history textbook, represents something more than a mere cinematographic achievement, prodigious as it is. These three documentaries constitute an act of profound historical and intellectual honesty. While political cinema irons out nuances in the pursuit of a given cause, these three documentaries are empathetically open to the imperfection and complexity of real life, and especially of war. While Saab's political sympathies are never obscured, her determination to avoid opportunistic demonisation provides us with a framework to untangle the causes of a conflict that degenerated into sectarian hatred. Refracted in their frames and echoed in their lyrical voice-overs are the clues to the possible interpretation of a conflict reduced to a confessional dispute whose origins were material, not religious. At the same time, the awareness that the dead and disappeared will never be redeemed or avenged traverses these three films like a shudder.

BIBLIOGRAPHY

Daher, Joseph (2016), *Hezbollah: The Political Economy of Lebanon's Party of God*, London: Pluto Press.
Haddad, Grégoire (1975), 'Primum vivere', *L'Orient–Le Jour*, 15 July.
Kassir, Samir (2010), *Beirut*, Berkeley: University of California Press.
Khatib, Lina (2008), *Lebanese Cinema: Imagining the Civil War and Beyond*, London: I. B. Tauris.
Labaki, Boutros (1988), 'L'économie politique du Liban independent, 1943–1975' [1973], in Nadim Shehadi and Dana Haffar Mills (eds), *Lebanon: A History of Conflict and Consensus*, London: Centre for Lebanese Studies and I. B. Tauris, pp. 166–80.
Nasr, Salim (1978), *Backdrop to Civil War: The Crisis of Lebanese Capitalism*, Middle East Research and Information Project Report no. 73, Tacoma, WA: MERIP, pp. 3–13.
Rouxel, Mathilde (2019), *Jocelyne Saab: la mémoire indomptée (1970–2019)*, Tunis: Nadhar.
Sayigh, Yusif A. (1962), *Entrepreneurs of Lebanon: The Role of the Business Leader in a Developing Economy*, Cambridge, MA: Harvard University Press.
Traboulsi, Fawwaz (2012), *A History of Modern Lebanon*, London: Pluto Press.
Zaccak, Hady (1997), *Le Cinéma libanais: itinéraire d'un cinéma ver l'inconnu (1929–1996)*, Beirut: Dar el-Machreq.

CHAPTER 6

Beirut, There Was and There Was Not[1]

Mark R. Westmoreland

> The city, however, does not tell its past, but contains it like the lines of a hand, written in the corners of the streets, the gratings of the windows, the banisters of the steps, the antennae of the lightning rods, the poles of the flags, every segment marked in turn with scratches, indentations, scrolls.
>
> – Italo Calvino, *Invisible Cities* (1997: 9)

MISE-EN-SCÈNE

In the early 1990s, the dust from the war had barely settled, leaving behind a landscape devastated by fifteen years of fighting and neglect. In the central district and along the green line running up Damascus Road, many buildings were collapsed or heavily marked by bomb blasts and bullet holes. Nostalgia for a bygone era blinded people from seeing post-war Beirut for what it was, or seeing it at all. Among those who were in exile, many felt that Beirut no longer existed: 'Beirut is a metaphoric place, a place that does not exist, except in film, in memories, as a souvenir', so declared film critic Ibrahim Al Ariss (in Hillauer 2005: 133). Many years after the war, the image of Beirut is still characterised by idyllic postcards of the golden age, 'reprinted in the thousands long since 1975, Beirut has been frozen in time' (Makdisi 2006: 202).

As part of the general amnesty agreement, the official stance insisted that the material remains of the war-torn city needed to vanish. Billions would be invested in the massive reconstruction of Beirut's Central District, BCD (Harb El-Kak 2001; Sawalha 2010). Solidere organised the project with the intent to re-mask the facades of ruin with splendid simulacra of an imagined pre-war

Beirut. By bulldozing much of downtown, Solidere presumed to sweep aside 'all the difficulties, problems, uncertainties, and hesitations' (Makdisi 2006: 210). As the materiality of a present Beirut became converted into representations of a past Beirut that had never actually existed, a triumphant futuristic fantasy of Beirut relied on people not looking beyond the refurbished surface image. This pre-war city paradise and the post-war one (re)built in its image thus imposed a nostalgic vision of Beirut unreconciled with what remained lost.

And yet, as access to the city centre became possible again after the amnesty agreement, young filmmakers, photographers, urban historians, architects, and particularly those returning from exile, were drawn to this site for their own projects. Some had opportunistic agendas like seeing the evidentiary authenticity of the ruinous buildings as realistic filmsets, in which the contemporary city served as a backdrop, a mere *mise-en-scène*, to tell their wartime stories. A strange slippage was happening in the city. Just as the BCD was about to be wiped clean, pushed into the sea and paved over, the ruinous landscape gained new life as part of a huge filmset. Beirut-as-a-filmset thus encapsulates the way the actual city is made to represent another version of itself, to become a stand-in for any catastrophic space, but also unable to represent itself. Using the material remains from the war – like ruins, but also mementos, photographs, film reels, and so on – as if they offer access to the past, enacts a kind of deceit that the past can be relived, the dead can be born again. Such a move neglects the burden these remains impose on the present and the traumatic excess that becomes flattened out in such an endeavour. Beirut-as-a-filmset thus highlights a central tension in the politics of representation that challenged artists in the so-called post-war period. Such projects would have to wilfully ignore the fact that these 'on location' ruins were not part of a civil war past, but rather part of a contemporary moment that is simultaneously haunted by the violence of the past, the silences of the present, and the blind faith in the future.

Others saw the ruinous landscape as emblematic of a moment that would quickly disappear into the past. Many filmmakers, artists and novelists turned to formal experimentation in ways that accentuated the inescapable paradox between representation and lived experience. A 'ruin-centred aesthetic' developed as a motif to mourn the irreconcilable tension between Beirut as a torn city and Beirut as a simulacrum of itself (Seigneurie 2011: 20). These works levied critiques of the reductive ways in which Lebanon had been represented, while also grappling with the vexed relationship between memory, mediation and materiality. Documenting these ruins before Solidere wiped the slate clean constituted an urgent salvage project that demanded a rescue mission attitude, premised not on preserving the past but on animating its present. Accordingly, the past cannot be held at arm's length and examined undisturbed. To hold the past in one's hand exposes us to radioactive material. Therefore, it takes courage to face 'the painful act of remembrance' (Makdisi 2006: 206).

The urgent task of artists and filmmakers thus required a two-pronged approach – one representational and one material – that deconstructs the redundant mythologies and reductive imaginaries about the city, while carefully collecting evidence of catastrophic conditions and (re)assembling these fragments into another kind of narrative. In the post-war context, it was believed that creative productions had to address the conditions that constitute a truthful image, a truthful narrative, and a truthful experience. And then navigate ways to share this response beyond oneself, whether with those 'in the know', clueless others, or antagonistic challengers. Perhaps there is some poetic justice in the way artists dismantle representational phantoms that had come to possess Beirut, but then excavate artefacts from the ruins as building blocks for a city they aspire to inhabit.

While the 1990s afforded many filmmakers a ready-made filmset of urban destruction, Jocelyn Saab's *Once Upon a Time, Beirut: Story of a Star* (1994) is ostensibly interested in the way Beirut had already become a filmset for an imagined city. At a moment when Lebanese cinema had ceased to exist, Saab enacts a cine-archaeology to excavate fragments from dozens of films set in Beirut, and reassembles them in ways that might elucidate taken-for-granted elements. Saab's intervention exposes the mythology of Beirut: 'although the myths associated with Beirut did so much over the years to enhance its wealth and fame, they were also largely responsible for its downfall' (Hillauer 2005: 180). In this chapter, I draw out the various references Saab has assembled to understand their critical

Figure 6.1 Leila and Yasmine dwelling in the film set

power and then I elaborate how the central plot signals the emergence of a robust critical paradigm of collecting and assembling archives in Lebanese art. Saab's film thus enacts a precarious form of research in which some aspects ultimately fail while others may momentarily strike a chord.

KAN YA MA KAN

Jocelyn Saab's *Once Upon a Time, Beirut* – an experimental re-editing of Beirut's cinematic record – is a complex film with multiple storylines and narrative threads, which revisits the multiplicity of experiences that have been reduced to simplistic clichéd narratives of Lebanon. And yet, the plot is a rather simple framing story. The film is set in present-day Beirut, at the beginning of the 'post-war' era.[2] The action follows two young women, Leila and Yasmine, on their journey to a secret cinema house where they hope to discover insights about the history of Beirut from Mr Farouk, who is also called 'Beirut's living memory' by the two girls. Farouk, Leila and Yasmine co-curate a mashup of films from different eras as a kind of cinematic voyage, each episode announced by a silent era title card. Through the magic of cinema, Leila and Yasmine do not merely watch these films but literally enter them as diegetic commentators as if on a magical expedition through time. On the surface, it is a simple and playful film that panders to any cineaste's deepest desires. But Saab does not give us easy access to these histories. *Once Upon a Time, Beirut* subverts the narrative to give greater dominance to an alternative poetics of narration premised on fragmented, non-linear episodes that begin in medias res and never seem to conclude. These vignettes operate on the register of myths and fairy tales. The film hints at this alternative narrative structure with its reference to the storytelling heroine Scheherazade.

After Leila and Yasmine arrive at Farouk's cinema, they make their way down into the bowels of the building and enter into a screening of the 1963 French film *Shéhérazade* directed by Pierre Gaspard-Huit and starring Anna Karina. As the Caliph of Baghdad marvels at Scheherazade's beauty, she dismisses his compliments: 'the beauty of a woman is nothing but an appearance. . . . A woman is only beautiful for a very short time, and she has a lot more years without that beauty.' Saab has clearly selected this scene as an allegory for Beirut's lost beauty. But if we look at the original tale, there is a more powerful subtext to this reference. Although more oblique in its allusion, the title of Saab's film is an intertextual reference to the *Thousand and One Nights*. In the English telling of a fairy tale, the opening line 'Once upon a time' is commonly understood to announce something fabricated. And yet, the exact rhetoric promises that this story happened *at* some time – 'once upon a time' – even if that exact time is forgotten or unknown. This allegorical tension between the possible and impossible is more precisely captured in the Arabic storytelling equivalent, *kan ya ma kan* – there was, there was not. Perhaps it happened, perhaps it did not. We may never know, but that is not really the point. A good storyteller, a traditional *hakawati*, will let their audience suspend such concerns of veracity for the sake of the story. Indeed, to captivate the audience is key to Scheherazade's tale-telling strategy.

In the *Thousand and One Nights*, Scheherazade is the last available bride in Sultan Shahryar's kingdom. After being betrayed by his first wife, Shahryar marries virgin after virgin in succession only to kill each one the day after the wedding to prevent any of them from dishonouring him with another act of infidelity. As the last virgin in the kingdom, Scheherazade volunteers to marry the sultan. In her cunning efforts to stave off the fate of certain death, she tells the sultan a seemingly endless series of stories, night after night, ending on a cliff-hanger just at the break of dawn, thus securing the sultan's curiosity and another day to live. After enduring this seemingly endless task of creating life in the face of certain death, the sultan has fallen deeply in love with Scheherazade and grants her a pardon.

But what kind of salvation is this? What could be more traumatic than surviving 1,001 nights of allegorical torture, weaving stories within stories, under the threat of death, to then be blessed with living happily ever after with your misogynistic tormentor? Although Saab does not spell this out, it seems more reasonable to situate Beirut's fate not to the natural cosmetic effects of ageing, but instead to an insidious and endless plot in which its protagonists must continue to tell dazzling, suspenseful stories in the hope of escaping catastrophe. Saab's film is about manifesting and inhabiting this allegorical world oscillating between experience and imagination, clarity and confusion. *Kan ya ma kan* thus provides a model of storytelling that brings both existence and non-existence into the same realm in order to imagine the impossible and articulate the possible.

In the early 1990s, Saab's film rehearses a set of post-war avant-garde aesthetics that triangulated complex memory between personal trauma and exile, political violence and amnesty, and ruinous and reconstructed cityscapes. Effective narrative strategies tend to be 'episodic and provisional, rather than a finished, self-contained form' (Nikro 2012: 5), experimenting with 'formlessness and narratological anarchy' (Makdisi 2006: 207). These tactics recognise that 'the past is a terrain that shifts kaleidescopically [sic] . . . a time of simultaneity and synchrony rather than a time of progress and redemption . . .' (Makdisi 2006: 208). These echo the avant-garde aesthetics in other contexts, which practise 'a range of cinematic strategies to consider elements of the past that are unseen, unspeakable, ephemeral, and defy representation' (Skoller 2005: xv). Laura Marks traces these temporal and structural experiments globally, in work that 'moves backwards and forwards in time, inventing histories and memories in order to post an alternative to the overwhelming erasures, silences, and lies of official histories' (2000: 24). This work is not calibrated for objectivity, but makes generative efforts 'through active and creative engagement, the outcome of which is never guaranteed' (Skoller 2005: xviii). So an experimental aesthetic must aim tactically in order to defamiliarise clichéd images by severing them from their context (Marks 2000: 46).

MACHINE-GUN EYES

Gaspard-Huit's film reel spools through the gate of the projector, fluttering and flapping its tail, leaving almost no image on the screen aside from a glaring white light, the hue of the lens, and the hum of the projector. Mr Farouk appears to wake from a spell and declares, 'I've lost track of time. I've been living so long in the darkness with my films.' Perhaps, partly imprisoned and partly seeking refuge, Farouk has spent thousands of nights in his cine-bunker, captivated by celluloid stories. He has screened one film after another, in the hope of – like Scheherazade – holding off the inevitable. He is the only one capable of showing Yasmine and Leila their city through a fairy-tale lens.

To set the stage and pose their question, Yasmine and Leila have brought a film reel that they want to share with Farouk. Mr Farouk's young assistant prepares the projector and dims the lights. The opening title card announces, '1914, Leila and Yasmine play a trick on Mr Farouk.' We see archival footage of people at seaside markets, accompanied by an extra-diegetic Oriental melody. As the scene builds, the film cuts to a new shot with a sepia filter to simulate an anachronistic film texture, and the frame pans to two young women inside the 1914 cinescape. It is Leila and Yasmine, introduced into the montage of the footage they have brought along. They announce, 'These are the only images that we've found of our city, Mr Farouk. They are undoubtedly very beautiful, but frankly, a little out of date.' The montage continues as Leila claims they have only found a 'head-spinning series of clichés':

> Beirut, the pearl of the Middle East,
> hidden in the blue casket of the Mediterranean.
> Lebanon, the Switzerland of the Orient.
> A haven of peace in the heart of a tumultuous region.

As children of the war, Leila and Yasmine are tired of the old and clichéd representations of Beirut. Yasmine declares: 'You know, nowadays, guys don't say to us: "you have beautiful eyes." They say: "You have machine-gun eyes."' Saab's intended audience for *Once Upon a Time, Beirut* was the generation who remember the civil war, but have likely been cut off from their earlier roots

(Zaccak 1997: 168–9). Leila and Yasmine, mostly speaking French, embody the cultural disconnect faced by Saab and her generation. Educated in French schools, Saab says, 'We didn't have contact with our origins. We were the generation that started looking for our roots, looking to see why we lost them' (Hillauer 2005: 173). Many Lebanese were raised abroad and had limited first-hand experience with the city, likely consuming only media depictions of Beirut. However, those who remained had to navigate a city cut down the middle by the green line, and through the ebb and flow of various checkpoints and the movement of the frontline. After the war, once they were allowed to enter sites that had been inaccessible and unthinkable, many Lebanese also had to make sense of a city with shifting boundaries and proximities.

So, what does the cinematic heritage tell us about the 'real' story of Beirut? What sort of gaps does it fill? 'In Lebanon,' Saab recounts, 'movie theaters only showed shallow entertainment – films that were mostly copies of American and Italian comedies' (Hillauer 2005: 174). Culling from dozens of films, Saab both acknowledges and mocks the cinematic fantasies that proliferated in the pre-war era. Thus begins a cinematic odyssey into Mr Farouk's secret archive of films. From temptresses to spies to villains, Saab shows us Beirut as an international playground, in which fantastic narratives of greed, seduction and political intrigue took place. Each scene moves between original film clips from global cinema and parody scenes where Leila and Yasmine enter the cinematic geography of these mashups as witnesses and commentators. An increasingly frenzied series of secret agents, voluptuous women, wiretapping and assassinations foreshadows a scene in which we are told Beirut is due to blow up in two days. Yasmine remarks, 'All these spies in Beirut at the same time. And nobody here seems to suspect a thing.' If we follow this fragmented and fantastic plotline, rather than another political exposé on the culpability of Lebanese and Palestinian militias as well as the Syrian and Israeli armies, should we believe that the destruction of Beirut was the result of a subversive conspiracy? A reggae soundtrack of 'La Marseillaise', the French national anthem, announces several scenes on French colonial and cultural influence.

Amid the Egyptian comedies and melodramas and the political intrigue in French, British and American films all set in Beirut, two figures stand out as locally identifiable everymen – Garo and Shoushou. With Leila and Yasmine overlooking things from a nearby window, in quick succession we see a drug-smuggling scheme, detective plots, checkpoints and a dead body, intercut with scenes of *Garo* (Gary Garabedian, 1965), in which the criminal outlaw climbs clandestinely over the city rooftops. Garo, the outlaw, is based on a real-life Robin Hood figure who undermined corrupt leaders in Lebanon in the early 1960s. The folk bandit was vilified and doggedly pursued by the police until he was finally killed. Garo is followed by a goofy cowboy figure entering Mr Farouk's theatre. The actor playing the cowboy is Khodr Alaa Eddin, playing

Shoushou, the role that made his father, the theatre and TV actor Hassan Alaa Eddin, famous. Shoushou (also Chouchou) evoked a humble fool with a ridiculously huge moustache, comical voice and silly behaviour, revealing social ills through the guise of a pitiful jester.

Cowboy Shoushou starts a playful game of shootout with the protagonists. As the girls take cover behind a row of seats, he says, 'Come on, it's only a joke. It's only a film.'

'It's only a film? Are you sure?' asks Leila. 'Films are not a joke.'
'And what is that hole in your hat?' probes Yasmine.
'It must be a moth hole. These old films are full of them.'
'Kan ya ma kan,' Mr Farouk recounts, 'I'm going to tell you a story and in two hours you can dream.'

In contrast to the tragic subtext of Scheherazade, Farouk's story contains an unlikely love story from the silent film era. Princess Daoulah ('nation') elopes with the aid of a cursed dwarf to marry Prince Salam ('peace'). Upon uniting with Peace, Nation kisses the dwarf with gratitude, immediately breaking a curse to reveal the dwarf's true identity as the Prince of Beirut. Yasmine responds, 'They will laugh when we tell them that Beirut is, in fact, a legend of peace.' Unimpressed, she tells Mr Farouk that she prefers 'the historical facts like in the books'.

Relenting, Mr Farouk appoints Shoushou's son to show the girls 'the real Beirut, without lies or illusions'. On a sandy beach with the girls, Shoushou's son and his donkey aim to teach them a series of historical facts and figures – the nationalisation of Iran's oil, the nationalisation of the Suez Canal, the overthrow of the Iraqi monarchy, US marines landing in Lebanon, and so on. At the end of this scene, Shoushou's son walks into the sea and disappears. Has another spell been broken, or has he given up and sacrificed himself to the sea? Transported back into contemporary Beirut, finding themselves walking along the corniche with Shoushou's donkey, the girls quickly seek a return ride to Farouk's cinema with their new history teacher, the donkey.

But Mr Farouk rebukes them for abandoning history, and he sends them to a hippie enclave, the depiction of which is intercut with archival footage of refugees fleeing across the collapsed Allenby Bridge in 1967. The footage reveals a sense of solidarity with displaced Palestinians. The film continues to meander through 'history lessons' that show cinematic dramatisations of militia training and anti-American street protests. With a sense of cyclicality, Leila evokes Marx's corrective of Hegel when she says, 'History doesn't repeat itself, it stutters.' In fact, Marx's claim that history occurs first as tragedy and second as farce may provide some logic for understanding the film's dizzying array of plots and people, as well as Saab's political persuasions.

Eventually the taxi driver returns with a second film reel, which Leila and Yasmine had accidentally left in his cab. The film is spooled onto the projector and starts to play. The scene opens at a madrassa, an Islamic religious school, with various teachers commenting on the notion of truth – all with contradictory metaphors. A student exposes the ruse and calls truth a 'monkey'. As the clip ends, there is general agreement among the other students that the student provocateur is wiser than the masters. The last shot in Saab's film shows Mr Farouk's young assistant, the inheritor of this cinematic Beirut as well as the real one just outside the cinema, laughing at the joke as the screen fades to black. Could it really be that truth is just a shapeshifting prankster and the youth will merely laugh at their elders arguing over its true nature?

LIKE YOU, I HAVE FORGOTTEN

Following the opening credits. The first shot of Saab's film is an epigraph from *Hiroshima mon amour* (Alain Resnais/Marguerite Duras, 1959), another film about traumatic memory:

> Like you, I have forgotten. Like you, I wanted my memory to be inconsolable, a memory of shadow and stone. I struggle for myself, every day, with all my might, against the horror of no longer understanding the reason for remembering. Like you, I have forgotten. Why deny the obvious need to remember? Listen to me, listen to me once more, it will start again.[3]

Ventriloquising the French protagonist in *Hiroshima mon amour*, Saab acknowledges that memory is withdrawn and forgetting is cyclical. Unparalleled by any other concept, memory emerged as a master conceptual paradigm in post-war Lebanon (see, for example, Haugbolle 2010; Sawalha 2010; Volk 2010; Larkin 2012; Nikro 2012). But rather than recovering memory and surfacing a 'specularization of the past' (Skoller 2005: xv), scholars have been more concerned with the structures of forgetting, be they personal silences or official amnesia. This elegiac process of contemplating 'loss without presuming to explain it' demonstrates 'the courage to see the irrecuperability of pain that utopic triumphalism must airbrush away' (Seigneurie 2011: 12, 17).

While at face value Saab's film would seem to be a film of memory and maybe also history, I would argue that the film also performs forgetting as an inevitable companion. While Leila and Yasmine are our guides as they are transported from the darkened space of the theatre to other cinematic worlds, they only vaguely gesture to their own memories. Early on in the film, Yasmine tells cowboy Shoushou, 'One day, I'll tell you about my Beirut filled with lies . . .' Later in the film, reflexively sitting in front of a dressing room mirror, she recounts sheltering with Leila from a bombing as their parents listened to communist music. A memory of a deceased friend comes to mind. But Leila quickly admonishes Yasmine's memory, 'Don't bring that up again.'

How do you tell a story of Beirut when forgetting is more prized than remembering? How do you tell a story when truth, like memory, is multiple and contradictory? Saab's history lesson gives us reference points but refuses to make sense of the forces that led to the war in any causal or conventional way. In Saab's hands, Beirut is a story of bullet holes and moth holes, devastation and decay, spectacle and stagnation, mythologies and clichés, blindfolds and filmstrips. And yet, for all her innovation and experimentation, the ending seems too easy, like a short-circuit that allows us to end on a comedic note. Perhaps this gesture betrays Saab's eternal optimism in the face of life's hardships, or it may simply relinquish any earnest effort to make sense of the senseless.

Although I do not want to treat these film clips with evidentiary authority, one might argue that our protagonists' ability to enter bygone moments 'in search of images of their city before the destruction' (Hillauer 2005: 179) betrays the reality that those scenes are no longer accessible. Jalal Toufic contemptuously asks, 'Is there a more effective way to hide that the images are inaccessible than to have the characters enter in them?' (2000: 68). Although Saab is not above reproach, I suggest another reading of her experimental remix that combines representational and material tactics for disrupting the integrity of the images. If the clips are considered indexical representations, this assumes their irrefutable relationship with the past. If the film clips are considered material objects, this assumes their undeniable relationship with the present. By 'creating a collage of the mythical and real city of Beirut' (Hillauer 2005: 180), Saab destabilises the position of time by recourse to media artefacts.

While Leila and Yasmine move through the imaginary landscapes of several films, including their own, Saab's creative geography draws attention to the devices used to meld cinematic space, rupturing the rules of the Hollywood paradigm that restricts the ability to jump through time for continuity (Bordwell et al. 1985: 30). Screenwriters' manuals warned that 'unmotivated jumping of time is likely to rattle the audience, thereby breaking their illusion that they participate in the lives of the characters' (Bordwell et al. 1985: 43). Saab either rejects this belief or is utilising its anxious capabilities to disorient our reference points. As such, the rattled viewer becomes aware that he or she is not a participant in this imagined world, but rather a mediated witness. Confronted with this radical reality of montage jumping us through time and space, Saab's film takes us on a narrative journey through the cinema of Beirut with two time-travelling women on a rescue mission. Yasmine and Leila move through these filmic geographies and diegetic temporalities with apparent ease. That is, in fact, the magic of cinema: to captivate and transport us to faraway places and different time periods.

Figure 6.2 Leila peruses Mr Farouk's film vault

Instead of farce or tragedy, however, I see a catastrophe. I adopt Saab's experimental gesture and read her film through non-linear and intertextual montage. As such, I have taken the liberty of imagining an alternate ending in her 'narratological anarchy', not premised on re-education, but enacting modalities of forgetting as critical responses to 'the fragmenting force of memory' (Nikro 2012: 5). I see Haydar in Borhan Alaouié's *Beirut the Encounter* (*Beyruth El-Likaa*, 1981) taxiing home from the airport. He has failed to deliver a cassette love letter to Zeina before departing Beirut to study abroad. This undelivered message in a state of immanent deterioration is inscribed with a message of catastrophe, but the contents of this artefact, whether farce or tragedy, are testimony for Zeina's ears only, a Zeina that ceased to exist as soon as she boarded her flight. Likewise, I imagine Leila and Yasmine's forgotten film reel in the back of the taxi, not returned to them at the theatre, but ripped from its case and unspooled out the car window, writhing unplayed on the dusty and busy city streets.

MATERIAL REMAINS

The film opens with a taxi driving through war-ravaged city streets, exposing bombed-out buildings on either side. A man in a wheelchair navigates rapidly ahead of the vehicle. Two young women – Yasmine and Leila – sit in the back seat blindfolded. Yasmine pulls off her blindfold, and her internal monologue voices worry: 'They'll think we're being kidnapped. Then again, it's no longer in fashion in Beirut.' Saab is, of course, making an intertextual reference to other films that depict a hostage being blindfolded and taken to a secret location. Yasmine continues aloud, 'I want to see the secret way to his mysterious hiding place, his Ali Baba's cave filled with treasures, his cinecittà. I can't wait to get there.'

I argue that the secrecy of the location is secondary to the prerequisite gesture of blinding. That is, the girls must reattune their vision in order to not accept the ruinous urban landscape at face value, while preparing to see anew the marvellous and enchanting depictions of the city retained in the cinematic record as holding another kind of reality. This is a reflexive gesture, materially supported by the delivery of two cans of film played as bookends to the epic cinematic voyage. Reflexivity enacts a restructuring of spatial visuality rather than an invisible erasure of it.[4]

Saab chauffeurs us through this ruinous filmset half blind, to arrive at Farouk's hidden cinema hall, a place with inherent double meanings, as both a reference to motion pictures and the place where they are shown. Saab's filmset is both the physical location of Mr Farouk's secret film theatre and the assembled cinescapes mashed up in Saab's remix. During the war, cinema halls became the site of refuge for many cineastes. Farouk's secret cinema is like a living archive, an accessible vault hosting these film reels. Farouk beckons Leila and Yasmine as they climb through stacks of film reels and past stacked shelves. They read out a series of different titles to each other. Farouk recounts his life story with cinema from the age of six, later running Rio Cinema, and eventually ten cinemas. He promises to show them 'his' Beirut, 'the city of love'. He leads them to a huge vault of films that the women explore.

Rather than inhabiting present-day Beirut as a filmset for a timeless backdrop of the civil war, Saab takes us to dwell in the ruins of cinema, the celluloid film reels of Beirut's long twentieth century. Saab has said that this was her first film not about the war, but instead on history (Zaccak 1997: 168). In order to address this history, Saab has to leave the present war-torn landscape, removing both the protagonists and the audience from this material reality, and create another space assembled from a collection of cliched storylines and cinematic spectacles. A slight shift in perspective reveals a prominent material dimension to the various depictions.

Farouk's darkened bunker of cinematic contraband is in fact Saab's filmset. His secret archive of cinema is a fairy tale. But this recasting of a cinema hall and the audio-visual strips of past filmsets enacts a mode of collecting media artefacts and displaying archival materials that ricochets across art practices in post-war Lebanon. In this way, Saab prefigures the important role of the archive in catastrophic aesthetic practices, which cultivates tactics for reflexively excavating personal and idiosyncratic media collections, placing artefacts into larger mediated contexts, and advancing alternate modalities of credibility that disrupt, disorient and destabilise dominant modes of knowledge production. Saab's reflexive gesture of simultaneously situating her protagonists within the physical space of a post-war cinematic archive and diegetically within the space of these pre-war and wartime films 'foregrounds the constructed nature of narrative forms and the materiality of the film medium' (Skoller 2005: xv). The blindfold, the film vault and the unviewed film reel left in the back of the car serve as iconic modes for structuring visuality. And the reflexive materiality of a singular film reel opens lines of inquiry through the entire multifaceted apparatus of production, dissemination and preservation, thus pointing to the infrastructures of connectivity for those departing for exile and those remaining at home. Mundane media artefacts – family photos, love letters, cassette recordings, film reels – become surrogate souvenirs for people, places and moments that have vanished in one manner or another. The assembly and display of personal mementos constitute a collection of fragments made in the face of a disintegrating world. Highlighting tension between the immaterial recordings and material objects enacts opportunities for rehearsing models of catastrophic research.

While our characters were conducting their own research in the celluloid archive as a history lesson, the film also exemplifies Saab's own act of creative research, assembling found footage, creating contiguous scenes, and remixing them to draw out patterns of analysis. Saab most likely assembled her materials (at least partly) from magnetic tapes rather than celluloid strips.[5] I imagine Saab sourcing the fifty films[6] through her media and journalism connections, perhaps recorded at home, off satellite TV reruns or available as a knock-off at the local video store. Some of the films have been dubbed from English to French or have layers of subtitles inscribed for different audiences, revealing an ever more complex social biography of these cinematic artefacts. This materiality also hints at the mobility of media and the processes of duplication and remediation that shapes the artefact's social life as it shifts forms across media ecologies and historical geologies. Cine-archaeologists excavate 'the material elements of the past as they exist in the present – objects, images, narratives, documents, detritus' (Skoller 2005: xvii–xviii), and then reassemble fragments in 'the gaps between these recorded images' (Marks 2000: 21). Marks shows how intercultural filmmaking strategies bestow mundane objects with 'auratic, embodied, and mimetic' faculties (2000: xiii). Saab, among other artists and filmmakers, specifically bestows media objects with these qualities, elevating their form to the same status as their content. This is achieved by de-emphasising their representational affordances and accentuating their material qualities. In this way, the media objects in this film refuse their taken-for-granted representational meaning and compel us to consider their role within a set of social relations and mimetic practices that underline their status as artefacts of war.

In many regards, Saab's effort with *Once Upon a Time, Beirut* is impressive for its scope of collected content, its finesse in (re)creating cinematic worlds (geographies and temporalities), and her critical ability to expose the various representational tropes that have presented Beirut as a fairy-tale landscape. Saab had high aspirations for her film: 'I am waiting for someone in Lebanon to regard my films as heritage, just like I gathered the heritage of others' (Khatib 2008: 42). By situating her project in an underground vault of film reels, she articulates the archive as an aesthetic device, charged with ambivalence about memory and materiality in 'post-war' art. As part of a larger effort to register the instability of catastrophic legacies in 'post-war' Lebanon, Jocelyn Saab's *Once Upon a Time, Beirut* lures us into a fairy-tale version of Beirut, destabilised between the possible and the impossible, between there was and there was not, *bayna kan ya ma kan* . . .

NOTES

1. Very different versions of this essay have previously appeared elsewhere (Westmoreland 2008, 2009). In this version I depart from some of my earlier arguments. A decade later, and with an eye to reflexive materiality, my re-viewing of the film revealed new things to me. This essay tries to enact the same strategies of montage as exemplified in Saab's film, while acknowledging that the transduction from film to text invariably participates in creating a new and different mashup.
2. While the civil war officially culminated in the disarmament of the militias as per the Taif Agreement, artists and intellectuals generally regarded the ensuing period with a great deal of scepticism and argue that the war simply became expressed in different ways.
3. The reference to *Hiroshima mon amour* goes further than the opening epigraph, drawing formal inspiration from Resnais's use of flashbacks and temporal ruptures to create a fragmented narrative structure, in which past and present coexist in non-linear relations (Bordwell et al. 1985). Resnais and Duras aimed to shatter time. As quoted by Kent Jones (2015: n.p.), Resnais said, 'The present and the past coexist, but the past shouldn't be in flashback.'
4. This point is brilliantly argued by Walid Raad about Maroun Bagdadi's 1991 film *Out of Life* (*Hors la vie*), which portrays the abduction of a French photojournalist by Shi'a militants during the Lebanese civil war. Raad (1996) argues that blindfolding the intrepid photojournalist literally obstructs the ocular superiority of his profession.
5. When writing her overview of Lebanese cinema, Lina Khatib (2008: 48) remarks on the disorganised collection at the Lebanese National Cinema Centre, in particular that they had no catalogue or organisational system to search the archive's content. I had a similar experience several years earlier, and was surprised at how incomplete their collection was.
6. Saab credits twenty-four Western films, twenty-six Arab films, and twenty-four song credits.

BIBLIOGRAPHY

Bordwell, David, Janet Staiger and Kristin Thompson (1985), *The Classical Hollywood Cinema: Film Style & Mode of Production to 1960*, New York: Columbia University Press.
Calvino, Italo (1997), *Invisible Cities*, London: Vintage Books.
Harb El-Kak, Mona (2001), 'Post-war Beirut: Resources, Negotiations, and Contestations in the Elyssar Project', in Seteney Shami (ed.), *Capital Cities: Ethnographies of Urban Governance in the Middle East*, Toronto: Centre for Urban & Community Studies, University of Toronto, pp. 111–34.
Haugbolle, Sune (2010), *War and Memory in Lebanon*, New York: Cambridge University Press.
Hillauer, Rebecca (2005), *Encyclopedia of Arab Women Filmmakers*, annotated edn, New York: American University in Cairo Press.
Jones, Kent (2015), '*Hiroshima mon amour*: Time Indefinite', *The Criterion Collection*, 13 July, <https://www.criterion.com/current/posts/291-hiroshima-mon-amour-time-indefinite> (last accessed 22 December 2020).
Khatib, Lina (2008), *Lebanese Cinema: Imagining the Civil War and Beyond*, London: I. B. Tauris.
Larkin, Craig (2012), *Memory and Conflict in Lebanon: Remembering and Forgetting the Past*, London: Routledge.
Makdisi, Saree (2006), 'Beirut, a City without History?', in Ussama Makdisi and Paul A. Silverstein (eds), *Memory and Violence in the Middle East and North Africa*, Bloomington: Indiana University Press, pp. 201–14.
Marks, Laura U. (2000), *The Skin of the Film: Intercultural Cinema, Embodiment, and the Senses*, Durham, NC: Duke University Press.
Nikro, Norman S. (2012), *The Fragmenting Force of Memory: Self, Literary Style, and Civil War in Lebanon*, Newcastle upon Tyne: Cambridge Scholars.
Raad, Walid G. (1996), *Beirut . . . (à la folie): A Cultural Analysis of the Abduction of Westerners in Lebanon in the 1980's*, Rochester, NY: University of Rochester, Program in Visual and Cultural Studies.
Sawalha, Aseel (2010), *Reconstructing Beirut: Memory and Space in a Postwar Arab City*, Austin: University of Texas Press.
Seigneurie, Ken (2011), *Standing by the Ruins: Elegiac Humanism in Wartime and Postwar Lebanon*, New York: Fordham University Press.
Skoller, J. (2005), *Shadows, Specters, Shards: Making History in Avant-garde Film*, Minneapolis: University of Minnesota Press.
Toufic, Jalal (2000), *Forthcoming*, Berkeley: Atelos (A Project of Hip's Road).
Volk, Lucia (2010), *Memorials and Martyrs in Modern Lebanon*, Bloomington: Indiana University Press.
Westmoreland, Mark R. (2008), 'Crisis of Representation: Experimental Documentary in Postwar Lebanon', doctoral dissertation, The University of Texas at Austin, Anthropology.
Westmoreland, Mark R. (2009), 'Post-Orientalist Aesthetics: Experimental Films and Video in Lebanon', *Invisible Culture: An Electronic Journal for Visual Studies*, 13, 37–57.
Zaccak, Hady (1997), *Le Cinéma libanais: itinéraire d'un cinéma vers l'inconnu (1929–1996)*, Beirut: Dar el-Machreq.

CHAPTER 7

A Mother and Daughter Reunion: How Jocelyne Saab Shot her Last Documentary, *My Name is Mei Shigenobu*

Yomota Inuhiko

As a film historian and critic, the Years of Lead in the 1970s are my burden, which almost became fatal. When the Red Army (RA) in Japan split off into countless groups, the United Red Army (URA) – one of the most radical groups – fought a gunfight against the police in 1972. The youngest member of the group was my age. They killed each other while hiding themselves in a winter camp. The shocking scandal was one of the causes of the decline of the New Left movement in Japan in the early 1970s. The Japanese Red Army (JRA), another group derived from the RA, built a base in Beirut, working voluntarily for Palestinian refugees. Japanese women's weeklies portrayed Fusako Shigenobu, the leader of the JRA, as a female hero. My classmates and I wanted to get information on them, but Beirut was too far away for a Japanese university student – even though I had lost almost all passion for political activity inside Japan. Campus life in the early 1970s in Tokyo was, I remember, so miserable that I could hardly survive the decadent violence among the many political sect conflicts. Bombings and other acts of terrorism took place often in Tokyo, and it exhausted me deeply.

More than thirty years later, in 2008, I was part of the production committee when Koji Wakamatsu, one of the most radical film directors in Japan, proposed to shoot the historical docu-fiction *The United Red Army*. I also published two volumes of memoirs about my political engagements in the late 1960s and early 1970s. In 2015 I published *Terrorism and Film*, an account of directors who deal prominently with political terror in their work. As a visiting professor at Tel Aviv University, I wrote and published on Zionist propaganda films of the early twentieth century, comparing them with the Manchuria films in the 1930s, and my deep interest in the JRA's involvement in the Palestine question has also brought me to Beirut on research. These travels, professional and personal, brought me closer to Jocelyne Saab. So close, in fact, that I assisted her with her research and worked voluntarily as an advisor on her last documentary.

My very first encounter with Saab's work was overshadowed by political and cultural censorship. In 2007 the third annual Arab Film Festival organised by the Japan Foundation in Tokyo included a retrospective of Egyptian cinema. The plan had been to open the festival with Saab's film *Dunia* (*Kiss Me Not on the Eyes*, 2005). However, this screening was cancelled at the very last minute, and instead they screened *The Yacoubian Building* (Marwan Hamed, 2006), a comedy that had been a big hit the previous year. I was disappointed and did not understand why the cancellation had taken place. The rumour was that someone in the diplomatic context had opposed the opening screening of *Dunia* and criticised the film, saying it could not represent Egyptian society. If anything, this made me more curious.

I finally met Jocelyne Saab in Paris, in 2016 when Nicole Brenez and I were collaborating for my lecture and screening at the Cinémathèque Française. Prof. Brenez introduced me to Jocelyne at the dinner table. I told her about the *Dunia* scandal in Tokyo and asked her about some further details, as I was ignorant of the Sufism tradition of dancing. After that evening, I visited her frequently for lively discussions about things such as Palestine, Jean-Luc Godard, terrorism in cinema, and so on, as I lived very near at that time. I found that she was interested in the JRA. She asked me to explain more details on the group. One day in 2016 she told me that she was planning to shoot a documentary about family problems among the JRA members. The theme was to be the relationship and reunion of a mother and daughter. She told me that it would be her last film.

A work of art cannot be reduced to the question of its creator's biography alone. Using the artist's life as a lens through which to view it, however, can grant us a deeper understanding of their work. This is especially true when the artwork in question is left unfinished on account of the artist's untimely passing, as was the case for Walter Benjamin, Pier Paolo Pasolini, and also Jocelyne Saab. For example, it is only when you acknowledge his long exile in Paris that some of the complex fragmental texts written by Benjamin in his last days can really be understood. Likewise, in order to truly understand the meaning of Pasolini's notorious film *Salò, or the 120 Days of Sodom* (1975), one needs to bear in mind his unfinished work. As for Jocelyne Saab, her last short piece of documentary is hardly intelligible without the context of her other unfinished works.

Throughout her lifetime, Saab harboured towards her mother what might best be described as a complicated mixture of love and hatred. She often told me how she thought of her mother with ambivalent emotion. Born in Beirut in 1948 to an affluent Maronite Christian family, from a tender age Saab was forced to come to terms with the fact that, as far as her mother was concerned, her birth had come as a disappointment. She had hoped for a son to take over the family banking business. Finding herself with a second daughter instead, she entrusted the young Jocelyne's upbringing to her own mother (Jocelyne's grandmother) and maid, after which she scarcely ever looked back.

As a young girl, Saab was overwhelmed by her mother in every sense of the word. A corpulent, magnanimous woman with a fondness for socialising, she held frequent parties at the family's hilltop manor, at which she was always the centre of attention. She spent her mornings riding through pine forests on horseback, read Sartre and Camus, and enjoyed sunning herself at the beach. Jocelyne, a shy child given to bouts of daydreaming, initially attempted to imitate her mother in these pursuits, but to no avail – on finding Jocelyne's bikini, her mother took to it with scissors and sent her away to a strict missionary school. Such stifling treatment, a constant feature in the director's young life, led her to look elsewhere for examples of how to live. She found one, thankfully, in her father, a lifelong Gandhi admirer who had spent his youth hopping from one adventure to the next throughout Iran, India and Indonesia.

A string of misfortunes cemented the growing discord between mother and daughter. After Saab's father died in 1981, the Israeli army's siege of Beirut came a year later, during which Saab's childhood home (which had once belonged to her paternal grandfather) was burnt to the ground. From 1985 onward Saab relocated, first to Paris then Cairo, the distance between her and her mother growing until eventually they did not speak at all for twenty-five years. One of the decisive factors was the issue of Lebanon's Palestinian refugees: whereas Jocelyne felt great sympathy for their plight, considering herself an ally, her mother regarded them as nothing but a nuisance. The next time Saab came face to face with her mother was in Beirut in 2017. By now, the once-stifling matriarch was ninety-one years old, and her frail, shrunken frame a far cry from that of the socialite queen who had once terrorised Jocelyne as a child. Indeed, so pitiful was the image that Saab hardly recognised her as the woman she had come to despise, and she found it within her there and then to bury the hatchet, resolving to make peace with her mother after all these years.

The fraught relationship with a mother figure is a recurring motif in Saab's work, and I would say it manifests as a borderline obsession. At times the mother figure is the oppressive matriarch stifling her modern daughter in the name of traditional culture; elsewhere, in a more symbolic context, she serves as an allegory for the city of Beirut and the land beneath it. She even takes the form of film and poetry themselves, archives of cultural memory that serve as edifying nourishment for the protagonists. The mother figure is something to be rebelled against, escaped from, and finally to be overcome in the fulfilment of a rite of passage. One obvious example is when the heroine in *Dunia* rebels against her famous mother, but finally accepts her in order to reach the Sufi-inspired cosmological consciousness of the earth.

This mother–daughter relationship returns explicitly when, towards the tail end of her life, Saab was working on a documentary about Fusako Shigenobu, former rebel leader and founder of the JRA, and her daughter Mei (sometimes transcribed as 'May'). At its core, the film set out to depict the story of a daughter whose life is upended by her mother, but who decides to live devoted to her mother in spite of this fact. Though sadly left unfinished as only a seven-minute short, had it been completed, it likely would have served as the apotheosis of Saab's fascination with the mother–child dynamic. I confess that I experienced quite complex emotions when Mathilde Rouxel kindly showed me the piece just after the director's death. But before I go into more detail regarding this unfinished film, it is worth briefly discussing the mother figure in Saab's most famous and widely discussed work.

THE MOTHER FIGURE IN SAAB'S FEATURE FILMS

The figure of the mother takes a variety of different forms in Saab's fiction films. Firstly, in *Dunia* (2005), she appears neither as a metaphor nor as an allegory, but instead as a very real psychological threat to the protagonist, whom she traps ambivalently somewhere between love and hatred. The eponymous heroine is a university student engaged in an idealistic search for representations of love in literature. By advancing in her studies, she is also trying to escape the sizeable shadow cast over her by her deceased mother, a legendary belly dancer. Her extreme devotion to idealism comes at a price, however; once repressed, the body will always take its revenge. Indeed, Dunia loses her way when she neglects her physical existence and has to face her mother's enormous shadow. Welcomed with open arms by her mother's former dancing companions, Dunia herself studies the art of belly dancing under a male instructor who idolises her mother. Through the medium of dance, she arrives at mysticism, experiencing a rapturous, trance-like state as she dances as if the whole universe is her audience. It is dance that shows Dunia a path to reconciliation with her mother; with this accomplished, she is free to achieve unity with the world on a higher plane.

What's Going On? (2009), another story of a rite of passage, is reminiscent of the kind of German Romantic *Märchen* once penned in the nineteenth century. The film is reminiscent of Novalis's masterpiece, *Heinrich von Ofterdingen: The Tale of the Blue Flower* (1800). Its protagonist is a naive young man, unversed in the art of love. Unlike Dunia, it is not dance that leads him to a state of communion with the world's essence, but rather the omnipresent poetry of life itself. In highly allegorical fashion, the film tells a story of the world's regeneration as accomplished through a symbolic return to the mother archetype in a Jungian way. Our protagonist meets Lilith – Adam's first wife and his independent equal, according to Talmud and Christian tradition of the medieval age – who relays to him some advice; nursing an ailing heart, she also serves as an allegory for the city of Beirut itself, still toiling under the painful scars of war. With Lilith as his guide, the lovelorn youngster searches for a lost garden, a journey that brings him face to face with his doppelgänger in the library of a mountain monastery. To restore Beirut to its former glory, he must travel down into the belly of the earth and locate the 'stone womb'.

The mother figure is represented by the rocks and mountains: Mother Earth in all but name. Through an act of symbolic copulation with the land itself, the protagonist regains balance between body and spirit; he then attempts to restore purity to the world at large by means of healing and revitalising the ravaged city of Beirut. As in *Dunia*, so too here dance plays an essential role. The object of the protagonist's affections is a dancer who seems to embody the earth. Saab's choice of location for their first meeting is particularly symbolic: what appears to be a nondescript vacant lot is in fact the former location of the director's childhood home, destroyed during the Israeli siege and since refashioned as a car park. Its inclusion lends an autobiographical edge to what is otherwise a highly abstract film. For Saab, the burning down of her childhood home in 1982 constituted a loss of her roots in the city. If any symbolic rebirth is to take place, she seems to suggest, it must begin with a return to her origins.

As such, in *Dunia* and *What's Going On?*, the motif of the mother is explored both in her capacity as stifling presence and as an allegory for Mother Earth herself. At first glance, *Once Upon a Time, Beirut: Story of a Star* (1994) seems like a happy-go-lucky musical taken straight from the imagination of a cinephile. Yet buried deep within the film's layers of meaning, we can see at work within its young female protagonists the conflicting forces of attachment and rebellion towards the mother. The maternal figure in question takes the form of a huge quantity of film reels housed inside a derelict movie theatre, which the owner projects one after another for the benefit of the two wide-eyed protagonists. Before long, they become so entranced that they find themselves entering the world of the screen – singing, dancing and acting as characters within the various films they are watching. In sociolinguistic terms, we might describe the relationship of the protagonists to the films as that of the Saussurian *parole* to the *langue*.

Here, the mother's 'womb' the girls return to is more than simply the past century of Lebanese (and Egyptian) cinema; it represents the huge memory repository of the city of Beirut itself. Yet this womb lies wounded and abandoned. With the real Beirut transformed beyond all recognition by the repeated waves of destruction visited upon it, it is the Beirut committed to film that ironically appears as a timeless utopia, swallowing up the protagonists whole and demanding their unwavering dedication. But entranced though they are by this maternal archive, the two young women also criticise it, arriving at their own conception of history in the process. In its opposition to the cloying, 'mothering' space of films as entities that encourage a rejection of thinking critically about the past, the film hints at its Nietzschean stance on the irreversibility of history. Hope and loss are interwoven: hope, in the form of a desire to challenge historical amnesia and hold onto our memories; but also a sense of loss at history's no longer being *la dolce vita*. For the girls at the heart of the film, their fall from utopia means being cast from the pacifying, pleasurable cocoon of the cinematic mother. In its depiction of their severing of the temptation to go back, the film emerges as a declaration of independence from the shackles of memory.

In these three films, then, the mother appears alternately as a threatening 'other' stifling the protagonist, as a symbolically charged manifestation of the city/land, and as a huge memory repository in the form of celluloid itself. This multiplicity of guises speaks volumes about just how important and integral to Saab the theme of confrontation with the mother figure actually was. For what would have been her last film, she returned to the documentary form to deliver what one might expect to be her defining statement on the subject. Here was her chance to resolve the final issue fundamental to her work: when faced with the ultimate 'other' as one's own flesh and kin, how to weather intense confrontation without looking the other way, and extend an offer of reconciliation afterwards?

FUSAKO AND MEI SHIGENOBU, MOTHER AND DAUGHTER

A brief introduction to Fusako and Mei Shigenobu – the subjects of the documentary – as well as the Japanese Red Army is in order. The Shigenobus are descended from an old samurai family hailing from southern Kyushu, the westernmost of the Japanese mainland's four main islands. Fusako's father, Sueo, came to Tokyo as a young man, where he became a nationalist; many of his friends participated in the failed coup d'état of 1932 and were put to death shortly after. Miraculously escaping punishment, Sueo crossed over to Manchuria, where he stayed until Japan's wartime defeat in 1945. Upon returning, he opened up a grocer's shop in a Tokyo residential neighbourhood, after which he distanced himself from all political movements. He got married and raised his children, the second of whom was Fusako, born in 1945.

Twenty years later, Fusako enrolled at Meiji University, where she majored in history during the peak years of the 1960s Japanese student movement. Around this time, a growing contingent of students fed up with the stifling conformism of the Japanese Communist Party began calling themselves the New Left, modelling their views on those of Trotsky and Mao. Fusako participated in one such faction, the Socialist Student League, as part of which she spent more and more nights holed up inside barricaded university buildings on campus. Upon arriving home, she would then receive an extra dose of education in the form of political conversations with her father. Indeed, it was down to Sueo's influence that she wrote her graduation thesis on pre-war Japanese fascism.

The period of 1968 onwards was a time of great upheaval for Japan's student movement. The Communist League Red Army Faction, which declared armed struggle against the state, was formed in 1969. Fusako leapt at the chance to join; its leaders, however, were soon arrested one after the other, throwing the organisation into disarray. Eager to establish international bases for their operations, nine members of the Red Army Faction hijacked Japan Airlines Flight 351, landing in North Korea, while another group – what would soon be known as the Japanese Red Army – headed for Beirut. Here they fought alongside the Popular Front for the Liberation of Palestine (PFLP), famously staging a gunfight with Israeli troops at Lod Airport (near Tel Aviv) in 1972. Fusako, who had arrived in Beirut the year before, was a central member of the RA, involved in the planning of all its major operations. Meanwhile, members of the Red Army Faction still in Japan formed an uneasy alliance with a group with whom they had severe ideological differences – frictions that self-imploded in 1972 with a spate of purges, followed swiftly by a bloody stand-off with the police.

In 1973 Fusako gave birth to Mei in Beirut, naming her after the month of the shoot-out at Lod Airport (the name also doubles up in Japanese as the word for 'life'). When asked about Mei's father, Fusako has always refused to be drawn beyond the scantest of details, stating only that he was a 'Palestinian warrior who died'. Mei's childhood was anything but typical. She lacked a nationality and a birth certificate. Intent on raising her daughter as a fully-fledged Japanese, Fusako spoke in her mother tongue to Mei at home, dressed her in kimono, and schooled her in her native country's culture and traditions. She even taught her classical poetry. Outside of the house, however, where being recognised by the Mossad could leave them vulnerable to kidnapping or even assassination attempts, the young mother and daughter were forced to conceal their identity, referring to one another by fake names – Mariam and Angela. They rehearsed scenarios for what to do should one of them be captured, and survived from one day to the next through frequent changes of address, sometimes even of schools. After graduating from the American University of Beirut, Mei went on to do a Master's, though even then she never once let slip so much as a word regarding her true identity, not even to her closest friends.

All this was to change in 2000 with the arrest of her mother in Osaka. Twenty-seven years old and without even a single piece of documentation able to prove her existence, Mei succumbed to a tumultuous crisis of identity. For the first time in her life, there was no need to hide the fact that she was

Japanese – but neither did she have anything to vouch for the fact that she was. Relief came in the form of film director Koji Wakamatsu and Fusako's lawyer, who travelled to Beirut and campaigned tirelessly for Mei to be instated with Japanese citizenship. Passport in hand, she 'returned' to her mother's country for the very first time, where she joined the effort to campaign on behalf of Fusako's release. She remained in Tokyo for a decade, achieving modest fame as a television news anchor, before finally returning to Beirut in 2011. Nowadays, Mei works as an international journalist focused primarily on Middle Eastern affairs. Fusako, meanwhile, is currently serving out a twenty-year jail sentence in Tokyo – she is due for release in 2022, when she will be seventy-seven years old. In interviews, Mei has stated that while her mother lived for the noble cause of revolution, her own cause is much more modest: that of living for her mother.

JOCELYNE SAAB'S ENCOUNTERS WITH THE JAPANESE RED ARMY

Not long after Saab began working as a television journalist, a strange twist of fate brought her into perilously close contact with the Japanese Red Army. In 1973 Saab joined the Paris-based TV station FR3, after which she visited Libya as staff on the channel's flagship special report programme, *Magazine 52*. An interview with Colonel Gaddafi completed, she was on her way back to Benghazi Airport one day when she noticed something was amiss. It was six o'clock in the morning. There on the runway, a stream of passengers was hurriedly disembarking from a plane: Japan Airlines Flight 404, recently hijacked by the JRA. Quickly grasping the severity of the situation, she put in a call to a Paris radio station from a public phone in the airport, explaining events down the line as she witnessed them happening. Archival footage of these events, including close-ups of the JRA perpetrators as they were loaded into a Libyan army vehicle, is included in her ten-minute documentary *Kadhafi: l'islam en marche* (1973). Importantly, the incident served to imprint the JRA indelibly on the young director's mind.

More than four decades after this first encounter, it was Saab's conversations on the topic with me that led her to the idea of a film portrait of the movement's ringleader and her daughter. As a film researcher by trade, I am also on close terms with Fusako and ex-RA soldier Masao Adachi, connections that led to my presence on the production committee for Koji Wakamatsu's *United Red Army* (2009). The immediate impetus for Saab's idea came when I showed her *Children of the Revolution* (Shane O'Sullivan, 2011). This documentary takes a sensational subject – the lives of Fusako Shigenobu and German Red Army faction founder Ulrike Meinhof – but tells it through the personal gaze of their daughters. Through interweaving interviews, the film makes plain the sharp contrasts between the experiences of Mei and Bettina Röhl (Meinhof's daughter) growing up: whereas Bettina claims to feel no connection whatsoever to her mother's life, preferring to stay silent when pressed on the topic of the German Red Army, Mei speaks sympathetically and admiringly of Fusako and of her trust in Japanese culture, which she says provided her with a pillar of valuable support from halfway around the world. On watching the film, Jocelyne was powerfully struck by Mei's story. She also felt confident that, with the chance to interview Mei herself, she would be able to shed a different light on the subject.

At Saab's request, I wrote a letter to Fusako in her Tokyo jail cell and established contact with Mei over Facebook. Fusako wrote back immediately, expressing her desire to support the project in whatever capacity she was able. It took a little longer to put Mei and Jocelyne into direct contact, but eventually Mei too granted her consent to appear in and cooperate with the production. For Saab, the stakes could not have been higher: completing the film would be a way of putting the previous bad blood between her and her own mother behind her once and for all. It was to stand as a symbol of their reconciliation.

JOCELYNE, FUSAKO AND MEI: AN UNFINISHED FILM

A variety of hurdles first needed to be overcome before production on the film could begin in earnest. Most pressing of these was the need for Saab to familiarise herself with the basic facts surrounding the JRA and its founder. Hoping to facilitate this process, I delivered books written by Fusako to Saab's studio in Paris, where I brought her up to speed on the origins and nature of Japan's New Left movement. I also translated a number of Fusako's *tanka* poems (traditional short verse) into English and spoke with Saab at length about the former revolutionary's sensitivity and intellect.

In February 2017 Saab went to Beirut to meet with Mei for the first time. They instantly connected. As she listened to Mei recount the story of her childhood, Saab was struck by the sheer power of its narrative – this story of a Japanese outlaw and her daughter living in hiding from the authorities, meticulously rehearsing scenarios lest one of them be arrested or kidnapped; their practice of adopting false identities outside the house, immediately changing names and moving away if ever they aroused suspicion; in short, doing whatever it took to survive. However, Saab was unable to get Mei to confirm the name of her father. This was a source of frustration for the director, having modelled her own self-realisation on the image of her father, the adventurer. Forced to adjust course, Saab decided to narrow her focus, homing in exclusively on the relationship between mother and daughter.

Considering the peculiar life she has led, it is easy to see just how essential the act of keeping secrets was in preserving all that Mei knew and cherished growing up. Perhaps for this very reason, her answers to Saab's questions often took the director by surprise. On the subject of motherhood and their relationship to it, a considerable gulf existed between the two women's perspectives. For Mei, who had no personal experience of having been persecuted or resented by her mother, Saab's insistence on trying to get her to open up on the topic – as if suspecting her of deliberately withholding information – must have been perplexing. On the other hand, Saab was understandably growing restless. Her myeloma, diagnosed before work on the film began, showed no signs of abating, leaving her perpetually exhausted as she worked. Halfway through production, she let Mei in on what she herself had only recently come to realise: this would be her last film.

The film's structure went through a number of changes during production. As filming Fusako in her prison cell was not possible, Mei's testimony would form the film's backbone; this was to be supplemented by depictions of two key periods, 1972 and 2000, for historical context. In 1972, directors Wakamatsu and Adachi visited Beirut to film the PFLP's armed struggle in the Golan Heights and mountains of Jerash; it was during this trip that they first met the young Fusako. Later, in 2000, Wakamatsu returned after Fusako's arrest to help obtain Japanese citizenship for Mei and bring her to Japan. With no footage remaining at all of the second expedition, Saab initially planned to reconstruct these scenes using actors, though she subsequently changed her mind to incorporate a more stylised aesthetic upon learning of Japan's prowess in the field of animation.

By the time the second synopsis for the film was finally completed in 2018, the main themes had crystallised in Saab's mind. The film was to be neither a political treatise on Palestinian refugees and the JRA, nor was it meant as a historical assessment. Instead, it was to be a personal tale of inward struggle: that of a mother who rebelled against her own country before continuing her fight abroad, and a daughter raised in the shadow of a motherland she had never known. In Fusako's attempts to pass on to her daughter the language and culture of her country of birth lay a nostalgia for the very nation she had once been so eager to leave; Mei, meanwhile, had grown up nursing a nostalgia for a place she had never even visited. Behind these personal nostalgias also lay a political one: that of the Palestinian refugees, now living in fear and degradation, for the homeland they had been forced from. Finally, one last theme came to the fore, one I had mentioned to Saab myself. It was something Fusako had once written about from her jail cell, in a poem describing the young Mei's unique spin on a much-loved childhood game: the theme of hide-and-seek.

In July and October of 2018 Saab finally made two long-awaited trips to Beirut to film Mei. The resulting footage was edited into a seven-minute short film. Jocelyne passed away in January the following year. The short fragment, titled *My Name is Mei Shigenobu*, represents at once a condensed realisation of the spirit of Saab's original synopsis while also containing just enough to hint at what form a fuller-length treatment of the subject might have taken. In the absence of this fuller version, it falls to the viewer to approach the short document we do have with the eyes of an archaeologist, working with fragments to imagine the whole.

MY NAME IS MEI SHIGENOBU (2018)

My Name is Mei Shigenobu is a quiet, contemplative film with a brief running time of just over seven minutes. It unfolds against a bluish-tinged background, and is underpinned by a deliberate, almost weighty piano refrain. The film begins by announcing its theme with a few lines of text, written in Saab's non-native English: 'Things were here one day. Then they have been lost for a while. Things disappeared in front of the subject. How to face these objects of sadness? This is nostalgia.'

In the film's first shot, Mei gazes out to sea from the sun-drenched boardwalk of Beirut's Manara district. Suddenly, the image switches to one of a young Fusako standing atop a cliff, busy filming something with a camera crew – a scene taken directly from Kazuya Shiraishi's *Dare to Stop Us* (2018), a depiction of Koji Wakamatsu's small group around the turn of the 1970s. When the shot returns to the Manara coastline, the weather has changed: a steady rain falls in quiet sheets, choppy waves breaking noisily along the shoreline. During summer, the restaurants here bustle with activity; now they sit bare and empty, their tables folded away. We hear Mei's voice: she is talking about how from a young age she was told to keep their identity secret; about how, as a toddler of only three or four years old, she asked her mother why they had to live this way, like floundering fish poking their heads above the water's surface in search of oxygen. For a brief moment, an image of Mei's face is superimposed with that of her mother's.

Next, the camera follows Jocelyne and Mei as they climb the stairs of an empty restaurant in the rain. They appear to be talking intimately; Mei runs her hands affectionately through Jocelyne's hair. She mentions feeling perpetually anxious as a child, never sure when the Mossad might catch up with her mother. A brief clip of footage: Fusako after her arrest in Osaka, being led in handcuffs through a bullet train, followed by the sound of Mei's voice reading aloud in Japanese a poem written by her mother. Titled 'Mei's Hide-and-Seek', it constitutes the heart of the film, and as such deserves to be quoted here in full:

> Mei enjoys nothing more than hide-and-seek.
> Mother plays the seeker and says to Mei,
> 'Hide yourself quickly so that Mummy cannot find you!
> Hide yourself while Mummy counts to ten.'
> But whenever Mother finishes counting, she always finds Mei with her eyes closed.
> Mei thinks she is invisible, saying, 'You can't find me, Mummy!'

A MOTHER AND DAUGHTER REUNION 123

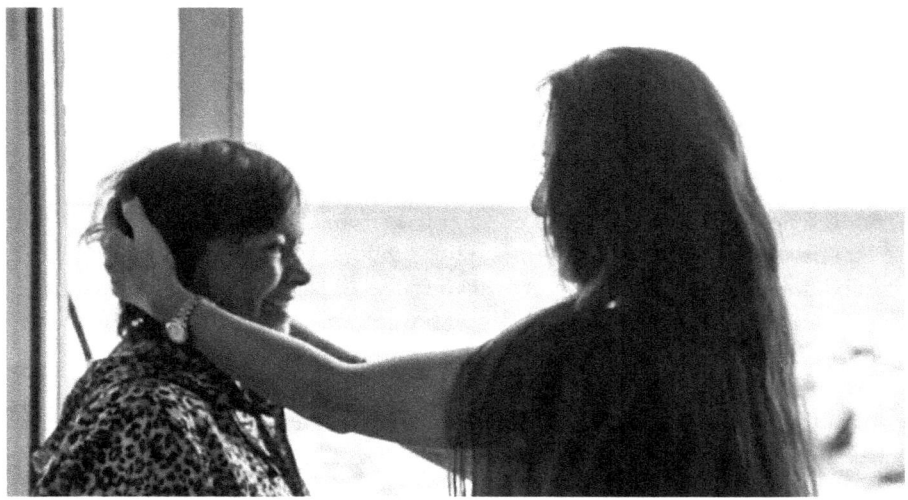

Figure 7.1 Mei caressing Saab's hair in *My Name is Mei Shigenobu*

Figure 7.2 Original manuscript in Japanese of Fusako Shigenobu's Mei's 'Hide-and-Seek'

Mei is cute, so cute.
Cats and chickens love to come and sit beside her.
'You can look for me now, I'm ready!' calls Mei.
This is how she plays hide-and-seek.

As a young child, Mei believed that she could hide herself simply by closing her eyes. The poem ends on a close-up of Fusako as a young woman, a short snippet of footage sourced from a 1973 documentary, *Shigenobu Fusako no kiseki*, by Yoshiko Yamaguchi.

The film closes with another paragraph of written text. It begins: 'Mei shares with her mother another kind of nostalgia' – that of the Palestinians among whom they lived, 'deprived of freedom and memory', a people forced to live 'in untold humiliation'. Fusako lived among them in Beirut in the belief that by doing so she too might recover the time and space she and her daughter had lost. After abandoning Japan, Fusako went on to become a prisoner of the country in her own imagination; just as ironically, Mei's acquisition of Japanese citizenship was in a sense occasioned by the loss of her mother. The text concludes: 'Nostalgia testifies to the ironic contradiction [separating] mother and daughter: so different and yet so close.'

The beating heart of *My Name is Mei Shigenobu* is undoubtedly Fusako's poem, 'Mei's Hide-and-Seek'. At first glance, the reference to the universally enjoyed children's game seems unremarkable. But in Mei's case, played in her own idiosyncratic style, it takes on a whole host of layered meanings. For Fusako and Mei, hiding was a way of life. They spent their lives on the run and in disguise, forever evading the Mossad and the Japanese authorities. Further compounding matters, Fusako's duties as the leader of the JRA meant that she often had to disappear for stretches without warning. Mei learned how to survive by being thrust into the company of people she did not know – forced repeatedly to move house, city, even country without so much as an explanation. In a very real sense, she grew up watching her mother play hide-and-seek for twenty-seven years.

In fact, hide-and-seek was a dress rehearsal for the day of reckoning they both lived in fear of. For Mei, it likely also served as a subconscious method of coping with and alleviating, through a form of sanitised play, the pain and anxiety of reality itself. By encountering the terrible threat of the Israeli secret service or Japanese authorities in the form of her mother-as-seeker – her mother whom she trusted implicitly – she was able to allay the fear she felt, thereby keeping it at a distance.

What to make of Mei's tactic of closing her eyes during hide-and-seek instead of hiding in a more traditional manner? Put simply, her innocent gesture represents a rejection of the rules of the game. By standing still, she of course makes herself an easy target when the time comes for her mother to find her. But in reality, it is her mother who has constantly skirted between the poles of presence and absence, there one day, gone the next. Regardless of her feelings on the matter, Mei has been forced to play hide-and-seek for as long as she can remember. For the young child, scrunching her eyes closed is simply a means of making the unbearable bearable. Mei is searching for a way to make sense of the harsh reality of her mother's absence, and to tolerate it. At the same time, she also harbours a strong desire to be found – to let her mother find her. By foregrounding Mei the child's unique spin on hide-and-seek, the film hints at a possible means of psychotherapy for Mei the adult, still yet to recover from the fresher crisis of identity occasioned by her mother's sudden arrest. Finally acknowledged by society for the first time as an adult, Mei is extending to her mother – who has disappeared again, perhaps indefinitely this time – an offer of reconciliation. Though only a short fragment of what a completed version might have been, the film nevertheless brims with the potential of regeneration, a revival of the bond between mother and daughter.

The second half of the film introduces the motif of the women's hair. In the 1970s Fusako's beauty was mythologised, the image of her black, shoulder-length hair printed indelibly on the minds of a generation. Nearly thirty years later, in the footage of her being shackled and led away by the police, her hair is cropped short, reminiscent of the holy saint in Carl Theodor Dreyer's film *The Passion of Joan of Arc* (1928). The significance of the image is not lost on Saab, though here it is the long, beautiful hair of Mei that is emphasised, forming a connection with the previous shots of her mother as a young woman, strong and rebellious. Elsewhere, Mei can be seen running her hands tenderly through Saab's hair. Having bridged the gap between presence and absence, the film goes one step further, using the medium of the three women's hair to emphasise the intimacy and affinity that exists between them.

For the film's central location, Saab chose the Al Rawda Café, situated on the Mediterranean coast. Summer is long gone; the restaurant's chairs and tables are all folded away, the space empty except for the lone figure of Mei. She occupies the same spot as Saab herself in one of her earlier documentaries, the melancholy *Letter from Beirut* (1978), in a scene in which the director sits writing a letter to a friend in Paris. Exactly forty years later, Saab returned to this very same location to film what would become her final missive.

BIBLIOGRAPHY

Shigenobu, Fusako (n.d.), *Mei no ikuji enikki* メイの育児絵日記 [Mei's Childhood Picture Diary], unpublished.

Shigenobu, Fusako (2001), 重信房子. *Ringo no ki no shita de anata wo umou to kimeta* りんごの木の下であなたを産もうと決めた [I Decided to Give Birth to You Under an Apple Tree], Tokyo: Gentôsha.

Yui, Ryoko (2011), 由井りょう子. *Shigenobu Fusako ga ita jidai* 重信房子がいた時代 [The Era of Fusako Shigenobu], Tokyo: Sekai shoten.

CHAPTER 8

Jocelyne Saab and CRIFFL: Dismantling Boundaries and Making New Routes for Asian Cinema in Lebanon

Némésis Srour

> You have to act, even if your action is a comma, a semicolon in the wake of History.[1]
> – Jocelyne Saab, Forum des images, Paris, 19 November 2017

Known for her work as a war reporter, for her documentaries and her fiction films, Jocelyne Saab, however, is not only a filmmaker or an image maker. Though she has explored creating images in diverse forms and with various media – photography, art installations, films or art video – little light has been shed on her role as an agent in developing cinematic links between Lebanon and Asia. A firm believer in Lebanon's integration into the Asiatic continent, her attitude contrasted with the country's general attitude, mostly looking West towards Europe and the United States.

In her endeavour to unearth this Asian commonality, always through and with cinema, Jocelyne Saab created, in 2013, the Cultural Resistance International Film Festival of Lebanon (CRIFFL), bringing Asian movies to Lebanese screens. While Lebanon did have a history of circulation of Hindi films and of Hong Kong 'kung-fu movies', this circulation of popular commercial films operated in the margins of non-elite screen practices. Under-appreciated by the educated population who preferred to watch European and Hollywood films, the history of circulation of Asian films in the Middle East remains a neglected one. By bringing Asian films to the forefront with CRIFFL, Saab's work went on to bridge a gap: reconnecting the country with a history of circulation of Asian films and, at the same time, legitimising these Asian films – through the form of a curated film festival – as an art form, paving the way for non-reductionist outlooks on films from Asia. Moreover, Saab wanted to curate Asian films that would connect with the local Lebanese audiences, and not only with the upper middle classes used to watching Western cinema. CRIFFL could be regarded as the first festival dedicated to Asian films in Lebanon and that, in itself, was a political act.

I met Jocelyne Saab through our shared love for Asian cinema and our ties with Lebanon in 2012. I worked with her on different projects, I eventually joined the CRIFFL team in 2014, as an assistant curator for Indian films. This chapter, focusing on Saab's links with Asia and on her work as a cultural agent with CRIFFL, formulates the hypothesis that she contributed to the production of a pan-Asian history of Lebanese cinema and of cinema in Lebanon.

CIRCULATION OF ASIAN AND INDIAN FILMS IN LEBANON: A HISTORY IN THE MARGINS

Film Distribution in Lebanon: The Power of Hollywood

In the 1950s and 1960s, up to the Six Day War, statistics collected in reports for UNESCO show a prevalence of English-language films, and more specifically American films, being screened in Egypt, Iraq, Jordan, Lebanon, Libya, Morocco and Tunisia. At a time when commentators observed a decline in cinema attendance, linked to the departure of many European residents following the independence movements, Hollywood managed to make the transition and attract local Arab audiences. According to Georges Sadoul,

> this decrease would seem to be mainly due to the disappearance of non-Arab spectators, but if we had statistics for the various population categories, they would likely establish that the number of Arab spectators has generally increased, in each country, after its independence. (Sadoul 1966: 130)

In the Arab-speaking world, Lebanon presented considerable advantages for Hollywood majors. Lebanon was regarded as a lucrative territory with its thriving cinema industry. The country was also open to Western cultural products and had a liberal commercial policy, with an open legislation for foreign films. In fact, in the 1960s a report insisted that 'The Lebanese Government does not impose any restrictions on the importation of films into the national territory; importation is "controlled" by means of a customs duty set at 50 Lebanese pounds per kilogram of imported film' (Monaco 1966: 143). Structurally, the arrival of foreign films in the country was still not under the supervision of a state body. The presence and distribution of films was based on private initiatives and market logistics, with no requirement to preserve national cinema, for example, via a quota system or legal favouritism of Arab films in general. Moreover, this small country was of vital economic interest in the region, since 'with an attendance index of 26.5 cinema tickets per year, [Lebanon was] an "overdeveloped" country for its exploitation' (Sadoul 1966: 129). It alone represented two-thirds of the Egyptian market for a population ten times smaller (Khoury 1966: 228). Thus, these factors allowed Beirut to secure its place as the central location for Hollywood regional offices, allowing it to become a centre of American film distribution in the Middle East region.

In the 1960s, American companies had seven regional offices in Beirut that supervised the distribution of their films in a large part of the region, even reaching into Africa: Lebanon, Syria, Iraq, Egypt, Jordan, Iran, Turkey, Cyprus, Kuwait, Bahrain, Sudan, Eritrea, Ethiopia, Somalia, Libya and Saudi Arabia. The centrality of Beirut distributors was also felt in the Egyptian film industry, whose films were distributed in the Gulf, Iraq, the Arabian Peninsula and Sudan, again via Lebanese distributors (Thoraval 1996: 103). While 'Beirut thus happen[ed] to be the vital centre of U.S. film distribution for the entire Middle East' (Jabre 1966: 172), the city saw on its screens, understandably so, the pre-eminence of American productions. In 1964, of the 503 imported films, 273 films came from the United States, representing 54.27 per cent of foreign films. Despite their hegemony in 1964 in Lebanon, American films nevertheless registered a certain decline. Between 1960 and 1961, they fell from 64 per cent of programmes to 56 per cent, but still occupied almost exclusively the programme of eight premiere cinemas in Beirut. This resulted in a monopoly of 77 per cent of all cinemas, and 82.5 per cent of all weeks of the year. In view of these figures, it is obvious that this left very little room for other film industries, especially since one of the major problems 'consist[ed] in the fact that cinema owners, bound by their obligations with American companies, ha[d] only a tiny number of weeks when they [were] free to screen films other than American films' (Jabre 1966: 172). Egyptian films occupied second place, just after Hollywood, with more than 15.5 per cent of the Lebanese market share in 1964. The prevalence of these two strong industries stymied the possibilities of Asian films' access in the country, especially since Italy, Great Britain and France each occupied about 10 per cent of the foreign films in the country.

Yet, the reputation of Lebanon as the centre of distribution and exhibition of films attracted Indian distributors. However, Asian movies were rarely screened in first-class cinema theatres, unlike Hollywood and European productions.

Non-elite Spaces: Localising Bollywood and Kung-fu Movie Screenings

At the end of the 1960s a family of Indian distributors, whose business was primarily established in Iran, discovered the potential of the Lebanese market through their network in Tehran. At first, they were a general trading company, operating between Bombay and Tehran, before seizing the opportunity of Iran's booming market for cinema in the 1960s.

In Iran the growth of the cinema industry was the result of a government policy that sought to encourage this mass leisure activity, facilitating the construction of new cinemas by limiting taxation on this type of building. The increase in attendance can further be explained by demographic change through the development of an urban middle class in the 1960s, and the economic migration of rural people to the big cities (Thoraval 2000: 27). The young, urban population thus made up the bulk of the cinema audience, in a country where most cinemas were concentrated in Tehran: 120 cinemas in the capital in 1975, compared with twelve in Isfahan and thirteen in Shiraz, for example (Thoraval 2000: 28). The popularity of films, where 'long lines characterized the cinema, which made money regardless of the quality of the films' (Issari 1989: 76), enabled a lucrative business. A foreign film could bring in up to seven times its cost, thus offering a more than interesting return on investment. As Mohammad Issari explains, 'These lucrative returns for commercial films and the tax exemption for the construction of new cinemas encouraged the growth of the film trade in Iran and enabled the government to achieve the goals set by its 1958 plan' (1989: 77). It is in this favourable context for cinema that the Indian film *Sangam*, directed by the iconic Raj Kapoor in 1964, appeared on Iranian screens and made the fortune of the Indian merchants' family. It was also in Tehran's booming market that Indian distributors met Lebanese distributors in the 1960s.

Although the Hollywood majors had local offices in the Iranian capital until the 1970s, Iran was also part of the territories supervised by regional offices based in Beirut. Lebanese distributors therefore travelled to Tehran to distribute the American films they were mandated to distribute. Through this channel, the Indian distributor family discovered the lucrative potential of the Lebanese market, a territory still virtually untouched by Indian films. This period of the 1960s corresponded indeed to a golden age for cinema exhibition in Lebanon. In 1961 the attendance index in Lebanon was four times higher than in France and ten times higher than in Egypt. Hence, the Indian distributor opened an office in Beirut in the late 1960s, a few years before the outbreak of the Lebanese civil war. However, in Lebanon, Hindi films continued to be a social marker. If the first great Indian successes managed to fit into the environment of first-class cinemas, for an audience of 'good taste', very quickly the displacement in time and space pushed these Indian films to the margins of the sub-cinema circuits, alongside karate and kung-fu films or spaghetti westerns. As the Lebanese film critic Mohamed Soueid recalls:

> In 1967, following the unexpected success of the Hindi film *Al-'Ibadah* [العبادة original title: *Aradhana*], with heroine Sharmila Tagore and director Shakti Samanta, the Pigalle became the only venue for the projection of the sung and lyrical melodramas imported from Indian studios.

> Distributor Zouheir el-Sabban, one of Mohammad Khalid el-Sabban's sons, is bringing Indian production back to Lebanon. It is true that his late father was at the origin of the distribution of Indian melodrama, but his role was first to organize the programming of Indian films. (Soueid 1996: 72)

With the arrival of the Sabban family, Indian productions began to accumulate on the screens of the Pigalle cinema in Beirut, and the cinema welcomed an important audience, most of whom came from both Indian and Pakistani communities. In addition to this community audience, the Armenians accounted for about 70 per cent of the Saturday screening audience, according to Soueid. The author goes on to compare the Pigalle's strategy with that of the Alphonse cinema, which was mainly aimed at an audience from the French community, while the Pigalle distinguished itself 'by attracting an audience of minorities and those from the category of emigrant workers, working and residing on Lebanese territory' (Soueid 1996: 72). He adds:

> The spread of Indian melodrama to different halls at the back of the al-Burj district has shed light on these cinema halls, which respond to popular and general taste, and to the pleasure of social classes outside the elite. These social classes have found in the melodrama a show in which their daily lives of misery and poverty are projected. (Soueid 1996: 72)

The analysis of audiences in terms of minority communities or foreign migrant workers echoes the strategy of exoticisation of audiences found in the Greek case in relation to Indian films, as highlighted by Dimitris Eleftheriotis (2006: 101–2). For Eleftheriotis, his work, dominated by the desire to collect data above all, observes the division of audiences into two categories: the middle class, who perceive Indian cinema with an ironic distance, and the working class, poor victims of ideological misidentification. In this rhetoric, Indian film remains deeply rooted in a form of 'Otherness', either as an exotic product of another culture or as the source of low entertainment for an 'other' audience (Eleftheriotis 2006: 109). Similarly, in the Lebanese case, this cinema is perceived as popular entertainment, practised by 'marginal', 'other' populations, first identified by their community origins (Indian, Pakistani, Armenian) and then by their social class. This analysis recalls that of Georges Sadoul in 1965 during the conference 'Arab Cinema and Culture' under the aegis of UNESCO. According to the conference report, 'Mr Sadoul then shows how the Arab working class ensured the success of Indian films. He wonders whether Indian films are not a deviation from their daily reality for this social class' (Interarab Centre of Cinema & Television 1965). The analyses of Soueid and Sadoul clearly contradict each other, since one sees in them an identification of popular audiences with the images on the screen, while the other sees them as an escape route. In both cases, this vision contributes to confining Indian cinema to an exoticism acceptable to non-Lebanese audiences, where elitist contempt joins a compartmentalisation of society, operating a division between the Lebanese and the Others.

This brief history of the presence of Asian films in Lebanon – with a focus on Indian films – shows how much of a political act it was for someone like Jocelyne Saab, in the 2010s, to bring Asian films back to Beirut and throughout Lebanon, as part of a film festival with a strong artistic vision and editorial policy.

A POLITICAL ACT – LEGITIMISING ASIAN FILMS AS A CATEGORY THROUGH CINEMATIC SPACES

The Importance of Space: Metropolis, where the Good Movies Go

Jocelyne Saab was aware of social geographies, especially in her home country. As such, when she conceived of the festival, the location and the cinema where the festival was to be hosted was in itself a political statement. As evidence of this political choice, the first edition of the festival in November 2013 was named 'Tripoli International Film Festival of Lebanon', in honour of the city, at a time when it had witnessed a number of violent attacks. Still, in 2013 the festival actually took place simultaneously in Tripoli and in Beirut. The choice to bring the festival to Beirut and other cities asserted another political act via its geographical and spatial existence. The first challenge for Saab as a cultural agent was to legitimise Asian films in a country that remembered Bollywood and kung-fu cinema only as part of popular entertainment. Accordingly, the famous Metropolis cinema in Beirut was the very best place to inaugurate a film festival in Lebanon. Part of the Empire Cinemas exhibition network, located in the upmarket district of Ashrafieh in Beirut, the Metropolis cinema was dedicated to hosting festivals and independent films. Yet, it was – as it has not survived at the time of writing this chapter[2] – quite a unique and elite space in the Lebanese cinema exhibition landscape.

The Empire firm has been an important historical actor in the field of Lebanese exhibition. Georges N. Haddad opened the first cinema in Beirut in 1919, the Cosmograph on the Place des Canons. Very quickly, from one cinema hall it turned into a network named Empire since 1926, and the Empire cinemas were in tune with international releases. As early as 1954, the chain managed simultaneous film releases with London, Paris and New York. As time went by, the Empire House established itself as the main and exclusive distributor for certain Hollywood majors.[3]

Yet, while the Beirut of the 1950s and 1960s is often described as 'a paradise for film lovers' (Thoraval 2003: 42) with superb cinemas, booming film production, and a powerful distribution network well established throughout the region, the 1970s were detrimental to the burgeoning Lebanese film industry. The civil war, which exploded in 1975, devastated the country and undermined the film distribution system, hitherto monopolised by Lebanese companies. Not only did the war paralyze production, it also reduced the infrastructure to ashes: the Baalbek Studio was repeatedly looted, while other studios simply disappeared. Cinemas, considered as the embodiment of depravation and westernisation, suffered irreversible damage if they were located on the 'dividing line' in Beirut. The Lebanese civil war also profoundly disrupted the exhibition sector, as the bombing of cities made going to the cinema dangerous if not fatal. As a result, 'most Lebanese opted for the safe environment of their homes to watch videos', especially since the acquisition of VCRs was facilitated by the development of 'illegal ports along the Lebanese coast' (Kamalipour and Mowlana 1994; 169). Although exhibitors tried to adapt to the country's explosive situation, offering films in the morning knowing that the streets of West Beirut were deserted after 5 p.m., distributors estimated in the mid-1980s that 50 per cent of the population had lost the habit of going to the cinema (Borsten 1984).

Yet, during these critical times, the Empire company seems to have tried to keep going, as they related in their official chronology of their website in 2015:

> 1976 – A Safe Bet
> Undeterred by outbreak of civil unrest, Empire transforms the auditorium of Casino Du Liban into a luxury theatre. Movie lovers fleeing the violence in Beirut sought refuge in the safety of Jounieh where their passion for movie-going continued unabated.
> 1978 – From Simple to Multiplex
> Daringly a raging Lebanese civil war reaching critical heights, Empire developed yet another movie-going innovation, launching the first 5-screen multiplex of its kind in the Middle East at an obscure location at the time called Zouk, calling it Espace Cinemas.
> 1982 – Flying the Flag
> Empire II & III theaters open their doors to an Ashrafieh clientele in the upscale Sofil Center, becoming the flagship theaters of the Empire chain. (Empire Cinemas 2015)

The 'flagship' theatre of the Sofil Center was actually the Metropolis cinema, thought of, since its beginning, as an elite and exclusive space. Its contemporary programme hosted, for instance, a repeat of the Cannes Critics Week, of the ARTE Film Week, the Director's Fortnight Retrospective, or contemporary Lebanese Film Festivals such as Ayam Beirut Al Cinema'iya. It has released Lebanese films, including Mai Masri's documentary *Beirut Diaries:*

Truth, Lies and Videos (2006), the latest feature of Borhane Alaouié entitled *Khalass* (*Enough*, 2007), as well as renowned director Ghassan Salhab's third feature *The Last Man* (2006). It is also the place of choice for, and actually the only one open to programming, foreign arthouse films. Symbolically, it made sense to open the CRIFFL in this most fitting space, the Metropolis cinema, where the festival's film selection resonated with the cinema's curation history and audience. However, at the same time, CRIFFL was supposed to be more than an arty festival, and the typical audience at Metropolis is bourgeois and middle class. Saab's goal was to reconnect Asian films with a non-cinephile audience, bridging the gap between the idea of an elite film festival and a choice of films where cinema acts as a social weapon, while re-enlivening the days of Asian screenings in Lebanese cinema halls.

When CRIFFL Remakes Once Upon a Time, Beirut: *The Act of Reconnecting with the Screening History of the City*

The act of creating and making CRIFFL happen can be seen, in many ways, as a continuation of Saab's cinematic gesture as a filmmaker. I argue that the touring festival was an enactment of a long-time ideal, brought to light in her film *Once Upon a Time, Beirut: Story of a Star* (1994), unearthing the cinematic archives of a city and rebuilding Lebanese and Beirut history and memory through cinema. There is, however, a prior milestone to the festival for this enactment, which only confirmed the necessity for Jocelyne Saab – both as an artist and historian – to make cinema, cities and history connect. In 1992, feeling a duty of memory, she launched a huge project to reconstitute the Lebanese Film Library. She travelled the world, managed to gather more than 400 films that evoke Lebanon and then carried out the immense archival work.

As Mathilde Rouxel explains (see Chapter 17 in this volume), *Once upon a Time, Beirut: Story of a Star* is the culmination of a larger project that Jocelyne Saab led over more than three years, entitled *Beirut, a Thousand and One Images*, and her objective was the foundation of a Lebanese Film Library. The project did not come into being in this form, but screening cycles of the films she gathered were organised both in Lebanon and worldwide over the next decade.

In the 1990s, when Lebanon was just emerging from a fierce civil war, there was not yet an environment conducive to setting up a national film library. Yet, some years later, in her endeavour to reconnect cinema and the city, Saab came across the project of Kassem Istanbouli, who was aiming to revive the Al-Hamra cinema hall, in Tyre, in southern Lebanon. The young actor and director reopened the doors to Al-Hamra after more than twenty years of closure, bringing it back to life as a cultural centre for the city. Before it became the Teatro Istanbouli Al-Hamra, the newspaper *Al-Akhbar* reported the following:

In mid-1938, the owner of a café in the coastal town of Tyre in southern Lebanon bought a 35mm projector and set off on an adventure. He took a sheet, usually used as a tablecloth, hung it on a wall adjacent to his café, and turned on the machine . . . And just like that, the first cinema [in Tyre] was born. (*Al Akhbar* 2014)

All that remains of the old Al-Hamra cinema today are the memories of former spectators who still remember the action films, westerns, and Indian and Egyptian films they saw there. Proof of this is Saab's collection of recovered posters of Indian films, which had disappeared, like so many silent testimonies stolen by the relentless course of time.

It is clear, then, that Indian films circulated beyond the capital. Indeed, they also travelled as far east as the Beqaa, as witnessed by the owner of the current Stargate Cinema in the city of Zahleh, Elie Ghattas. Before building this multiplex cinema at the end of the 1990s, the family owned several cinemas in Zahleh, until they closed down with the Battle of Zahleh in 1981. Elie Ghattas remembers showing Indian films in his early cinema venues. At the time, he told me, 'the Hindi film was doing well but with the war and the closure of the cinemas in Zahleh, the Indian film disappeared'.[4]

As the Lebanese civil war put an end to the circulation of Asian films in the country, the aim of CRIFFL was to reconnect with that heritage of Lebanese cinema-going, and to make people remember their past cinematographic experiences. In fact, in testimonies by spectators, they state that when they discovered the festival, it took them back to the time when they used to watch Indian films on the big screen in Zahleh. In order to reconnect to the cinematographic history of each city where the festival took place over the years, Jocelyne Saab's curatorial choice of film for each city took that aspect into account. CRIFFL was therefore not only about bringing new Asian films to Lebanon, it was, in fact, enacting a cure for a form of cinematic amnesia.

As the festival aimed to address spatial segregations, which had taken the shape of social or political divides, cinematic space was at the core of CRIFFL's curatorial practice. The festival wanted to tackle Lebanon's ingrained geographical disparities. This was not only a part of the 'internal' reflection: Jocelyne Saab would also endlessly fight, on the external front, for a Lebanon that would take its place and role in the Asian continent. Cinema, for her, was a constructive tool to show how much the Lebanese have been and continue to be connected to Asian countries in their social and political realities.

Reclaiming Lebanon as Part of Asia through Cinema: When the Hindi New Wave Connects with Local Lebanese Audiences

The curatorial choices of film programmes draw a parallel between, on the one hand, the circulation of Jocelyne Saab's own artistic work throughout Asian countries and, on the other hand, Saab bringing together Asian films to be screened and celebrated in Lebanon. Two important meetings shaped CRIFFL's curation of Asian and Indian films in particular. In 2006, Saab's film *Dunia* was selected for the Osian's Cinefan Festival of Asian and Arab Cinema which takes place in New Delhi and was founded in 1999 by Aruna Vasudev. The friendship between the two women developed through the Network for the Promotion of Asian Cinema (NETPAC). NETPAC had been founded in 1990, also by Vasudev, at the end of a conference organised in New Delhi at the request of UNESCO to promote a better understanding and recognition of Asian films and directors. NETPAC took as its official magazine *Cinemaya*, founded by Vasudev in 1988. Another essential encounter was with the founders of the Vesoul Asian Film Festival, Martine and Jean-Marc Thérouanne, which a NETPAC delegation attends every year to award a prize. Jocelyne Saab relied on these two networks' international contributions over the years for the screenings of Asian films during CRIFFL.

These international experiences forged Saab's knowledge and experience of the commonalities between Lebanon and other Asian countries. She would become a go-between figure between both cultures, a true pan-Asian agent, and CRIFFL became the physical act and space of transmission. This significantly contributed to the strong curatorial line of CRIFFL, to select films for screening that created a sense of 'shared reality' between Lebanon and Asian countries. This was also clearly present in the formulation of the aims and objectives of the festival:

> This event, directed and supported by director Jocelyne Saab, brings together in its programming films from Asia and the Mediterranean that question issues that echo the situation in Lebanon.
>
> Through its history and its geographical location, Lebanon is at the crossroads of the Euro-Mediterranean, Arab and Asian worlds. The festival's main objective and the basis of its programming is to confront cinematographic works from these worlds and to draw, through them, a portrait of their different cultures, to draw the common issues that affect Lebanon itself: exchanges and conflicts of values, religions, political systems. (CRIFFL n.d.)

CRIFFL's programming for the centenary of Indian cinema during its first edition in 2013 'deliberately chose to shake up conventions' (CRIFFL n.d.). The festival thus justified its curatorial choices on its website:

> If usually old traditional films and Bollywood cinema are put in the spotlight, the festival has chosen to privilege the young generation with two exceptional films: the first, *Ship of Theseus* [2012], directed by Anand Gandhi, a director-scriptwriter in his thirties. Already famous

throughout India for his television series scripts and for the awards he has received, he has made a magnificent film that tells a long story in the manner of the *Thousand and One Nights*, but which deals with a subject of burning topicality: using the theme of organ transplants to question the metaphysical relationship we have with our bodies, he questions the human being and his difference with others. If I see the world through other eyes than my own, am I still the same person?

[. . .]

Salma [2013] is the film of a woman, Kim Longinotto, who tells the extraordinary story of the greatest poetess of South India, locked up for twenty-five years for being born a woman. With the connivance of the prisoner, she managed to pass her texts on pieces of toilet paper or paper bags, and was able to transmit her poetry to the world. Without keeping any hatred of the traditions that locked her up, she freed herself through the words of poetry. (CRIFFL n.d.)

The Centennial Evening took place on Saturday, 16 November 2013 in Beirut at the Metropolis cinema and in Tripoli at the City Complex at 8 p.m.

While the Lebanese audience would still associate Hindi films with boring and dramatic pieces full of song and dance, the discovery of the Hindi New Wave came as a double shock: first, that of an extremely modern cinematic style, and second, the discovery of a shared reality with India. In the selection for its 2014 edition, the documentary *Powerless* (Deepti Kakkar and Fahad Mustafa, 2014) showed that the electricity problem was not specific to Lebanon, as it portrays an Indian Robin Hood of electricity who illegally connects poor families to the state-owned networks. The third and last edition to date, in 2015, was more modest, in terms of number of films, geographical location (the festival only took place in Beirut) and duration, for economic and financial reasons. Yet, one of the flagship guests was Anurag Kashyap, the internationally renowned figure of the 2010s Hindi New Wave.

His film, *Gangs of Wasseypur – Part I* (2012), was screened on 9 November 2015 at 9 p.m. at the Metropolis cinema hall. The hall was full, mainly with students, since the festival had renewed its partnership with high schools and universities in the framework of the 'Young Critics' competition. The students had to produce a review of a film of their choice, and those who chose Anurag Kashyap's film were amazed to discover an Indian film that was so far removed from the stereotypes they had in mind. It was not a tearful melodrama, but a gangster action film that kept them on the edge of their seats for more than two hours. The context of the film, which mentions rivalries between the Sunni and Shiite communities, also helped to bring this Indian film closer to the experiences of the Lebanese spectators. They were surprised to find in this film a community with habits and religious references that were entirely familiar to them.

Figure 8.1 Poster of the second edition of the Cultural Resistance International Film Festival of Lebanon, 12–17 November 2014

A masterclass with Anurag Kashyap at the University of Fine Arts provided a space for dialogue between the students and the director. During this session, the director showed them an unfinished version of a short film he was working on. The film follows a young married woman who one day decides to remove all the hair from her genitals. Astonished by this change, her husband accuses her of having a lover. Interested in this peculiar and intimate image of a couple, the young people wanted to know more about sexuality in India, about private space and love relationships. Comments were also made about the feature film, and the students were surprised to learn about the Muslim communities in India. Seduced by the style of Kashyap, the young people discovered another kind of Indian cinema, far removed from the stereotypes they had held onto from the familiar Bollywood films. Anurag Kashyap's cinema brought to light a shared reality, be it social, political or even emotional, between India and Lebanon. And, in that moment, Jocelyne Saab felt she had succeeded in her endeavour with CRIFFL.

CONCLUSION

In an in-depth interview, Saab reflected on the developments in her career, and concluded:

> I think what makes my career special is that I have always wanted to remain coherent; I have always been ready to fight to defend what I believed in, to show and analyse this Middle East that I was so passionate about in the midst of change. Yet the day came when I grew tired, or rather, when my eyes grew tired; I could no longer see anything – there was too much death, too much suffering. I then moved on to fiction. I wanted to develop, to work the image differently. The third period of my career came when doors shut down on me, especially with *Dunia* in Egypt, which was censored. I turned to photography. A new way of making images, alone, so as not to stop. Today I'm back to moving images, to cinema, to video. (CNC 2019)

In this chapter I have demonstrated that there was also a fourth very productive period in Jocelyne Saab's artistic life, where she took the role of a political and cultural agent and activist. There is more to her artistic gesture than an act of encapsulating images, be they archives, documentaries, fiction or visual art. With the Cultural Resistance International Film Festival of Lebanon, she acted towards making the cinema space a political space and to introduce a different understanding of Lebanon as part of the large Asian continent, in all its facets and wealth.

With CRIFFL, Saab reminded the Lebanese that there is a quality arthouse cinema outside of Europe and Western countries; with that, she participated in legitimising Asian cinema in Lebanon. With CRIFFL, she reminded the Lebanese that their cinema halls used to screen Bollywood and kung-fu movies; with that, she reconnected the audiences to the local history of the cinema halls while curing a form of amnesia. With CRIFFL, she reminded the Lebanese that their struggles were not that different from the ones lived in India or other parts of Asia; with that, she reclaimed Lebanon as part of Asia through cinema. Through all these actions, CRIFFL aimed to build bridges across the divides between the Lebanese people: the social gap between elite and popular audiences and the geographical divide between the capital and the rest of the country. The festival was meant as an act of peace, with art and cinema as its sole weapons. At a time when Lebanon is living through the darkest hours of its history – questioning its mythological essence as the phoenix always ready to rise from its ashes – one cannot help but wonder what Jocelyne Saab's take on it would have been. I think she would have thought, and said again, 'You have to act, even if your action is a comma, a semicolon in the wake of History.'

NOTES

1. These are Jocelyne Saab's words during the Q&A following a screening of *A Suspended Life* curated in 'Un état du monde', an event organised by the Forum des images in Paris, on 19 November 2017. Original quotation in French: 'Il faut agir, même si ton action est une virgule, un point-virgule dans l'Histoire.'
2. The Metropolis cinema has not survived: at the time of writing, the cinema has ended its partnership with Circuit Empire. Instead, they plan to open a cinematheque.
3. In 1958 the company obtained exclusive distribution rights for United Artists' films for Lebanon and Kuwait. In 1964, when Columbia Pictures closed its Beirut office, it appointed Empire as exclusive distributor for the Middle East. In 1988 Empire became the exclusive distributor of 20th Century Fox in Lebanon and the Gulf, before pursuing its expansion into the Gulf market.
4. Author's interview with Elie Ghattas, 24 April 2014, Zahleh.

BIBLIOGRAPHY

Al Akhbar (2014), 'Al-Hamra Cinema Hopes to Revive Tyre's Cinematic Golden Age', *Al Akhbar* English, 14 November 2014, <http://english.al-akhbar.com/content/al-hamra-cinema-hopes-revive-tyre%E2%80%99s-cinematic-golden-age> (last accessed 2 August 2016).
Borsten, Joan (1984) 'The Show Goes On – Under the Gun', *The Los Angeles Times*, 15 July 1984.
Centre National du Cinéma et de l'image animée (CNC) (2019), 'Disparition de la réalisatrice Jocelyne Saab, précurseur d'un nouveau cinéma libanais', CNC, 14 January, <https://www.

cnc.fr/professionnels/actualites/disparition-de-la-realisatrice-jocelyne-saab-precurseur-dun-nouveau-cinema-libanais_917245> (last accessed 4 December 2020).

Cultural Resistance International Film Festival (CRIFFL) (n.d.), website, <http://culturalresistance.org>, unavailable, archived by the Association of Jocelyne Saab's Friends.

Eleftheriotis, Dimitris (2006) '"A Cultural Colony of India": Indian Films in Greece in the 1950s and 1960s', *South Asian Popular Culture*, 4: 2, 101–12.

Empire Cinemas (2015), <http://www.empire.com.lb/AboutUs/History> (last accessed 9 December 2015).

Interarab Centre of Cinema & Television (1965), 'Cinéma et cultures arabes. *IVème Conférence de La Table Ronde* organisée avec l'aide technique de l'UNESCO', Beirut: Interarab Centre of Cinema & Television.

Issari, Mohammad A. (1989), *Cinema in Iran (1900–1979)*, Metuchen, NJ: Scarecrow Press.

Jabre, Farid (1966), 'L'exploitation au Liban', in Georges Sadoul (ed.), *Les Cinémas des pays arabes*, Beirut: Interarab Centre of Cinema & Television, pp. 170–6.

Kamalipour Yahya R. and Hamid Mowlana (eds) (1994), *Mass Media in the Middle East: A Comprehensive Handbook*, Westport, CT and London: Greenwood Press.

Khoury, Lucienne (1966), 'Perspectives du cinéma libanais', in Georges Sadoul (ed.), *Les Cinémas des pays arabes*, Beirut: Interarab Centre of Cinema & Television, pp. 228–33.

Monaco, Eitel (1966), 'Exploitation, distribution, importation des films', in Georges Sadoul (ed.), *Les Cinémas des pays arabes*, Beirut: Interarab Centre of Cinema & Television, pp. 164–5.

Rouxel, Mathilde (2018), 'Jocelyne Saab, cinéaste témoin de la cinéphilie libanaise', in Jean-Paul Aubert, Cyril Laverger and Christel Taillibert (eds), *Les Représentations de la cinéphilie*, *Cycnos*, 34: 1, 111–27.

Sadoul, Georges (1966), 'Géographie du cinéma et monde arabe', in Georges Sadoul (ed.), *Les Cinémas des pays arabes*, Beirut: Interarab Centre of Cinema & Television, pp. 127–34.

Soueid, Mohamed (1996), *Ya fu'adi u'sirat sinamai'it ᶜan salat Birut alrahla*, Beirut: Dar Al Nahar.

Thoraval, Yves (1996), *Regards sur le cinéma égyptien (1895–1975)*, Paris and Montreal: L'Harmattan.

Thoraval, Yves (2000), *Les Cinémas du Moyen-Orient: Iran, Égypte, Turquie (1896–2000)*, Paris: Séguier.

Thoraval, Yves (2003), *Les Écrans du croissant fertile: Irak, Liban, Palestine, Syrie*, Paris: Séguier.

PART III

Liberating the People, Freeing the Body

CHAPTER 9

Guerrillas, Border Crossings and Internationalism: The Liberation of Non-Arabs in Jocelyne Saab's Early Documentaries

Stefanie Van de Peer

Jocelyne Saab was a Lebanese-French pioneer of women-led non-fiction filmmaking in the 1970s, with an idealism that stood out as courageous and ground-breaking. She was not perceived favourably by the establishment as she embraced the feminist, anti-imperialist and internationalist atmosphere of the decade. Instead, she carved out her own niche through a multifaceted point of view on some of the greatest political issues of her time. Her films are 'influenced by western journalism and documentary, but their sustained rhythm, efficient images and economy of means give her work a special cachet' (Hottell and Pallister 2011: 112). Saab's earliest war reportages already showcased a proclivity for the poetic power of painfully truthful images. She was a filmmaker who believed in the long-term impact and meaning of intellectual movements. The 'osmosis' between fiction and non-fiction in her work reflects her own border-crossing reality, which remains relevant – in particular in the three non-fiction films discussed in this chapter – as the films retain their integrity more than forty years since they were made.

In this chapter, I discuss three of Saab's early documentaries, looking at the filmmaker's revolutionary interests in *Iraq: War in Kurdistan* (1974), *The Sahara is Not for Sale* (1977) and *Iran: Utopia on the Move* (1980). These three films show how Saab rejects the label of 'Arab' filmmaker, and how her internationalism led her to report on territories where borders were crossed, both literally and metaphorically. In *Iraq: War in Kurdistan*, made for French TV channel FR3's programme *Magazine 52*, Saab chronicles the Iraqi responses to the Kurdish independence movement in a lucid, essayistic manner. Her prominent voice-over explains all sides of the conflict in Iraqi Kurdistan, through the lens of an internationalist on the side of the underdog. In *The*

Sahara is Not for Sale her docu-journalism looks at the Western Saharan conflict from all possible viewpoints, excluding no one, and interlacing these testimonies with contemplative visions of the desert, which looms so large over (or under) the conflict. As an independently shot film, supported by the Moroccan government and partly funded by Algerian TV, this film is testimony to the ongoing complexity of the conflict in what is often called the last colony on the African continent. It was Saab's second long feature documentary (after *Lebanon in Turmoil*, 1975), and the personal consequence for her was that she was unable to visit Morocco for the next two decades. The personal and visual quality of these journalistic documents sets her apart from other reporters from that period, and her direct engagement with the significance of borders and self-rule shows Saab's idealistic journalism. This type of visual political analysis is also showcased in *Iran: Utopia on the Move*, initiated by Japanese TV channel NHK, in which her observational commentary encompasses Iranian society as a whole and aims to understand what this early revolution meant for the (Muslim) world. Avoiding the sensational elements of the media, which often associates Islam with antagonism towards the 'West' (Said [1981] 1997), this film instead shows a deep interest in the human stories behind the Iranian revolution and its failure. Interviewing people from all walks of life, Saab shows how the common people are being misled by their leaders. This film is an early example of her interest in the Asian world, rejecting the West's assumptions that the news is filtered through its channels.

In all three films, Saab focuses on young people, whether these are idealistic soldiers and young students working for a Kurdish national identity, Sahrawi children and women describing their nomadic lifestyle, or Tehrani students raising their fists to proclaim their revolutionary fervour. Through her activist, emancipatory audio-visual work, Saab ensures that her contemporary as well as future international audiences understand the global consequences of seemingly local conflict. Although reportages and journalistic documents often do suffer from diminishing relevance, Saab's work remains acutely relevant, as the Kurdish and Sahrawi fights live on in the twenty-first century, while Iran remains at the centre of the international journalistic gaze. Her vision of the Middle East is one that showcases its diversity through language, culture, literature, art and ways of living. Ceaselessly criss-crossing the region, her gaze and her voice embrace the region's many faces and its plurality of voice. In what follows I first engage with the personal and political circumstances in which Saab made these three early documentaries, and then I analyse in detail the visual and spoken qualities of the films. Audio and visuals are both considered, as they highlight the indexical correspondence and the ironic juxtapositions of information through Saab's personal and political involvement with her subjects.

PERSONAL AND POLITICAL CONTEXTS

Although Saab had made short films as a young reporter in Lebanon, it was when she arrived in Paris that she really dedicated herself to audio-visually mapping contemporary issues in the Middle East and bringing these to the forefront. As a journalist for French TV, at the time she was one of the only women in this milieu, 'which earned her the contempt of some, and the trust of others' (Rouxel 2015: 16). She stands out, not just because she is a female journalist in the male media world of the 1970s, and because she is an Arab working in a French context, but also because her petite figure, which often appears briefly in her films, is complemented with a confident voice and a critical gaze. Around the time when Saab made *Iraq: War in Kurdistan* (1974), she was also working on ten- to fifteen-minute reportages about Palestine and the Golan Heights for French TV. When, in 1975, the Lebanon war broke out, she moved away from working for French TV and became an independent reporter to go to Beirut and make *Lebanon in Turmoil* (1975), her first feature-length film and one of the most highly regarded films about the initial stages of the Lebanese civil war. This independence as a filmmaker also provided the opportunity for her films to be screened internationally. Through these experiences she could now evade the constraints of the reportage format and give shape to her own form of filmmaking: her language became increasingly personal and more poetic (Rouxel 2015: 21). In this section I pay attention to the personal and the global context in which Saab was working at this time, in order to show how her internationalism, her broad view, was shaped by her Lebanese roots, her French lived reality and the tendencies in global news media.

From 1975 until 1977 Saab dedicated herself entirely to the Lebanese cause, but then decided to film global revolutionary movements and the ensuing conflicts. The form of her documentaries underwent considerable change at this time. While her earlier reportages were made as a journalist on commission, her independence and the experience in Lebanon – which made her question the (im)possibility of representing the personal trauma of war – forced her to find a particular visual and political language that suited her sense of social justice. Moving away from the personal experiences of Beirut under siege was necessary in order to liberate her voice and gaze and commit to an outward-looking advocacy. This new visual language was not only committed to establishing her own vision for justice, it was also entirely dedicated to giving shape to a platform where she could really listen to the oppressed and the intricacies of their experiences. This language encompassed a nomadic, free and flexible position that enabled her to speak with everyone, on all sides of any conflict. That unexpected and multiple point of view gave this female reporter the capacity to balance journalistic objectivity with a powerfully subjective activist fervour. This approach is encapsulated in her presence during or immediately after the revolution takes place, as she explains very complex situations at the outset of decades-long problems. As such, Saab's films remain relevant, putting things in a clear contemporary perspective in hindsight.

In the 1970s and 1980s there was a global trend in the news media to shift focus away from majority political consensus towards a more critical journalism. Media histories show the new power of journalists to expose scandals, hold politicians to account and search for social responsibility. Likewise, advances in satellite and other technologies allowed the television news media direct coverage of international events. The conflict in Iraq and global suspicion of Iran made the region of the Middle East a hot topic of debate. Indeed, Saab's films could be read in the context of a large number of TV and film documentaries dedicated to Iran and Iraq, as the Cold War was a global conflict implicating most countries. For example, France supported Iraq, and even supplied weapons (including nuclear weapons). *Iraq: War in Kurdistan* can be seen in this context, while it also expresses an anti-establishment sentiment, as Saab opens up the debate and includes different voices to the representation of the complex conflict. The world was opening up to a wider TV audience, as movements for equal rights, independence and freedom of the press continued into the 1970s.[1] If the late 1960s in France had been characterised by cultural-universalistic conflicts, the conflicts of the 1970s were of a 'corporalist-particularistic-materialistic nature' (Boudon 1979: 669). Nevertheless, Saab remained an idealist working in the spirit of universal humanism based on solidarity with the oppressed, interested in new ways of constructing open and thriving societies. At the end of the 1970s the Iran hostage crisis dominated the global news, and so Saab's film *Iran: Utopia on the Move* could be seen in that context. But she is decidedly *not* interested in the American side of the hostage crisis – for her that crisis remains a footnote at the end of the film. Instead, she turns her camera and microphone to the people in the streets, who instigated the utopian anti-imperialist rebellion and are now dealing with the consequences of a failed revolution. The irony of the situation does not escape the filmmaker, as is apparent from her title, but there is a stubborn consistency in her concern for the oppressed: women, children, students and revolutionaries.

Although Saab is preoccupied with the lived reality of Arab peoples, as illustrated by her many films about and set in Lebanon, Palestine and Egypt, she is not limited to those national contexts. She is an internationalist, interested in non-Western cultures that suffered at the hands of imperialists and are reclaiming agency. The fact that her interest, knowledge and experience encompass the Middle East and North Africa shows her resistance to Western dominance. In that sense, her films provide the context for global crisis from a Western perspective, not the other way around. At the same time, there is an awareness that the majority of her audience, or perhaps rather the initial audience, is not Middle Eastern at all – especially in her earlier work. *Iraq:*

War in Kurdistan was made for French TV, *The Sahara is Not for Sale* premiered in cinemas in France, and *Iran: Utopia on the Move* was made for and distributed by Japanese TV channel NHK and later broadcast on European channels.[2] These international audiences have to be shown that the Middle East is not a monolith, but a vast region dominated by cultural, religious and linguistic diversity. These three films showcase the particular fights of Kurdish, Amazigh and Iranian revolutionaries. Saab's critical internationalism here focuses on non-Arab Middle Eastern testimonies of conflict, at the basis of which lie imperialist, colonialist and essentially racist tendencies, condemned by the filmmaker.

VISUAL LANGUAGE AND ACTIVIST FILMMAKING

In a piece on activist filmmaking, Angela Aguayo (2006: 6) explains that non-fiction film often makes intense use of persuasion techniques. She identifies three main historical stages through which the activist film has developed, which have changed the emphasis both within activist work and about these films. These move from John Grierson's 1930s ideals about bringing about social change through creative filming techniques, to the more 'objective' tactics that emphasise the role of the witness and the agency of the audience in the 1960s, and then the digital age's changes in diverse online platforms, including social media. The activist filmmaker has, by and large, changed from one who focused on the *image* for social change and developed through a focus on the voice-over and synchronous *sound* towards a more testimonial platform. This conceptualisation of the activist film is integrated into the development of technology, as the increasingly lightweight 16 mm cameras used by Saab were adapted and improved to enable synchronous sound in the 1960s and 1970s.

Alongside these changes and adaptations, I would add the importance of global idealist cinema movements in this era: the consequences of the 1968 movements were felt acutely by worldwide activist filmmakers. Indeed, an important aspect that influenced Saab in her development towards finding her own filmic language in her films was the changes in world and Arab cinema in the period leading up to her making the films under discussion here. She was still a young filmmaker at the time when important revolutions in cinema were taking place: not only the anti-establishment sentiments in French cinema after 1968, but also the Third Cinema and New Arab Cinema manifestos at the end of the 1960s and beginning of the 1970s. These global anti-establishment trends need to be acknowledged as major influences on filmmakers everywhere, in particular those, who – like Saab – are concerned with social justice and the rights of the oppressed. As I have shown at length elsewhere (Van de Peer 2017), New Arab Cinema pushed filmmakers to embrace the reality of everyday life over the grand discourses a sentimentalist cinema had become used to. Third Cinema similarly preferred an engagement with the real, with the lower classes and with those whose lives had been ignored by the establishment for too long. Both manifestos called for transparency of perspective, while they also strongly believed in the ability of active, engaged audiences to act upon calls for change. Saab's particular response to these changes in the audio-visual at this volatile time was to incorporate a conscious and confident voice-over to complement her emancipatory gaze, to experiment with sound and camera angles, and to acknowledge her own role as the creator of the films by appearing in them. Filming people during lulls in conflict, violence and protests enabled her to engage their tired but passionate viewpoints at moments of particular clarity.

Whereas Aguayo's assertion that activist films in the 1960s and 1970s focused on speech and testimonial aspects enhanced by synchronous sound to the detriment of the aesthetic elements of the image rings true, Saab also highlighted the particular visual qualities of her interviewees and her surroundings, wherever she was filming. In *Iraq: War in Kurdistan*, Saab shows how the people are victim to a corrupt leadership, whichever side of the conflict they find themselves on. She shows both how the central Iraqi government is not living up to its promises made in 1970 regarding autonomy for the Kurdish north, as well as the split within the Kurdish resistance, into those loyal to Mustafa Barzani and those more pragmatic about their immediate future. At the same time, she also calls out the Kurdish leadership for its collusion with Iran and the American imperialists and concludes that 'there is a difference between support for Kurdish demands and support for the Kurdish people. Supporting the Kurdish people does not mean supporting the Kurdish democratic party or its election.' The clarity with which Saab illustrates this highly complex political imbalance is reflected in what is on the screen. The level of personal involvement in her documentaries is clear not only from the way in which she herself physically features on screen as interviewer, but also from a sense of ideological alignment. Iraqi Kurdistan is filmed entirely under grey clouds and endless rain – a reflection of the grey areas and the complete lack of black and white clarity. Travelling shots of the empty streets in Sulaymaniyah, Kirkuk, Mosul and Irbil show the abandoned shops and houses, empty cities that held promise, which is shown in the contrasting archival footage of public celebrations on 11 March 1970, when the autonomy plan was announced at the end of the first Iraqi–Kurdish war. The failure of this plan and the Iraqi insistence on the Arabisation of the oil-rich Kurdish territories resulted in the 1974 conflict under scrutiny in the present film. Now, Iraq's constant presence in a region that was declared autonomous causes increasing concern.

Using maps of the regions to illustrate the territorial disputes as well as travelling shots of the diverse landscapes she criss-crosses in Iraq and Kurdistan, Saab indexically shows the diverse nature of the people inhabiting the landscape. Juxtaposing images of tanks and soldiers by the side of the roads with empty, static combine harvesters in the fields, Saab's allegiances are clear. She explains that national and regional borders are the result of human interventions in shaping the identities of the people living there. Most importantly, these borders need to be crossed in order to – literally – get all sides of the story. As such, she furtively crosses the border into the contested areas of Kurdistan, in her white Volkswagen Beetle (which also appears in some of her Lebanese films), in order to document the Iraqi army's mistreatment of the Kurdish people.

However, she was kidnapped by Iraqi soldiers and subsequently released with the aid of the French embassy (Rouxel 2015: 39). While the potential sensationalism of this border-crossing and the repercussions is entirely avoided, the footage of the border-crossing act in her Beetle did make it into the film, to clarify Saab's ethical and ideological concerns and priorities, on the side of those treated unfairly by their powerful leaders.

This unfair treatment of those victim to leaders interested only in power and wealth is also at the basis of *The Sahara is Not for Sale* (1977). Once again, Saab was one of the first (female) journalists to visit the Sahrawi Arab Democratic Republic. She built close trust relationships with her subjects in order to disentangle the complex political reality behind the sensationalist headlines. As an independent journalist, Saab was able to gain both support from the Moroccan government and funding from Algerian television. While audiences in 2020 have access to a huge corpus of films made about the Sahrawis and the Polisario Front, in the 1970s this film was a rare document of a volatile conflict. Activist filmmaking from or about Western Sahara often focuses on cultural creativity, exemplified by songs, poetry, and the kind of grass-roots democratic movements built on oral and deeply intellectual thinking. Saab was a front runner of this trend.

The issue of the ownership of Western Sahara continues to be a highly politicised and sensitive one for the surrounding countries. While there is no space here to go into much detail, it is important to note that Moroccan filmmakers have consistently treated this conflict with a response emphasising the liberation from the previous Spanish occupation. In contrast, Algeria seemingly has a more supportive stance towards Western Sahara, but this is mostly due to its ongoing conflict with Morocco. Saab illustrates that, although the Sahara is a desert, the territory is very rich in natural resources – an incentive for the surrounding countries to have a vested interest. Although she was given a permit by the Moroccan government to make the film on the basis of her submitted plans, the film and filmmaker were both banned from Morocco. This level of confidence about being on the side of the revolutionaries is rooted in a relationship of trust achieved through acts of modesty and solidarity. Her awareness of her position as a filmmaker and the inclusion of herself in the frame show courage and commitment to what we now know was a revolution that did not fail as such, but that has gone on for so long now that it is very often forgotten, a consequence used by the Moroccan government as a tactic in its continued oppression of the Sahrawis.

Saab's camera draws close-up attention to several kinds of 'common' people, most admiringly women and children, and students. The women and children are important from the very beginning of the film, because – although this is a film about war and conflict – they are the true inhabitants of the desert, who have a right to their space and their way of life in this beautiful place. As such, they embody the central motive for the conflict. Interviews to the camera as well as recorded songs, poetry and performances shape their testimonies, both of violence and suffering and of a real sense of pride in the righteousness of the rebellion. As such, they represent the lived experience of the Sahrawi people.

Likewise, Saab offers the camera and her microphone to the combatant soldiers from all sides of this conflict. The camera lingers on the guerrilla fighters' faces as they passionately debate or amuse themselves in times of quiet boredom. She films them at rest, in the sand dunes, smiling at the camera and relaxing between fights. She talks with them on and off camera, showing her solidarity with and understanding of their cause. In contrast, through clever juxtapositions in the montage, Saab explicitly shows how commanders of the Moroccan army misunderstand their opponents and the desert landscape.

Figure 9.1 Polisario fighters relaxing in the desert and talking to Saab

While the Moroccan soldiers vastly outnumber the Polisario fighters, and their weapons are much more sophisticated, they are not winning this conflict.

The filmmaker also engages with leaders of all sides, either in original or in archival footage: Hassan II (king of Morocco, 1961–99), Houari Boumediene (Algeria's president, 1976–8), Mokhtar Ould Daddah (president of Mauritania, 1960–78) and Mohamed Abdelaziz (secretary general of the Polisario Front, 1976–2016). While all are certainly charismatic, Saab juxtaposes their speeches with one another in such a way that their propagandistic discourse is foregrounded and shown to be out of touch with reality in the desert.

It is the desert that becomes the most dynamic interlocutor for Saab, as it is the space and time between speeches and battles that reveal the absurdity of the David and Goliath-style conflict. The abundance of space and time comes to inhabit the question of whether there is any sense in the power of leaders that are out of touch with the people. Indeed, as much as Saab is a filmmaker focused on a multifaceted conflict, at no point in the film is there any evidence of fighting, until the very end. She shows a battle between Moroccans and the Polisario Front at Zarouat, in a yellow haze of sand and smoke, half-obscuring a bloody attempt to dislodge a bullet from the torso of a fighter. A close-up of this body in pain after such a long, slow and detailed depiction of landscapes and discourses brings home the filmmaker's commitment to the fighters opposed to the barbarity committed by those with a lot less knowledge of and insight into the intellectual spirit of the people.

In a central act of solidarity, Saab calls out the visual propaganda put on by the governor of Samara, a Morocco-controlled town in the Sahrawi desert:

> For the camera, the governor has set the scene for a calm city and a happy population that poses no political problems for the new leader. Men were ordered to regroup in the square, while the women had put on their finest attire, a sign of prosperity, and simulated the gestures of daily life, for 13 hours, while it is 37 degrees and a sandstorm looms.

And it is with the sound of wind and a sandstorm that Saab ends the film, immediately after showing the fallen soldier's pain. She loves the desert and the endless landscapes, and uses the timeless emptiness of the desert landscape to illustrate the senseless violence, which becomes ever more painful as we get the benefit of hindsight, and realise that this conflict is still ongoing.

Similarly, in *Iran: Utopia on the Move* (1980), landscapes and borders are as important as people. Just as she provides extremely high-angle shots of the crowds at rallies and speeches in Tehran, Saab includes silent travelling shots of the roads she takes beyond the city. As she travels throughout Iran, Saab highlights the humanity of the places she visits, interviewing people from all strata of society. Stubbornly interested in those areas she is technically not allowed to visit, she films previous centres of learning and universities as they are transformed into centres where mullahs are trained. She shows the extreme poverty of people living in the volatile border area with Afghanistan (which is occupied by the Soviet Union at that time), Iran's Kurdish regions, and those areas in Tehran where the drug cartels are in power. As such, once again Saab does not avoid danger or conflict. She crosses borders, both physical and moral ones. The physical borders are crossed in an effort to show the international relevance of the revolutionaries and the conflicts. The crossing of moral borders is inspired by a journalistic passion for plurality and unbiased reporting on the most complex issues of the day, but also by a curiosity that is elevated by emotional commitment and 'transformed into a kind of duty of memory' (Rouxel 2015: 71).

When it comes to reporting on Iran in 1980, the main focus of the global media was on the US hostage crisis. Instead, Saab was concerned with the experience of the revolution by the people, both in the capital city and in the country. As such, filming young women and men, workers and students, politicians and farmers, and idealists as well as religious leaders, she showed not only an anti-imperialist stance but also a concern with the common people, in order to move beyond the exoticisation of Iran and of Islam, towards a considerate and humanist representation of a country undergoing quick political, religious and social changes. One example is the discussions around the points of view of several young women on wearing the veil. It was in April 1980 that it was

Figure 9.2 Young Iranian women discussing the hijab

decided in Iran that women working for the government and in official institutions would wear the hijab. Considering that the early 1980s in Iran saw the introduction of the still-contested mandatory dress code including the hijab, this film is still a document of particular social relevance. It seems especially poignant then that this image and discussion appear exactly in the middle of the film. It comes across as an issue that needs to be treated with much care and sensitivity, enfolded within the film between the layers of many other hotly debated social issues.

This careful enfoldment and sensitivity may seem uncharacteristic of a courageous feminist reporter like Saab, but it is precisely in moments like these that she reveals her very effective way of building trust relationships with her interviewees and her idealist belief in the individual's right to express herself. As a woman having grown up in the Middle East, she is acutely aware of the power of self-expression, and her own expression is certainly a part of that. Saab appears physically in most of her films, but it is perhaps in *Iran: Utopia on the Move* that her courage as a woman crossing the boundaries within patriarchal societies is most visible. Her body language, which displays an intense interest in her interviewees by turning towards them – even towards those she is clearly not in favour of – stands out, as she is a small, slender woman with short hair surrounded by tall, bearded men in long robes. This small stature may have become a tool in gaining the trust of her interlocutors. Indeed, linking the visual directly to the aural was a particular characteristic of Saab's early films, in the exploration of indexical relationships between what she shows and what she says, using the words 'here' and 'there' in the voice-over. This relationship between the visual and the spoken is experimented with through ironic juxtapositions.

FEMINIST VOICE-OVER AND SOUND

In documentary studies, there tends to be a strong opposition to the authority of the voice-over narrator. Stella Bruzzi argues that the voice-over should not be burdened with a bad reputation. Different uses and experiments with extra-diegetic voice-over narration in documentaries show the potential of non-didactic, democratic voices. Self-reflexivity and subjectivity by the director aid the voice-over in its effectiveness and in the possibilities it offers to be critical and interpretative. In addition, Bruzzi shows, the voice-over in documentaries from the 1970s offers a distinctive feminist perspective: there are 'various ways in which the classic voice-over has been modified and its rules transgressed through the insertion of ironic detachment between image and sound, the reflexive treatment of the narration tradition and the subversion of the archetypal solid male narrator' (Bruzzi 2006: 47).

A common reaction to voice-over is that narration suppresses the voices of the subjects. In fact, in Saab's films the voice-over establishes a complex relationship between the director and her subjects – it becomes a subversive tool. A woman's voice is confrontational, especially in the 1970s and 1980s TV universe, where male voice-overs dominate (in many ways, they still do in 2020). A clear, well-spoken female narrator subverts patriarchal authority. The very presence of a female voice tampers with the unity and the universality of the male voice-over: it creates a critical distance (Bruzzi 2006: 64). In the 1970s and 1980s, women's journalistic documentary voices gained prominence, and signalled a lack that had until then been masked by the maleness of the voice. Indeed, it is crucial to look at the many ways in which the voice is used in Saab's documentaries and in reportage, especially because of her fluent blend of documentary narration with journalistic exposition, essayistic argumentation and often also elements of dramatic literature or epic poetry.

Iraq: War in Kurdistan starts with a male announcer or newsreader framing the topic of the reportage in the wider (French) context: 'On the Baghdad side, they see things differently. The Kurds are rebels supported by imperialism.' Saab immediately undercuts this with a much more balanced introduction to the complexity of the problem in Kurdistan, showing the poetic precision in her knowledge: 'Sulaymaniyah, the historic capital of Kurdistan, today emptied of its inhabitants who joined Barzani, suffered a siege. Kirkuk, Mosul, and Irbil – the main border town in a region that has been declared autonomous – are surrounded by Iraqi divisions.' However, rather than painstakingly 'explaining' everything through the voice-over, Saab chooses to interview a wide variety of people, in order to maintain a sense of journalistic objectivity but also, most importantly, to find the voice of the people. In *Iraq: War in Kurdistan*, she records injustice and violence, because she is more interested in humanity. She wishes to hear everyone's voice, 'in order to denounce the unfair' (Rouxel 2015: 45). Through interviews with people from all sides of the conflict, Saab gets to the heart of the problem. Interviews with men in the streets, both Arabs and Kurds, result in clarity about what is at stake: not just independence or autonomy, but ownership of the oil-rich regions and cities. Where initially Saab asks the questions (edited out of the interviews) and adds longer critical reflections in voice-over, later on in the film the interviewer's questions are left in, as they are short and quick, and get short and quick answers, revealing the heart of the issue. At first, the statements are about understanding and respect: 'the Kurds are our brothers' and 'we respect their revolution and everything else. [. . .] If they accept autonomy we will live in good harmony. [. . .] We are part of the same house, of the same people.' However, the interview soon leads to statements that contradict those assertions: 'We will never give them the city of Kirkuk, it is an Arab city.' And so, as soon as the conversation turns to oil, the Arab interviewees become less accommodating and less fraternal: 'We will never accept. Arab oil to the Arabs. Why would we give them oil? It's our oil.' Hence, in the voice-over that reflects on this interview, Saab says:

> This is precisely where the shoe pinches. Supporters of Barzani demand the equitable sharing of the fabulous petroleum resources which the regions of Kirkuk, Khanaqin and Sinjar contain. For Baghdad, there can be no question. According to the Baathist leaders this would provide the Kurds with the financial means to proclaim full independence.

The combination of official interviews and casual conversations on the streets with a voice-over that reflects critically on what she witnesses and hears is what makes Saab's docu-journalism different from other TV reportages. Her in-depth knowledge of the region, her courage and insistence on getting all sides of the story, and her ability to gain the trust of those she speaks with, give her a unique insight into the complexity of the conflicts she covers. As Saab makes this film for French TV but knows and speaks Arabic fluently, she is both an outsider and an insider in Iraq. This offers her the opportunity to get close to the people she speaks to, in order to get to the underlying truth(s).

Three years later, and after her experience of the Lebanese war, her approach to the conflict between Moroccans and Sahrawis is similar. Interviews with politicians are complemented by on-the-ground conversations with students, women and soldiers. In voice-over, Saab explains the different sides of the conflict and the historical realities of the people living in the desert. This is complemented by testimonies, among others by a former student, an intellectual guerrilla fighter who engages with the historical argument Morocco uses about identity, belonging and nationality:

> I was a combatant, first against Spanish imperialism, then against Mauritanian colonialism and now against Moroccan repression. [. . .] Moroccans push the argument that they have historical relationships with us, that we were Moroccans before. But this is only an idea that suits Moroccan expansionism. The Sahrawis have been here since before Hassan II's grandfathers were around, and before Mauritania even existed.

Saab asserts that the film was made 'for those living in the Sahara, not in the name of this or that state' (Rouxel 2015: 69). Highlighting the opposing claims gives Saab the ability to reveal her own scepticism about the truth(s) at play in this conflict. Saab feels at home with students and treasures conversations with them in all the films under discussion in this chapter. However, once again it is when she moves away from interviews with intellectuals and soldiers, or with politicians and their official discourse, in order to speak to the people, that Saab finds the core of the conflict: while on the surface it may seem that the film is occupied with an empty space, a desert, the Sahrawis' territory is in fact very rich in natural resources such as ore deposits, phosphates and fish reserves in the Atlantic Ocean. The Sahrawis demand ownership of those resources, appropriated by the occupiers. Therefore, 'the film intervened in order to revive their words and their right to speak out, asserting their presence in front of an audience' (Rouxel 2015: 69). Saab was making a film for a people who want to liberate themselves and who do not (as the Moroccan occupation continues in 2020) give in to political pressure from an occupier that denies them their freedom.

An acute sense of anti-imperialism and political awareness is also at the heart of *Iran: Utopia on the Move*. The voice-over reflects on the importance of the students and intellectual movements' contributions to the revolution, while the street interviews result in discussions about sensitive issues relevant to the Iranian population. Indeed, the film opens with quotes from Ali Chariaati, one of the ideologues of the Iranian Revolution, thus encapsulating a sense of both hope and disillusionment:

> The revolutions of the last three centuries were inspired by philosophers.
> The philosopher understands things and speaks to the mind.
> The prophet feels things and speaks to the heart.
> – Ali Chariaati, 1933

Seeing the sea of people bowing down in prayer on the squares and in the streets of Tehran gives a sense of the scale of the revolution. The disappointment is all the more acute, as Saab reflects on the function of a revolution and her belief in intellectualism: 'Whatever the outcome of the revolution, living a revolution is to live a love story.' This optimism is balanced with her reflection that 'Everyone is a little philosophical today in Tehran.' The sense of regret about the revolution going in the wrong direction is clear, not only from the reflective voice-over caught between hope and regret: 'in Tehran everything happens in the street, as if after a long imprisonment at home, the Iranians burst out from an over-constrained frustration', but also from the interviews with the people in the streets: 'They proclaim that this is the revolution of the dispossessed, for it is they who overthrew the Shah. But since then, nothing has changed, and we no longer agree.' The painful realisation that there is no longer an alignment between the people and those in power impacts on the further development of the film.

Jocelyne Saab arrived in Tehran only two years after the revolution. Her analysis of the situation emphasises the side of the disenfranchised, those that had most to gain and thus also most to lose in the revolution. She shows that Tehran is a fast-growing metropolis, where the promises made by mullahs on TV about relocating the poor to the most prosperous city resulted in 'five hundred thousand new arrivals in Tehran's shanties', where two million people already suffered from overcrowding. Handing the microphone to everyone, including very poor city dwellers, she includes the people's voices: women working the red-light district, who 'have been sent for retraining in needlework classes', and, controversially, heroin addicts.

But she moves beyond the Tehran-specific situation. She explains that she is in Iran discussing a revolution in the context of the Cold War. There is, on the one hand, the increasing influence of Russia in Afghanistan, on the border with Iran. On the other hand, the revolution is the result of anti-Shah and anti-American sentiments. What arrived instead was a religious state, increasingly oppressive, as Khomeini declared an Islamic Republic. In order to put the disillusionment in perspective, Saab offers an internationalist perspective of the revolution, offering insight into the situation not only of those in Tehran city centre, but also in cities like Qom, and on the borders with the Kurdish regions and Afghanistan. As she returns to the Kurdish regions, where the developments of the revolution complicate the already volatile issue of Kurdish autonomy, she shows that both external, internal and complex transnational Kurdish issues determine the conflict. This leads to the assertion that what is the heart of the problem, once again, is the financial inequalities between social classes, and more specifically between those who have access to the oil-rich areas in Iran and those who do not. And *that* is a direct consequence of external superpowers and their interests in and dependence on Iran's oil reserves. As such, the film reveals that beneath the philosophical, political and religious layers are diverse real-life oppressed people who have been deceived by a co-opted revolution and leaders unwilling to compromise for the good of the people.

CONCLUSION

I have shown that all three of Saab's early films under consideration in this chapter reveal her commitment to and belief in the power of revolutionary movements. Even though the three revolutions discussed in the films fail to a certain extent, Saab retains a sense of optimism, loyalty and respect for those fighting against imperialism. In essence, Saab brings a humanism and solidarity to the people both in her early reportages, her independently made documentaries, and her films funded by and made for a foreign TV channel. Whichever stage a revolution is at, 'living a revolution is to live a love story', a love story enacted by all sides of a conflict that has a bearing on global solidarity and international relationships. Different from Western journalism on the Middle East where the focus, as Edward Said has shown, is so singularly on Islam, in Saab's films there is an opportunity to learn to understand one another, wherever in the world we are and in whatever circumstances or times we are watching her films. Hindsight tells us that her understanding of the situations she analysed was almost prophetic, but in effect it is her tenderness with the visual representation of spaces and her compassionate effort to listen to people's statements that promote an international understanding of and solidarity with the liberation of every person and every place she turns her camera to.

NOTES

1. The freedom of the press had been tested and confirmed in 1971, in a widely mediatised scandal referred to as the publication of the Pentagon Papers in *The New York Times* and *Washington Post*. The newspapers won a Supreme Court battle against the government to publish the contents of the Pentagon Papers without risk of further government censorship.
2. The edit of the film that is known now, and which I used for this chapter, is different from the broadcast on Japanese TV. Saab handed the footage to NHK, who created their own version, while she made the film we know independently.

BIBLIOGRAPHY

Aguayo, Angela J. (2006), 'Activist Filmmaking', in Ian Aitken (ed.), *Encyclopedia of the Documentary Film: Volume I*, London: Routledge, pp. 6–9.

Boudon, Raymond (1979), 'The 1970s in France: A Period of Student Retreat', *Higher Education*, 8, 669–81 <https://doi.org/10.1007/BF00215989> (last accessed).

Bruzzi, Stella (2006), *New Documentary: A Critical Introduction*, London: Routledge.

Hottell, Ruth and Janis Pallister (2011), *Noteworthy Francophone Women Directors: A Sequel*, Lanham, MD: Lexington Books.

Rouxel, Mathilde (2015), *Jocelyne Saab: la mémoire indomptée*, Beirut: Éditions Dar An-Nahar.

Said, Edward [1981] (1997), *Covering Islam: How the Media and the Experts Determine How We See the Rest of the World*, London: Vintage.

Scriven, Michael and Emily Roberts (eds) (2003), *Group Identities on French and British Television*, New York: Berghahn Books.

Van de Peer, Stefanie (2017), *Negotiating Dissidence: The Pioneering Women of Arab Documentary*, Edinburgh: Edinburgh University Press.

CHAPTER 10

'Talking about something much larger': Script Development and Creating Metaphor and Meaning in Jocelyne Saab's *Dunia*

Margaret McVeigh

> I received many threats of death already when I was shooting [*Dunia*] and when the film went out [. . .] because [. . .] the image was strong and I think they didn't realise that it was strong because I didn't tackle the problem in a direct way [. . .] but in fact I was talking about something much larger.
>
> – Jocelyne Saab (2016)[1]

This chapter considers the narrative and aesthetic decisions Franco-Lebanese writer/director, war correspondent and documentary filmmaker, Jocelyne Saab, faced in writing and making the feature film *Dunia* (*Kiss Me Not on the Eyes*) (2005). *Dunia* was a 'reinvention' and exploration of many real issues facing Arab women at the time. The film took writer/director Saab seven years to make, was filmed in Egypt and produced in Egypt, France, Libya and Morocco, and was selected in competition for the Sundance Film Festival. Confronted with stark issues facing women in then-contemporary Egypt, documentary filmmaker Saab, no longer able to consider making stories with real images about Middle Eastern conflicts, turned to the fictional world of feature film. In *Dunia*, Saab deploys metaphor and experimental narrative techniques to blend truth and reality in creating the story of Dunia, a young Egyptian student of dance and poetry whose journey to 'free her body and dance with her soul' resonates with cultural meaning.

This chapter, based on my 2016 interview with Saab at her Paris home, takes an interdisciplinary approach to consider the creative decisions she faced while researching, writing, directing and co-producing *Dunia*. In discussing Saab's multifaceted creative process of developing story, metaphor and meaning for the screen, it melds the established field of Screen Studies and the emerging fields of Script Development and Screenwriting (Batty et al. 2017). To this end, it includes a textual and structural analysis of the narrative and aesthetics of *Dunia*, to consider how Saab adapts reality in her work, including her creative treatment of reality, via metaphor, as one way of exploring the 'truth.'

Craig Batty et al. (2017) interrogate the definition of script development, noting that different perspectives have emerged in defining what script development in the field of screenwriting means. In particular, they note that

> The literature on script development – whether explicit in its focus or implicitly referring to its practice – is wide, varied and multi-faceted; and [. . .] arguably fragile and still emerging, in the sense that it does not collectively purport to add incremental, scholarly insights into the practice, and/or does not necessarily refer to other literature. (Batty et al. 2017: 240)

They highlight the facet of script development that involves the individual and their negotiations with self in the development of ideas. They note that considerations of plot, character, story, theme and emotional impact are paramount, but they also question 'what development actually entails: which aspects of screenwriting craft beyond plot are used in/by/for script development, and what tools are used to achieve this?' (Batty et al. 2017: 228). However, they do not mention the importance and power of metaphor as a tool in the creation of story and meaning. This chapter contributes to the field of Screen Studies and Screenwriting by considering metaphor as it contributes to and underlines the script development considerations of 'plot, character, story, theme and emotional impact'. I investigate the script development decisions Jocelyne Saab makes around metaphor in *Dunia* and analyse the tools inspired by metaphor in cinematic storytelling including *mise-en-scène*, colour, character movement and cinematography.

JOCELYNE SAAB, WRITER/DIRECTOR: CREATING MEANING FOR THE SCREEN

Jocelyne Saab is widely recognised as one of the most important political and artistic filmmakers of the Arab world. She worked as a newsreader, journalist, war reporter, filmmaker and artist photographer and lived between Beirut, Paris and Cairo. She was a news reporter during the civil war in Lebanon and then a war reporter in the Middle East and Iran. As Stefanie Van de Peer notes, this 'really brought her to the front line, in the field, as a war reporter. The physical risks she took to report on the war in Lebanon made her the first woman in the Arab world to bear witness to the horrors of war around the globe' (2017: 55). Saab directed more than thirty documentaries, as well as four feature films screened worldwide. She filmed in Lebanon, Egypt, Iran, Syria, Kurdistan, Western Sahara and Vietnam. Saab was the main writer for all of her films, with the exception of *Beirut, Never Again* (1976), *Letter From Beirut* (1978), *A Suspended Life* (1985, which was written by Gérard Brach) and *One Dollar a Day* (2015, to which Etel Adnan contributed).

In our interview, one of the first questions I asked her was why – after almost thirty years as a reporter and documentary maker – she switched from documentary filmmaking to feature filmmaking. Her answer was simple. Saab said she moved to fiction filmmaking when she found 'the truth was too hard to tell'. It is the way in which Saab renders this truth via the tools of cinematic storytelling – specifically metaphor – that I explore in this chapter. Elsewhere, I have discussed the ways we may conceive of truth and reality in documentary and fiction film (McVeigh 2018: 70). In this chapter, I reaffirm my discussion of the parameters around truth and reality as presented in fiction film as a means of illustrating the 'truth' explored by cinematic storytelling as noted by Macedonian writer/director Milcho Manchevski:

> Every piece of art has to contain the truth. But, not the truth of what happened. It needs to contain the truth of how things are – and the difference between what happened and how things are, is what is important. Is it the events (and by extension the facts) of what happened, or is it the emotional and conceptual underpinning and thus understanding of how things are? (Manchevski 2012: 70)

In order to explore how this 'truth' is presented in *Dunia*, we may consider the ways in which both filmmakers and audiences create, experience and comprehend a cinematic narrative via tools such as metaphor, with 'a certain trust and faith in the artwork to render, not the factual truth, per se, but the importantly shared experience of trusting what artist and audience can see and feel together: what feels real becomes the world we inhabit' (McVeigh 2018: 70).

In screenwriting theory, the central precept of metaphor is a compelling tool used to create narrative, as well as the formal elements of form, style and visual sub-text. Screenwriter Paul Schrader (*Taxi Driver*, Martin Scorsese, 1976) emphasises the power of metaphor in underscoring narrative, thematics and aesthetics in discussing the central metaphor of *Taxi Driver*:

> To be a writer you should first examine and confront your own most pressing personal problems. When you find your problem, then come up with a metaphor for it. A metaphor is something that stands in place of the problem. It is not like the problem; it is another variation of the problem. Where this first came to me was with *Taxi Driver*; the

problem was loneliness. The metaphor was the taxicab. The steel gaudy coffin floating through the sewers of New York, an iron box with a man inside who looked like he was in the middle of society, but in fact he was completely alone. The metaphor of the cab is so powerful that it can be treated as a metaphor for loneliness. (Schrader quoted in McGrath and MacDermott 2003: 14)

In what follows, I consider how Saab uses metaphor to represent or allude to reality and in doing so uncover the 'truths' that she wishes to create for audiences via the use of metaphor to represent 'the problem' in the cinematic narrative of *Dunia* (2005).

METAPHOR AND MAKING MEANING IN *DUNIA*

On her inspirations for *Dunia*, Saab has noted that she had always wanted to make a feature film in Egypt, as Egyptian neorealist films were the films she saw growing up. However, she was also aware she wanted to make a film that distanced her from the reality of war as investigated in her documentary work, and instead make a fiction film that commented on social reality. On this creative dichotomy, Saab says:

> At the same time there was a dream of making a feature film because I was raised with Egyptian films on TV. There was only the beginning of television when I was a child and there were only black and white Egyptian films [. . .] which were in a way imitating Italian Neo-Realism films. So, it was a dream for me to go there and make a feature. But [. . .] we were still in war and that changes you. You don't have enough distance to talk about everything. That's my story.

In her exploration of the lingering emotional and sexual atrocities committed against young women in contemporary Arab society in *Dunia*, Saab has taken elements of the neorealist style so inspirational to her and developed a feature film with a complex and experimental narrative structure, aligned with an equally complex use of metaphor.

In her discussion of Saab's documentary work, Van de Peer notes that 'Saab's earliest experimental documentaries [. . .] deal with an enfolded historiography as they are unfolding their matryoshka doll structure, and reveal a preoccupation with the future' (2017: 82). In *Dunia* the multi-strand narrative structure is akin to that of a tapestry with independent coloured strands of metaphor and meaning. The film has at its core Dunia's quest to be both an educated woman and the daughter of her mother, a belly dancer, a profession regarded by her culture as akin to being a prostitute. One of the key themes of the film is Dunia's driven struggle to find her identity reflected in how she searches to express desire through both her study of dance and in classic Arabic poetry, which becomes the subject of her Master's thesis. While on one level these key narrative threads appear to trace the reality of her quest to become a dancer and be a student, the potential pathways that her life could take are actually reflected in her relationship with the adults in her life – her teacher, her husband and the women in her family.

'Dunia' is the Arab word for 'life' or 'world' and is the name of the main character, Dunia, played by Egyptian actress Hanan Turk (Mostafa 2015: 46). Dunia is a student of belly dance and Sufi poetry and she aspires to be a professional dancer like her famous mother. *Dunia* is also an exploration of real issues facing Arab women in life. We follow Dunia's journey via a number of elliptical and interweaving narrative strands. All of these strands reflect the constraints of a traditional past, the promise of a liberated future and the failure of the institutions of society to liberate women. While Saab's stylistic and narrative work in *Dunia* displays vestiges of a neorealist style, it is deeply symbolic and metaphorical in its treatment of reality. For example, in the film's intimate roving camera work we are made party to the conversations between Dunia and her female friends and relatives as she weaves her way through life in streets, public institutions and apartments in Cairo. Ironically, while Dunia studies the poetry of desire, she suffers emotional and psychological distress from being circumcised as a little girl – a fact which is only alluded to very late on in the narrative. As Van de Peer notes, Saab's work is connected by the overarching theme of 'identity-formation and coming-of-age experiences of urban women' (2017: 57). *Dunia* exposes perhaps the most confrontational of the realities facing Egyptian women today: that of female genital mutilation.

The opening images of *Dunia* introduce the stylistic and symbolic elements that will be embroidered into the narrative tapestry of the film. In handheld documentary-realist style we first follow Dunia as she weaves through the busy streets of Cairo. We also see the unexpected but delightful image of a bright red, heart-shaped taxi light atop a taxi. We learn later that this taxi belongs to Dunia's seemingly independent working-woman friend, Inayate. We then see the title sequence.

In a previous piece (2018) I have considered *Dunia*'s elliptical narrative structure and proposed that each narrative strand was metaphorically reflective of a potential pathway that Dunia's life could take. I categorised four main strands: the quest for freedom of expression through Sufi poetry and learning, the quest for love via traditional marriage or true partnership, the quest for freedom of expression/self-identity through dance, and lastly, the pathways of tradition as reflected by the roles of women in her life (McVeigh 2018: 75).

Figure 10.1 The heart atop the taxi

In this chapter, I revisit this earlier discussion to build on observations regarding narrative as metaphor, in order to consider Saab's use of metaphor as developed via *mise-en-scène* and cinematography, including symbolism, colour and movement, which drive both plot and theme.

POETRY AS METAPHOR

The narrative strand that deals with Dunia's quest to educate herself is deeply significant. It provides the overarching metaphor of Dunia's desire to escape tradition in her search for liberation through a mastery of Arabic poetry and dance. To this end Saab presents key story moments in her elliptical use of narrative, rather than a complex plot-driven narrative. These include the moments in which we learn that Dr Bashir, Dunia's mentor in poetry, wishes to publish an uncensored version of the erotic Arabian story of Scheherazade's *Thousand and One Nights*. In one of the tragedies of the film we later learn he is blinded by unknown authorities in retaliation for this insurrection. As I have observed elsewhere,

> It is in Dunia's encounters with Bechir [Bashir] that much of the multifaceted and beautiful symbolism and metaphor around seeing reality and divining the truth is developed. Dunia's thesis is on Love in Arab Poetry, ironically the poetry of erotic desire, which women like Dunia (whom we later learn has been circumcised) are unable to experience sexually. (McVeigh 2018: 76)

As I also noted previously, in an early sequence of the film Dunia listens to a lecture given by Dr Bashir and is heckled for noting that 'A kiss is forbidden.' In a later sequence Dunia tells Bashir, who is now blinded, that 'when I first met you, I was scared of your eyes'. The ability to see the real with one's eyes is the ultimate irony, and acts as a metaphor for the ability to see the truth, because now this learned man literally cannot see. One of the pivotal scenes in the crystallisation of Saab's use of this metaphor is in the music shop scene where Dunia and Bashir meet. In the background we hear the soundtrack to the song 'Kiss Me Not on the Eyes' by the famous Egyptian singer and composer, Mohammed Abdel Wahab, who was noted for his passionate love songs (Mostafa 2015: 46). This song, 'Kiss Me Not on the Eyes', also became the title for the film when it was released in English. It is in this scene that the lines of the song become deeply metaphorical. In Dunia's relationship with Bashir, we see what her life could be like, as he opens her eyes to the honesty and acceptance of real love. This is particularly evident in the scene where Dunia and Bashir sing together: 'Kiss me not on the eyes / A kiss on the eyes means parting / Leave our goodbyes without kisses / Leave me hope.' Dunia says to Bashir, 'Our songs speak only of sad tears and suffering' and Bashir says in response, 'This is what I wanted to tell you. We are afraid of love and of pleasure, we steal them. But you can't dissociate pleasure from Arabic literature.' As Saab noted in our interview, the themes of *Dunia* – including the desire to experience pleasure and self-actualisation – are emblematic of what she as a director had hoped for a modern Arab woman: 'She had better things to do than marriage, [. . .] why hide behind the veil of traditions to get her freedom?'

RELATIONSHIPS AS METAPHOR

Saab's sustained use of the metaphor of seeing, as developed in Dunia's relationship with Dr Bashir, and her use of the metaphor of desire, as developed in Dunia's quest to study the poetry of desire, is masterful and pivotal to the overall narrative and meaning of *Dunia*. The importance of this metaphor as a way of showing how young Arab women like Dunia can escape the strictures of practices like female circumcision is also highlighted in Saab's use of metaphor in Dunia's relationship with her boyfriend and husband, Mamdouh. One of the key themes of the film is Dunia's desire to find her identity reflected in the ways in which she searches to express her own desire. The film portrays her struggles to come to terms with her physical desires, sensations and movements through dance, through the memory of her late mother, as well as through the idea of pleasure and sexual desire as expressed in classic Arabic poetry.

However, in the development of Dunia's relationship with Mamdouh, we can see how the patriarchal strictures and impositions placed on women in society thwart a woman's ability to be herself and claim her identity. Dunia is able to express her personality and have an equal footing in the relationship when she and Mamdouh are only girlfriend and boyfriend. During this period of their relationship, when he pushes her for intimacy, she resists him and the potential compromise of her reputation. Eventually she gives in to his proposal of marriage and we see a happy Dunia marry in a beautiful white wedding dress. It is interesting to note that scenes of Dunia and Mamdouh in their bedroom were challenging to film, as in Egyptian films male and female actors are not permitted to touch. However, once Dunia and Mamdouh are married, she is no longer free to be herself and have an equal footing in the relationship. This is particularly evident as we see her facing the attempts of her husband to control her in the marriage by demanding that, for example, she put her hair up and stop learning to dance.

Perhaps more pertinent to the metaphorical power of the image is the research Saab did and the inspiration she found in reality for the pivotal scene where Dunia declares her need to have independent thought and for her husband not to be privy to what she is thinking. Dunia confronts Mamdouh with who she is and why she needs to be herself in one of the most compelling scenes of the film. She says the dreaded words, 'We have to talk', and continues: 'You want my body, take it. But I can't kiss you. From here to there it's mine alone. I'll look for pleasure in there. My head is my kingdom. I won't share it. Anybody can fill this bed. But here. No.'

Figure 10.2 *Dunia*, 'From here to there it's mine'

In discussing the inspiration for this scene, Saab notes its basis in reality. In her research for the film, she conducted many interviews with young female Beaux Arts students whom she felt may have been more liberal in discussing their approach to contemporary sexual reality. However, she said she was still shocked by what she learned, in particular when she learnt of how the girls were sexually 'broken upside down' and how men still did not know how to treat them as modern women. One girl in particular, who had been circumcised and had boyfriends, stood out. Saab told me:

> The girl was speaking on a more private level [. . .] she was having boyfriends, she'd hidden, she was living normally her sexuality [. . .] so we met [. . .] and she talked to me much more frankly about her life. She said 'I had a relationship with a boy and he didn't understand what my feelings were and I explained to him that this was mine' and she did this gesture. I thought my God I've got my scene at the moment she did that! (Jocelyne frames the space between the top of her head and her chin with her hands as does Dunia in the movie scene.)

In her script development of *Dunia* it is evident that Saab's documentary-style research and background as a reporter strongly inform the fictional elements of her film, which in turn inform the development of metaphor and meaning in, for example, this scene where character gesture is as important as dialogue.

COLOUR AS METAPHOR

I have proposed that in the film the potential pathways that Dunia's life could take are represented in the lives of Dunia's seemingly liberated taxi driver friend Inayat, Inayat's traditional mother and daughter Yasmine, who in her youth represents the promise of a liberated future, as well as her female professor, Arwa. The tragic irony of the film is that despite living in this household of women, in the film's climatic scene, the grandmother circumcises her own granddaughter, Yasmine.

Saab's use of colour and carefully orchestrated colour palette as metaphorically underlining Dunia's relationships with these women in her life is one of the striking features of *Dunia*. It underlines the truths and themes she is developing across all the narrative strands. The colour red is set up from the start as a significant metaphor. As noted earlier, we first see Dunia's friend Inayat, an outspoken taxi driver with a red heart as the light on the top of her taxi. Dunia is always dressed in red, the colour of desire, passion and love. Saab also notes that Dunia was dressed in red because 'She was determined [. . .] She is in red because she has already been genitally mutilated. Red is the colour of blood, red is the colour of desire. There are many meanings for the colour of red.' Dunia's female friends and family are dressed in colours that symbolise their status as females in Egyptian life. Through this use of colour, they also metaphorically represent the potential pathways through which Dunia could live out her life. Saab notes:

> The popular woman was green. Green is the colour of the country. Of Islam. Life. Of hope. She is hope, she was going to be protecting her daughter. The intellectual was in blue. It was a soft colour to say she thinks. That she has been saved from mutilation? The sensual woman is black.

The colour red is also inspiration in the closing scenes of the film, where Dunia appears to be liberated: she is dancing dream-like on a plateau with the city behind her. As Anny Gaul notes, 'The film achieves its resolution not with a relationship or on a stage, but in a performance through which Dunia finally embodies the ideas she has struggled with, unties her mother's scarf from her wrist and sends it to the wind' (2011: 5).

One of the most visceral uses of the colour red as metaphor can be seen in the pivotal circumcision scene, only obliquely referred to in the narrative. Early in the film we witness, from the point of view of Dunia – who is a sort of voyeur to the action – the first conversation between Inayat and her mother, about having Yasmine's clitoris cut. Next, we witness, again from Dunia's perspective, the grandmother preparing Yasmine for the circumcision. She is bathing the girl whilst advising her that 'it's just a small wound. To be clean. You'll be a real woman. Be respectable. What do you say?' In the final sequence of this narrative strand, during the actual circumcision, Dunia is witness to Yasmine being hunched in a reflection of the exact position Dunia assumed at the start of the film, when she declared she has not seen her body. The grandmother advises: 'Come on, my pretty. What are you afraid of? We are about to remove a small good for nothing piece of skin so you grow up to be beautiful.' It is ironic, 'it seems no matter what Dunia is doing to liberate herself, the reality is that the tradition of female mutilation continues a generation later' (McVeigh 2018: 80). Again, in stark neorealist style, we are confronted with the razor used to perform the circumcision and the red blood that is the result of the operation. As if we were Dunia, we hear Yasmine's tortured screams as the operation is performed on the kitchen table.

Dunia has been unable to change the relentless course of tradition. She confronts Inayat and Yasmine's grandmother with the truth: 'You've done it. Made her just like you. You think you are protecting her, but you put her out [. . .] You wanted to make her a lady but, in the end, you butchered her.' Saab does not dwell on the scene. But the final image of the film is prose text, noting the stark facts of genital mutilation of young girls in Egypt: 'According to Amnesty International and the UNDP, 97% of Egyptian women are genitally mutilated.'

Ultimately, Saab's inclusion of the circumcision scene was, as she notes, 'born of her desire to expose a confronting truth in Egyptian society. This, in turn, grew out of her documentary work and her desire to make films about women in society as a reflection of elements of herself' (McVeigh 2018: 81). She said:

> I was always giving attention to women as if it were my own image reflected in a mirror [. . .] I decided it was enough to talk about war and I was at a moment of my life I should speak about gender. And, in fact, reality, as I felt in my own country that I couldn't, even in my family, express myself as I wished. And there was a sort of mental excision and I needed a subject to write this. (Saab in McVeigh 2018: 81)

However, while the exposure of the startling facts and truth around female genital mutilation is a part of the film, it is not the focus of the film. Saab notes:

> The drama is built from within the psychology of these young circumcised women [. . .] It is a disturbed sexuality. The whole movie is a projection of what we can be because it shows an image of a young woman who chose herself, and who could be free. This is what they didn't tolerate in the movie.

For Saab, 'This was the truth of the film – Saab's observation in Dunia's resolution to be herself and to confront tradition in order to free herself' (McVeigh 2018: 82).

DANCE AS METAPHOR

Dance as a driver of narrative and dance as the creation of meaning via metaphor is set up from the very beginning of the film. In this narrative strand, we first see Dunia at a dance competition where she attempts to dance like her dead mother. She is confronted by the judges and assumes a foetal sitting position in response. This is a pose Yasmine will also assume as she tries to resist circumcision later in the movie. Dunia wraps her hands around her knees and declares that she has never seen her body, as women are not allowed mirrors in her society. Saab said that Dunia is the 'story of a girl who buys a mirror to watch herself. She needed to see her body.'

Perhaps the most aesthetically beautiful and metaphorically constructed scenes of the film are those of the actual dance sequences where we see Dunia learning the art of Sufi dance from her dance master. He continually challenges Dunia to express her body and free herself. Saab discusses the way in which she developed the dance narrative in tandem with the ideas she wished to explore. The intricacy of the way in which Saab created a hybrid of the classical-traditional dance mastered by Dunia, the daughter of a famous belly dancer, is based on the in-depth research by Saab the documentary filmmaker but also on her ability to create a fictional story that comments on life as it is via the metaphor of the dance. In our interview she said:

> I studied dancers and then we had to construct Dunia, because dancing was kind of a 'bad' thing for women. I had to work on codes. I had to invent an Arab dancing style that was related to classical dance, because classical dance is accepted by the bourgeoisie [. . .] I had to invent a dance located between oriental dance, Sufi dance and classical dance, [. . .] so as to upgrade dancing. I did not want people to say that my hero, Dunia, was a belly dancing girl in a pejorative way. So, there were a lot of things to work on. You have to be from the region to understand. This is very interesting, because that is what makes the film so rich, if you know about all these details. Why is she studying Sufism? Because Sufism liberates the body. It allows you to pass through your body.

In the closing scenes of the film, the colour red, associated so closely with Dunia's state of mind and her preoccupations, and the style of dancing she has mastered to express herself, come together. It is a dream-like sequence, where Dunia is dancing on a plateau with a panoramic view of the city of Cairo behind her. This dance is the one that expresses her sense of liberation. As noted earlier, she releases her mother's scarf from her wrist and throws it to the

Figure 10.3 *Dunia*: the final dance

wind. The closing song reverberates with poetic hope: 'You are Dunia. You are the world. You are Dunia. You are life.'

Saab notes of Dunia's liberation in the film:

> You see, when you get into gender problems – and for women the gender problems are deep – the way to treat them, it took me seven years, it was long and hard [. . .] but Dunia is a sort of turning point film in the Arab world. Nobody treated a subject like this and went as far [. . .] It's the first film that talks so clearly about a young woman without treating the cliché image of the relation with the man [. . .] Here the woman is totally liberated, and this had to come from a liberated filmmaker and that is why it took me such a long time.

Although Saab explored and exposed many truths in her film via her intricate use of metaphor, the reality of the treatment of women in Egypt she was exposing was shocking. She notes, in our interview:

> I wasn't conscious of the impact I was going to have with images in trying to shape the image of a young woman who is just trying to find herself, to decide what she wants to be. She wants to become a dancer, after all it's just natural. But this was a bad thing in the country because her doing Arab dancing is like saying she is a whore [. . .] I was shaping in my idea the image of a young free modern Arab woman. Then when the film went out and the culmination of the film was the scene of the genital mutilation [. . .] I took a huge problem, which had been there for 4,000 years, and talked about it very easily and even showed the scene of genital mutilation in a very smooth way, not in a pornographic way, nor to show shock. This made them crazy and the whole society was against me. I received many death threats when I was shooting and when the film went out, because the image was strong. I think they didn't realise that it was strong because I didn't tackle the problem in a direct way, it was like climax and it's as though I had delivered a family secret hidden for so many years.

'TALKING ABOUT SOMETHING MUCH LARGER'

In Saab's discussion of the reception of *Dunia*, she demonstrated her ability to create both the poetic and the philosophical through a masterful ability to use metaphor. Van de Peer's observation of Saab's documentary work, of its 'non-linear structure, poetic voice and the trust she places in her audience when it comes to understanding the experimental representation' (Van de Peer 2017: 59), can also be applied to her fiction work in *Dunia*.

In the field of screenwriting, one of the most complex elements in developing a script for a poetic visual story is the ability to create metaphor to deploy and inform the language of cinema – narrative and image via cinematography, *mise-en-scène*, editing and sound – with a masterful hand. *Dunia* and Saab's opus stand testament to her work as one of cinema's great unsung poets. Through the subtle and clever writing, and specifically, as I have shown here, the complex interweaving of several metaphors in this film, Saab does not only talk about the details of poetry, relationships, dance and colour, but about 'something much larger': the universal metaphysical and physical experiences of growing up and finding freedom as a woman in the Arab world.

I conclude with a comment from Jocelyne, as she expressed herself in our interview. She shows how her fictional work is grounded in the reality of what she proposes to explore via metaphor:

> For me, coming from documentary, you must observe reality very well, because from this reality you will invent new things. This is cinema – to invent a new language. Everyone is an entity and has to express themselves in the most authentic way and not be afraid of stories you have to tell.

In her brave and relentless metaphorical and literal work in *Dunia*, Saab has managed to expose the concrete and contemporary realities of life for women in the Arab world that for many may still go unobserved. In her life and her art, she was not afraid to face and uncover age-old truths.

NOTE

1. All original quotes in this chapter come from an interview I conducted with the filmmaker in Paris, 4 September 2016. The aim of the interview was to discuss her fiction film *Dunia* for the Griffith Film School course, Asia Pacific Film Online developed and taught by Jocelyne's good friend and colleague, Dr Anne Demy-Geroe, who introduced me to Jocelyne. Thank you, Anne.

BIBLIOGRAPHY

Batty, Craig, Stayci Taylor, Louise Sawtell and Bridget Conor (2017), 'Script Development: Defining the Field', *Journal of Screenwriting*, 8: 3, 225–47.
Gaul, Anny (2011), 'From Dance to Transcendence', *Jadaliyya*, 13 June, <http://www.jadaliyya.com/Details/24084/From-Dance-to-Transcendence> (last accessed 4 December 2020).
McGrath, Declan and Felim MacDermott (2003), *Screencraft: Screenwriting*, Mies: RotoVision.
McVeigh, Margaret (2018), 'When the Truth Becomes Too Hard to Tell. Jocelyne Saab & Dunia (2005)', in Davinia Thornley (ed.), *True Event Adaptation: Scripting Real Lives*, London: Palgrave Macmillan, pp. 67–86.

Manchevski, Milcho (2012), *Truth and Fiction: Notes on (Exceptional) Faith in Art*, New York: Punctum Books.
Mostafa, Dalia Said (2015), 'Jocelyne Saab: A Lifetime Journey in Search of Freedom and Beauty (Lebanon)', in Josef Gugler (ed.), *Ten Arab Filmmakers: Political Dissent and Social Critique*, Bloomington: Indiana University Press, pp. 34–50.
Saab, Jocelyne (2017), 'Dunia: Director's Note', <http://www.jocelynesaab.com/dunia/EN/JocelyneSaab.html> (last accessed 4 July 2017).
Van de Peer, Stefanie (2017), 'Jocelyne Saab: Artistic-Journalistic Documentaries in Lebanese Times of War', in Stefanie Van de Peer, *Negotiating Dissidence: The Pioneering Women of Arab Documentary*, Edinburgh: Edinburgh University Press, pp. 28–55.

CHAPTER 11

The Feminist Cinema of Jocelyne Saab: Women's Relationships and the Philosophy of Dance in Four Fiction Feature Films

Maram Soboh

Working as one of the first young, female Arab war correspondents in countries like Iraq, Libya and Kurdistan, among others (Brenez 2016), impacted and enriched the personality of Lebanese director Jocelyne Saab. All her experiences from the beginning of her journalistic career contributed significantly to the formation of both her humanitarian and artistic sides. They also gave Saab the incentive to break with the traditions of her own bourgeois class and its conservative mindset in order to live her life freely and outside the constraints of tradition and conservatism.

Her journalistic work exposed Saab to hugely complex humanitarian issues, and she engaged with interviewees on a humanistic level, regardless of their identity, affiliations or race. Indeed, she lived alongside her subjects, and experienced their intense moments of fear, panic and hopelessness. Throughout these rich and varied experiences, Saab became especially interested in the suffering of women, and the particularities of their worlds. I want to argue here that this realisation was a major turning point for her, both psychologically and intellectually. She fearlessly and passionately covered in her work women's painful realities, and foregrounded how women were robbed of their freedom and independence, and became victims of oppression and socio-economic, political, religious and cultural restrictions.

When she was twenty-two years old, Saab worked for national Lebanese radio, where her programme about pop music was entitled *Les Marsupilamis ont les yeux bleus* (*The Marsupilamis Have Blue Eyes*) (Brenez 2016). The programme was suspended because Saab violated the station's rules. These rebellious characteristics of her personality and work accompanied her and indeed grew stronger when she picked up the camera. As an Arab woman herself, observing and experiencing the Arab world and its many iterations, she knew what women face at the hands of Arab men, their social and familial constraints, and she was aware of the constant persecution of their rights: the physical and verbal violence women endure through forced marriages and bullying, and the elimination of their intimate sexual pleasures through female genital mutilation. As such, the issues dealt with by Arab women became central to Saab's own identity as well as the concerns she raised in her films. Even in some of her hardest-hitting documentaries and reportages, she never lost sight of this particular priority. For example, in her 1973 interview of Muammar al-Gaddafi in Libya, Saab includes questions about his vision for Arab women (Al-Mashhad 2017).

In this chapter, I dive deeper into the representation of women and feminism in Saab's four feature-length fiction films, *A Suspended Life* (1985), *Once Upon a Time, Beirut: Story of a Star* (1994), *Dunia* (*Kiss Me Not on the Eyes*, 2005) and *What's Going On?* (2009). I look at the representation of women and the relationships between women in these films, and compare these with the relationships between women and men in her films. I will do this through an in-depth analysis of the personalities and depictions of the women, as well as through a close reading of Saab's cinematography. I then engage with Saab's philosophy of dance, and how she uses dance to free the Arab woman from restrictions. This leads to a description of the particular type of feminism Saab subscribed to through her films.

It is clear how her deep cultural awareness, and the audacity with which she raised controversies, earned Saab both severe criticism and high praise. One well-known example is the way in which her most famous film, *Dunia*, which is set in Egypt, was met with protests from 80 million Egyptians (Habechian 2019). These reactions on the extreme ends of the spectrum are also illustrated in the prizes she won and the name she managed to make for herself in the film world. She won numerous awards for her documentaries, and some of her fiction features did exceptionally well throughout the world: *A Suspended Life*, for example, was screened at the Director's Fortnight of the Cannes Film Festival in 1985 (Démy-Geroe 2019), while she received distinctions for *Dunia* at global film festivals, including Carthage and Sundance.

STRONG AND FREE HEROINES

Arab film critic Ibrahim Al-Arees says about Saab: 'From this creator [. . .] we will simply discover that her firm world is a feminine world with distinction' (2018: 17). Saab wrote most of her films' characters by herself. She wrote the first draft of the script of *A Suspended Life* in 1981, before giving it to the famous French scriptwriter Gérard Brach (Farid 2016: 78–9). In 2008 she asked the Lebanese poet Joumana Haddad to collaborate with her on the script of her last feature film, *What's Going On?*.

A Suspended Life (1985) is the first fiction film Saab wrote in her career. It is the story of Samar (Hala Bassam), a teenage girl who has just arrived in Beirut with her family from the south of Lebanon after the bombing of their house by the Israeli army, which occupied southern Lebanon after 1978. She makes a friend in these horrible conditions, and all around them is destruction. With her family Samar lives as a refugee in the southern suburbs of Beirut and, as Saab said, she is lively, energetic and strong: 'She is an incredible and strong girl from a war generation, which always amazes me and I can never understand it and I might envy her on how she is' (El-Cinema n.d.a). Samar brings water to her family at the shelter and looks for bricks in the suburban houses, helping her father in his endeavour to build a house and deal with the loss of their house, which was destroyed by the war. She has a happy spirit and spends most of her time in the company of her friends, dancing and singing Egyptian film songs.

In *Once Upon a Time, Beirut: Story of a Star* (1994), Yasmine (Michele Tyan) and Leila (Myrna Maakaron) are two young girls at the age of twenty, film lovers, who dance and laugh a lot. They live in a Beirut destroyed by the Lebanese civil war, and want to get to know the beauty of their city from before the cataclysm. They go to Mr Farouk, who is known to be the greatest cinephile in the city and owns many Arabic and foreign language films, such as *Al-Hob Al-Kabeer* (*The Great Love*, 1968) by Egyptian director Henry Barakat. The film was shot in Beirut, which was then considered the Paris of the Middle East. Throughout the film, which highlights the central presence and beauty of Beirut in Arab cinema, Yasmine and Leila's story weaves in and out of the fragments of cinema history projected onto the screen by Mr Farouk. The magical element emphasises the girls' youth, and their high spirits are shown through their dancing and singing as they discover the rich past of their destroyed city.

In 2005 Egyptian star Hanan Turk gave shape to Dunia in Saab's eponymous and most famous fiction feature. Saab wrote Dunia as a very smart but complex and multifaceted character. Dunia (whose name means 'the world') represents a large segment of women in the Arab world. As such, she is a woman who suffers and struggles with the traditions and customs of a closed society. Dunia is from Luxor and she is twenty-three years old. Her father fell in love with her mother, famous dancer Asmaa, but her parents separated shortly after she was born. Her quest to understand life takes Dunia from Luxor to Cairo to become a student. She lives in a neighbourhood where conservative beliefs dictate that women's bodies should be covered in modest ways. Dunia wears a veil in public and takes off her shoes when going up the stairs in her building late at night, wary of what the other residents might think or say about her, especially as her reputation also depends on that of her mother, whose profession as a dancer gives people the impression she was a prostitute. While she prepares her Master's thesis, Dunia participates in a dance competition, discovering her physical and emotional inheritance from her mother. The topic of her study is the concept of love in Arabic poetry. Like the majority of Egyptian girls, Dunia is circumcised, and through dance and poetry she discovers how the trauma of that experience has had an effect on her body and soul. She marries Mamdouh but does not feel any sexual pleasure. She reads about love and orgasm in Arabic poetry but is unable to experience either. The combination of dance and poetry helps her to experience the longings of her soul, her spirit and her body.

Lastly, in *What's Going On?* (2009), Saab tells the story of Khouloud (Khouloud Yassine), who is actually a character in a novel written by the fictional author Jalal Khoury, also a character in the film. Khoury is the son of a tailor and writes his novels on pieces of cloth that are cut as if they will be stitched together. Khouloud is a dancer, and she has a heart condition. She also works as a waitress at a restaurant and sleeps on the roof of one of the buildings. She does not talk much, is observed from a designated distance and speaks to the imagination, as she is produced by it. Anyone who wants to win her heart must understand her through reading the book that is being written by her.

It becomes clear then, that the combination of literature and love, and the importance of dance are central to Saab's fictional work. These art forms and concepts are also in large part very personal to Saab. Like Saab, her heroines are strong and do not accept the limits or the curtailment of freedom inherent in their realities. They are courageous, adventurous and long for their freedom.

Figure 11.1 Khouloud wakes up in the book about her life

WOMEN'S RELATIONSHIPS

Perhaps more than the personalities of these female protagonists, it is especially telling to contextualise the young women in their immediate environments, and the manner in which they respond to events and circumstances. It is, in fact, the inner world of these women that brings them together. For example, at the start of *A Suspended Life*, Samar shows how she trusts her female friend to such an extent that she feels able to confide in her about losing her virginity. She also tells her friend about her mother's wish to let Samar undergo reconstructive surgery, to make her a virgin again. This topic is severely taboo in the Arab world. But in Jocelyne's film, Samar's friend keeps the secret and does not tell anyone. In spite of their young age, the girls both understand that Samar would suffer the consequences of an affected family honour. Likewise, in *Once Upon a Time, Beirut*, Leila and Yasmine are very close young female friends. They bond over their love of cinema. They share their goal in the film, of getting to know their beloved Beirut the way it was before the war.

In *Dunia*, it is likewise the friendship between Dunia and the other women in the film that is most interesting. Firstly, Inayate is one of Dunia's closest friends. At work people call her 'Asta Inayate', or 'Mr Inayate'. She is an independent woman and a taxi driver, but in Arab society driving a taxi is very much a man's occupation. Inayate behaves spontaneously and freely, both in the internal world of the flat and outside on the Cairo roads, where she eats,

Figure 11.2 Leila and Yasmine dress up like actresses

laughs and smokes a hookah. She is also the one who agreed on Dunia's marriage to Mamdouh, because Inayate wants the younger woman to be happy and marry for love. As Inayate represents love, she has put a heart logo on the taxi she drives around. She also believes in sensual and sexual expressions of love, and approves of Dunia's marriage in that playful way, stating that sex is important in a relationship. Inayate has been married before and is experienced, and she teaches Dunia about how to please her husband sexually. Inayate suggests that Dunia dance nude in front of Mamdouh to entice him. These intimate conversations and the advice that Inayate gives Dunia indicate a very close trust relationship, which leads to a deep friendship.

Dunia is also very close to Yasmine, Inayate's daughter. She is a teenager whose body is going through hormonal changes. Their friendship is based on their love of dancing. There is even a sensual admiration from Dunia towards Yasmine. Dunia's gaze, emphasised through looks and touch, follows Yasmine closely as she dances and takes a bath. There is also a level of envy in Dunia's admiration for Yasmine. She wants her younger friend to live freely and to enjoy her body. However, one of the most difficult scenes in this film is when, without Inayate's consent, Yasmine's grandmother enacts illegal female circumcision on the girl. Dunia witnesses this violent act secretly, and it causes traumatic recall for Dunia, as her own circumcision is now the cause of her failure to enjoy her marital relations and to develop as a dancer. During the circumcision scene, witnessed through Dunia's gaze, we experience her anger and sadness when Yasmine screams in pain.

After that happens, Dunia flees with Yasmine to a hotel, where they meet Jamalat, the hotel manager. Dunia and Yasmine find refuge and safety at the hotel, more so than at the Egyptian hospitals where circumcision operations are performed legally. Dunia arrives at the hotel with an unconscious Yasmine. At first, Jamalat hesitates about letting them stay, but her solidarity with the younger women wins the inner struggle between her caring side and her professional role. On the one hand she is afraid that their presence might cause her and the hotel serious trouble, but on the other hand she understands what Egyptian conservatism is like for young girls and she starts to feel sympathy with them. As Dunia and Yasmine start to feel safer there, they stay for some time.

Dunia also cultivates a specific relationship with her thesis supervisor, Dr Arwa. Arwa is single and open minded, she is willing to be open-minded and flexible as a scholar. She urges her students to think independently and meditate. She is portrayed with a short-cropped haircut, which makes her stand out in Egyptian cinema, where short hair is associated with men. When Dunia announces to Arwa that she is getting married to Mamdouh, Arwa's remark is 'The most important thing is to be free.' Her honesty about this indicates that there are no barriers in their friendship, as does Dunia's knowledge and Arwa's openness about the man she has an intimate relationship with. Later, Dunia takes refuge with Arwa, as she wants to learn about sensuality and seduction in order to spice up her marriage with Mamdouh, because Arwa has that experience. The teacher tells Dunia not to have sex with Mamdouh unless it is her own desire to do so, something that is clearly an emancipatory statement unusual in Arab cinema.

We could say that the older women in Dunia's life represent a motherly presence, a maternal role that Dunia lacks so tragically. The film also problematises the role of the mother figure in the performance of circumcision. In spite of this complex motherhood, Dunia does maintain a special relationship with her mother Asmaa, even if she is physically absent. The only direct reference to Asmaa is in the black and white photographs hanging on the back wall of the hall where Dunia is being trained. As Asmaa was such an admired star of dance, she lives on through her daughter that way. Indeed, she is always present in her daughter through her art, as an inspiration and in the scarf that Dunia wears on her wrist. Although Dunia does not have a clear memory of her mother and seeks other mother figures in the older women around her, it is through self-expression and physical discovery that Dunia experiences the love for her mother.

Apart from these Dunia-centred relationships, there are also female friendships between other women in the film. One interesting example is the relationship between Arwa and Inayate. Dunia brings them together in a friendship based on mutual openness, but the friendship between the two women develops independently from Dunia. There is even a suggestion of sensual (and even sexual) attraction between the two women, which is highlighted in a sequence in the taxi, where Arwa and Inayate are positioned very closely together, and meaningful looks are exchanged between them as Dunia sits in the back seat and observes these looks clearly. Likewise, in the scene in Inayate's kitchen, where Dunia is being instructed in the sensuous ways of lovemaking, this meaningful look of mutual attraction is exchanged under Dunia's gaze.

Next to these very constructive female friendships, the relationships between women in Saab's films can also be destructive. In *A Suspended Life*, for example, the relationship between Samar and her mother is quite confrontational. On the surface, Samar's mother constantly gives her orders to do different kinds of tasks inside the shelter. If we look on a deeper level, her mother is actually trying to hide or overcompensate for Samar's non-conventional girlhood. Samar has lost her virginity, and her mother fears that her father will kill both of them, as in Lebanese society at the time, a girl's honour was everything, according to the popular saying: 'Honour is like a matchstick, you can ignite it one time only.' Accordingly, her mother forces Samar to undergo reconstructive surgery, in order to save the family's honour and find Samar a husband.

A similar relationship of domination linked to gendered traditions and the dominant gaze of a conservative society is staged in *Dunia* between Yasmine and her paternal grandmother, Um Antar. Yasmine's grandmother is from the generation adhering to customs and traditions. She constantly reprimands

Yasmine because she dances at home and on the street. As she is a teenager now, and she has started to develop a bust that shows through her clothes, her grandmother does not approve of the friendship between Dunia and Yasmine, as she notices how Dunia touches Yasmine's waist. In order to contain her granddaughter, and perhaps also to not see Yasmine follow in Dunia's free footsteps, she decides to circumcise her, apparently to protect her and safeguard her dignity and as per Egyptian customs.

Likewise, Um Antar also does not approve of the physical relationship between Inayate and her husband (Um Antar's son), and she controls the household and imposes decisions on Inayate's family by interfering in their private matters. Dunia recognises this controlling behaviour as that of her own paternal grandmother, who represents the majority of the Egyptian population, whose attitude towards the art of dancing is negative. Dancing is seen as a dishonourable profession or pastime, and the dancer is seen as a prostitute who reveals her body. She wants Dunia to forget her mother primarily because she was a dancer who, in her eyes, brought dishonour to their families.

RELATIONSHIPS BETWEEN WOMEN AND MEN

In Saab's fiction features, the male protagonists mostly respect and even encourage the development of women's freedom. They serve the narrative in the women's quests for their individual goals. But in setting her films in the conservative contexts of Middle Eastern cities, Saab also allows space for the complexities inherent in love relationships. For example, in *A Suspended Life*, Samar and Kareem are brought together by war. Kareen is a painter and calligrapher. He is affected by the war, which thwarted him and left a deep sadness inside of him. He lives in a large mansion in the southern suburb of Beirut. He does not join the fighters, who in fact target and enter his house during his absence. Kareem and Samar's many meetings lead to her falling in love with him, as she needs someone by her side during this difficult period of her life in which she struggles not only with the changing nature of her own teenage body but also with the ravages of war on her city, her surroundings, her family and her identity. Kareem is the only male available to fulfil her desire.

In *Once Upon a Time, Beirut*, Mr Farouk represents the living memory of pre-war Beirut. He has collected hundreds of films and has archived them at the old cinema where he lives. It is his role to accompany two young girls, in search of their identities and their past, in their quest to discover the reality of a past Beirut. He helps Leila and Yasmine to navigate their way through these films, in order that they can gain insight into the history they have in common with the generation that destroyed their city. He helps them to discover the past they have never known.

In *Dunia*, Dunia's relationship with her husband Mamdouh is highly complex, as are many relationships between men and women in Saab's fiction films. While Mamdouh initially seems genuinely in love with Dunia, he becomes increasingly selfish and controlling once they are married. As such, he represents a large cohort of young Arab men who believe that they have to be central to their wives' lives, and that they in fact own their women's bodies. Although Mamdouh and Dunia marry for love, when they make love, he fails to understand her physical needs and wonders why she does not react to his sexual advances. He finds her sexually cold. It is when she bravely expresses unwillingness to share her mind with him, expressing her mental freedom as opposed to her physical entrapment, that a real antagonism creeps into their relationship. Mamdouh thinks the marriage allows him to control Dunia and limit her freedom. He no longer wants her to practise her dancing or participate in the competition, where people can see her body; the stigma of the dancer as prostitute remains firmly in place in Mamdouh's eyes.

When Dunia is introduced to Sufi thinker Bashir (Mohamed Mounir) by her thesis supervisor, Dr Arwa, her world changes. Bashir is to help her in developing her thesis on the concept of love in Arabic poetry. Bashir is attacked by extremists and he loses his sight, because they presumed that he had published porn in the form of his book entitled *One Thousand and One Nights*. At the start of the film, his relationship with Dunia remains superficial, but it grows into a friendship based on mutual respect, and later also into a relationship rooted in desire. As a mentor, Bashir frees Dunia's mind from reactionary ideas and beliefs, and helps her to know the meaning of love, the art of communicating with her soul and spirit. He also frees her physically, when their relationship becomes one of a shared desire evoked by the harmony between their bodies and minds. In contrast with the fraught relationship with her husband Mamdouh, Dunia does permit Bashir to touch her head, the area which she would not allow Mamdouh to touch. Bashir summarises their relationship by saying, 'I give you like you gave me.' This same type of physical and emotional mentorship is reflected in Dunia's relationship with her choreographer, who was also her mother's choreographer a long time ago. She seeks him out specifically to train for the competition she is participating in. When Dunia feels unable to dance freely because of the physical trauma of the circumcision and the sexual limitations she experiences, he trains her to belly dance like her mother. He manages to loosen up in Dunia the freedom of expression she needs to dance. He says, 'I want Dunia, the real Dunia.'

The 'real' is perhaps harder to achieve in *What's Going On?*. In this film, Khouloud is a dancer with a heart condition, sprung from the imagination of writer Jalal Khoury. Together with Lilith and Joumana Haddad, she is a character in his novel. The writer's voice and gaze are central, and observe the characters as he creates them. Khouloud wants Nasri to understand how to love her. Lilith has to lead Nasri to understand the world of women, and to be equal with her. Haddad, the prostitute who married an elderly man, left the profession, and gave Nasri insight into the old romantic love from her era. Khouloud experiences a real need for a person who understands how to love her. In the scene when Nasri wants to kiss her, she moves her face away, but when he picks her up from the airport, she is very comfortable and feels happy, as she has finally reached her goal of love. Again, like in *Dunia*, the duality of physical desire and emotional balance becomes clear through the symbolism of the woman's development through literature.

AESTHETICS AND CINEMATOGRAPHY: SAAB'S FEMINIST CINEMATIC LANGUAGE

One of Saab's strengths is her reliance on the medium shot. The medium shot is employed in most of the scenes in which female characters appear and share inner secrets. Many male directors tend to take extreme close-up shots of women's bodies, in particular in intimate scenes or during dance sequences. Saab stays further away to include groups of women and bring them together physically, also including the (female) viewer in the scene. For example, in *What's Going On?* Saab stabilises the movement of the camera at a slight – respectful – distance, that also signifies the fictional nature of Khouloud's existence, and creates a medium shot so that we can see Khouloud's entire body, dancing freely inside the frame. Likewise, in *Dunia*, there is a scene in the small kitchen that includes Dunia, Dr Arwa and Inayate. All three women are visible in the shot when Dunia asks for advice on seduction and sensuality. In these intimate moments, Saab stabilises the camera and takes a medium shot of them to enable us as viewers to see their bodies without excluding any one of them. In this shot the filmmaker succeeds in bringing the viewer into the sexual world of women, thus emancipating not only the women in the film, but also the viewers of the scene.

When Saab depends on close-up shots, for example in *A Suspended Life*, it is to get closer to the inner feelings of a character. Samar sits with her family, watching television. Again, Saab stabilises the camera for a close-up shot that shows Samar in company but alone with her thoughts about Kareem. In *Dunia*, when the three characters Dunia, Dr Arwa and Inayate are sitting together, Saab takes a close-up shot of Dunia's face when she reveals what her husband has said about her sexual performance and how he describes her as a cold person. Then the camera moves to a close-up of Dr Arwa's face, as she explains that she prevented her mother from circumcising her, and how she influenced her aunt to not let her daughter go through with the operation. Next, the camera moves to a close-up of Inayate's face as she confesses that she gave Antar an ultimatum when his mother indicated she wanted Yasmine to be circumcised. Through extreme close-ups, Saab enables the viewer to understand the women's intimate feelings, anxieties, fears, and the psychological, physical and sexual damage circumcision causes them.

The intimacies of female conversations or confessions, expressed through the medium shot and the close-up, are also central to the silences in Saab's fiction films. The filmmaker uses silence as an expressive language that explores the female characters' innermost thoughts. For example, in *What's Going On?* the female characters speak only a few words. In *A Suspended Life*, in the last scene, when Karim is killed and the children take Samar to the beach, among all the chattering of the children, Samar keeps very quiet. Likewise, in *Dunia*, when the protagonist joins Bashir at the coffee shop, he is singing while she is completely silent. With these silences, Saab is able to deliver a strong message about her female characters, by giving the viewer a space to go deep into the female mind and explore their hidden worlds.

The details that make the silences and close-ups stand out are also inherent in the background frames in Saab's films. She consistently choses to meticulously construct *mise-en-scènes* intimately related to the narratives. This can be linked to Saab's talent for and extensive experience in the field of photography. In *Dunia*, for example, she herself decorated the location of the scene in which Inayate's taxi is standing in front of a store. Once again, Saab uses a medium shot to include the mannequins in the shop window wearing underwear. The inclusion of these dolls in the shot becomes meaningful to the understanding that the film is about women and their private intimate lives. In the coffee shop scene in *Dunia*, Bashir is talking to Dunia about spirituality and mysticism as Saab stabilises her camera to take a medium shot that includes a huge wall painting of Umm Kulthum, the legendary Egyptian singer. Dunia mirrors the position of Umm Kulthum's head on the wall. Both of them belong to the same community and society. Freedom unites them. Those who know Umm Kulthum can read in this shot a reference to her song 'Give Me Back My Freedom, Release My Hands', as Dunia wants to be liberated from the customs and traditions of her society.

As well as the *mise-en-scène*, colours are central to Saab's symbolic and aesthetic attention to detail. In *Dunia*, Saab uses the colour red for the walls of Dunia's room, the walls of the hotel where Bashir resides, and for Dunia clothes (Abd al-Kareem 2017). The colour red represents passion and love, as well as harmony between the human body and life. In Egypt it specifically also symbolises destruction in the culture of the pharaohs. Saab's goal was to let Dunia achieve harmony between her body and her life. Circumcision destroyed her life and prevented her from experiencing a normal life with her lover. But in the film, Dunia does not only represent herself. She also represents 'the world', and therefore women all over the world, who are oppressed and fight for their freedom. In the Egyptian context in which the film was made, she represents all girls who were and still are suffering from the effects of circumcision on their bodies, their souls and their lives.

Saab worked hard on both technical and photographic elements in all her films. In *Dunia*, in a scene where Dunia wraps her nude body in plastic, Saab stabilises the camera at a close distance and surrounds her on the left side with a narrow frame. The camera then moves closer and closer to Dunia's body. Next, Saab takes a close-up shot of her face, so that we see her looking at her own body and then at the round mirror hanging on the wall. With all these technical and photographical layers, Saab creates huge depth in this scene. She makes us feel what Dunia feels about her nude body, lacking a connection between mind and body. She is packaging her body as if it is a piece of furniture. Similarly, in *What's Going On?* there is a scene that places Khouloud, Nasri and the author in what looks like a swimming pool. But when the cameras take a medium-long shot, the frame reveals Khouloud lying on the floor, Nasri at a distance away from her, and the writer standing between them, holding a book. In this scene Saab implies that the author's power over the book is what stands between Khouloud and Nasri, complicating the love that could potentially grow between them.

BY WAY OF CONCLUSION: SAAB'S FEMINIST PHILOSOPHY OF DANCE

In 2017 *Daif wa March*, a TV programme on France Channel 24, hosted Jocelyn Saab. The presenter said, 'She learned dancing as a child and did not continue, but it became a syndrome for her, and she took a philosophy and reflected it in her films, adding that the circular dance movement represents her life' (France 24 2017). Since her first fiction film, *A Suspended Life*, Saab has highlighted her philosophy about dancing. In the film, Samar and her young teenage friends dance freely and have fun on the debris left by the Lebanese civil war. There is also a scene where Samar is watching TV in the shelter. On the screen is dancer Naima Akef, dancing in *Tamr Hinnah* (*Tamarind*, 1957), a film by director Husain Fawzi (El-Cinema n.d.b). Dancing is one of the few pleasures available to Saab, and a way to express what lives inside her and her female characters.

In 1989 Saab filmed a documentary entitled *Les Almées, danseuses orientales* (*Bellydancers*), about young Egyptian women learning to dance, specifically belly dance. There is also a sequence of Egyptian dancer Samia Gamal, who was hugely popular during that period, as well as a sequence of dancer Dina, who is still active as a performer. The film includes archival material of other famous dancers like Naiemeh Akef and Tahia Carioca, as well as footage of a Paris-based group of women learning Middle Eastern dance, accompanied by a man. Likewise, in *Once Upon a Time, Beirut*, in the films shown by Mr Farouk for Yasmine and Leila, there is plenty of footage of Arab dancing, for example dancer Samia Gamal from the film *Sheharazade* (1946) by Egyptian director Fouad El-Jazairly (El-Cinema n.d.c).

Saab's philosophy of dance really matured with *Dunia* (Jarjoura 2019). She has a deep understanding of the world of dancing and its styles. She also knows the intricacies of the constraints put on women's bodies in the Middle East (Al-Atasi 2014). Therefore, Saab has chosen two styles of dancing to symbolise Dunia's freedom. She wants Dunia to be free from traditions and male power so that she can start to belong to herself, expressing herself through a body that experiences the sensations she had lost to circumcision. Firstly, Dunia practises belly dance, an entirely feminine dance that uses every part of a woman's body, 'from her head to her heel' (Belghiti 2012: 137). Saab wanted her audiences to move away from associating belly dance with pornography (Ketu Katrak in Hussein and Hussein 2014). Likewise, when Dunia dances for Mamdouh in their bedroom, the audience is urged to understand that dancing is a tool for self-expression, and so Dunia is not trying to provoke her husband but is expressing herself as belonging to her own body. The second style of dancing central to *Dunia* is the mystic dance (Dancing on the Edge n.d.). What Dunia learns from Bashir is Sufi mysticism, an ideology in which dancing dervishes turn and move three times anti-clockwise around the dance floor. Her choreographer trains her in this type of dance, but in the ballroom she keeps experiencing frustration due to her physical restraints and the traumatic relationship with her body. However, once Bashir and Dunia have made love, and she experiences her first orgasm, she dances joyfully and victoriously, as if she has conquered something difficult after bitter suffering.

In her last feature film, *What's Going On?*, Saab stayed true to this philosophy of dance, but this time in a new and surrealist film. For this, she sought the help of gestural dancer and pantomime actress Khouloud Yassine to play Khouloud in the film. Yassine is a master in using her body language and her facial expressions when she dances in the gardens (Dortmund Cologne International Women's Film Festival 2012). It is my contention that Saab chose this type of dancing specifically to make the viewer think and imagine what is going on inside the head of the woman. Saab has said, 'I am not asking the viewer to understand everything, but to dream for a while' (Al-Siyabi 2018). The kind of dancing used in her last fiction feature serves to let our imagination create its own world, and to perform or think through kinetic embodiment.

Through her interest in women, their bodies, minds and their self-expression through dance, Saab achieved an aesthetic of resistance to resignation. She wanted the world to become a better place, and her strong belief in humanity's potential is evident in her beautiful and strong films, which express powerful feminist statements about beauty and movement.

BIBLIOGRAPHY

abd Al-Kareem, Mohamad (2017), 'Colors for the Pharaohs', *Al-Arabiu Al-Jadid*, 25 July.
Al-Arees, Ibrahim (2018), *Film w jami῾ya fy āl-῾ālm āl῾rby. Al-qāmūs āl-naqdi li-muḫrijin* (*Film and Society in the Arab World: A Critical Dictionary of Filmmakers*), Beirut: Center of Arab Unity Studies.
Al-Atasi, A. (2014), 'The Philosophy of Dance', *Al-Quds Al-Arabi*, 21 November.
Al-Mashhad (2017), 'Juslyn ṣa῾b fy ālmašhad' ('Jocelyne Saab in Perspective'), BBC News A῾rabi, 6 July, <https://www.youtube.com/watch?v=2r0WREG0kek> (last accessed 4 December 2020).
Al-Siyabi, Bin Mohammed (2018), 'Gestural Representation or the Art of Gestural Representation', *Al Watan*.
Belghiti, Rachid (2012), 'Dance and the Colonial Body: Re-choreographing Postcolonial Theories of the Body', PhD thesis, Montreal University.
Brenez, Nicole (2016), 'Jocelyne Saab: Multiple Methods of Censorship', *Each Dawn a Censor Dies by Nicole Brenez*, 15 March, <http://lemagazine.jeudepaume.org/blogs/each-dawn-a-censor-dies-by-nicole-brenez/2016/03/15/jocelyne-saab-multiple-methods-of-censorship/> (last accessed 22 December 2020).
Dancing on the Edge (n.d.), 'Khouloud Yassine', *Dancing on the Edge: Urgent Artistic Dialogue With the Middle-East*, <https://dancingontheedge.nl/artists/khouloud-yassine> (last accessed 4 December 2020).
Démy-Geroe, Anne (2019), 'Jocelyne Saab – A Woman of Grit, a Filmmaker of Substance', *Asian Pacific Screen Awards*, 22 January, <https://www.asiapacificscreenawards.com/news-events/vale-jocelyne-saab> (last accessed 4 December 2020).
Dortmund Cologne International Women's Film Festival (2012), 'What's Going On?', <https://frauenfilmfestival.eu/index.php?id=981&L=1> (last accessed 4 December 2020).
El-Cinema (n.d.a), 'Alhabu alkabir (1968)', *El-Cinema*, <https://elcinema.com/work/1549917> (last accessed 4 December 2020).
El-Cinema (n.d.b), 'Tamuru hana (1957)', *El-Cinema*, <https://elcinema.com/work/1746298> (last accessed 4 December 2020).
El-Cinema (n.d.c), 'Shhrzad (1946)', *El-Cinema*, <https://elcinema.com/work/1008667> (last accessed 4 December 2020).
Farid, Samir (2016), *Muḫrijin āl-aflām fy āl-῾ālm āl῾rby* (*Film Directors in the Arab World*), Cairo: Dar al-hilal.
France 24 (2017), 'Juslyn ṣa῾b muḫrija w ṣaḥafya lubnānya' ('Jocelyne Saab, Lebanese Film Director and Journalist'), France 24 Arabic, 9 February, <https://www.youtube.com/watch?v=WL4mPYXeG04&feature=youtu.be> (last accessed 4 December 2020).
Habechian, Hauvick (2019), 'Juslyn ṣa῾b : muḫrija fy dawāma alšuruq' ('Jocelyne Saab, a filmmaker in the turmoil of the Middle-East'), *An-Nahar*, 7 January, <https://www.annahar.com/article/922594> (last accessed 13 October 2019).
Hussein, Iyad Muhammad and Amr Muhammad Hussein (2014), 'Sufi Dance and Symbolism of Dance Movements: Whirling a Model', *Journal of Babylon Center for Humanities Studies*, 4: 3, 73–95.
Jarjoura, Nadim (2019), 'Juslyn ṣa῾b: nihāya muġāmara āktišāf āl-film' ('Jocelyne Saab, The End of the Film Discovery Adventure'), *Al-Arabiu Al-Jadid*, 9 January.

CHAPTER 12

Exile, Gender and Empowerment in Jocelyne Saab's Films: *Gender Café* and *One Dollar a Day*

Corinne Fortier

> Was this a story about the sacred? The sacredness of human life?
> – Opening credits of *One Dollar a Day*, Jocelyne Saab, 2016

Jocelyne Saab deals with three main topics that are central in all her work: war, exile and gender. The theme of gender is also one of the central topics of six short documentaries of 4 minutes each, made in 2013 and brought together under the title *Le Café du genre* (*Gender Café*), which was commissioned by the Museum of the Civilizations of Europe and the Mediterranean (MuCEM) located in Marseille, France. This series of films deals with expressions of gender, body and oppression. In this chapter, I will focus especially on the fifth film of this series, entitled *Table de la danse et de l'orgueil*, or *The Table of Dance and Pride*, with the subtitle 'Interview with the Dancer Alexandre Paulikevitch in Beirut', a short that deals with homosexuality in the Arab world. I will also analyse Jocelyne Saab's last artistic production, entitled *One Dollar a Day* (2016). In this short art video of 6 minutes, the filmmaker observes daily life in a Syrian refugee camp in Lebanon, and especially those of women and children, dealing with anthropological issues related to gender, disaster (Glowczewski and Soucaille 2011) and survival.

As an anthropologist and film director, I will discuss and compare these two different works in an anthropological way. I hope to show that even when Jocelyne Saab delves into very different topics – a homosexual dancer on the one hand and refugees on the other – her overall concern is with the oppressed, those on the margins of society. The two films discussed in this chapter both engage on a deep level with emotional and physical pain, and even if they are different in subject matter and approach, the common element is the expression of suffering and the corporeal pain of a way of being that is non-normative.

Bringing these oppressed people into the centre of her film world, Jocelyne Saab shows her humanism and empathy with those who suffer from repression and the failure of the world to look after its people, especially those most in need of support. Nevertheless, her films also show the agency and strength in the people she puts at the centre of her screen. Ultimately, these two films are about empowerment and accountability.

THE TABLE OF DANCE AND PRIDE

Gender Café is set after the 'Arab revolution' in 2013 and portrays a number of Middle Eastern artists and researchers, specially from Egypt, Lebanon, Turkey and the Maghreb, dealing with women's realities and also with homosexuality. The first one is entitled *The Table of Walid Aouni, the Green Mad Man*. After having danced with the French choreographer Maurice Béjart, Walid Aouni became the director of the Egyptian Modern Dance Company at the Cairo Opera House, creating engaged shows dealing with the oppression of women, topics that, after the 'Egyptian revolution', force him into exile in Beirut. In this film Jocelyne Saab is particularly interested in his performance dealing with the status of women wearing the veil due to the influence of Islamist movements: since the 1970s, the hijab was promoted by the Muslim Brotherhood in Egypt, and the niqab was introduced by the Wahabites of Saudi Arabia in the 1990s (Fortier 2017a).

The second film of *Gender Café* is entitled *The Table of the Painter of the Pharaohs and the Dancers*, with Adel Siwi. Adel Siwi is an Egyptian painter who is also worried about the progress of fundamentalism in his country, which promoted the defiance of women's bodies as related to pleasure. The third film, *The Table of the Magazine on the Body*, with Joumana Haddad, is a portrait of Joumana Haddad, who created in Lebanon the feminist magazine *Jasad* (*The Body*), which was censured because it promoted the freedom of women. The fourth film, *The Table of the Golden Okra*, with Melek Ozman and Cuneyt Cebenoyan, is about a competition in Istanbul, named the Golden Okra – the word 'okra' refers locally to a vegetable looking like a little penis – organised each year by an association that promotes gender equality in Turkey, which rewards the films considered the most macho of the year. The sixth film, *The Table of Exigency*, with Wassyla Tamzali, is an interview with the Algerian feminist Wassyla Tamzali, who asserts that emancipation of women in the Arab world depends on their own control of their bodies.

In this study, I focus on the fifth film of this series, entitled *The Table of Dance and Pride*, with the subtitle 'Interview with the Dancer Alexandre Paulikevitch in Beirut'. In this 'interview', as in the others in the series, the spectator never hears the voice or sees the face of Jocelyne Saab, but only those of the subject – there is no explicit interaction between them. The filmmaker follows the protagonist, the Lebanese choreographer Alexandre Paulikevitch, when he is dancing and when he is protesting for women's rights and is preoccupied with his LGBTQI activism. Saab films him as he puts on make-up to prepare himself for a performance and cross-dresses during his performance. Saab films two of Paulikevitch's performances, as she did with Walid Aouni, the famous Egyptian choreographer in the first film of *Gender Café*. In this case, however, the performance is not public but accomplished for the purpose of the film. And through the work of Paulikevitch, the focus is less on women's oppression than on discrimination against the gay community, and its physical and emotional suffering.

Alexandre Paulikevitch dances the *baladi* dance, literally meaning 'local', and he does not call this dance a 'belly dance', most likely because of the colonial and female connotations of that term. In the Arab world, men's and women's dance is very similar. For example, it is not unusual for men to dance together during weddings or at private celebrations, tying a scarf around their pelvis to emphasise the movement of the hips (Fisher and Shay 2009). But this type of dance becomes transgressive when it is performed by a cross-dressing dancer, as is the case of Paulikevitch when he presents himself cross-dressed during his performance in Jocelyne Saab's film. At the beginning of *The Table of Dance and Pride*, Paulikevitch is looking at himself in the mirror and putting on make-up, especially kohl, a staple of make-up in the Arab world. He is transforming himself for his performance, a gesture that corresponds to a type of feminisation. And in the filmed performance, he is dancing in a red 'oriental costume' usually used by a feminine dancer.

At a performance at the Institut du Monde Arabe in 2017 in Paris, he wore a red tutu. That costume has connotations of the female ballerina, but Paulikevitch does not hide or cover the bulge of his genitals, the way a transvestite would. This can be read as conforming to the Lacanian process of masquerade, which carries echoes of Judith Butler's gender performance. I refer to the notion of 'masquerade' as it was first introduced by Joan Rivière ([1929] 1994), and which was taken on by Jacques Lacan ([1964] 1973), according to whom the masquerade refers to a certain portrayal of femininity – a notion that echoes Judith Butler's notion of 'performance' in *Gender Trouble* (1990).

As such, Alexandre Paulikevitch's dance does not constitute a sexual inversion, but rather an over-exposure of his masculine virility, as he emphasises his muscles and the visible bulge of his penis when he moves. It is not a feminine but a masculine body that appears and asserts itself by dancing as an object of desire. In an interview with *Le Monde* he explained: 'it is also a tool of gender liberation. By surfing on the codes of the feminine and the masculine, by playing with them too, we subvert them, and we get out of the gender binary. I am sure that in the future there will be a multitude of genders' (in Boisseau 2018). As such, the dancer questions the codes of gender and of the genre of dance in his performance.

The feminisation of men is forbidden by Islam, as the Qur'an provides a clear affirmation of sex difference, exemplified in the verse (92: 1–4): 'That which created the male and the female' (Arberry 1980: 595). Already in Medina, at the time of the Prophet in the seventh and eighth centuries, the classic Arabic term *mukhannath*, which means 'the effeminate', was known through a Hadith stating that Mohammed 'cursed effeminate men (*al-mukhannathin mina al-rijal*) and mannish women (*al-mutarajjilat min an-nisa*)' (Nawawy 1991: 435). The *mukhannath* also practised music, singing and dancing (El Feki 2013). The etymology of this term, *mukhannath*, refers to sweetness, curvature and languidness, qualities that were considered specific to women (Boudhiba 1979: 55). But despite its protestations, this Hadith actually provides evidence of the existence of men with effeminate behaviour. A *mukhannath* does not necessarily cross-dress, but he does demonstrate erotic movements (Lagrange 2008). As American historian Everett Rowson confirms, 'There is considerable evidence for the existence of a form of publicly recognized and institutionalized effeminacy or transvestism among males in pre-Islamic and early Islamic Arabian society' (1991: 671).

The figure of the Medinese *mukhannath* existed throughout the Persian, Ottoman and Arabic worlds (Fortier 2019a). Although this figure was referred to by a vernacular term specific to each society and historical period – with the exception of Iran, where until the nineteenth century the word *mukhannath* itself was used (Najmabadi 2005: 5) – these terms often have the triliteral Arabic root k-n-th (e.g. in the word *khuntha*, which designates the 'hermaphrodite' in Muslim jurisprudence), indicating the Arab-Persian influence of the *mukhannath* figure throughout time and space. These various figures share characteristics with the *mukhannath*, such as being beardless and practising singing and dancing. In general, facial hair is considered an immediately perceptible element that clearly demonstrates the physical differences between the sexes. The beard, and to a lesser extent the moustache (*shārab*), are the visible markers of masculinity, and of the superiority that is attributed to men. Likewise, their particular practice of singing and dancing makes them stand out as effeminate, especially in ritual ceremonies where they become objects of desire for other men (Fortier 2020). Similarly, in Jocelyne Saab's film Alexandre Paulikevitch did not appear as a hairy man, he has no beard or moustache, but he has long, feminine hair that he uses as a visual and moving element during his performance, which actually makes him look 'effeminate'.

Figure 12.1 Alexandre Paulikevitch sensually uses his hair while dancing

In *The Table of Dance and Pride*, the performance by Alexandre Paulikevitch is accompanied by some sentences spoken in Arabic over the music. In the music, we hear the words 'I'm going to fuck your sister.' As Paulikevitch explains in the film after this performance, it refers to insults that he has overheard in the streets, referring indirectly to his homosexuality. This type of insult, as I analyse it, is an indirect way of saying 'I'm going to fuck you' but the person who says it is masking his repressed homosexuality by stating that he will fuck someone's sister. Paulikevitch explains in the film that he incorporated this insult and the stigma in order to exorcise – through the dance – the violence related to homophobia. By dancing, he turns shame into pride, as indicated by the title of the film. In his performance, he shows a homosexual body that is proud to dance a feminine dance through a masculine body. Embodying that paradox, he allows himself to experience and perform on the stage, challenging international audiences, not only Lebanese ones but also those of Europe, where it is also still a taboo subject.

At the end of the film, Alexandre Paulikevitch explains that he belongs to the Lebanese association *Helem*. This Arabic word means 'hope'. *Helem* was the first LGBTQI association in the Arab world. It was established in 2004, before other similar organisations saw the light of day in the Middle East.[1] Jocelyne Saab's film shows Paulikevitch during a protest with *Helem* against women's virginity tests, which are seen as constituting a kind of rape. These virginity tests were carried out by the Egyptian police on women who were protesting in Tahrir Square in 2011. The action of the tests served to deny the women access to the public space (Fortier and Monqid 2017). In the Arab world, there is a counterpart of this female test for homosexual men. The police in Egypt and in Lebanon are allowed to conduct anal tests on men, through which they enter an egg-shaped object into the anus, in order to check its elasticity, as 'proof' of the man's practice of sodomy and of his homosexuality.

Whereas the term 'homosexuality' has been in use in the West since the nineteenth century (used either to refer to a particular sexuality, or to the attraction of a person to someone of the same sex), in the Arab-Muslim world the term only really emerged recently, in the 2000s, under the influence of international LGBTQI associations.[2] As such, the practice of naming masculine homosexuality in terms of anal intercourse is still common (Fortier 2017b). Alexandre Paulikevitch claims in the film that homosexuality remains penalised in Lebanon, to the extent that one can be imprisoned for a year for homosexuality (Art. 534 of the Penal Code). As such, he denounces the hypocrisy of his home country, when he explains that bisexuality is almost normative for men not only in Lebanon but throughout the Arab world.

In a second sequence of Alexandre Paulikevitch's performance, his whole body is bandaged like a mummy. He continues to dance despite these restraints: first with an arm, then with his shoulders, and then the torso and the abdomen, in an astonishing vertical serpentine movement. At this moment, the spectator understands that the dancer is performing not only an erotic dance but a contemporary dance. As Paulikevitch explains just after the performance, this for him represents his mutilated body in reference to the numerous wars in Lebanon. As such, his body becomes the metonym for the pain suffered not only by a gay man in the world, but by a gay man in Lebanon and in the Arab world as a whole. Being from a country ravaged by war, Paulikevitch links his pain as a gay man and a gender-defying physical dancer to the scars of his country, but also implicitly testifies to his own and his country's strength in persisting in spite of the pain and the wounds. Jocelyne Saab films Paulikevitch's performance when he shows his body in pain. At the start of the film her camera maintains a distance from this suffering body, but progressively, she comes closer as if she wants to assist him, and she comes even closer when he frees himself from his ties, thus underlining his victory. The woman filmmaker treats the body in pain not with pity but with empathy. Saab's gaze is not curious or intrusive, but it is a concerned and caring gaze; it is not a 'male gaze' (Mulvey 1975) but a 'female gaze'.

ONE DOLLAR A DAY (2016)

As in *The Table of Dance and Pride*, the main issues dealt with in Jocelyne's Saab last film *One Dollar a Day* are violence, discrimination and war, but also dignity, resistance and survival. At the start of the film, the opening credits present the context in a mix of objective narration giving information about places, dates and statistics, and in subjective narration, where Saab affirms her physical presence in the field: 'In the autumn 2015, I went to the Beqaa valley, near the Syrian Border. The war in Syria had been raging for four years. Over 500,000 people had already died. Six million people were now refugees [. . .]'. Saab has in fact devoted several films to the wars, especially the one that ravaged her country, Lebanon, for fifteen years (1975–90), the ramifications of which are still felt acutely throughout the Arab world.

Beyond the Lebanese civil war, she has also shown a consistent interest in the displaced, in refugees and in the people's struggles. She has a special interest in the Palestinians, whose struggles she discusses in three films produced around 1974: *Le Front du refus* (*The Front of Refusal*), *Les Palestiniens continuent* (*Palestinians Keep Fighting*) and *Les Femmes palestiniennes* (*Palestinian Women*). There was also a special interest in the Saharawis, depicted in her 1977 film *Le Sahara n'est pas à vendre* (*The Sahara is Not for Sale*). The making of these films did lead to incidents, including censorship by French television, the confiscation and destruction of her camera equipment, as well as violence against her, for example at the film festival in Tangier in Morocco, which she attended with her son, seventeen years after filming in the Western Sahara (Brenez 2016). The filmmaker asserts:

> I have often been ready to put myself in danger in order to create and bear witness to the great moments of history that I found myself witnessing. Nevertheless, I believe that what makes my journey so special is that I have always wanted to remain consistent and have always been ready to fight to defend what I believed in, to show and analyse this Middle East in the throes of change that fascinated me. (Saab in Rouxel 2019)

As a result, Jocelyne Saab's biography (Rouxel 2015) echoes that of the exiles, to the extent that she came to settle in Paris and in Cairo after the bombing of her house in Beirut in 1982, and filmed herself amidst the ruins of her home in *Il était une fois Beyrouth* (*Once Upon a Time, Beirut: Story of a Star*, 1994). In an interview I conducted in Paris with Jocelyne Saab in 2018, she told me she had lost all her 'souvenirs' (photos, pictures and objects of her family . . .) in the bombing of Beirut. Unlike war's destruction and erasure of memory, filming is a way to reconstruct and recreate memory. In addition, while Saab could have died in this bombing, filming her body in the middle of these ruins is also a way to affirm that unlike her house that has been destroyed, she herself is still standing, feeling more creative and combative than ever, as shown by the making of this film. By shooting *One Dollar a Day* in a Syrian refugee camp in Lebanon in 2015, for one of her last artistic productions three years before her death, Saab testifies once again about human disasters created by the successive conflicts in the Arab world, and – most importantly – about the resilience of the displaced populations. Saab believed that as a filmmaker, she could change the gaze of viewers and raise awareness of civil society; as she said, 'We cannot legislate, but we can act where they do not act, and mobilise public opinion' (in Rouxel 2019).

In *One Dollar a Day* we do not witness any men. The spectator can deduce from this absence of men on the screen that most of them died in the war in Syria. The film's opening credits remind us that in 2015, 500,000 people had already died in this war. In the film we see only women and children, and they testify to the social role of women for the survival of the group. According to the point of view given by the woman filmmaker, in this film (and unlike the patriarchal dominant ideology which affirms that men are pillars of society) Saab makes visible that women are in fact the pillars and guardians of the perpetuation of society. In this film she emphasises the empowerment of women, even in extreme and desperate circumstances. In the refugee camp, despite the disaster, women continue to manage daily life and raise the children. We are spectators of their everyday life: a woman cradles her child, children play ball games. The spectator perceives the quietness of this refugee camp.

But a shrill soundscape contrasts sharply with the ostensibly peaceful day-to-day images, pointing out that danger is imminent, and that behind this seemingly peaceful daily life hides a past of war, a war which is still present in Syria. One sentence of the opening credits confirms this meaning of the 'sound contrast' experimented with in the film: 'Over there, the overwhelming noise of fighting, here only deafening silence.' The shrill soundscape also evokes an uncertain future for the children of the refugee camp. The refugee camp appears as a *non-lieu*, a non-place, a concept coined by the French anthropologist Marc Augé (1992), who used it to express a transient space, a place with no spatial or temporal referents, where time is suspended and where there is no future.

One Dollar a Day also does not contain any words: not from the people filmed, nor from the filmmaker in voice-over. The women of the refugee camp do not complain about the disaster of their situation and do not speak at all, but they are living. They do not beg but they claim their rights and show their empowerment by holding up a document from the Office of the United Nations High Commissioner for Refugees (UNHCR) testifying that they are entitled to one dollar a day per woman and child to live off, a small sum that they do not always receive in reality, and which gives the film its title.[3] Although the direct gaze is often discouraged in documentaries, Saab films these women and children that way: they are looking frontally at the viewer and challenge him or her, awakening his or her responsibility and the fact that he or she is concerned by their dramatic situation. The document from the UNHCR, which testifies

Figure 12.2 When an advertisement billboard becomes a home

that the refugees are entitled to one dollar a day per woman and child to live off, contrasts strikingly with the huge billboards advertising jewels and other luxury items. The contrast between these two worlds comes to a head when the irony becomes tangible in the fact that the refugees' tents are made of the plastic advertising tarpaulins for Louis Vuitton bags.

The simultaneity of such paradoxical images in the same space is shocking. Jocelyne Saab takes this logic to its end and then reverses it. She takes the camera to Beirut and confronts the viewer with the contrast between the daily lives of the people in the camps on the one hand, and those in the city on the other hand. Through this contrast she establishes a juxtaposition of values and images, and thrusts the truth of inequality upon us. Beirut is a city dominated by advertising imagery, and Saab takes up the public space of these images of luxury with images of the humanitarian slogan 'How to live with one dollar a day'. As such, she opposes the consumer logic of the city with the reality of survival in the camps.

Moreover, while many might not want to be confronted with stark images of the Syrian refugees in Beqaa, Jocelyne Saab represents them in the very heart of Beirut, in an almost heroic way. As such, she succeeds in ensuring that the plight of the Syrian refugees in these camps is not forgotten by the people of central Beirut. Her black and white photographs of the children in the camps are blown up to a very large format, and are adorned with gold and bright colours, like Byzantine icons. These icons are very present in Lebanese Orthodox churches, which may have inspired Saab, who came from a Christian family.[4] Then she

EXILE, GENDER AND EMPOWERMENT 197

Figure 12.3 Sacred images of Syrian child refugees in the port of Beirut

exposes them in the middle of Beirut, suspended from cranes. It is a gesture that aims to give back to these children – whose portraits stand out against the azure sky – their majestic, sacred, angelic and iconic character, in contrast with the media images, which often portray these children as a possible danger. The term 'sacred' is used by Saab herself in one of the sentences in the opening credits of the film when she asks, 'Was this a story about the sacred?'

Through these large images, placed in central Beirut, that confront the privileged Beirutis with the harsh reality of the Syrian refugees just beyond the limits of their city, Jocelyne Saab highlights not only the presence of the refugees, but also the consumerism of the city dwellers. The installations of the humanitarian slogan and the painted photographs enable the artist to resettle the space of the camp – at least in images and words – within the city itself, in a spatial and political sense. It is hence not a question of inserting advertising images into refugee camps as permitted by cinematographic effects, but of inserting the very material of the camps, where the tents are made from billboards, into Beirut. Likewise, it is not a matter of merely inserting the slogan 'How to live with one dollar a day' or photos of children from camps on billboards in the sky of Beirut, but rather of installations made within and of the city's urban material. This film is based on artistic interventions in the core of the city, which the inhabitants of Beirut cannot ignore, and as such, it has the potential to directly impact social reality.

The strength of these installations lies in the interpenetration of two contiguous worlds that coexist: the consumerist world of Beirut, and the precarious world of the refugee camp. In its turn, the film that shows and juxtaposes these images brings together two realities that coexist without intersecting. Lebanon carefully keeps them apart, both spatially and socially. It is as if the film, and therefore its artist, confronts us with our ability to forget about what we do not see. What we do not see is 'lost in sight', in both the real and in the psychoanalytical sense – that is, it does not exist (Pontalis 1999). In Jocelyne Saab's hands, film has the immense power to show us what we cannot or do not want to see. Her art testifies to what we would like to ignore. She makes appear that which we would like to see disappear (Fortier 2019b). The cinema screen, like the migrants' tent canvas, is undoubtedly a fragile refuge, but it allows them to survive in images and can save life from indifference.

CONCLUSION: THE 'SACREDNESS OF HUMAN LIFE'

In *One Dollar a Day*, although we witness the human disasters created by the successive conflicts in the Arab world and especially in Syria, as in *The Table of Dance and Pride*, which portrays Alexandre Paulikevitch, a dancer struggling with the stigma of homosexuality in Lebanon and in the Arab world more widely, Jocelyne Saab puts emphasis on the vitality and empowerment of the people. Her films allow us to question our responsibility, our resignation or our mobilisation. Until the end of her life she worked courageously to produce films that reflect the struggles of people to control their territory as well as their own bodies.

Her films also show the struggle of people to survive, especially in her last film, where the struggle for staying alive with 'one dollar a day' for Syrian women refugees in the Lebanese camps reflects in a mise-en-abyme: Jocelyne Saab herself struggled to stay alive at that time. While filming *One Dollar a Day* she knew she was seriously ill. Like the future of the children of the camp, which is compromised, the future of Saab herself was at stake, as she explains in the opening credits of the film: 'At the time I had no idea that this would become a part of my own inexorable struggle, as my life slipped through my fingers . . . Was this a story about the sacred? The sacredness of human life?' The 'sacredness of human life' is the key concept at the heart of all Jocelyne Saab's films. Even if the films cannot save lives, they can give to the protagonists and to the filmmaker a kind of eternity, and so restore to life the sacred dimension it deserves.

NOTES

1. Such as the following movements and organisations: *Lambda Istanbul* in Turkey in 2006, *Kif Kif* in Morocco in 2008, *Bedayā* in Egypt, Iraqi LGBTQI, *Abū Nuwās* in Algeria, *Aswat* (the voice) and *Qaws* (the rainbow) in Palestine.

2. The term 'homosexual' in modern Arabic is the words *mithlī* and *mithliyya*, masculine and feminine derivatives of the word 'same', antonyms of the term 'heterosexual': *ghayrī* and *ghayriyya*, which refers to the notion of otherness. The word 'bisexual' in Arabic is also built on the notion of 'two': *thunaʾī* and *thunaʾiyya*.
3. Personal communication with Jocelyne Saab, Paris, 2018.
4. Jocelyne Saab also set up an exhibition of these photos at the French Institute in Beirut in 2017.

BIBLIOGRAPHY

Arberry, Arthur J. (trans.) (1980), *The Koran Interpreted*, London: George Allen & Unwin.
Augé, Marc (1992), *Non-lieux*, Paris: Seuil.
Boisseau, Rosita (2018), 'À l'IMA, Alexandre Paulikevitch mêle féminin et masculin', *Le Monde*, 19 April, <https://www.lemonde.fr/scenes/article/2018/04/19/a-l-ima-alexandre-paulikevitch-mele-feminin-et-masculin_5287821_1654999.html> (last accessed 7 December 2020).
Boudhiba, Abdelwahab (1979), *La Sexualité en Islam*, Paris: Presses universitaires de France.
Brenez, Nicole (2016), 'Jocelyne Saab, les voies multiples de la censure', *Jeu de Paume*, 15 March, <http://lemagazine.jeudepaume.org/blogs/each-dawn-a-censor-dies-by-nicole-brenez/2016/03/15/jocelyne-saab-les-voies-multiples-de-la-censure/> (last accessed 7 December 2020).
Butler, Judith (1990), *Gender Trouble*, New York: Routledge.
El Feki, Shereen (2013), *Sex and the Citadel: Intimate Life in a Changing Arab World*, New York: Pantheon Books.
Fisher, Jennifer and Anthony Shay (eds) (2009), *When Men Dance: Choreographing Masculinities Across Borders*, New York: Oxford University Press.
Fortier, Corinne (2017a), 'Derrière le "voile islamique", de multiples visages. Voile, harem, chevelure: identité, genre et colonialisme', in Anne Castaing and Élodie Gaden (eds), *Écrire et penser le genre en contextes postcoloniaux*, Berne: Peter Lang, pp. 233–58.
Fortier, Corinne (2017b), 'Intersexuation, transsexualité et homosexualité en pays d'islam', in Rémy Bethmont and Martine Gross (eds), *Homosexualité et traditions monothéistes: vers la fin d'un antagonisme?*, Geneva: Labor et Fides, pp. 123–37.
Fortier, Corinne (2019a), 'Sexualities: Transsexualities: Middle East, North Africa, West Africa', in Suad Joseph (ed.), *Encyclopedia of Women and Islamic Cultures* (EWIC), online, Leiden: Brill, <http://dx.doi.org/10.1163/1872-5309_ewic_COM_002185> (last accessed 7 December 2020).
Fortier, Corinne (2019b), '*Welcome!* Des réalisateurs engagés: Philippe Lioret, Fernard Melgar, et Jocelyne Saab', *Vol spécial*, *La forteresse* et *Le monde est comme ça* de Fernard Melgar, *One dollar a day* de Jocelyne Saab', in Corine Fortier (ed.), *Les Migrants, ces nouveaux héros. Quête de l'ailleurs, quête de soi, et créations filmiques, Science and Vidéo. Des écritures multimédia en sciences humaines*, 9, <http://scienceandvideo.mmsh.univ-aix.fr/numeros/9/Pages/default.aspx>(last accessed 7 December 2020).
Fortier, Corinne (2020), 'Troisième genre et transsexualité en pays d'islam', in Corinne Fortier (ed.), *Réparer les corps et les sexes*, vol. 2, *Intersexuation, transidentité, reconstruction mammaire, et surdité, Droit et cultures*, 80 <https://journals.openedition.org/droitcultures/> (last accessed 15 March 2021).
Fortier, Corinne and Safaa Monqid (2017), 'Le corps féminin en contexte arabo-musulman: entre autonomisation et domination', in Corinne Fortier and Safaa Monqid (eds), *Corps des femmes et espaces genrés arabo-musulmans*, Paris: Karthala, pp. 9–19.

Glowczewski, Barbara and Alexandre Soucaille (2011), 'Présentation', in Barbara Glowczewski and Alexandre Soucaille (eds), *Désastres, Cahiers d'anthropologie sociale*, 7, 11–22.
Lacan, Jacques [1964] (1973), *Le Séminaire. Livre XI, Les quatre concepts fondamentaux de la psychanalyse*, Paris: Seuil.
Lagrange, Frédéric (2008), *Islam d'interdits, islam de jouissances*, Paris: Téraèdre.
Mulvey, Laura (1975), 'Visual Pleasure and Narrative Cinema', *Screen*, 16: 3, 6–18.
Najmabadi, Afsaneh (2005), *Women with Mustaches and Men without Beards: Gender and Sexual Anxieties of Iranian Modernity*, Berkeley: University of California Press.
Nawawy, [Imam] (1991), *Les Jardins de la piété. Les sources de la tradition islamique*, Paris: Alif.
Pontalis, Jean-Bertrand (1999), *Perdre de vue*, Paris: Gallimard.
Rivière, Joan [1929] (1994), 'La féminité en tant que mascarade', in Marie-Christine Hamon (ed.), *Féminité mascarade. Études psychanalytiques*, Paris: Seuil, pp. 197–213.
Rouxel, Mathilde (2015), *Jocelyne Saab: la mémoire indomptée*, Beirut: Éditions Dar An-Nahar.
Rouxel, Mathilde (2019), 'Portrait de Jocelyne Saab', *Les Clefs du Moyen-Orient*, 8 January, <https://www.lesclesdumoyenorient.com/Portrait-de-Jocelyne-Saab.html> (last accessed 7 December 2020).
Rowson, Everett K. (1991), 'The Effeminate of Early Medina', *Journal of the American Oriental Society*, III: 4, 671–93.

CHAPTER 13

Twilight Reflections in Single Frames and Short Sequences

Samirah Alkassim

Jocelyne Saab was one of the most adaptive and versatile women filmmakers of her generation. This is evidenced by the creative work she produced in her later years that took her literary voice, documentary eye, and personal experience of the Lebanese wars and those of its surrounding countries, into photography, video art, and cultural curatorial practice while crossing geographic borders. This chapter will examine the works of her later years in light of their adaptive elements, particularly as the more flexible formats of video art, photography and installation allowed for greater freedom to explore issues that were of increasing concern to her: the culture wars between East and West; Arab women and Western feminism; the negative impact of increasing religiosity; and the refugee crisis resulting from regional wars. Describing herself as 'a cartographer of the human condition' (*Imaginary Postcard*, 2016), she sought to understand the world around her as it continued to change, never losing the capacity to find wonder in a single frame or visual utterance.

Beginning as a journalist in the early 1970s, Saab stepped into extraordinary opportunities, but she also took creative risks. She belonged to the second wave of Arab feminism which dealt head on with issues of visibility (Naccach 2019) and more broadly participated in a collective struggle with language, using the language of the 'Master' to enter the 'Master's house' (Trinh 1989: 85) through which she honed her creative voice. Saab used the languages associated with colonialism – French and English – in her documentary and experimental works (less so in her narrative fiction), sometimes for pragmatic reasons related to obtaining foreign funding, which she readily admitted (Mostafa 2019: 37). This may have invoked for her the 'guilt' of women who find themselves compromising certain values to attain other freedoms (Trinh 1989: 11), particularly in the absence of film funding and production infrastructures in Lebanon and the region in general, but such tactics do not diminish the radical nature of her work, which challenges hegemonic ideologies including those that pertain to representation.

Her work is unique because it is multifaceted. From the brutal realities captured in the Beirut documentary trilogy – especially *Beirut, Never Again* (1976) and *Beirut, My City* (1982) – to the experiments with image and text of her later years, a continuous thread is the importance of (and relationship to) language. But it is less a matter of the 'language of cinema' or of a specific mode of writing/filmmaking – although they are no doubt important – and more a question of who speaks and how meaning and expression emerge from language, particularly in the films that reflect on the dissolution of place and the complexity of identity during Lebanon's long war: Saab spoke from a position of being both inside and outside, as a privileged multilingual Lebanese who could move between East and West, and who lived at times in exile. In the war trilogy – *Lebanon in Turmoil* (1975), *Beirut, Never Again* (1976) and *Letter from Beirut* (1978) – she frequently laments the loss of identity and even memory, yet it is precisely her struggle to express this loss through the limitations of language that distinguishes her work. It is this movement between things, and the inevitable poetry emerging through language in the liminal spaces, specifically as they connect to her later work, that is the subject of this chapter.

At the outset, it is worth noting how often Saab collaborated with writers in her work (Etel Adnan in *Beirut, Never Again* and *Letter from Beirut*; Roger Assaf in *Beirut, My City*; Joumana Haddad in *What's Going On?*, 2009) and made reference to writers (Ali Chariaati in *Iran: Utopia on the Move*, 1980; Fouad Negm in *Egypt, The City of the Dead*, 1978; Orhan Pamuk in *Imaginary Postcard*; excerpts from several Arab and North African writers and poets in her last feature film *What's Going On?*). It is also significant that the protagonist of her last feature film is arguably a book, which an author cannot write until the contained narrative about finding love is closed, and that the protagonist of *Dunia* (*Kiss Me Not on the Eyes*, 2005) studies Arabic poetry and dance, through which she finds a form of emancipation and symbolic compensation for the loss of sexual pleasure due to her childhood excision (all the while disturbing the border between the sacred and the profane). This emphasis on writers as intellectuals with social agency, and literature as a vehicle of political and social emancipation, reinforces the importance of language in Saab's work.

ON ABJECTION

> To listen, to see like a stranger in one's own land; to fare like a foreigner across one's own language; or to maintain an intense rapport with the

means and materiality of media languages is also to learn to let go of the (masterly) 'hold' as one unbuilds and builds.
— Trinh T. Minh-ha, *When the Moon Waxes Red* (1991: 199)

We can read Saab's work as speaking and giving form to the abject, in terms of the horrors of war (the war trilogy; *Strange Games and Bridges*, 2007), marginalised people (*Children of War*, 1976; *The Sahara is Not for Sale*, 1977; *Egypt, The City of the Dead*; *One Dollar a Day* (2016)) and controversial subjects (*Dunia*; *Gender Café*, 2013). This attraction to push the envelope, to speak with and to focus on the subaltern, to reveal their situations to the world, requires and entails passage between things that appear to be sealed off from each other even within one country, crossing geographic, social, linguistic, ethnic, cultural, cinematic, sexual, generic, real and imaginary borders. This crossing of borders (and in the case of Saab, her accompanying affinity for bridges) has been theorised as a particular aspect of the abject, which feminist writers have identified as characteristic of specific genres (horror, science fiction, experimental films) and de-colonial perspectives (Creed 1993: 8–15).

Trinh T. Minh-ha elaborates on Kristeva's notion of the abject in relation to the concept of difference, which is more aligned with multiplicity than (dis)similarity: 'There are differences as well as similarities within the concept of difference. One can further say that difference is not what makes conflicts. It is beyond and alongside conflict' (1991: 150). Trinh critiques the (Western) idea that conflict must be a principle component of story and discusses her emphasis on voice and silence in her films (e.g. *Naked Spaces*, 1985) to demonstrate this concept of difference. Rather than one unified voice-over commonly found in conventional documentary, she uses multiple voices that do not compete with each other and silence. Silence for her is important as a political act in undermining patriarchal and hegemonic systems. Rather than in automatic opposition to speech, it is 'a will not to say or a will to unsay, a language of its own' (Trinh 1991: 151).

Trinh notes that occupying a position of difference in filmmaking sometimes necessitates a 'restructuring of experience' and disruption of patriarchal film codes and conventions. To do this, Trinh argues, one can use familiar language (including words, images, and both cinematographic and editing techniques) differently, 'in contexts whose effect is to displace, expand, or change their preconceived, hegemonically accepted meanings' (1991: 151). Doing so would arrive at a difference in defining the 'cinematic'. We certainly see this in Saab's later works, but we can see traces of this engagement of making films from 'a different stance' in all of her films (Trinh 1991: 151).

For Trinh, this notion of difference as distinct from not otherness involves, for those who take agency, the intertwining of both, affirming 'I am like you' while simultaneously pointing to the difference; and reminding 'I am different' while unsettling any notion of otherness (Trinh 1991: 152). In Saab's films, difference works to expose the gaps and cracks in the systems of filmmaking and film viewing – so as to deny the viewer the illusion of a stable world: 'Listening to new sounds, speaking in a different way, manifesting the Formless' (Trinh 1991: 164). This concept of difference is more clearly present in Saab's experimental and installation works, as there are no limiting rules about order, structure, coherence, realism and cinematic codes of narrative. But one could argue that all her work engages with articulating different kinds of difference distinguishing their subjects, from her more conventional documentaries to her work in fiction. For example, one of Saab's lesser-known films, *Iran: Utopia on the Move* uses conventional documentary structures with voice over, interviews, news footage, and location shooting to reveal the heterogeneity and cultural complexity of Iranian society. It presents footage of the alluring religious council that promised return to the country's core cultural values as an answer to Western interventions that had supported the Shah and class oppression; it also reflects on the critical location of Iran, strategically and precariously positioned between divergent US and Russian oil interests; and it attempts to hear from the people, both men and women, to learn about their aspirations at that critical moment.

In the documentaries about issues that are more personal, objectivity is served between brackets, where the poetic power of the image to speak beyond words is used to capture unique moments in time. One striking example is *The Ship of Exile* (1982) about the departure of Yasser Arafat and the head officers of the Palestine Liberation Organization (PLO) aboard the *Atlantis* to Greece from Beirut in 1982. Although there is a commentary (in French with English subtitles) and although there are two scenes where Arafat responds in English to an enquiring young Saab, about 'what now', the power of this document is spoken most allegorically in the silent moments as a haunting representation of the close of a chapter in the PLO's story as the victorious representative body of the Palestinian people. Viewed from the historical vantage point, and if viewed following *Beirut, My City* (both 1982), it closes a chapter for the political aspirations of the Palestinians while opening a new chapter of nightmare for all who inhabited Lebanon at that time, particularly the Palestinian refugees. That chapter had already begun with the Israeli invasion of Lebanon of 1982 that had precipitated the siege of Beirut and the PLO's subsequent departure. About a month following the PLO's departure, the Sabra and Shatila massacres (resulting in approximately 3,000 casualties of mostly Palestinians; see Cobban 1985: 131) would be conducted by Phalangist militias under the watch of the Israeli army. It is worth noting that *Beirut, My City* ends with the people's tearful farewell to the departing PLO fighters: one stage of horror would soon be surpassed by something far worse.

In Saab's fiction films, difference is written into cinematic style, characters and plots, but dialogue is also used to convey characters who stand out against the grain, often resulting in more performativity than we normally find in the dialogue of drama films. This is particularly pronounced in *Dunia*, in Dunia's audition scene and interactions with Dr Bashir, as well as in the scenes of her friends Inayate and Dr Arwa, and scenes with Inayate's mother-in-law and daughter. In some ways this film abounds with clichés, yet they serve a performative function that advances the subject of the film: the struggle for women's sexual and social emancipation in a patriarchal society where such freedoms are increasingly denied. The opening sequence pays homage to another beloved film, Mohamed Khan's 1988 *Dreams of Hind and Camelia* (about the friendship and thwarted dreams of two women who work as maids), in a scene where Inayate, played by Aida Reyad who acts as Hind in Khan's film, cleans the interior of her taxi, which she drives to make a living. It is impossible to dissociate *Dunia*'s beginning from the tragic ending of *Dreams of Hind and Camelia* (where Hind and Camelia are dropped off in the desert, robbed and humiliated). As we begin with recognition and homage, there is little room to imagine that this film might surmount the tragedies of the former, given the social, economic and political realities of Egypt of the last forty years that foreclose such a possibility. But where *Dreams of Hind and Camelia* brings us melodrama through various established film codes, *Dunia*'s film language ruptures the cinematic codes to give us only the woman's point of view, in search of pleasure and power over the body and voice in an environment that increasingly circumscribes these things (Naccach 2019).

AFTER *DUNIA*: FROM HAUNTED GARDENS TO BELOVED CAFES

All the work Saab produced in the last twelve years of her life departs from classical forms.

It seems that the negative reception of *Dunia*, which came with death threats and banishment from Egypt, hastened Saab's subsequent focus on the critique of state-sanctioned heteronormativity and the violence thereof, before her final preoccupation – circling back to her earlier work – on death and the precarity of life. In these last works, we can see her interest in challenging and critiquing the contingency of identity and binary views of the world by parodying the symbols and icons of otherness (*What's Going On?* and *The Opposite of Occidentalism* part of the *Sense, Icons and Sensitivity* exhibition, 2007), asserting a will to unsay and to play with form.

Saab's last statement in feature form was *What's Going On?*, which she described as a surrealist film, although it has a clear narrative progression from beginning to middle and end. Her other works in this period are all short form, each no longer than 6 or 7 minutes, each created for the purpose of exhibition in gallery spaces. *Strange Games and Bridges*, *Sense, Icons and Sensitivity* and *Gender Café* are all ripostes to her previous work. The last film, *My Name is Mei Shigenobu* (2018), spirals back to the material of the war, but gives a face, time and space to the daughter of the founder of the Japanese Red Army, Fusako Shigenobu, who lived for thirty years in Lebanon before her eventual arrest in Japan in 2000. It is as if in the coda of her life, Saab was speaking to a traumatic memory, to catch up with time.

Strange Games and Bridges (2007)

Saab's first exhibition opened at the National Museum of Singapore. Here she returns to re-edit her work: in this installation she uses footage and still frames from her earlier documentaries *Lebanon in Turmoil*, *Children of War* and *Beirut, My City*. Scenes of death and destruction, soldiers at rest, children playing at war, and shattered detritus from a destroyed city are projected on multiple screens simultaneously, many of which are suspended, using scaffolding and ramps for the spectator to travel across levels in the space. While these moving images are time-bound, they are also timeless in their universal anti-war message.

Capturing a magnitude of loss, these 'poetic' documentaries highlight Beirut's ephemeral and mythologised image (the 'Paris of the Orient', etc.) in contrast with the horrors and abjection of war. Their critique of Beirut's pre-war publicity image, via shattered storefronts, mutilated business signs and dismembered mannequins (see Berger 1972: 131) remains striking in this non-linear presentation, and will be a theme Saab returns to in her exhibitions *The Opposite of Occidentalism* from *Sense, Icons and Sensitivity* and *One Dollar a Day*.

The spectator walks through the space via a ramp and stairs that go from the ground to the second level. Projected on large, suspended screens are excerpts from Saab's war films (*Lebanon in Turmoil*, *Children of War* and *Beirut, My City*) that correspond to the following titles in the programme notes that demonstrate the juxtapositions of the life and death, the sacred and the profane in the madness of war: WALKING IN WAR, a floor of broken mirrors projected on the ground screen; KILLING MANNEQUIN, the remains of mutilated mannequins displayed on television sets encased in gabions (stone-filled wire cages used in civil engineering); TOY FIGHTERS, three men on bar stools during a firing interval projected with the accompanying sound of a music box winding and unwinding; STRANGE GAMES, children playing at massacring each other as catharsis after witnessing the real thing, projected on the lower level in the centre of the room; MOTHERS, faces of women projected on the second-level screen who are the witnesses of this merciless tragedy; ENGRAVING, a 'bas-relief of corpses' extracted from *Beirut, My City*, which resemble Phoenician sculptures. Saab includes a more personal reference with an image of her destroyed house (as a result of Israeli bombing in 1982), titled, MY BURNED HOUSE, also an excerpt from *Beirut, My City* (Strange Games Bridges 2017).

In her programme notes, Saab described this as a return to a 'paradise lost' of the garden of spirits (*djinn* in Arabic), which can be understood as the place of trauma that erupts from the image as a haunting (Strange Games Bridges 2017). This exhibition, if not an exorcism, is an experience to share with others as a warning about the unspeakable horror and madness of war. Saab also likened this 'floating garden' of images to the layering of epochs left partially open for the passer-by to appreciate, but also so as never to forget Beirut's (and the region's) history as one of cycles of civilisation, destruction and reconstruction. Reworking the allegorical possibilities of her previous work in this non-linear format demonstrates the paradox of attempting to express trauma (the aporetic; see Rastegar 2015)–always an incomplete process – that can find some type of catharsis through art.

What's Going On? *(2009)*

Co-written by feminist writer Joumana Haddad, this experimental feature is about a man's search for an idealised love in the city of Beirut. An ironic statement in response to Beirut being named the World Book Capital in 2009, which Saab found hypocritical given the high degree of censorship of writers and filmmakers alike (Eilmes 2012), her pleasure in playing with language is evidenced in the opening lines of the opening frames of epic oriental tales:

> Here, Asia begins while the sun is falling and setting, and one more night adds to the thousand nights already said, one more night, one long night in Beirut. And we only visit his palace, and we only discover Africa, when he laughs loudly. It is inside the mouth of the writer: she swallows the characters in the book, she restores them by hand, the one who writes . . .

The film consists of an author and a tale surrounding a man and woman who cannot reconcile the time of their different desires. The author has the dual task of being the writer (of a book of empty pages) and a clothing designer, both of which require him to dictate form, yet creation seems to resist being designed. The central conflict is the elusive nature of love, despite the (male) lover's attempts to capture the (female) beloved. The lover, a bit of a lothario who must find the heart, is in need of a compass; the beloved, a dancer, who wants to explore and express her body in time, needs a heart transplant. She appears in total self-possession until the lover expresses his desire to make love, which ushers in her loneliness. He must learn to embrace emptiness and death before he can learn to love, something Lilith (the first wife of Adam in Jewish folklore who dwells among the statues atop the buildings) decides to show him. She leads the lover to where he can learn to speak to the beloved through Arabic literature at the imagined Souk Okaz[1] and on a journey through the heart (mountains) of Lebanon.

Even the beloved tries to instruct the lover by directing his reading through her book titled *L'Enfer* (*Hell*). The author tries to sew together the heart but even this is unsuccessful in bringing the lovers together. The lover must be initiated into the realm of the split self, the 'I/i' in the scene where he is split in two, the stronger one teaching the weaker one to memorise lines of poetry in classical Arabic. It is only this submission to split subjectivity that brings the lover and the beloved together, not to fill each other but to fill the pages of a book.

The author who presides over nearly every scene with his book of empty pages is only able to fill it in the end after the lovers are reconciled, after the lover discovers how to speak to the beloved through poetry and literature. The focal meeting point is a giant book on a rooftop, where the beloved, who is a dancer, sleeps, and which the lover watches obsessively from a nearby roof. When they do meet at various points, he speaks to her in French and she backs off, responding in Arabic. It is only towards the end, when he leaves some books for her in the giant book, that she speaks in French, reading the books he has left her.

The Souk Okaz, where Lilith introduces the lover to literature, is ironically housed in the Burj building, which was a Phalangist sniper's post demarcating the border between East and West Beirut during the war. While Saab has claimed this film is about a city without war, it is impossible to ignore the meaning of the site of the Souk Okaz, although clearly the film seeks to rehabilitate a place of death and carnage to tell a tale of love that requires the protagonists to learn the language of love. In this film the garden metaphor appears again, but in contrast to its haunted meaning in *Strange Games and Bridges*, it is one that allows for rehabilitation as a 'place where opposite things can talk to each other' (Eilmes 2012). This leads by extension to the importance of the cafe, elaborated in the next piece below.

Gender Café *(2013)*

The cafe in the Arab world has historically been a place for people (often exclusively for men) to gather, talk, socialise and discuss (world) events, its clientele reflective of the degree of social openness or conservatism in its local setting.

Gender Café turns the traditional cafe into a virtual gathering place for six activist artists to analyse the problems of gender oppression and state-sanctioned violence against the (specifically female) body that still persist to this day in the Middle East and North Africa. This six-channel installation is in conversation with *Dunia* and *What's Going On?*. There are six 'tables', each featuring a specific artist or writer (from Lebanon, Egypt, Turkey and Algeria), whose work deals critically with the relegation of women (and others) to the realm of the abject as a function of institutionalised violence against the body.

The first segment, *The Table of Walid Aouni, the Green Mad Man*, features choreographer Walid Aouni who played the choreographer in *Dunia*. It begins with a performance of two men pushing giant ink rollers over a woman, as Aouni says to the camera, 'Once upon a time, there was a choreographer in the Cairo Opera of Egypt. He was a defender of women's rights.' His face is in silhouette, painted in green, wearing a bald cap. The voice explains that he was nicknamed 'the Green Mad Man' after the famous painting by modernist Egyptian painter Abdel Hadi Al-Gazzar, due to the controversy aroused by his performances, which ultimately disrupted his career in Egypt and led to his exile in Beirut. We see performances he directed as he discusses how politics in the Arab world are so consuming that they can lead to madness. We return to the first performance of a woman and men with ink rollers, only now the woman runs out, stands on top of an ink roller, grabs the motorcycle helmet of the man, puts it on her head, and pushes the man down so she can roll over him.

The second segment, *The Table of the Painter of the Pharaohs and the Dancers*, introduces us to painter Adel Siwi who recounts noticing how people danced out of sheer joy when Hosni Mubarak was toppled in 2011. He describes how dancing from pure joy is a natural instinct of the body setting itself free, 'as a part of that ultimate freedom we're pursuing', which transformed his approach from focusing exclusively on the human face to painting women dancers: 'to rehabilitate the notions of joy, pleasure, and the creative power of the body'. Inserted is a clip from *Dunia*, of plump belly dancers, showing only their torsos, who celebrate Dunia's desire to take up the dance. Siwi's last question indirectly answers itself, explaining why the abject is constructed in systemic oppression, defeat here referring to what was lost in the revolutionary struggles in the region: 'Why is it the body that has to bear the full burden of the soul's defeats?'

The third segment, *The Table of the Magazine on the Body*, features Joumana Haddad, the feminist author who plays Lilith in *What's Going On?*. The video incorporates an excerpt from the film with commentary from Haddad. Her voice recalls first encountering Lilith in a dictionary and immediately identifying with her, as a woman 'not willing to negotiate or settle for a compromise with authority [. . .] I realised she was my mother.' This recognition became the impetus to start her own magazine, *Jasad*, a literary and artistic journal about the body and other taboo subjects in Arab society. She discusses the problem of denial, taboo and shame with which the body is viewed in Arab society, and the backlash against her for the controversy unleashed by the journal: 'Alas, we live in a region where, if things are not specifically named, we tend to believe they are non-existent.'

In the fourth segment, *The Table of the Golden Okra*, we meet film critic Cuneyt Cebenoyan and filmmaker Melek Ozman who established the 'Golden Okra Academy' in Istanbul, a jokey collaboration which gives annual awards to films, for homophobia, misogyny and sexism. Standing in his library holding the jar of pickled okra, Cebenoyan explains that in Turkey an okra stands for a small penis, and that giving this prize to an actor or director implies that 'he has a little penis'. At one of the Golden Okra award ceremonies, an apologetic (male) recipient of the award says,

> During the few other awards ceremonies we have attended, we kept wondering how we could thank people, but here we have been wondering all along how we should apologise. I hope we will learn from it and never come back here again.

Ozman, who also founded the Filmor Women's Cooperative, explains that they chose this title for the award because the okra is the most suitable symbol for discussing sexism, chiming well with indigestion and resonating perfectly with the intended sexual connotations.

In the fifth segment, *The Table of Dance and Pride*, we meet Lebanese artist Alexandre Paulikevitch whose performances disrupt heteronormative ideas of femininity and masculinity. We see this in his performative interpretation of belly dancing, which refuses the delivery of abundant corporeality commonly associated with the female body. He explains that his creative work is informed by the physical, psychic and verbal abuse he has endured as a gay man in Lebanon: 'I think the key word of this work is exorcism. I wanted to exorcise the violence.' His performance art is connected to his queer activism in Lebanon: we see him participating in a demonstration against the sexist crackdown by government forces via 'tests of shame' (virginity tests and rectal examinations) on gay people and those working to decriminalise homosexuality (HRW 2012). This is another facet of the struggle Joumana Haddad contends with in Lebanon, where violence is the response to art and activism that seek to emancipate the body.

The Table of Exigency is the sixth segment, which features Algerian writer, feminist and lawyer Wassyla Tamzali, who analyses two contrasting images from Egypt that reflect the recent revolution in the Arab world: the scene from *Dunia* where Dunia tells the jurors of a dance competition that she has never seen her own body, while she pulls her dress around herself versus the image

Figure 13.1 Alexandre Paulikevitch shatters gender codes of 'oriental dance', in *Gender Café*

of the naked young Egyptian woman who shared this image as a political statement on the internet in 2012. The cinematic image from *Dunia* displays the secular tradition 'that dictates that women be deprived of their body in their own eyes', says Tamzali; whereas the viral internet image shows how a single frame of a naked woman on the internet can have a viral impact but no sustained political agenda, with more than five million clicks on her picture. 'It's a revolution that goes through the woman's body and emancipation.' We then see the iconic footage from Egypt of the woman protestor who was beaten by the police, exposing her blue bra beneath her black veil, which a police officer immediately tried to cover, revealing, in Tamzali's words, the obsession with woman's sexuality that begins and ends with violence. While *Gender Café* was originally a six-channel installation, Tamzali's 'table' is an appropriate conclusion to the video sequence, suggesting that the law (and its language) are essential in the struggle for human rights, both as tools in the battle and as codified conclusions. The issue of human rights in the wake of the (thwarted) revolutions of the Arab Spring is a strong element of Saab's subsequent works, either as a direct subject or influential undertone.

Imaginary Postcard *(2016)*

An ode to a bridge (Osman Gazi Bridge) uniting Europe to Asia across the Bosporus, this 6-minute film is also a meditation on mortality, as Saab explains her attempt to understand what this bridge means to her, where it leads. Connecting to a more utopian interpretation of bridges in her previous work (*Strange Games and Bridges*), here she ponders where it leads her:

> Didn't I already know how fragile I am? How this bridge that links Europe and Asia is in the end the only solid structure that I can hold onto in order to continue my journey. But isn't this frail bridge actually only as solid as the image that Turkey is today trying to portray as itself? Isn't this for me a story of something sacred? How many minutes, how many hours did it take for me to understand that this inexorable journey is one in which life escapes me? I have to understand what this bridge is guiding me towards.

The bridge is examined from many different framings, corresponding to her description of it as a 'poetic manifestation of love' that privileges neither East nor West. But this is how she would like to imagine it, despite the historic and political turbulence in the region. Her quest to understand has another context in the aftermath of the Arab Spring and the afflicted revolutions, with the creation and renewal of centres of power and global proxy penetrations that have resulted in more death, destruction and refugees.

Saab concludes by quoting from Orhan Pamuk's book *Istanbul: Memories and the City*, her voice switching from English to French as the medium framing of the bridge and water slowly pulls out to a wider shot: 'But here we have come full circle . . . for anything we say about the city's essence says more about our own lives . . . and our own states of mind. The city has no centre other than ourselves.' Curiously, this line echoes one of her first creative statements made in her 1976 documentary *Beirut, Never Again*, in its reflections on war, the destroyed city, and its people. The end circles back to the beginning.

One Dollar a Day *(2016)*

This photographic exhibit and 6-minute film attempts to place recently displaced refugees (of the Syrian war) from the margins of the Beqaa Valley to the centre of public discourse in the city of Beirut. Remembering the Palestinian refugees who came more than sixty years before, and whose exposure of Lebanon's class problems in their liberation project became the tinder for sectarian conflict, here Saab attempts to humanise the new figures of abjection.

The photography exhibit is composed of images of children and their dwellings covered by large advertisement canvases they were given (promoting the good life of perfumes, designer clothes and jewellery) to help resist the elements. Unnaturalistic colour tinting has been added in some photographs, to draw attention to the sky and ground as reversed fields, and to render some of the children as 'angels' rather than figures of our pity. These photographs emphasise the contrasts between the empty promises of the publicity image and the precarity by which these refugees live.

The video, by contrast, gives us a silent 'documentary', although there is a soundtrack composed of one long, uninterrupted violin composition that creates a sense of suspension, apprehension and anticipation. Everything takes place against this sonorous background as if the recording is just a prelude to something momentous yet to come. It begins with a reflection on discovering this refugee camp in the Beqaa Valley and noting enormous statistics for the casualties of war: 500,000 deaths and 6 million refugees. Travelling shots show us a refugee camp in the distance, and a mound of tyres, after which flow a series of stationary framings of women silently holding their United Nations High Commissioner for Refugees (UNHCR) refugee identity papers, sometimes clutching or being clutched by a child. This is followed by panning across a row of crouching women – some hiding their faces – who hold identity papers among their children. A woman walks out of a housing unit towards the camera and hands her paper to an offscreen hand, followed by a close-up of the paper which provides data on this woman: picture, name, file number, date of birth, country of origin: Syria.

The refugees are then placed within the city, in a reversal of the publicity image: a dusk shot of a busy city intersection with an illuminated advertisement case shows an image of the woman holding both her baby and her identity paper. Another image shows a different woman in a different display case on the other side of an overpass. It is large and bright enough to command the

Figure 13.2 Cafe goers and Syrian refugees inhabit the same space, one as an image the other does not see, in *One Dollar a Day*

attention of the passing cars. A third advertisement case has a black image with words in white text, 'Comment vivre avec un dollar par jour' ('How to live on one dollar a day'). The electronic billboard shows the woman with identity papers in the background of an outdoor cafe. The people passing by do not appear to look at these images, suggesting indifference and desensitisation to the 'reality' of their surroundings, as opposed to the fiction and mythologisation offered by advertisements. Meanwhile, in the city, cranes pull into the sky huge images of the refugee children, women, and the following line: 'Comment vivre avec un dollar par jour' ('How to live with one dollar a day'). John Berger (1972) famously discussed this power of the publicity image as envy for the dream deferred of the good life and the glamour it promises but which has not been attained. Here, the publicity image is shown to be interchangeable with the refugee in a simulacral swap that consumers do not seem to notice. This is a chilling statement on twenty-first-century humanity.

The video ends with words from Etel Adnan, conveying a warning about the coming generation of the displaced who will no doubt want to attain a decent quality of life and possibly return home, as their Palestinian brethren do. As Saab's past films attest, such aspirations, if not met, bode ill for the future of Lebanon:

> The destroyed cities continue to crumble, the precarious shelters have been shown.
>   In your name juicy arms contracts were honoured.
>   For this reason, you're afraid of (the dignity of) these women,
>   And this common future that they seem to carry.

My Name is Mei Shigenobu *(2018)*

An unfinished work, this 6-minute portrait of Mei Shigenobu relies on silence as the 'will to unsay' articulated by Trinh. It is not a film 'about' Mei but rather a fusion of energies in revisiting a place that invokes nostalgia for both Saab and Mei. Mei is the daughter of Fusako Shigenobu, a woman who was the founder of the Marxist Japanese Red Army group allied with the Popular Front for the Liberation of Palestine in Lebanon. She grew up in a very protected yet insecure situation among other children and families of the Red Army and Palestinian freedom fighters. Under constant threat of being discovered and assassinated by the Israeli Mossad, Fusako and Mei moved around a lot so as to conceal their identity. In 2000 Fusako was arrested in Japan and was sentenced in 2006 to twenty years' imprisonment for her participation in the activities of the Red Army (McKirdy 2017).

Following the visual introduction to Mei, a beautiful woman with long black hair looking out at the Mediterranean sea, there is a reimagining of the scene behind the iconic photo (which we also see) of Fusako Shigenobu posing for a photograph holding a Kalashnikov, layering images of women's emancipation in the image of Palestine liberation solidarity. This is the one of two instances of archival material used in the film, as if to briefly provide an explanation for Mei's displacement.

As Mei describes her childhood in Lebanon, of living with secret identities, having to change her identity and school at the arrival of any students who might be in the foreign diplomatic community, we see her from different framings. Mei walks slowly up a long flight of stairs with an ageing Jocelyne to a favoured spot, an outdoor cafe, now vacant but one we have seen before in her other films (*Letter from Beirut*, *Once Upon a Time, Beirut: Story of a Star*). The camerawoman, Jocelyne and Mei fix the shot, and Mei plays affectionately with Saab's hair. She walks through the empty cafe, clearly a place to which Jocelyne had great attachment.

Television footage of Fusako Shigenobu's arrest in 2000 (in Japan) shows a dignified if somewhat fragile captive being escorted in handcuffs onto or off a plane, waving and smiling victoriously to the crowd. This is where the emotional tone shifts. Mei's tears roll down her cheek as we hear her voice speaking in Japanese recounting a memory of a game of hide-and-seek her mother used to play with her, which may have also been a way to instruct her in how to avoid being caught. The unfinished film ends with a reflection:

> Mei shares with her mom another kind of nostalgia, carried by the Palestinian struggle. Palestinians were deprived of freedom and memory, living

Figure 13.3 Mei Shigenobu recalls her childhood in Lebanon, in *My Name is Mei Shigenobu*

in untold humiliation. Fusako lived among them in Beirut as if she could recover time and space she lost. Nostalgia testifies to the ironic contradiction which opposes mother and daughter, so different but so close.

But what is this nostalgia? It is more than a fusion of personal attachments to memory, place, and a time of energised Marxism; it also expresses a collective absence (and for many a longing) of the concept of women's emancipation that has nothing to do with religion.

In this last statement, Saab circles back, between temporalities, but also between the idea of East and West. It is a movement and theme frequently returned to in her work, whether focusing on Beirut's many faces before and during the war, or the bridge that connects people and ideas, or the garden that is sometimes haunted and sometimes fantastic, or the cafe where people discuss emancipation. It was a lifelong engagement, a personal struggle with the hegemony of language and an attempt to unsettle its structures. There may appear to be multiple personas or types of filmmaker in the figure of Jocelyne Saab. But it is this openness to different forms and a refusal to 'settle' into one form (an auteur, a documentarist, an experimental filmmaker, a photographer, an installation artist) that demonstrates a resistance to settling the 'I' of subjectivity, which Kristeva saw as disrupting the (unchanging) 'logic of identity' (Trinh 1991). In Saab's explorations of borders and their imaginings, the areas they demarcate lose their form: East is no longer East, West no longer West. There is just formlessness (Trinh 2013: 161) and the world.

NOTE

1. The Souk Okaz was a pre-Islamic market located in Ta'if, Saudi Arabia, where poets and storytellers gathered among the merchants, athletes, musicians and revellers.

BIBLIOGRAPHY

Berger, John (1972), *Ways of Seeing*, New York: Penguin.
Cobban, Helena (1985), *Palestinian Liberation Organization: People, Power, and Politics*, Cambridge: Cambridge University Press.
Creed, Barbara (1993), *The Monstrous-Feminine*, New York: Routledge.
Eilmes, Éléna (2012), 'Interview with the Lebanese Filmmaker Jocelyne Saab: "My Country Was a Beautiful Garden"', *Qantara.de*, 17 August, <https://en.qantara.de/content/interview-with-the-lebanese-filmmaker-jocelyne-saab-my-country-was-a-beautiful-garden> (last accessed 1 December 2020).
Human Rights Watch (HRW) (2012), 'Lebanon: Stop "Tests of Shame". Authorities Order Anal Examinations on Men Charged with Homosexuality', *Human Rights Watch*, 10 August, <https://www.hrw.org/news/2012/08/10/lebanon-stop-tests-shame> (last accessed 30 June 2020).

McKirdy, Andrew (2017), 'Imprisoned Japanese Red Army Founder Shigenobu Holds Out Hope for the Revolution', *The Japan Times*, 8 June, <https://www.japantimes.co.jp/news/2017/06/08/national/imprisoned-japanese-red-army-founder-shigenobu-holds-hope-revolution/> (last accessed 7 December 2020).

Mostafa, Dalia Said (2015), 'Jocelyne Saab: A Lifetime Journey in Search of Freedom and Beauty (Lebanon)', in Josef Gugler (ed.), *Ten Arab Filmmakers: Political Dissent and Social Critique*, Bloomington: Indiana University Press, pp. 34–50.

Naccach, Nessrine (2019), 'Entrées par effraction. May Ziade et Jocelyne Saab: les mots et les images à l'usage de la "des-orientale"', *TraHs: Trayectorias Humanas Trascontinentales*, 6, <https://www.unilim.fr/trahs/index.php?id=1833&lang=es> (last accessed 7 December 2020).

Rastegar, Kamran (2015), *Surviving Images: Cinema, War, and Cultural Memory in the Middle East*, Oxford: Oxford University Press.

Strange Games Bridges, 'The Work' (2007), 28 June, <http://strangegamesbridges.free.fr/EXPOstrange/pages%20english%20ok/creation.html> (last accessed 2 December 2020).

Trinh, T. Minh-ha (1989), *Woman, Native, Other: Writing Postcoloniality and Feminism*, Bloomington: Indiana University Press.

Trinh, T. Minh-ha (1991), *When the Moon Waxes Red: Representation, Gender and Cultural Politics*, New York: Routledge.

Trinh, T. Minh-ha (2013), *D-Passage: The Digital Way*, Durham, NC: Duke University Press.

PART IV

Advocating Poetry

CHAPTER 14

A Suspended Life: A Cinematic Fall

Marie Chebli

'*Nous tombons*', writes René Char, 'We Fall'. '*Je vous écris en cours de chute*, I write to you as I fall. *C'est ainsi que j'éprouve l'état d'être au monde*: that is how I understand, how I undergo, the state of being in the world.'[1] This is the feeling we get as readers of *Alice's Adventures in Wonderland* by Lewis Carroll ([1865] 2013a). We fall in a literary realm when we read or in apperception when we screen a film. The fall is a doorway or the expression of another perceptive paradigm. Alice and her readers are constantly falling, gliding, slipping from one scene to another, from one realm to another and getting more and more confused about who they are. Alice's adventures leave her quite nameless: she becomes a series of events as she 'falls' from one 'space' (scenery-narrative unit) to another. Her story unfolds as she goes deeper 'into the rabbit hole'. She is not what we might call a proper 'subject'. Instead, Alice is always physically becoming a tall, small, huge, unproportioned little girl in an irrational world, yet the way she functions, her persona, is not altered by her physical transformations. Her movements and physical transformations are conducted by the diegetic space she finds herself in, thus proposing the scenery as a narrative element more than a diegetic one. In Jocelyne Saab's film *A Suspended Life* (1985), the main character, Samar, is similar to Alice, and the film's scenery and structure echo those of Wonderland and *Through the Looking Glass* (Carroll [1871] 2013b). During the film, Samar leads us through deserted spaces and hidden doors that no one seems to see or know about; she will take us to ruined places where life has become mad. We follow her into narrative 'units' that can be autonomous, disengaged from the film. We speak of units because they are spatially presented as such: the pink house is a unit, the destroyed mosque is another, and the theatre is yet another unit.

Samar is a young, fierce and childish woman, not quite a girl and not quite a woman, being both and neither at the same time. The film is sewn together around this peculiar character and takes place in a ruined Beirut: a wonderland filled with mad people evolving in a queer social construct, and each inhabiting a unit. Samar and Alice are both shifting characters being directed in and by a mad world, crossing and visiting 'units'. Samar will be mutilated, in order to erase a 'fault' and become a 'pure girl' once again, a suspended creature between realms (womanhood, childhood). Samar is thus a kind of Peter Pan creature;[2] a fairy-tale creature that will not transform at the end of this story and 'grow up' or 'die'. She is not like any other 'classical' suspended character that eventually gets out of its situation and lets linear time get hold of it.

In *A Suspended Life* Samar embodies both the tragic reality of a young woman living and *embodying* (as in containing and expressing) the destruction of her society and the horrible banality of it. She becomes a symbol of sorts, an idea, a figure that, as theoreticians, we mistreat and try to hold within frames. And unlike Peter Pan or any other figure who evolves from realm to realm, from frame to frame, Samar is peculiar, because she is just like Alice. The two girls guide us through a timeless narrative where past and present tense are equivalent,[3] where they do not 'evolve' but remain the same character with the same psyche. As such, they provoke the destruction of a period-like time pattern where we cannot move in a derivative structure from scene to scene, from action to reaction in a logical, causal fashion. Alice and Samar move around in an unconstructed narrative from one independent unit to another. We follow them into the presentation of an *ob*scene world. *Ob* as in the Latin prefix connoting an overturning, which also means collapsing, falling and facing. The two women evolve outside of a frame-like narrative because they are not contained by the units they pass through. Time, for example, does not flow in them since their identities do not change. As they move on, the units (time–space) are shown as obscene: folding and unfolding into themselves as an arabesque figure (see Marks 2010). The film's narrative structure presents on the surface a linear movement: Samar follows her dream, meets her charming prince, he dies, she moves on. And, underneath that surface or coated by that surface, another kind of structure emerges, which I will try to reveal in this chapter.

The two 'girls', Alice and Samar, cannot be considered as either subject or object in a verbal (action) sequence. Their adventures, both wild and banal, are based on and formulated by paradoxical sentences: 'I must be *growing small* again', says Alice (Carroll [1865] 2013a: 14; my emphasis), whilst Samar speaks in enigmatic paradoxical poetic sentences where she *draws and erases* life at the same time, where she *knows unknowable* things. Finally, the two girls evolve in a narrative where everything exceeds the frame instead of being contained by it. In Alice's story, it is her physical transformations and paradoxical phrasing that accompanies this movement. In *A Suspended Life*, Samar is the exceeding element: she is the city, she is motherhood. She is civilisation. In this chapter, I will investigate the similar structure between Carroll's novel and Saab's film in a 'unit'-like fashion.

FIRST, WE FALL

Alice falls 'down, down, down' (Carroll [1865] 2013a: 3) and the fall cannot come to an end. She wonders if she will fall right through the centre of the earth and land on the opposite surface of the globe. She gets sleepy along the fall and nonsense fills the narrative, the language, the geography and spatial representations: '"Do cats eat bats?" and sometimes, "Do bats eat cats?" for, you see, as she couldn't answer either question, it didn't much matter which way she put it' (Carroll [1865] 2013a: 4). Nonsense is created by a paradoxical narrative, and as such it introduces a paradox in logical phrases, turning them over, reversing subject and object. Likewise, 'Samar goes through the door' could be equivalent to 'the door goes through Samar'. Does the diegetic space express a volition of some sort and call for Samar to respond to it in a certain way, or is it the other way around? Does Alice's environment call upon her to shape-shift by drinking and eating? It does indeed, and it underlines how every movement, every action made by a character, is initiated within the surroundings (space and scenery). The surroundings become narrative elements instead of diegetic ones.

Figure 14.1 Samar finds Karim's pink house and enters its inner courtyard

In Figure 14.1, the nonsense operates as such: 'Samar meets the door' is equivalent to 'The door meets Samar.' Samar is carefully invited towards the door by the positions of the jars that initiate her movement. The lighting softly reveals her white dress, drawing her contouring shadow, which springs out of the adjacent jar and is projected onto the white wall. The light then gently enters the pink door and slowly fades. Even the colouring is designed to make the audience feel the concentrating sensation of the junction between spaces, and the tension held between Samar and the door. The pink door is presented as a *Narnia* closet, a rabbit hole, an entry to a world within a world. Samar and Door meet: they evaluate and gauge each other silently and decide to unite (to fall, René Char might say). Sense is directional and the paradox is carefully composed between the arrangement of the surroundings and the trajectory of the girl. But in Carroll's story, the paradox is pronounced by Alice, whose transformations leave her disoriented: 'which way which way?' (Carroll [1865] 2013a: 8). Growing or shrinking, opening up or shutting down like a 'telescope', she says (Carroll [1865] 2013a: 10).

Alice's transformations disorient her. They are rooted in language and phrasing. She cannot see how her body is affected and how it is changing. She cannot help herself as she enunciates distorted poems or lessons. The disorientations of Alice are literary. The paradoxical direction Samar leads and undergoes are cinematic: they are noted in the phrasing and in the verbal quality of the narrative, but they unfold in a cinematic situation of sound and image. Samar finds a hidden pink door, she is silent, her feet brush the ground, and the frame is constructed in a way that holds all these tales in one situation. The young woman goes towards the pink door and we understand that that door has been luring her. The main musical theme of the film carried by a soft but intensive flute suggests that there is no urgency in this scene, only a concentrating sensuous, hypnotic quality. 'It is as if action floats in the situation' (Deleuze [1985] 1989: 4).

Nothing else is happening. It is just a girl walking towards a threshold, or the threshold calling the girl, but that is how all stories begin. The intense quality of the scene is constructed through two paradoxical readings of it. First, the simplicity, the banality of the act. Then, the complexity of the scenes it generates in our minds, connecting all fairy tales. 'Girl enters a door' / 'door calls a girl' are not specifically propositions made by Saab's film, or by Carroll's novel: they are found as a point of no return in a great number of stories, and those stories fill up our viewer's mind when we face Saab's image. We are facing, here, the birth of a mythological idea: where an action does not correspond to a certain character but to all humans in certain circumstances. We can qualify this scene as a 'pure optical and sound situation'. The Deleuzian expression 'pure optical and sound situation' describes certain scenes in the Italian Neo-Realism films, and Ozu's cinema. It comes from the crises of the sensory-motor situations (a narrative based on causality – action and reaction, movement scaled by timing and montage: a cinematic representative modus operandi). When the reality is such that it can no longer be faithfully represented by a traditional narrative structure, another type of narrative image emerges, says Deleuze, an image that is linked directly to time: 'where the movement is the perspective of time' ([1985] 1989: 22).

Saab does not present us with a plain and visible abstractive process, but initiates that peculiar feeling of the 'out of time – out of space' narrative through the use of these 'units' and 'pure optical and sound situations'. Through them, she connects her film to the wide network of stories and images. All stories, here, respond to one another. The film does not speak of dates, clear locations or specific characters that we can pinpoint in history. All of that is removed from a destroyed Beirut. Saab takes us through a mythological tale as she erases a certain historical depth of field and concentrates on what is left alive.

In the eyes of Lévi-Strauss ([1977] 1995), mythology is amongst other anthropological theories, a description of the permanent structure between people. The sociological anthropological narrative of a myth is an 'out of time' narrative as in an 'eternal' story, because it is a description and an interpretation of a cultural modus vivendi concerning permanent patterns of social interactions. A fairy tale is a specific narrative structure where we only focus on the interactions and certain psychologies of the main characters. If Saab draws on both structures, she defines cinema in Lebanon or about Lebanon as both. Her film is an 'out of time, out of space' experience, everything is destroyed and there are only human interactions, interpretations and perceptions left. There is no other information in this film. In the film's context we understand that action is not initiated by a character, a subject, but it is a consequence of how the character becomes a witnessing object (an element on which an action is produced or incarnated) subjugated to his or her world. Lévi-Strauss dedicates a chapter to the relation between myth and history. He explains that, working on mythological and historical literature, he finds that they are intricate. But the main difference between history and mythology is that 'Mythology is static' and history cannot be perceived as static or a closed system. Lévi-Strauss also finds that in Western civilisations:

> in our own societies, history has replaced mythology and fulfils the same function, that for society without writing and without archives the aim of mythology is to ensure that as closely as possible – complete closeness is obviously impossible – the future will remain faithful to the present and the past. (Lévi-Strauss [1977] 1995: 42–3)

By studying both, Lévi-Strauss reveals the anthropological cause of the invention of mythology and history: to placate, ease and define a perceptive paradigm for time and events. If societies shed their mythology in a context of never-ending destruction, it will sprout again out of the lack of historical thought. Just like plants break out of stone graves. Lebanese cinema, bursting out of a war context, is compelled to raise a mythological pattern out of the impossibility of writing history. Lebanese film directors in that context do not work for any other reason than for the urgency to try to overwrite what used to be history. In *A Suspended Life*, Saab is fully enrolled in this movement of cinematic work on mythology.

DEAD FERTILE SPACE

A Suspended Life opens on a cemetery, where a long pan movement leads us to a man, Karim, picking flowers from a tomb. Whilst the frame concentrates on him, the soundtrack leaves the quiet cemetery to a conversation between two girls. The camera follows the sound to a visual. We meet Samar, who has had another dream about this man, Karim, and his grand house. She says that the dream must be followed.

Beirut here is a network of 'dead forces' (Deleuze [1985] 1989: 7), a cemetery. Flowers, as 'force vive' or 'life force', are picked from tombs as we shift towards a visual of the dreaming girl who is going to pursue the realisation of

Figure 14.2 The first image of the film is a silent pan shot of a Beirut cemetery

her dream. Saab opens the filmic narrative with two movements. First, the film opens to a dream, a vision that leads the clairvoyant girl, and the spectator, into the destroyed Beirut: like Alice we fall into a dreamland. Second, the death potency or 'dead force' that is Beirut spurts out a vital thrust. The tombs in the cemetery around Karim are perforated and broken by plants that have sprouted out of them. As the film rolls on we realise that Samar is not a character per se; she is the exploration of a vision. She is the vital thrust (little flower and fierce plant) that will keep Beirut alive, renewing it, sprouting from it and reinventing it. Samar does not represent a person but 'her-self', which is extended to the entire city, if not wider. The death potency of Beirut is rendered palpable and immanent in the long pan on the cemetery. Sprouting from a cemetery, a floral motif – the little white flower echoing the girl in the white dress – becomes, in this reading of the film, a narrative element. Slowly contaminating the story, becoming the story. And in the end, exceeding it.

In this way, the film opens in an abstractive process, melting objectivity and subjectivity together. The processes of abstraction as defined by Wilhelm Worringer ([1908] 2014) is a subjective experience of empathy and immanence, where the feeling of being a part of the living thrust of the world is anchored in the spectator. An abstract aesthetic experience is the rendering of that feeling as a series of forces conducted by presentational movement and not representational ones. In other words, the aesthetic experience in abstract art functions through distorting the idea of subject (spectator) and object (work of art) by leading us into a form of contemplation and absorption that provokes self-alienation, as empathy does, and by doing so the constructed identity (self-objectivation) shatters.[4] For a brief moment, in this abstractive aesthetic experience, we experience René Char's 'Fall', we lose our handles on our fixed identity and 'melt', like Alice does, in a situation that qualifies us as abstract.

TIME AND MONTAGE

The opening credits of the film, following the introduction held between the cemetery and the two girls, is presented in a sequence of five static shots. Five different images of endless pathways in and out of Beirut accompanied by Siegfried Kessler's flute (the main musical theme in the film). The montage puts us 'in the eye' of a peculiar roundabout that has been crafted with cameras. The screen is shown as the meeting place of all those roads leading to numerous horizons. Like Beirut, the film is a central connector of narrative lines (or units) that, in this particular case, disengage us from the concepts of beginning or ending. There is only the way we enter a unit and the way we get out of it; the concepts of beginning and ending are necessarily subjective ones and produced in consequence of a linear perception of time in one's self. We

Figure 14.3 Inside the pink house, Samar enters a new room with a grid on the floor and is compelled to cross it accordingly

are led as spectators from one line-unit to another through Samar's wanderings and dream followings. This defines the film as an atomist structure that exposes 'units' of 'time–space' as explored and linked together by camera and sound. Thus presented we see that the fundamental structure of the film is roughly in the image of a cinematic dot connecting different lines together. The dot functions as a 'point of view' that puts all the lines in perspective and as concentric to it. That particular radiating point or crossway shapes the world as a network linking horizons together.

The concept of 'becoming' can be illustrated by a crossway, one point connecting two or more states and tending towards them. On the first page of *The Logic of Sense* Deleuze says:

> As it eludes the present, becoming does not tolerate the separation or the distinction of before and after, or of the past and future. It pertains to the essence of becoming to move and to pull in both directions at once. Alice does not grow without shrinking and vice versa. (Deleuze [1969] 1990: 1)

In other words, the specificity of 'becoming' is not 'to be' in the present tense. Meaning that any personal identity is undermined in the process. Alice loses her name and Samar extends it out of any personal consideration. Time and self-evolution are perceived in a different paradigm here. Time is not some unidirectional dimension we live in, rather it is a dimension we create by living and representing our life through a narrative causal process. So, if we use a different narrative process, we will create another perceiving paradigm for time, losing our causally constructed identity (Worringer's self-objectivation) along the way.

Alice's physical transformations (initiated by her environment) cause the readers to jump-cut from scene to scene. In the first chapter of *The Logic of Sense* ([1969] 1990), Deleuze takes the example of the growing Alice and says that the event of growing from a form 'A' to a form 'A+' is becoming 'A+', but it is considered as 'becoming' from a certain time-sensitive point of view in the evolution of Alice. From a specific point in time we can see her becoming bigger or growing, but from another moment in time we see that 'A' becoming 'A+' is equivalent to 'she was smaller – shorter than now'. Becoming and reducing, leading us to the different points of existence (bigger or smaller), are relevant and logical only if time is a unidirectional vector. They pertain to the existence of the present tense (bigger *than*, smaller *than*). But if the present tense is lost, 'becoming' and 'reducing', as 'beginning' and 'ending', are folded into one another and cease to mean anything.

To be able to comprehend that multidirectional perception of time, we must see time as a grid on which we move (like a chess board). Time is thus not represented as a linear string from beginning to end, but as a grid that provides crossways of autonomous units that we inhabit or visit. We then become a sort of series of the abstractive experience of those units. In this way, Samar's movements are identical to Alice's. Their transformations, becoming (falling in love) and reducing (getting mutilated), do not alter who they are and how they function in their stories. In Samar's case we clearly are projected in abstractive processes. Time and characters, in both stories, do not function in progressive unidirectional levels as would a classic videogame. Alice and Samar do not change (their perceptions, their modus vivendi are maintained), they do not become another version (an adult one) of themselves as we jump from scene to scene.

In the multidirectional time grid of *A Suspended Life*, the concept of the main character's personal identity is torn in paradoxical directions (nonsense). Being forever suspended, Samar is always torn, always moving from one roundabout to another, entering and leaving units, becoming and reducing without changing her suspended state or the way she stiches the film together. There is no sense at all, no meaning, no morality, no ending, nothing. The film is the nonsense wandering of a teenage figure dancing around barefoot in a broken city. As we plunge into her story, we realise that these 'units' – Samar discovering the pink house, Samar grabbed by the hand and going to the shore with children, Samar becoming the mother, the sister of all in the destructed theatre – are eternal. Eternity being a moment that has no beginning and no ending. These units, which Deleuze would call 'pure optical and sound situations', are carried by banal situations and yet unfold in a quiet intensity that delivers us with the experience of a pure moment where time does not flow, where time is not felt since the character is absorbed in its situation. Not only is time not 'felt', but it cannot in these eternal moments be represented as linear either, it is not able to change us from one state to another. The character becomes a sort of 'infinite identity', and the spectator is held in a suspended state. Deleuze says:

> The paradox of this pure becoming – with its capacity to elude present and intensify it, is the paradox of infinite identity (the infinite identity of both directions, or senses at the same time – of future and past, of the day before and the day after, of too much and not enough, of active or passive, and of cause and effect). (Deleuze [1985] 1989: 2)

In the pink house, whilst discovering the rooms within the rooms, Samar takes off her slippers and childishly places her feet only on the connecting dots of the grid. A child's moving pattern from one crossway to another, letting the lines on the ground guide her. Samar moves on the crossway of our grid – keeping the units of the squares and the categories carefully untouched. She does not linger, or enter a unit, but keeps her footing carefully on its border. She sees everything inside the unit; her position makes her clairvoyant. Concentrating the frame on that particular pattern is a poetic form *only* if we understand it as the montage modus operandi: jump-cutting from the corner of one unit (crossway) to another is the pattern stitching the movie together in a map-making fashion.

BODY ALTERATION AND NAME LOSS

Physical transformation is treated curiously in the cases of Alice and Samar. In *The Logic of Sense*, Deleuze says that a disoriented Alice loses her name: 'these reversals as they appear in infinite identity have a consequence: the contesting of Alice's personal identity and the loss of her proper name' ([1969] 1990: 3). The first consequence of 'becoming' is losing our own 'handles', the known qualities that define us, like our name, surname, eye colour, behavioural traits. Alice forgets her name, and this loss of memory is an event producing a before-and-after situation, putting us into a causality narrative again. At the loss of her name, Alice experiences the incapacity of representing herself:

Dear, dear! How queer everything is today! And yesterday things went on just as usual. I wonder if I've been changed in the night? Let me think: was I the same when I got up this morning? I almost think I can remember feeling a little different. But if I'm not the same, the next question is, Who in the world am I? (Carroll [1865] 2013a: 13)

Alice cannot get hold of her name, the tool that permits her to 'handle' herself, which can unite the representation and the feeling of Self. Frustrated by this inability, she starts crying a river, literally, whilst shrinking. But she does not notice her transformation, and only factually deduces it: 'I must be growing small again' (Carroll [1865] 2013a: 14), maintaining the paradoxical movement in the way she phrases it. She does not feel herself physically transform as she is in a dissociated state. Similarly, while Samar acknowledges the mutilation inflicted upon her, she does not scream or run away – she seems stoically to witness it. As such, the main event is not the physical shifting of Alice or Samar, but referring to the concept of falling out of a perceptive realm and into another, we understand that the main event of Carroll's novel, and the main effect of Saab's film, is the loss of the representational paradigm.

Alice cannot represent herself – re-present as in repeating the pattern of self-presentation, recognising one's self through sameness. Repeating sameness is the antidote to 'becoming'. It is sterile and limiting. Reducing is an act of expansion, and the loss of a name permits Alice to not be trapped as a figure in a frame or a character in a narrative unit. The act of repetition shows a lack of invention, of exploring possibilities (units) and creating spaces and bodies that can live through impossibilities. Being nameless is the great power of Alice. Within her, everything is possible and she can become everyone. Being nameless is thus the first consequence of literary abstraction and it is also its first cause. Unlike Alice, Samar does not forget her name. On the contrary, she stretches her name onto the whole city, rendering visible the life thrust that takes root in the ruins. The meaning of the Arabic name 'Samar' is 'a conversation of loved ones under the moonlight' and the girl says that she is the city, she is Beirut, under the moonlight. Saab presents us with a cinematic samar held by her main 'infinite' character. Samar speaks as a clairvoyant mythological creature, saying that she is thousands of years old, talking of the moon and lovers, putting us and Karim in a dream-like situation: forced to perceive the world differently.

The 'samar' is the harmonious quality of love between people. As love is the connecting affection between elements that can resonate in rhythm together, thus constituting a viable system, the word 'samar' echoes the vital thrust mentioned earlier. The word 'samar' shifts from name, to noun, to adjective, always proposing the quality of affection, harmony and joyous vital rhythm between people. The girl knows this, yet she cannot write her name correctly. She cannot transcribe it from spoken to written letters arranged in a certain significant manner. If Alice becomes nameless, Samar's name exceeds her. Although Karim teaches her to write her name, it cannot be written by her hand.

And so, very much like Alice, as we go deeper into her story, Samar undergoes a form of name loss. Both characters are unable to produce a representative thought of themselves, since they evolve in an abstract realm. If Alice cannot speak it, Samar cannot write her name. Like Alice, Samar does not express pain, but deduces that she is undergoing a transformation, witnessing it passively. For example, in the 'operation' scene, we see Samar stretched out on a long table while one woman describes her work on the girl as delicate embroidery, and another is at last satisfied. The girl in this scene is silently, calmly looking at the ceiling, expressionless. Again, we are projected into an intensive 'pure optical and sound situation' that holds violence and banality in a simple frame but refers to a million stories. Both Alice and Samar shift their name to the representative realm and disconnect automatically from it as it should represent them. Samar is the web lighting up Beirut, causing life to sprout out of it, and Alice is without a handle that presents the extendable unity of a little girl. In the end, two movements (that echo what I exposed earlier about eternity, infinite identity and abstract aesthetic experience) can be identified. The first one is the loss of one's handle on one's own representative identity. The second movement is a declaration of identity as a cartographic motion. Samar breaks the wheels of the traditional sensory-motor film and of the narrative with only her name and transposes it as an eternal moment governing the life thrust of a civilisation, thus reaffirming the filmmaker's will to describe the destructed Beirut life not as documented history but as cinematic mythology writing.

CONCLUSION

This chapter has tried to reveal the narrative structure underneath the linear one. The double filmic narrative produces a form that explodes the boundaries between fiction and documentary, and responds to the European Neo-Realism movement. A slim, childlike figure wandering around in a ruined city will always be reminiscent of Roberto Rossellini's *Germany Year Zero* (1948), where fiction is an atomist (unit-like) construct of reality, and thus, fiction faithfully reveals the feeling of reality of the world. Fiction overwrites the purely documentary, the way mythology can overwrite history.

Even if *A Suspended Life* documents the Lebanese civil war, it also defines cinema as an experience to fall out of the concept of the 'subject's identity'. With her first feature film, Saab shows she is not only a journalist dedicated to a political cause; she is also a cinematic inventor (theorist and practitioner). The film stumbles, like Alice and Samar, working its way through the leftovers of

Beirut and its cinematic potential. The city, the girl and the film are suspended in a becoming, between two ways of being. As one of the founding figures of New Lebanese Cinema, Saab shows that Lebanese cinema may be born from Neo-Realism, but it stands out from it with a crystalline narrative, because in its own abstraction it does not kill its characters or trap them in a death potency. Saab does not follow in Rossellini's footsteps, where the child-like figure is violently absorbed by the death potency of the ruined city. Saab underlines the paradoxical act of reducing and expanding, as the oriental cinematic signature.

NOTES

1. My translation of the René Char poetic fragment in *Eloge d'une soupçonnée* (Char 1988).
2. The Peter Pan character is the embodiment of the conflictual state of refusing to leave childhood for adulthood. The representations of Peter Pan's body are the illustration of that 'in-between' unviable state. Making a character out of an unviable state is the proposition of studying the conflict as an event that affects the one who contains it until the forces exceed the container and transform it. Usually or classically, the conflict carried by Peter Pan figures resolves in the adherence of the suspended character to one realm (adulthood), or in its death.
3. In Joseph Frank's *The Idea of Spatial Form* (1991), the author applies Worringer's abstraction theory to modern literature. He underlines how the expansion of space in plastic arts is rendered in literature with the expansion of time: the melting of past and present, he says, is the equivalent of the destruction of the dimension of depth in pictures. Vanishing the limits of past and present is the act of fading out the historical context in which a situation is placed. Drawing only the literary motions and their tensions by defusing them from their context is the first movement of abstraction in modern literature. (Proust, Joyce, Pound and T. S. Eliot are to blame here.)
4. Not to be confused with self-subjectification. The concept of 'self-objectivation' developed by Worringer refers to 'the fact that the need for empathy as a point of departure for aesthetic experience also represents, fundamentally, an impulse of self-alienation that is all the less likely to dawn upon us the more clearly the formula rings in our ears: "Aesthetic enjoyment is objectified self- enjoyment". For this implies that the process of empathy represents a self-affirmation, an affirmation of the general will to activity that is in us. "We always have a need for self-activation." Indeed, this is the basic need of our nature. In empathising this will to activity into another object, however, we *are* in the other object. We are delivered from our individual being as long as we are absorbed into an external object, an external form, with our inner urge to experience. We feel, as it were, our individuality flow into fixed boundaries, in contrast to the boundaryless differentiation of the individual consciousness. In this self-objectivation, lies a self-alienation . . .' (Worringer [1908] 2014: 24).

BIBLIOGRAPHY

Carroll, Lewis [1865] (2013a), *Alice's Adventures in Wonderland*, London: HarperCollins.
Carroll, Lewis [1871] (2013b), *Through the Looking Glass*, London: HarperCollins.
Char, René (1988), *Éloge d'une soupçonnée*, Paris: Éditions Gallimard.

Deleuze, Gilles [1985] (1989), *Cinema 2: The Time Image*, trans. Hugh Tomlinson and Robert Galeta, Minneapolis: University of Minnesota Press.

Deleuze, Gilles [1969] (1990), *The Logic of Sense*, trans. Mark Lester with Charles Stivale, London: Athlone Press.

Frank, Joseph (1991), *The Idea of Spatial Form*, New Brunswick, NJ: Rutgers University Press.

Lévi-Strauss, Claude [1977] (1995), *Myth and Meaning: Cracking the Code of Culture*, New York: Schocken Books.

Marks, Laura U. (2010), *Enfoldment and Infinity: An Islamic Genealogy of New Media Art*, Cambridge, MA: MIT Press.

Marks, Laura U. (2015), *Hanan Al-Cinema: Affections for the Moving Image*, Cambridge, MA: MIT Press.

Worringer, Wilhelm [1908] (2014), *Abstraction and Empathy: A Contribution to the Psychology of Style*, trans. Michael Bullock, Eastford, CT: Martino Publishing.

CHAPTER 15

The City of Disasters and Dreams: Experiencing Beirut and its Urban Geography in Light of Jocelyne Saab's *Beirut, My City* and *A Suspended Life*

Gregory Buchakjian

> The modern fact is that we no longer believe in this world. We do not even believe in the events which happen to us, love, death, as if they only half concerned us. It is not we who make cinema; is the world which looks to us like a bad film.
> – Gilles Deleuze, *Cinema 2: The Time Image* (1989: 171)

A POSTHUMOUS ENCOUNTER

On a rainy morning in January 2019, three men visiting Sursock Museum's twin galleries stood for a while in front of a photograph. They gazed at a composition displaying a grand vestibule flanked with a double revolving staircase. Barely visible across an iron railing and overexposed by a ray of light falling from the upper left corner, a woman was seated on the ground. The photograph was taken in Qasr Heneiné, a mansion built in the mid-nineteenth century for a Russian or Polish aristocrat named Todorski or Podhorki. The nobleman was

> responsible for the exceptional interior decoration, most particularly the Alhambra-inspired grand salon with its marble fountain, multifoil arches, muqarnas, friezes and lavish stucco ceilings inlaid with mirrors. It is an 'imagined Orient' turned into stone and plaster, and one of the earliest examples of such a Moresque interior in Beirut. (Bodenstein 2005: 193–4)

In the early twentieth century, a French doctor, Justin Calmette, inhabited the residence and occasionally organised masquerades in its extravagant setting. When the declining Ottoman Empire joined the Central Powers in World War I, Dr Calmette was forced to leave as the citizen of an enemy nation (Buchakjian 2017a: 50). The United States rented the place for their consulate, swapped it temporarily with the Netherlands and came back. Then, in 1936, Marie Mezher and her husband Dr Joseph Heneiné moved in and Dr Heneiné used part of the house as a clinic. In 1968, Mrs Mezher-Heneiné converted the drawing room into a restaurant named 'Le Petit Palais'. After her death, in 1970, the restaurant closed down and the apartment remained empty. In 1976 war-torn Beirut, among the thousands of civilians who had been expelled from their lodgings, five Shia Muslim families found shelter in the uninhabited space. With makeshift structures made of wood and cardboard, they subdivided the Heneiné mansion into a configuration that 'resembles the structure of a small village or a secluded quarter in a traditional Arab city' (Bodenstein 1999: 151). In the early 2000s, refugees returned to their homes. Around 2010, real estate developers who had acquired shares in this property and were erecting nearby a skyscraper named 'Cielo' lodged construction workers in the hall. Nevertheless, heirs of the Heneinés managed to put an end to this informality, so that in 2015, while I was completing my research and artistic work on abandoned dwellings in Beirut, Qasr Heneiné was empty and locked. It took me three months of negotiations with the various stakeholders to gain access and take photographs of the interior.

A few days after this visit, I obtained a copy of *Ghazl Al-Banat* (1985), known as *Une Vie Suspendue – L'adolescente Sucre D'amour* in French and *A Suspended Life* in English. At that time, Jocelyne Saab's first feature had never been publicly shown in Lebanon and was extremely difficult to find. The film became a fixation after I read Ghada Sayegh's PhD dissertation about Lebanese cinema, as the paper included the screenshot of a scene that was obviously situated in Qasr Heneiné (Sayegh 2013: 133). Sandra Bsaibes, who was sitting beside the staircase in the above-mentioned photograph, and I watched *A Suspended Life* together. What we experienced during the screening was an extremely strange sensation. The similarity of points of view between Jocelyne Saab's frames and my images made us feel we had been transposed into a picture shot thirty-two years before. On that rainy morning of January 2019, in the exhibition *Abandoned Dwellings, Display of Systems*, I was telling Achim Borchardt-Hume and Walid Raad this story and the coincidences that led me to the film. At that moment, in Paris, Jocelyne Saab passed away.

THE CITY OF DISASTERS AND DREAMS   237

Figure 15.1 *Abandoned Dwellings. Tableaux*. BF622-Zokak el-Blat _ 02'09'2015 (Gregory Buchakjian, 2015)

FILMING IN TIMES OF WAR

On 17 June 2009, *The Road to Peace* exhibition opened at Beirut Art Center. Curated by Saleh Barakat, the show aimed to investigate the production of visual artists during the 1975–90 war, putting together a haunting assortment of paintings, etchings, drawings, sculptures and photographs (Healy 2009). The selection devoted to Fouad Elkoury's *Civil War 1977–1986* comprised a diptych of deteriorated images depicting explosions. In 1980, Elkoury had worked as a set photographer for Volker Schlöndorff's *Die Fälschung* (*Circle of Deceit*, 1981), a feature that portrays foreign journalists in Beirut during the 1975–6 stage of the Lebanese war. After a day of working on a war sequence in the devastated city centre, Elkoury got his films developed but the job was rushed and the films were burned:

> For a long time the photographer was in a state of denial about the reality of this film shoot – because of this failure, because of the way the production blew up buildings without the slightest scruple, and because of the movie's somewhat orientalist perspective. (Buchakjian 2017a: 248)[1]

The Road to Peace was the first public appearance of this fruitless collaboration.

In the summer of 2016, Elkoury invited me to work on *Passing Time*, a book that would survey and question the archive of pictures he produced in Lebanon from the early 1960s to that day. For six months, we examined thousands of negatives, slides and contact sheets. In the batch that became the *Civil War* series, surfaced the camera rolls from *Circle of Deceit*. Apart from the ruined films, there were dozens of set pictures including the view of a Volkswagen Beetle cabriolet driving in a cloud of pink smoke. The vehicle was operated as a camera dolly for a tracking shot. Besides the driver, two people holding a movie camera are visible in the photograph. 'This is Jocelyne's car', said Elkoury. The Beetle appears in many of her films including *A Suspended Life* and *Beyrouth, ma ville* (*Beirut, My City*, 1982). In April 2019, the Department of Cinema and the School of Visual Arts at Alba – the Lebanese Academy of Fine Arts – organised the second *Ciné-rencontres* (*Cinema Encounters*) under the theme of 'Filming in times of war'. Elkoury's cabriolet photo was selected for the event poster. Ghassan Koteit and I asked Volker Schlöndorff whether Jocelyne Saab was one of the camera operators in the photo. He had his doubts, but he did have a surprise for us. In a video he produced for the *Ciné-rencontres* in which he expresses thoughts and memories about his Lebanese experience, Schlöndorff presents a wooden handicraft cabinet and explains it belonged to the family residence of Jocelyne Saab. When he was about to leave the country with the rushes of *Circle of Deceit*, Jocelyne asked him to take this object with him. Less than two years later, on the first days of the Israeli invasion of Lebanon, the Saabs' house was bombed and completely destroyed. Schlöndorff is still overwhelmed by her premonition of this fateful event.

FINDING REFUGE

The opening shot of *Beirut, My City* reveals a monumental facade with a portal cut into a grand arch bearing traces of smoke. In the subsequent frame, a woman stands inside the remains of an annihilated grand hall. Facing the camera, she says, in French:

> *Voilà.* This is my house; what remains of my house. *Voilà.* Here is my room. Here we were preparing a film. At the end of the day, that doesn't matter. These are only walls, after all. And we are all alive. Thinking of all the dead. It's true that this house is tradition. It hurts my heart. It's 150 years of history. It's my identity also. It's like for many people, the identity of the Lebanese who lose their homes, their properties. And as we don't know to whom to refer, we don't know any more who we are.

In the mid-nineteenth century, the De Freige family erected this imposing edifice on the Mar Elias/Abdel Kader street, opposite the one built for Todorski or Podhorki. 'De Freige was in love with an Austrian princess. To convince her to come, he designed for her a proper ballroom, enlarging the traditional central hall and increasing the height of the ceiling.'[2] In the early twentieth century, Saab's grandfather acquired the property with all the antiques and furniture it contained, including the piece that ended up at Schlöndorff's home in Potsdam. Saab was born and grew up in this fairy-tale setting that felt immutable. When she was a teenager, she went on her own in pursuit of the Palestinian cause. Thus, she remained in the eyes of people 'the girl of the *Qasr* (castle)'.[3] In 1978, the Qasr witnessed unforeseen events:

> After the first Israeli invasion of South Lebanon, thousands of refugees migrated to Beirut and families found shelter in our house. My sister wanted to kick them out and asked the Syrian army to do that. Her attitude upset me, and I requested the refugees to come back home. These are people from our country, and it was our duty to offer them hospitality. So, they moved inside the house and we became neighbours. An Armenian photographer working for Associated Press photographed us. He couldn't believe that the landlords of a castle would welcome poor people that way.[4]

Jocelyne Saab and her father shared the life of their new neighbours: 'Once a week, they cooked freekeh – grilled green wheat – and invited us for the meal.'[5] The way they reconstituted their rural life in the mansion fascinated her and triggered the idea for a film, *A Suspended Life*. Right before the beginning of the war, Maroun Baghdadi had already shot scenes of *Bayrout ya Bayrout* (*Beirut Oh Beirut*, 1975) – inside the Saabs' house (Saab in Millet 2017: iv–c). Location photographs taken in 1982 by Fouad Elkoury reveal an empty room of the Qasr, where filming was supposed to take place. However, its destruction changed the plans. In 1983, Jocelyne Saab resumed the project that became *A Suspended Life* and selected substitute locations: Qasr Heneiné was to replace her lost residence as the palace inhabited by exiled families. In addition, the similarly abandoned Qasr Ziadé, opposite Heneiné, served for scenes in Karim's studio, a middle-aged artist painting large scenes inspired by Arabic calligraphy, and the iconic Pink House, near the lighthouse, was chosen for the studio's exterior.

'LOOK, NOW, I'M ALIVE'[6]

The plot of *A Suspended Life* is a romance between Karim and Samar, a fifteen-year-old girl whose family found refuge in the abandoned mansion. Besides

Figure 15.2 Still from *Une Vie Suspendue* (*A Suspended Life*)

their age difference, which nowadays would make the film politically incorrect, they belong to ostensibly irreconcilable segments of society. Karim is the son of a conservative, upper-class Christian family. When saying goodbye, his father recites in French a famous quote by Georges Naccache, 'Deux négations ne font pas une nation – two negations don't build a nation', and his mother is worried about his unorthodox and unsafe lifestyle in West Beirut. The studio he lives and works in belongs to people who have left, so Karim is an informal dweller and a rebellious figure according to his community standards. Samar, who spends her time on the streets, alone and/or with other children, does not hesitate to break into houses. She barely knows how to read and write. In one of the film's most evocative scenes, Karim teaches her to spell her name. Samar's younger brother makes it clear he does not approve of her habit of hanging out with older men, while her father keeps things subtler. After she loses her virginity – it is left ambiguous whether the person responsible is Karim or someone else – her mother is introduced to a female doctor with the promise that the girl will shine again 'like a golden coin'. Executed in the kitchen of Qasr Heneiné, the hymen reconstruction surgery foreshadows the end of Samar's affair with Karim.

Intriguingly, toxic relationships are recurrent in cinema from the Lebanese war. In Maroun Bagdadi's *Liban, le pays du miel et de l'encens* (*The Land of Honey and Incense*, 1988), a little girl befriends a French hostage. The same director's *L'Homme voilé* (*The Veiled Man*, 1987) contains an explicit scene between sixteen-year-old Claire and a man in his forties. In *Circle of Deceit*, a German journalist who has split up with his wife, dates a former lover who moved to Beirut with her husband. After making love to her in the lavish 'traditional' house she inhabits, the journalist (incarnated by Bruno Ganz) runs across the city on fire and kills a man. In Borhane Alaouié's *Bayrût al-liqâ'* (*Encounter in Beirut*, 1981), Haïdar, a young man from the South who has migrated to West Beirut, has to 'cross' into the East to meet with a woman friend. 'Beirut does all it can to prevent encounters [. . .] the city is never as chaotic as the morning after the night before' (*Le Monde diplomatique* 1982: 13). These redundant impossible love stories express the fact that 'the city and its people shared a destiny during the war. Both lost their points of reference. The war changed the dynamics of interaction in Lebanese society, introducing new parameters of good and evil' (Khatib 2008: 62).

In both *Encounter in Beirut* and *A Suspended Life*, one of the main characters is a refugee who has found shelter in an abandoned residential unit of Beirut. *Encounter in Beirut* discloses a sober, white – almost virginal – and empty apartment in a modern building. In *A Suspended Life*, in contrast, the grandiose Alhambra-inspired decor abounds in picturesque details and anecdotes: women prepare *mulukhiyah* – leaves of *Corchorus olitorius* – seniors smoke shisha, and a goat needs to be taken care of. As Mathilde Rouxel points out, the house is perceived as a 'space of security and trust' (2015: 212–14). *A Suspended Life*'s having being produced after the disappearance of the house, this position might be seen as a cathartic reaction. Jalal Toufic writes that 'A filmmaker, thinker, writer, video maker or musician who in relation to a surpassing disaster still considers that tradition has persisted, never has the impression that he has to resurrect even some of what "survived" the carnage' (2009: 15). This assertion can be applied in reverse, as Saab was conscious that tradition was lost or at least broken, so that her works can be seen as an attempt to overcome the vacuum. Rouxel's reading opposes the protective house to the street, associated with danger. While Borhane Alaouié refrains from war violence and illustrates the city's deficiency through an inextricable traffic jam that makes Haïdar's journey impossible, in *A Suspended Life*, Saab alternates scenes where militiamen interact with the characters and raw shelling footage that was used as the core of *Beirut, My City*. Ultimately, *A Suspended Life* ends with the death of Karim, shot in the middle of the street by a sniper.

Within this lethal game, where 'the body of Beirut comes to mirror the bodies of its inhabitants' (Khatib 2008: 61), Saab composed an unannounced – and perhaps unconscious – mesmerising diptych expressing death and life. In *Beirut, My City*, after watching the horrors of Israeli bombings and graphic shots of burnt corpses, the spectator is brought into a school courtyard. A dozen entirely naked five- to ten-year-old boys are lying on the ground, their bodies covered with flies. Sick, starving, sad and lost, they lay bare the curse of Beirut's besieged population. Mirroring this spectacle that conveys the smell of death, *A Suspended Life* stages two girls, Samar and her best friend, talking and mimicking their sexual desires against the apocalyptic backdrop of the destroyed Sports City stadium. A few years before, in *Hamasat* (*Whispers*, 1979), Maroun Bagdadi followed the poet Nadia Tueni wandering through Beirut's shattered historical centre, lamenting its annihilation. However, these female presences in the ruins are very dissimilar from one another. Saab's teenagers, who are exploring their sexuality, use the wrecked infrastructure as a playground without any consideration for the tragedy that lies beneath, while Tueni, who incarnates elegance and dignity, refrains from breaking down in tears. Yet they all embody instincts of survival and resilience in the space of an utter calamity. They also prefigure the attempts, in the post-war years, to recover a city lost by its inhabitants. When, in 2009, I initiated *Tableaux*, I photographed performances inside abandoned dwellings, part of which is the picture of the vestibule of Qasr Heneiné, and the human presence was a repeated re-enactment of Tueni's aura. Apart from her presence itself, there was the fact that she 'died three years after the film was made and the movie was not released until the 2000s. As a consequence, her fragile presence in the filmed images and her recorded voice is something of a post-mortem apparition' (Buchakjian 2017c: 35). As I had not watched *A Suspended Life* until

Figure 15.3 Still from *Beirut, My City*

2015, for me it constituted more of a prequel than an inspiration. It generated considerable intellectual and emotional connections in my mind, and it was an immense source of pride for me to organise its first public screening in Lebanon, on 10 November 2016 at Sursock Museum.

THE AGONY OF UTOPIAS

'I chose images that gave a sense of the life that existed, or that re-enacted the life that was disappearing', said Jocelyne Saab about a sequence from *Beyrouth, jamais plus* (*Beirut, Never Again*, 1976) where militiamen are reading *Tintin* (Saab 2016). In *Beirut, My City*, an old man wearing white pyjamas roams a wrecked neighbourhood. In voice-over Roger Assaf says, 'When one has been touched, in his family or his relatives, we suddenly realised the intimacy of relations the besieged city had tied with death.' In a subsequent sequence, another old man waters plants while bombs are falling here and there. 'I did this garden alone', he says. 'Nobody helped me. The plant is stronger than their [the Israelis'] bombs. They are up [in the sky] and I am here.' These moments of resilience in the face of the disaster alternate with others that move into the burlesque, like in *Beirut, My City*, when a spy disguised as a madman cleans Saab's Volkswagen. 'There was a madman in the city: Abou'el rich. Beautiful poisonous flower in a gruesome gangrened city. When he was filmed, we did not know yet he was a spy. A disguised Israeli military', says the voice-over. The anecdote around Abou'el rich is the occasion for *Beirut, My City*'s narrator to expand further, in a statement:

> We also didn't know what Beirut was hiding, nor did the foreigner [the spy] or the insider really know it. Man always believes what he sees and what he sees didn't stop betraying him. The madman was not mad and the city was not what it seemed to be. Beirut: bordello city, prostitute city, stepmother city. This is how we used to perceive it before. This is how we used to talk about it. Finance, spying, aggressive and destructive modernity, the most arrogant political venality, the supermarket of all traffics and treasons, it was all this, Beirut. Apparently. What didn't have to happen for the image to revolve, for the optical illusion to crumble and the reality of stone to start speaking.

Rooted, deliberately or not, in the posterity of Roberto Rossellini's War Trilogy and Alain Resnais's *Hiroshima mon amour* (1959), the films of Jocelyne Saab, Borhane Alaouié and Maroun Bagdadi were conceived during an ongoing conflict, and thus, in most cases, were produced during times of respite. This is where *Beirut, My City* stands out as an exception, as it transpires during the 1982 Siege of Beirut, one of the most terrible episodes in the city's history. What Roger Assaf's voice pledges after the description of Abou'el rich goes into a political, social and theoretical manifesto that attains its climax in the film's grand finale, 'the farewell to the fedayeen, with an epic accent, an immense liturgy in honour of their departure was only the expression of this recognition'. Nonetheless, the pivotal moment of *Beirut, My City* lies in street scenes taken in Hamra. Once described as the 'Champs-Elysées of the East', it was 'unique in the Arab world for the speed of its metamorphosis, the neighbourhood hosted half of the city's foreign residents, attracted by its modernity' (Kassir 2004: 470). After the beginning of the war, Hamra lost most of its lustre. During the invasion, it literally became a court of miracles. Informal stalls obscured the displays of shops that were mostly closed, offering miserable merchandise for a crowd of beggars and cripples. Over this vision of an agonising urbanity on the edge of survival, Roger Assaf says:

> We used to say: 'I am from West Beirut' and at once we had a language and an attitude that went beyond the narrow norms of little communities. We could be Shia or Christian, Jewish or Sunni, Lebanese or Palestinian, faithfully, proudly, and be at the same time in the same space, someone from West Beirut, where the forms of a possible society, the one of a certain Arab dream and the unaccomplished desire of a condemned people survived. Agonising Beirut had the features of utopia. Being Lebanese and Arab, it was possible. Jewish and Palestinian, it existed. Muslim and Progressive, it was done. Woman and boss, they were both there. Anarchist and organised, it was common.

Roger Assaf's words express everything that secular and progressive Lebanese – and perhaps Arabs – would have dreamt of. During the 1982 siege, the remaining inhabitants in this wicked place had no choice but to develop solidarities that would shape a new social contract. As Roger V. Gould wrote about the Paris Commune, 'mobilization does not just depend on social ties: it also creates them' (1991: 719). Assaf's statement, which may sound as radical for the Lebanese establishment as the Commune was for the French bourgeoisie, never left my mind. It rang a bell when, on 17 October 2019, economic and financial recession triggered massive protests against the corrupted political elite, the confessional system, social and gender inequalities, environmental crises and many other misfortunes. The year 2019 was somehow as extreme as 1982, but in a different way: the population was not under the threat of bombardments and massacres but was facing the announced bankruptcy of the state and the private corporations, and imminent starvation. Demonstrators filled the streets, in Beirut and across the country, even in localities considered to be strongholds of the dominant political parties, instigating new ways of defiance every day. 'I think a lot of Jocelyne', said Yara Salem, a film student at Alba and one of the most engaged protestors. 'I watched her films in my tent on Martyrs Square', she added.[7] Yara is certainly not the only person missing Jocelyne. The revolution resembles her; it is feminine, profound, generous and excessive, like her.

In *A Suspended Life*, Saab filmed inside the historical Grand Theatre on what was at that time the demarcation line. The location was not without risks and one day a group of young men burst into the building brandishing guns. They kidnapped the crew: 'They locked us up in a cafe that functioned as a whorehouse and a gambling joint and sent my assistant to fetch a ransom, together with one of the kidnappers, while the others held us at gunpoint. She came back with a cheque for 3,000 Lebanese pounds and they let us go.'[8] Forty years later, the Grand Theatre is still derelict. Solidere, the private company in charge of the reconstruction of Beirut city centre, envisaged a conversion into a luxury resort, but the project never took off and the structure remained fenced off and inaccessible. On the first days of the revolution, the Grand Theatre and the neighbouring City Palace, better known as 'The Egg', 'The Dome' or 'The Bubble' – another relic awaiting an unknown fate – were implemented as instruments for debate, contestation and urban reinvention. One month after the beginning of the revolutionary process, demonstrators initiated the habit of knocking as violently as possible on the palisades of the Grand Theatre as if it were a percussion instrument. Whether this gesture was born out of frustration, despair, love, hate, desire or anger, it had something of a primitive cathartic ritual about it. The society of this country in agony was reclaiming the city.

In *Beirut, My City*, Roger Assaf concludes his manifesto with the statement that 'utopia is highly paid, and we didn't know yet that the bill would be diabolically increased'. At the time of writing this chapter, the fears of the Lebanese people were as high as their hopes.

NOTES

1. Volker Schlöndorff rejected the statement that 'the production blew up buildings without the slightest scruple' for the obvious reason it would have put in danger the lives of actors and crew (interview with Ghassan Koteit and Gregory Buchakjian, 24 September 2019).
2. Author's interview with Jocelyne Saab, 2 November 2015.
3. Author's interview with Jocelyne Saab, 2 November 2015.
4. Author's interview with Jocelyne Saab, 2 November 2015.
5. Author's interview with Jocelyne Saab, 2 November 2015.
6. Rohe 2018: 286.
7. Author interview, 12 December 2019.
8. Author's interview with Jocelyne Saab, 2 November 2015.

BIBLIOGRAPHY

Bodenstein, Ralph (1999), 'Qasr Heneiné. Memories and History of a Late Ottoman Mansion in Beirut', Master's thesis, Rheinischen Friedrich Wilhelms-Universität, Bonn.
Bodenstein, Ralph (2005), 'The Heneiné Mansion', in Ralph Bodenstein, Andreas Fritz, Hans Gebhardt, Jens Hanssen, Bernhard Hillenkamp, Oliver Kogler, Anne Mollenhauer, Dorothee Sack and Friederike Stolleis, *History, Space and Social Conflict in Beirut: The Quarter of Zokak el-Blat*, Beirut: Orient Institut, pp. 193–4.
Buchakjian, Gregory (2017a), 'Selecting, Sorting, Looking: An Archaeology of Fouad Elkoury's Photographic Career', in Gregory Buchakjian, Fouad Elkoury and Manal Khader (eds), *Passing Time*, Beirut: Kaph Books, pp. 223–48.
Buchakjian, Gregory (2017b), 'Une maison avec vue', in Gregory Buchakjian and Clémence Cottard Hachem (eds), *Traversées photographiques: le journal du Docteur Cottard*, Beirut: Arab Image Foundation, pp. 48–51.
Buchakjian, Gregory (2017c), 'The Lives and Deaths of Inhabitants in Abandoned Houses', *OAR: The Oxford Artistic and Practice Based Research Platform*, 2, 30–46.
Deleuze, Gilles (1989), *Cinema 2: The Time Image*, trans. Hugh Tomlinson and Robert Galeta, Minneapolis: University of Minnesota Press.
Gould, Roger V. (1991), 'Multiple Networks and Mobilization in the Paris Commune, 1871', *American Sociological Review*, 56: 6, 716–29.
Healy, Patrick (2009), 'Beirut Art Center Depicts Trauma of War', *The New York Times*, 6 July.
Kassir, Samir (2004), *Histoire de Beyrouth*, Paris: Fayard.
Khatib, Lina (2008), *Lebanese Cinema: Imagining the Civil War and Beyond*, London: I. B. Tauris.
Le Monde diplomatique (1982), 'Les générations éclatées', *Le Monde diplomatique*, September, p. 13.
Millet, Raphael (2017), *Cinema in Lebanon*, Beirut: Rawiya Editions.
Rohe, Oliver (2018), 'Look, Now, I'm Alive', in Nour Salamé and Clémence Cottard Hachem (eds), *On Photography in Lebanon: Essays and Stories*, Beirut: Kaph Books, pp. 286–95.
Rouxel, Mathilde (2015), *Jocelyne Saab: la mémoire indomptée*, Beirut: Éditions Dar An-Nahar.
Saab, Jocelyne (2016), Interview, *Magreb Orient Express*, TV5 Monde, 11 December.
Sayegh, Ghada (2013), 'Images d'après: l'espace-temps de la guerre dans le cinéma au Liban, du " Nouveau cinéma libanais" (1975) aux pratiques artistiques contemporaines (de 1990 à nos jours)', PhD dissertation, Paris: Paris Ouest Nanterre la Défense.
Toufic, Jalal (2009), *The Withdrawal of Tradition Past a Surpassing Disaster*, Beirut: Forthcoming Books.

CHAPTER 16

Fiction and Voyeurisms: For a Fantasmatic History

Léa Polverini

When television channel France 3 asked Jocelyne Saab for a short film about Alexandria in 1986, it was mostly supposed to be a tribute to Lawrence Durrell. From the British author, however, Saab kept only these words: 'Alexandria, princess and whore. The royal city and the *anus mundi*.' The phrase provided a mischievous subtitle to *The Ghosts of Alexandria* (1986), that seemed good enough to summarise both *The Alexandria Quartet* (Durrell 1962) and the declining city of which Saab was trying to recollect the image. Although '*anus mundi*' literally means 'old world', one might spontaneously think about a faecal world: a world that has been digested, processed and transformed by the passing years. Durrell's graphic formula pointed towards the idea of an organic memory of the city, and this is ultimately what Saab offers us through the figure of the storyteller. Indeed, *The Ghosts of Alexandria* barely displays any image of Alexandria; there is no archive – unlike in Saab's Lebanese films – to restore an atmosphere or to recollect a past event in order to preserve its memory, but the short film gives us scattered and fragmented, incomplete and impulsive stories: testimonies on the fringes of a polite society, nostalgic for a time that never quite existed, mixed with the banalities of today's everyday life. Alexandria's essence lies not in the cityscapes, but in its inhabitants' faulty memories and testimonies: voices replace urbanity, and the camera thus delegates its primary function to various casual narrators.

The art of storytelling is essential in Jocelyne Saab's work; from her very first reports in the 1970s to the last films of her career, she gradually moved towards a fictionalisation of history. It is not that Saab tried to rewrite it, but rather that she came to understand history as a set of discourses, often contradictory. Significantly, Saab mainly filmed drifting societies, either at war, morally challenged, or threatened by time passing by and oblivion: societies whose narratives were constantly changing and subject to caution. Her artistic journey is informed by the Lebanese civil war and the partition of Beirut that she first covered as a reporter from early 1975, insofar as the country's pluri-vocal history is as changing and conflicted as its confessional composition. In a way, Saab's work consisted in emancipating oneself from ideologies, to account for their fantasmatic and relative nature. In that respect, carrying the story of a lost Alexandria is quite similar to filming a dismantled and partitioned Lebanon, reshaped according to war factions: both are only fantasies, and produce imaginary spaces at some point. While criss-crossing Lebanon during the filming of *Letter from Beirut* (1978) and after passing ten checkpoints, Saab related: 'my itinerary belongs also to science-fiction. Can you imagine yourself visiting ten countries in less than five hours?' Faced with societies in crisis or disappearing societies, the line between fiction and reality becomes porous.

Through the study of a few films including both documentary and fiction (*Letter from Beirut*; *Beirut, My City*, 1982; *The Ghosts of Alexandria*, 1986; and *What's Going On?*, 2009), I propose a reading of Jocelyne Saab's cinema as an attempt to recompose vanishing worlds through fiction. Filming disaster and loss is like walking on a tightrope: one must be neither too complacent nor too compassionate. Saab opens a third way: her approach is that of a voyeur, but she paradoxically makes voyeurism an act of resistance. While voyeurism involves some sense of fictionalisation, in her hands it mostly becomes a way to transcend a chronological history. The weaving together of cinema and literature is also essential here, since Saab's films are written like some kind of poetic variations, especially considering the peculiar use of voice-over and the insertion of numerous literary fragments. This constitutive polyphony eventually opens an imaginary, almost mythical horizon.

FOR A VOYEURISM OF RESISTANCE

Voyeurism is an obscene gaze that usually implies the transgression of moral values, and especially that of bodies' dignity. This is obviously one of the first issues at stake when covering a conflict: how far should the testimony go? The question is not so much to decide what to show, but rather *how* to show it. In an interview with French journalist Jean-Marie Cavada, Saab explained:

> I did not want to show the war with its tanks, its shells, its corpses and its dead, but I always wanted to show the humans, those who suffered, those who lived and those who endured this war on a daily basis because I was part of this population. (Saab, cited in Rouxel 2015: 271)

In her war documentaries, Saab films what might be called the 'weak times' of the conflict: although she films during the disaster, it is as if the struggle had always already occurred. It still appears as a trace, and a memory. Saab films defeated bodies as ruins, and the city as an injured or decaying body, because the disaster is less about events than about the loss of landmarks. The backward editing of *Beirut, My City*'s opening is quite enlightening in this regard. When Jocelyne Saab appears in the middle of her former and now devastated house, she ends her speech by saying: 'We don't know who we are any more', just before the shot switches to an overview of bombings that quickly alternates with a close-up of dead bodies and badly injured victims. The temporality of events is compressed, and the mutilated bodies become symbols devoid of individuality. However, a singular quietude oozes from those shots. Saab does not show corpses for the sake of showing corpses. There is a constant refusal of martyrdom in her films, to prevent any vain heroisation, and any romanticising of the fights. Elsewhere, by emphasising it in a ludicrous manner in her film *Our Imprudent Wars* (1995), Lebanese filmmaker Randa Chahal Sabbag made a mockery of the obsession with martyrs which is very prevalent in the Middle East's visual and political culture. In contrast, Saab's shots keep a measured distance. In his reading of what Jacques Rivette called the 'Kapo's travelling' (1961), French critic Serge Daney wrote that 'innocence [is] the terrible grace given to the first comer. To the first one who simply performs the gestures of cinema' (1982: 5). Saab's voyeurism is paradoxically not an immoral voyeurism, but rather a moralisation of the voyeurism of images, which is partly unavoidable. This moralisation is especially achieved through editing: it is the effect produced by the alternation between close-ups of the bodies (voyeuristic shots) and panoramic shots of the city (de-voyeuristic shots). Far from indulging in a perverse or macabre voyeurism, Saab cuts loose from political party logic at this very moment, while revealing, and thus denouncing, their blind killings. When the Lebanese playwright Roger Assaf takes over the narration, he declares:

> And we will have to act quickly then, to track the consciences down, and show them with fresh images, their excessive blindness: the almost immediate vision of the mutilated corpses, enucleated eyes, scalped skulls, bodies disembowelled with axe blows, will repulse the world, and force a little the tolerated doses of voyeurism. But how will this carnage be different from the previous ones?

The opening sequence, in its naked horror, was necessary in order to fight against denial and oblivion, whether they are based on the total destruction of the country, or its reconstruction with the help of bulldozers – a society intending to remove all its ruins is far worse than the ruins themselves, since it would be condoning a world without history. And indeed, the rest of the documentary is dedicated to a rhapsodic remembrance of Beirut, as Assaf considers: 'The dates get mixed up nowadays. Images oppose to each other, they collide in your waking moments, to acquire the shape that memory will take when appearances will have melted away.'

The different sequences in *Beirut, My City* stand as a daydream supposed to revivify the story of a city both wrecked and persevering in its habits, oscillating between intimacy and collective experience: the death of friend Kamal, Abu Riché, the town's fake madman, the starving children, the proud inhabitants of West Beirut attending to their business amid rubble and under a hail of bullets, and so on. The images of horror and everyday life candidly coexist, and neither can overcome the other. The succession of small scenes shows us a fragmented and almost ahistorical Beirut: the city is constantly reconfiguring itself, everything is in motion, as shown by the countless cars, mopeds or bikes (someone even put wheels on the martyrs' crosses) which the people filmed constantly drive off-screen, as if endlessly running away. In *Letter from Beirut*, the camera itself circulates between buses and checkpoints.

FANTASMATIC RECONSTRUCTIONS

At the start of the documentary *Letter from Beirut*, there is a woman who phones a friend to exchange the latest news: which road has been blocked, where the militiamen are, who is shooting at whom, what the rumours of the day are, and so on. After hanging up, she continues this little puzzle game by comparing newspapers from 1970 and 1978, which present almost identical contents: 'As you see, nothing has really changed. Each year, each month got its massacre.' The state of permanent disaster in which Beirut finds itself knocks the meaning and the course of history out of kilter, and history suddenly seems to stutter, while being only able to accumulate interchangeable lines of attack. The newspapers that the woman flicks through are more fill-in-the-gaps texts, with wide white pages – the result of censorship, which erases even the prime minister's words. The real story of Beirut, in the end, is not what has been printed but what is missing: 'the game is to discover what has been said', jokes the woman on the phone. The absurdity of the situation provokes a sense of derision, through a bitter comic, which above all exposes the gradual meaninglessness of all things. These war chronicles work as riddles and turn history into a mere rumour: Beirut's history is a collective noise, but it is above all a bet on the future.

A little later in the film, Saab's friends meet in the evening and speculate about what will happen next, working out various scenarios for the future of West Beirut. But this discourse runs idle: there is no control over the future, therefore it is not so much a question of knowing what might really happen as it is of reinventing history, starting from a human community, through the power of words by

FICTION AND VOYEURISMS 251

those fantasising – war has already shown the precariousness of all certainty, and the inanity of all dialectical discourse. With children, this will be done through mime: reality is transformed into fiction; like actors, children replay the war with an innocent cruelty – so much so that Saab has been accused of having prepared the scene. In the end, Beirut's history becomes a matter of fiction.

Yet this rewriting of history has a much darker side, as soon as it enters the political discourse game. Saab's documentaries combine poetic speeches with propaganda speeches, rooted in history: this enlightens a constitutive polyphony, which refuses to solve the fate of the cities by offering a single narrative. That is what we see through the evocation of the Tel al-Zaatar massacre, in 1976. Two years later, Saab returns to the ruins of the Palestinian refugee camp with two former inhabitants, Abu Brahim and his wife. They point out through the rubble the location of their former home, and to that of their neighbours. But this memory is about to be replaced by the story of the winners: 'The bus does not come here any more. There are no passengers for a razed camp. But the road has been built by the Phalangists, in order to bring visitors to the spot of their victory.' Once inhabited, Tel al-Zaatar has become a pure manifesto, a war trophy conquered from the ruins – namely, the absolute negation of a city. By coming to pick a few leaves of vines that have grown through the ruins, Oum Brahim nevertheless reactivates the lost land's memory, by reproducing the gestures of a daily life long gone.

Figure 16.1 Abu Brahim and Oum Brahim indicate what used to stand in Tel al Zaatar before the bombings, in *Letter from Beirut*

Although she relies on a precise historical context, Saab rejects the imposture of writing a collective or personal history as a logical series: history is not made of lessons but is rather a matter of representing the experience of a debacle. In 'The Discourse of History', Roland Barthes theorised the confrontation between 'the chronic time of history' and that of discourse itself ('paper time'), which contributes to restoring 'a complex, parametric, non-linear time, whose deep space recalls the mythic time of the ancient cosmogonies, it too linked by essence to the speech of the poet or the soothsayer' (Barthes 1986: 120–31). If Barthes was writing about the historian's discourse, aiming to demonstrate that every historical discourse is 'essentially ideological elaboration', his apprehension of history as a reconstruction fed by mythical representations seems absolutely relevant to Saab's work, as her films play on collective imaginations to put the immediate reality into perspective. It is a lacunar, sutured history, that supports an aesthetic of the trace. Both Beirut and Alexandria are city-palimpsests fed by literary representations resonating with each other: Cavafy and Durrell in *The Ghosts of Alexandria*, the comments of Adnan and Assaf in *Letter from Beirut* and *Beirut, My City*, and a multiplicity of literary fragments in *What's Going On?*. The gaze at the disaster is supplemented by a poetic speech that wrests it from historical contingency. As if language was contaminated by the surrounding decaying spaces, the wastelands lead to an aesthetic of fragments: in the rhapsodic editing, but also in the commentary by the voice-over or the characters. Indeed, the commentary does not function as a narrative, but as a poetic testimony: there is no linearity, but a succession of vignettes trying to account for a disjointed reality. Just like the short prose poem by the Lebanese poet and artist Etel Adnan, recited at the end of *Letter from Beirut*:

> There was a time, when comrade Dostoevsky was lodging at the Orient Prince. He was eating at the Horseshoe. He was swimming, no kidding, at the Saint Georges. He was yawning at the American University of Beirut. And for his redemption, he was counting the typographical errors of the newspaper An-Nahar.

The writer, a literary giant turned into a simple 'comrade', travels through all the mythical places that have forged the image of Beirut as the cultural and intellectual capital of the region; but he travels through them as a dilettante, in the manner of Henri Michaux's jaunty Monsieur Plume (1963). It is a mischievous tribute, which oozes with burlesque, that Etel Adnan pays here to the city. Beirut's 'Golden Age' is only a succession of clichés whose prestige is immediately defused: one never does anything but yawn on the benches of the very venerable American University of Beirut, and one will buy its fame as well as its salvation by correcting the misprints of a newspaper that was supposed to inspire respect. Nostalgia is shown to only produce chimeras: it conjures up images of a past that never existed, but which is reconstructed retrospectively.

TIME AND FICTION

Given this, we should think of the specific temporality of voyeurism. Just like Khouloud's metronome in *What's Going On?* gives rhythm to a time that does not pass – a flat time – voyeurism creates fantasies that resist the passing of time. However, these images only testify to the fantasy of a vanished reality. Voyeurism is mostly a matter of reconstruction, which creates fictional witness-objects. *The Ghosts of Alexandria* is paradoxically quite interesting in this regard, since it presents a collection of testimonies without images: this documentary uses only speech to show a lost atmosphere. Unlike Beirut, Alexandria was not disfigured by war: its changes are mostly cultural and ideological. To capture this hectic era which cannot be restored through archives, Saab needs living bodies, memory-bodies – witnesses and historians. But how far back in time must we go to understand Alexandria's history? The one that is told is definitely unchronological, and overdetermined by poets: Lawrence Durrell, of course, and the Alexandrian Greek writer Constantine Cavafy, who is actually his primary inspiration.

In Durrell's *The Alexandria Quartet* (1962), Cavafy's poem 'The God Abandons Antony', published in 1911, is quoted several times – in Clea's translation. The poem initially represents Alexandria's fall for Mark Antony, when he learns of his defeat, inflicted by Octavian: 'With courage say your last goodbyes / To Alexandria as she is leaving.' Alexandria is seen as a city of loss, whose image is fleeting, always ready to disappear. It is the city that one cannot keep before one's eyes, the city which escapes from the gaze that would like to seize it: the voyeur must now become a *voyant*. The paronomasia is easy, Rimbaud's famous word provides us with the pretext, but still, it allows us to better understand what is at stake in the reconstruction of the city's history through poetry. The city does not have one truth, but several truths, which one can only grasp in the flaws of representation: it is only by telling the history of Alexandria as it has been a fantasy over the years that one can hope to grasp an accurate image of this ever-changing city. In the second chapter of *The Alexandria Quartet*'s *Balthazar*, the character of Darley mentions 'the polymorphous desires of the city', as if the city was self-determining. In fact, Alexandria is a city that reconfigures itself under the gaze of its architects, that is to say, those who put it into narrative.

Durrell's Alexandria is nothing but a fantasy, and so is Saab's in *The Ghosts of Alexandria*: it is written in the rifts and hazards of forgetful testimonies of upper-class old ladies who embellish their memories with anecdotes of the city's wealth and glory. It is an Alexandria that cultivates the discrepancies: from the mention of General de Gaulle to the day's menu, the tone remains the same. Alexandria is a city of decadences, written through multiple stratifications. The 'ghosts' of Alexandria are its remembrances, as well as its *passeurs* from another time. At one point, an old woman reads another poem of Cavafy's, 'I went', composed in 1905 and published in 1913 (Cavafy 2007). This time it is the decline of those who lived in Alexandria that Cavafy writes of, those who have drowned in the lights and intoxication of the city, seeking delights, real as well as imaginary. In the end, Alexandria is nothing but a mystification, and so is the so-called golden age of the country built on its cosmopolitanism, praised and already worn out by the famous Hellenistic, Roman, Coptic, Muslim Alexandria, little Egyptian Paris of the 1930s – before the Six Day War and the oil issues put an end to it.

Poetry must be considered to be a political necessity in Saab's work. Against macabre voyeurism, we should consider the idea of a storyteller's voyeurism, as a politico-poetic concept. After the experience of war and its impossibly crude representation, it was necessary to bear witness to Alexandria – that was the Egyptian period of Saab's work – in order not to talk about Lebanon any more. This would allow her to talk about it again later, but this time through an assumed fiction – *Once Upon a Time, Beirut: Story of a Star*, in 1994, and

Figure 16.2 The old lady reading Cavafy's poem 'I Went', in *The Ghosts of Alexandria*

What's Going On?, in 2009. Saab's attachment to what she called 'cultural resistance', formalised in 2013 when she set up the Cultural Resistance International Film Festival of Lebanon, sheds light on her use of fiction. It was then supposed to be a cinema that would heal the country's – and to a greater extent the region's – wounds, by making an act of memory, and a space for dialogue, through a visual language that escapes from war ideologies; an emergency cinema that is also, paradoxically, part of a longer moment in time. However, in what way could voyeurism represent an act of resistance? It destabilises reality's data through a fantasmatic gaze, and emancipates from expected representations – which would work as a condemnation – to open up a new horizon of possibilities. It is about discarding what Stéphane Mallarmé (1897) called the 'universal reporting': a language strictly assigned to its function of communication, and therefore expeditious and instrumental. In opposition to this utilitarian understanding of language stands a poetic discourse, which is a self-criticism of all its inherent means of expression, words or images. This is also a way not to get used to the horror. In Saab's cinema, the experience of loss creates new realities. As her documentaries switch to a poetic register, all those films are finally a kind of tribute to the cities that vanished and endure only by the organic memories of those who lived there. It is a similar, although smiling, ironic distance that we find in *The Ghosts of Alexandria* with the two old men sitting in the cafe, and reciting the alphabet to return to Alexandria's origins: 'Alexander the Great, Alexandria', they eventually recompose, as if the single name of the city could contain some truth of it.

FROM EROTICISM TO KNOWLEDGE

Yet there is another kind of voyeurism, the one towards a body targeted by a desire. The voyeur's gaze shapes things, is superimposed on its object, and aims to redefine it, if not to replace it: one reconfigures this object under the shapes of one's desire. One films war victims to denounce through their bodies this very war, one films city ruins to recall through them a previous state of history and, finally, one – Nasri, the protagonist of *What's Going On?* – takes pictures of the body of one's beloved to always keep her image, a form of timeless presence by one's side and under one's gaze. First standing on an observatory tower, Nasri soon hides behind the branches of a tree to take pictures of Khouloud standing behind a fence, as if she has become an animal: this *mise-en-scène* points out a form of captivity, until the final look to camera: Khouloud appears utterly captive by Nasri's eye. There is no insouciance of the bodies facing the voyeur: the pose is simply reversed. It becomes a pose when the voyeur triggers his camera. Besides, Nasri does not hide effectively, and quickly ends up showing himself in front of Khouloud, who stares back at him as if she were challenging him.

In any case, the voyeur's gaze is detached from historical reality and turns its objects into symbols. This implies a phenomenon of disconnection from reality and fictionalisation, if not mythification. This phenomenon is intensified in *What's Going On?* by a *mise en abyme*: Nasri is a voyeur, reinventing women through his gaze, but he is himself only a pawn under the gaze of the laughing poet, the poet-tailor at the origin of the film, who tries to recompose a whole world by means of allegories. Each feminine figure (from Nayla to Lilith, including Khouloud, Raïa the prostitute and the mourners) becomes a relay-character, drawing for Nasri the process of an initiation. Nasri's love for Khouloud – which is more of a quest – symbolises the access to knowledge which would result in finding the city's lost history.

From the top of his buildings, Nasri observes not only Khouloud, but also Beirut, multiplying the panoramic and high-angle shots: the woman, the city – 'Beirut, brothel city, whore city, shrew city', Assaf likewise announces. Once again, this is a deeply organic history, rooted in the bodies, as suggested by many symbolic elements, such as Khouloud's bed-book, whose pages become a new skin, or the heart that has stopped beating, which the poet anchors in his own book before finally stitching it up.

At some point, the images of a human body seen from the inside dissolve into the images of Lebanon's landscape. These come from a previous scientific report by Saab, *Fertilisation in Video* (1991), in which Saab filmed a fertilisation in vitro as a journey, hence a possible metaphorical interpretation: through the heart of the woman beats the pulse of the city. The dissolve also announces the grotto's pattern, which we see twice during the film. First, in the vagina-shaped cave,

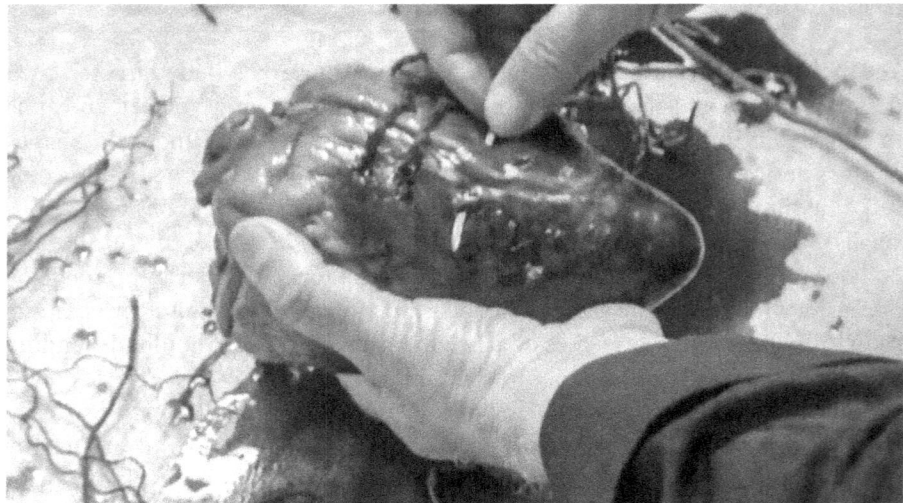

Figure 16.3 The poet mends Khouloud's heart, in *What's Going On?*

found in the Bekaa valley and rubbed by Khouloud's hands in a highly erotic scene: the birth of desire then becomes a rebirth, and the exploration of the body, a rediscovery of origins. The second occurrence represents a metaphorical death: still in the Bekaa, it is this time Nasri who attends his own funeral during the procession of mourners. The burial leads him to a cave as well, where he meets up with his double in front of twelfth-century incunabula. The double's appearance introduces a duplicity in the very filmic matter: first a visual redoubling, in the alternation of shots between Nasri and his double, then the alternation of voices, since Nasri's double repeats his words:

NASRI:	To learn is to remember, and to remember something, one must have learnt it before.
NASRI'S DOUBLE:	And to remember something, one must have learnt it before. And to remember something, one must have learnt it before.
NASRI:	He longed to know about self-empowerment and the thrill of choice.
NASRI'S DOUBLE:	He longed to know about self-empowerment and the thrill of choice.

The scene summons the Platonic notion of reminiscence: to learn is to remember, that is to say, to discover in oneself the path that leads to truth, yet knowledge is what has never been the present of an intentional conscience. One has to find a past self to find the lost memory of the city. Nasri then relates to an alter ego of Dante, who descends to the centre of the earth to reach knowledge – guided not by Virgilio, but by the demon Lilith, considered to be Adam's first wife in Jewish mythology. Significantly, his return to Beirut marks his reunion with Khouloud, who gives him a large volume of *Inferno*. A few shots later, Nasri's figure will replace the one of the poet-tailor, as shown in the poster that depicts him holding a book in front – instead – of his face.

MYSTICAL RESURGENCES

The garden's pattern is also interesting regarding this issue of remembrance. It is a recurring element in several of Saab's films, and calls up the *topos* of the *locus amoenus* – but a *locus amoenus* that would have been degraded, and which one is trying to restore. It is the image of the Palestinian cemetery in *Letter from Beirut* that recalls this *topos* through the commentary of the poet Etel Adnan:

> We arrive in front of artificial, plastic flowers. A woman comes to wash the tombs. Natural flowers are too expensive, people then use those

flowers, which are not flowers. Dead things, to celebrate the dead. It's true they last longer. To this people which have nothing, even flowers are forbidden.

During the war Beirut has nothing but gardens of the dead. The plastic flowers materialise a second death inflicted on the victims of the conflict, as they symbolically mark the absence of any possible new blossoming.

In *What's Going On?*, the image of the garden becomes a sign of the city's rebirth. Those who built the greatest empires – Nebuchadnezzar the Babylonian, Ramses II the Egyptian – are presented by Nayla as 'the world's greatest gardeners'. The city is conceived as an organism; and the art of gardens is an art of the living. Above all, it is an art that unfolds over time, and which is always in a process of cyclical evolution. Referring to a small territory, the garden appears as a microcosm. Significantly, it is the garden that is at the centre of Nasri's quest: in order to find Beirut again, to be able to make Khouloud's heart, which threatens to stop, beat and, more prosaically, to finally make love to her, Nasri must 'bring back to [her] all the city's gardens', threatened by the savage reconstruction of Beirut and its unbridled industrialisation. Just as Khouloud's heart is covered in roots, so Nasri will check the heart of Nayla's cactus by sticking a knife into it. As Mathilde Rouxel writes: 'it is as if making images of the body's contours was no longer enough: from now on, one must know the inside of it to allow its resurrection' (2015: 137). The woman's body and the garden's bodies are metonymies of one another, allowing one to reconnect with the city, but one must plunge into the intimacy of the bodies to rediscover a meaning for Beirut. This is incidentally the meaning of the epigraphic poem that opens the film and structures it:

> Beneath the roof of his palace,
> On the interior surface of his palace's dome,
> there is engraved, there is traced, there is tattooed a map – in brown – of Africa . . .
> The interior of his palace is rose, a very subtle rose,
> a rose hinting that of the tea-rose or of that ancient old
> Laurier rose.
> A moving rose, a very human rose, finally . . .
> [. . .]
> It's inside the mouth of the author:
> she swallows the protagonists of the novel,
> she restitutes them by hand,
> she, the one who writes . . .

The poem revolves around a wordplay on the polysemy of the French term *palais*, which means 'palace' as well as 'palate'. The dome of the palace it depicts, where one can read 'the thousand nights already spoken', is a metaphor for the poet's mouth, which is itself a metonym of the poetic word. The poet in his palace is a king, he takes on the role of the poet-Creator, and his mouth in fact is a world, which shapes his characters as the tailor cuts his cloth – the tailor, like the poet, is the one who draws signs, whether on a cloth or on a page. Being one of the multiple voice-overs, he introduces himself at the very beginning of the film:

> Whenever I start a new book, I think of you father and how I fail to meet your high expectations of becoming a great tailor, and settled for a modest writer. You would have taught me how to structure the cuts, to become familiar with the intrigues of scissors and to engulf with a swift glance the spectrum of figures. Hence your apprenticeship would not have been to no avail. Now for figuring out the characters of my book, I sketch the silhouettes, cut a curve and pin them on mannequins to shape and reconstruct them by hand, the hand – pardon me father – that writes.

Yet there is still one night to tell, 'one more long night in Beirut': the film opens precisely on the last, still blank, pages of the poet's book; and ends with his burst of laughter, which finally gives us a glimpse of his palate-palace: 'and we never visit his palace, we never discover Africa, except when he laughs to madness', states the poem. That is because at the end of his itinerary, Nasri manages to find – that is, to write – the history of Beirut.

There is thus an opposition between a chronological rhetoric, always faulted by Saab, and an incantatory rhetoric. Instead of a speech of truth, it would be a speech of vitality, which accounts for a feeling of the city, while building a mythical and poetic horizon. There is one last but essential figure then, the mystical Lilith, who carries on the role of voyeur-*voyant*. Unsurprisingly, the character is played by the Lebanese writer and activist Joumana Haddad, who wrote '*wdatou Līlīt* (*Lilith's Return*) in 2004, which is directly quoted in *What's Going On?*. In her volume of poetry, Haddad rewrote the myth of Lilith, while breaking with the Kabbalistic and biblical traditions. Lilith is the original figure of insubordination, a blasphemous woman-cosmos who gathers within herself all the opposites. Haddad's Lilith escapes the curses to which the sacred texts condemned her, to become a figure of positive emancipation, mistress of her own destiny. If Lilith left the Garden of Eden, it was to better find the gardens of Beirut. After losing Adam, she will guide Nasri through his initiatory quest, teaching him patience: one has to take the time of contemplation to access the knowledge of things. But above all Lilith is a figure of feminist revolt. She is the one who conquered the control of her own body, and who has withdrawn it from male desire – just as Raïa will do, as she was too weary to wait for the rest of the story, and finally abandons the role of prostitute assigned to her by the poet. Just like Lilith, virgin and libertine at the same time, all the women of *What's Going On?* refuse the advances of male characters: 'for my purity is the spark of debauchery / and my abstinence, / the beginning of possibility', Lilith affirms. By regaining power over their bodies, they open up a renewed narrative out of alienations: if Beirut is a living body, it is above all a question of liberating the women's bodies. This is the meaning of Raïa's incipit declamation of Le Clézio's *The African*:

> I have a few things to say about the face I was given at birth. First of all, I had to accept it. To say I didn't like it would make it seem more important than it was to me [. . .]. I didn't hate it, I ignored it, I avoided it. I didn't look at mirrors. I think years went by without my ever seeing it. I would avert my eyes in photographs, as if someone else had taken my place. (Le Clézio 2013: n.p.)

It is in front of a broken mirror that Raïa recites this text, as if to learn to re-tame, in fragments, a body that has become foreign to herself. The mirror obviously has a symbolic dimension here: mediatory object, it gives a vis-à-vis, splits the self's image to transform it into an otherness. And in fact, Raïa's voice soon blends with Nasri's, who takes the text over in canon, until the point of cacophony: to the body trying to find itself, echoing scrambled words. However, Le Clézio's text has been cut from a short fragment, thus clarifying that this feeling of dispossession was the one of a child, looking at his own face ('make it seem more important than it was to me as a child'). This mention disappears in Saab's film, as if to extend the time of self-recognition beyond the time of childhood. It is, in fact, a new birth that is at stake: by redoubling things, the mirror shows them as representation; and the issue is about giving back an image to mistreated bodies.

CONCLUSION

In his collection of essays *The Theatre and Its Double* (1970), Antonin Artaud wrote 'Let them burn down the library at Alexandria. There are powers above and beyond papyri. We may be temporarily deprived of the ability to rediscover these powers, but we will never eliminate their energy' ([1970] 2013: 5). It is eventually the same moral, if there is one, that we find in Jocelyne Saab's films: through the living, through the ruins, one can film ghosts. Saab brings about a new architecture of the cities based on memories, whether it is by re-poetising images of disaster, or by overcoming the absence of images through speech. Fiction therefore appears as a means to transcend violence, without concealing it. Accordingly, voyeurism takes on a sealing function: it is a gaze that reinvests its objects with desire, not to alienate them, but to give them an echo. Through the eyes of the voyeur, what was about to disappear makes history. A testimony voyeurism then, which is also a tribute to war victims, as an ultimate way to restore their dignity. This is probably how we should listen to Roger Assaf's words, when he states in *Beirut, My City* that 'the executioner revealed the victims' beauty, and the city's truth sprang from all the wounds inflicted on its living body'. Facing horror and oblivion remains the filmmaker's responsibility: that of producing images that are not oozing death but instead oppose resistance to propaganda speeches – as Assaf says, 'between the meshes of sordid and sublime'.

BIBLIOGRAPHY

Artaud, Antonin [1970] (2013), *The Theatre and Its Double*, trans. Victor Corti, London: Alma Classics.
Barthes, Roland (1981), *Camera Lucida*, trans. Richard Howard, New York: Hill & Wang.
Barthes, Roland (1986), 'The Discourse of History', in Roland Barthes, *The Rustle of Language*, trans. Richard Howard, New York: Hill & Wang, pp. 120–31.
Cavafy, C. P. (2007), 'I went', in C. P. Cavafy, *The Collected Poems: With Parallel Greek Text*, trans. Evangelos Sachperoglou, Oxford: Oxford University Press, p. 75.
Daney, Serge (1992), 'Le travelling de Kapo', *Trafic*, 4, 25 November, 5–19.
Durrell, Lawrence (1962), *The Alexandria Quartet*, London: Faber.
Haddad, Joumana (2004), عودة ليليت ('*wdatou Līlīt*'), Beirut: Éditions Dar An-Nahar.
Le Clézio, J. M. G. (2013), *The African*, trans. C. Dickson, Boston: David R. Godine.
Mallarmé, Stéphane (2009), 'Crisis of Verse' [1897], in Stéphane Mallarmé, *Divagations*, trans. Barbara Johnson, Cambridge, MA: Harvard University Press, p. 210.
Michaux, Henri (1963), *Plume*, Paris: Gallimard.
Rivette, Jacques (1961), 'De l'abjection', *Les Cahiers du Cinéma*, 120, June, 54–5.
Rouxel, Mathilde (2015), *Jocelyne Saab: la mémoire indomptée*, Beirut: Éditions Dar An-Nahar.

CHAPTER 17

Complete Catalogue of Jocelyne Saab's Artistic Output

Mathilde Rouxel

FILMS

La Maison libanaise (The Lebanese House)
Houses breathe with the lives of those who have lived in them.
　　Documentary, 1970, colour, Lebanon, 16 mm, 30 min.
　　Director: Jocelyne Saab, DOP: Hassan Naamani, Editor: TV Liban Canal 7, Production: TV Liban Canal 7. Unavailable.

Kadhafi: l'islam en marche (Gaddafi, The Green March)
The first convulsions of Libyan politics in 1973 and the country's tumultuous relationship with Egypt. Report on the hijacking of an airplane at Benghazi airport by the Japanese Red Army.
　　Documentary, 1973, colour, France, 16 mm, 10 min.
　　Journalists: Jocelyne Saab, Jean-François Chauvel, DOP: Gérard Simon, Editor: Magazine 52, Production: Rencontre, Pictures: Sygma, Copyright: INA France.

Portrait de Kadhafi (Portrait of Gaddafi, The Man Coming from the Desert)
A detailed portrait of a young head of state, admirer of Nasser, during the first days of the construction of a modern state in Libya.
　　Documentary, 1973, colour, France, 16 mm, 60 min.
　　Director: Jocelyne Saab, Editor: Magazine 52, Production: Rencontre, Copyright: INA France.

CATALOGUE 263

Moyen-Orient: Israël (Middle East: Israel)

The fourth Israeli–Arab war is in its sixth day. Syria and Egypt join forces to launch a surprise attack on Israel on the day of Yom Kippur. Tsahal is forced to fight on two fronts: the Golan Heights to the north and the Suez Canal and Sinai to the south. The conflict has never been bloodier, the fighting never fiercer.

Documentary, 1973, colour, France, 16 mm, 26 min.

Journalists: Geneviève Chauvel, Édouard Luntz, Jocelyne Saab, DOP and Sound: Egyptian team, Editor: Magazine 52, Production: ORTF, Copyright: INA France.

La Guerre d'Octobre (The October War)

In a village 100 km from Cairo, the Israeli air force has targeted a factory producing electronic parts. But the bombs destroyed the village, killing 141 people. Witness reports and comments.

Documentary, 1973, colour, France, 16 mm, 8 min.

Director: Jocelyne Saab, DOP and Sound: Egyptian team, Editor: Magazine 52, Production: ORTF, Copyright: INA France.

Moyen-Orient: Égypte (Middle East: Egypt)

The fourth Israeli–Arab war has been going on for more than two weeks. President Sadat orders the mobilisation of popular militias. The UN orders a ceasefire but Egypt is still in a state of war.

Documentary, 1973, colour, France, 16 mm, 8 min.

Director: Jocelyne Saab, DOP and Sound: Egyptian team, Editor: Magazine 52, Production: ORTF, Copyright: INA France.

La Guerre en Orient: Égypte (War in the Orient: Egypt)

The fourth Israeli–Arab war was finished a week ago. But the peace is fragile despite the arrival of the UN peacekeepers, and the local population is slow to accept the end of hostilities.

Documentary, 1973, colour, France, 16 mm, 8 min.

Director: Jocelyne Saab, DOP and Sound: Egyptian team, Editor: Magazine 52, Production: ORTF, Copyright: INA France.

Les Palestiniens continuent (Palestinians Keep Fighting)

Although peace has been declared, the Palestinians continue to fight Israel for the liberation of their territories.

Documentary, 1973, colour, France, 16 mm, 10 min.
Director: Jocelyne Saab, DOP and Sound: Egyptian team, Editor: Magazine 52, Production: ORTF, Copyright: INA France.

Golan, sur la ligne de front (Golan, On the Frontline)

This is the first report from the Syrian front line on the Golan Heights that the Israelis have just occupied.
Documentary, 1974, colour, France, 16 mm, 10 min.
Director: Jocelyne Saab, DOP and Sound: NBC team, Editor: Magazine 52, Production: ORTF, Copyright: INA France.

Irak: La guerre au Kurdistan (Iraq: War in Kurdistan)

Baghdad worries about Kurdish demands for independence supported by Iraq's neighbour and long-term enemy, Iran. Chronicle of a civil war waged against Iraqi Kurdistan.
Documentary, 1974, colour, France, 16 mm, 16 min.
Director: Jocelyne Saab, Journalist: René Lefort, Editor: Magazine 52, Production: ORTF, Copyright: INA France.

Les Femmes palestiniennes (Palestinian Women)

Palestinian women, the often-forgotten victims of the Israeli–Palestinian war, are given a voice by Jocelyne Saab.
Documentary, 1974, colour, France, 16 mm, 15 min.
Director: Jocelyne Saab, DOP: Hassan Naamani, Editor: Philippe Gosselet, Production: Jocelyne Saab, Copyright: Nessim Ricardou-Saab.

Le Front du refus (The Front of Refusal)

When peace proves impossible, all means are justifiable in defence of a political cause. That is what the suicide commandos argue, operating on the frontier separating the Palestinian territories from the land they refuse to accept as Israel. Jocelyne Saab films these adolescents, between sixteen and twenty years old, who train every day in a secret underground base to become suicide commandos.
Documentary, 1975, colour, France, 16 mm, 10 min.
Director: Jocelyne Saab, Journalist: Jocelyne Saab, Production: Jocelyne Saab, Copyright: Nessim Ricardou-Saab.

CATALOGUE 265

Les Nouveaux croisés d'Orient (New Crusader in the Orient)

Portrait of a French mercenary working in Libya, hired by the Phalange to train the militias. War leaves its traces; and for some, who see death as part of the job, it is a vocation.

Documentary, 1975, colour, Lebanon, 16 mm, 10 min.

Director: Jocelyne Saab, Journalist: Jörg Stocklin, DOP: Gérard Simon, Hassan Naamani, Sound: Marc Mourani, Michel Beruet, Editors: Philippe Gosselet, Marie-Jeanne de Susini, Production: Jocelyne Saab, Copyright: Nessim Ricardou-Saab.

Le Liban dans la tourmente (Lebanon in Turmoil)

Months after the incident on 13 April 1975, during which Palestinian civilians were gunned down by Phalangist militia, the numbers are even more horrifying: 6,000 dead, 20,000 injured, daily kidnappings and a capital city half destroyed. This film, a unique document about the Lebanese civil war, goes back to the origins of the conflict as seen by a society that went to war singing and with their heads held high.

Feature-length documentary, 1975, colour, Lebanon, 16 mm, 75 min.

Director: Jocelyne Saab, Journalist: Jörg Stocklin, DOP: Gérard Simon, Hassan Naamani, Sound: Marc Mourani, Michel Beruet, Editors: Philippe Gosselet, Marie-Jeanne de Susini, Production: Jocelyne Saab, Copyright: Nessim Ricardou-Saab.

Les Enfants de la guerre (Children of War)

Days after the massacre of Quarantina in a predominantly Muslim shanty town in Beirut, Jocelyne Saab found and met children who had escaped, and who were deeply traumatised by the horrific fighting they had seen with their own eyes. Jocelyne gave the children crayons and encouraged them to draw while her camera turned. She made a bitter discovery: the only games the children engaged in were war games, and the war would quickly become a way of life for them as well.

Documentary, 1976, colour, France, 16/35 mm, 10 min.

Director: Jocelyne Saab, DOP: Hassan Naamani, Editor: Philippe Gosselet, Production: Antenne 2, Copyright: Nessim Ricardou-Saab.

Sud-Liban, histoire d'un village assiégé (South Lebanon, History of a Sieged Village)

The ceasefire declared on 21 October 1976 gave the fedayeens the opportunity to reclaim this area, Fatah territory until it was abandoned in 1970, from

the right-wing militia. But Syrians and Israelis joined together to neutralise this 'autonomous force' of Palestinians and imposed a siege on two Lebanese frontier villages, Hanine and Kfarchouba, before attacking them.
Documentary, 1976, colour, France, 16 mm, 12 min.
Director: Jocelyne Saab, Commentary: Jocelyne Saab, Editor: Antenne 2 France, Production: ORTF, Copyright: Nessim Ricardou-Saab.

Beyrouth, jamais plus (Beirut, Never Again)

The year 1976 marks the beginning of Beirut's Calvary. With a child's eyes the filmmaker follows for six months the daily destruction of the city's walls. Every morning, between 6 and 10 a.m., she roams around Beirut while the militia on both sides rest from their night of fighting.
Documentary, 1976, colour, Lebanon, 16/35 mm, 35 min.
Director: Jocelyne Saab, Commentary: Etel Adnan, DOP: Hassan Naamani, Jocelyne Saab, Editor: Philippe Gosselet, Voice-over (English version): Jocelyne Saab, Voice-over (French version): Jörg Stocklin, Production: Jocelyne Saab, Copyright: Nessim Ricardou-Saab.

Pour quelques vies (For a Few Lives)

Portrait of Raymond Eddé, candidate for the Presidential elections and fervent opponent of the religious war. During the 1975–6 conflicts he and his team had actively searched for people killed in the war, whether they were Christian, Druze or Muslim.
Documentary, 1976, colour, Lebanon, 16 mm, 17 min.
Director: Jocelyne Saab, Production: Jocelyne Saab, Copyright: Nessim Ricardou-Saab.

Le Sahara n'est pas à vendre (The Sahara is Not for Sale)

This documentary from the heart of the desert shows the conflict between the Algerians and the Moroccans at El-Aiounet, the Saharan resistance on the Polisario Front.
Documentary, 1977, colour, France/Morocco/Algeria, 16 mm, 75 min.
Director: Jocelyne Saab, DOP: Olivier Guéneau, Sound: Jean-Michel Brun, Editor: Philippe Gosselet, Production: Jocelyne Saab, Copyright: Nessim Ricardou-Saab.

Égypte, la cité des morts (Egypt, The City of the Dead)

In this portrait of Cairo, 'mother of the world', Jocelyne Saab searches for the city's origins. While her own city, Beirut, is being torn to pieces, in the City of the Dead she finds the traces of a lifestyle and traditions that are also disappearing in the face of increased globalisation.

Documentary, 1977, colour, Lebanon, 16 mm, 35 min.

Director: Jocelyne Saab, DOP: Hassan Naamani, Sound: Juan Pablo Molestina, Editor: Philippe Gosselet, Music: Sheikh Imam, Lyrics: Ahmed Fouad Negm, Production: Jocelyne Saab, Copyright: Nessim Ricardou-Saab.

Lettre de Beyrouth (Letter from Beirut)

Three years after the start of the civil war, the filmmaker returns to her city for several months. Living between this war-torn country and a country in peace, she tries to readapt to daily life in Beirut. Public transport in the city no longer exists, but the filmmaker gets an old bus up and running, provoking a disconcerting return to normality in this city at war: people climb onto the bus, which they see as a place of security.

Documentary, 1978, colour, Lebanon, 16 mm, 52 min.

Director: Jocelyne Saab, Commentary: Etel Adnan and Jocelyne Saab, DOP: Olivier Guéneau, Sound: Mohamed Awad, Editor: Philippe Gosselet, Production: Jocelyne Saab, Copyright: Nessim Ricardou-Saab.

Iran: l'utopie en marche (Iran: Utopia on the Move)

The Iranian revolution leads to the Shah's downfall and installation of the Islamic Republic. Avoiding the more sensational elements of the news, this film questions Iranian society as a whole to try to understand what this wave of change means for the Muslim world.

Documentary, 1980, colour, Lebanon, 16 mm, 52 min.

Director: Jocelyne Saab, Journalist: Rafic Boustani, DOP: Olivier Guéneau, Production: NHK, Copyright: Nessim Ricardou-Saab.

Le Bateau de l'exil (The Ship of Exile)

After living clandestinely in Beirut to escape the Israeli forces, the head of the PLO, Yasser Arafat, leaves Lebanon aboard the *Atlantis* for a new exile in Greece and then Tunis. He talks about his destiny and the future of the PLO.

Documentary, 1982, colour, Lebanon, 16 mm, 12 min.

Director: Jocelyne Saab, Commentary: Jocelyne Saab, Production: TF1, Copyright: Nessim Ricardou-Saab.

Libanais, otages de leur ville (The Lebanese, Hostages of their City)

Jocelyne Saab films the city of Beirut destroyed by the Israeli bombardments, revealing the extent of the destruction and the suffering of the victims.

Documentary, 1982, colour, Lebanon, 16 mm, 6 min.
Director: Jocelyne Saab, DOP: Hassan Naamani, Production: TF1, Copyright: INA France.

Liban: État de choc (Lebanon, State of Shock)

Reza, a photographer from the SIPA Agency, disguised himself as a stretcher bearer and was able to infiltrate the Palestinian refugee camps of Rashidiyyeh and al-Buss near Tyre and Sidon in Lebanon, at the moment of the Israeli attack. The horrors that Reza witnessed, and that his photos revealed, left him deeply traumatised. Back in France, he speaks about it on camera to Jocelyne Saab. He describes a scene of collective denunciation and a round-up organised by the Israeli army in Sidon.

Documentary, 1982, colour, Lebanon, 16 mm, 6 min.
Director: Jocelyne Saab, Journalist: Marc Leclerc, Production: TF1, Copyright: INA France.

Beyrouth, ma ville (Beirut, My City)

In July 1982 the Israeli army laid siege to Beirut. Four years earlier Jocelyne Saab saw her 150-year-old childhood home go up in flames. She asked herself: when did all this begin? Every place becomes a historical site and every name a memory.

Documentary, 1982, colour, Lebanon, 16 mm, 37 min.
Director: Jocelyne Saab, Commentary: Roger Assaf, DOP: Jocelyne Saab, Assistant: Mirwan Khoury, Editor: Philippe Gosselet, Music: Rafic Boustani, with the participation of: Hassan Naamani, Jean-Marie Anglès, Dina Haidar, Boutros Rouhana, Mixing: Paul Bertault, Lab: AUDITEL, Production: Jocelyne Saab, Copyright: Nessim Ricardou-Saab.

Une Vie Suspendue – L'adolescente Sucre D'amour (A Suspended Life)

Samar is a young girl born during the war. Forced to live as a nomad, she grew up among fighters, learning to live in a country at war. The daily challenges she faces in life contrast with her love of Egyptian romantic comedies, until one day a chance meeting with Karim brings these two parts of her life together. A love story at the heart of a war.

Fiction, 1985, colour, Lebanon/France, 35 mm, 90 min.
Director: Jocelyne Saab, Script: Gérard Brach, Translation: Tahar Ben Jelloun, DOP: Claude La Rue, Music: Siegfried Kessler, Actors: Jacques Weber, Hala Bassam, Juliet Berto, Production: Balcon Productions, Copyright: Nessim Ricardou-Saab.

L'Architecte de Louxor (The Architect of Luxor)

The architect and philosopher Olivier Sednaoui, a disciple of Hassan Fathi, explains how he built his mud-brick house, which brings together the infinitely small and the infinitely huge, as the Egyptians from the era of the pharaohs did, in a harmony largely forgotten by the end of the twentieth century, and which he tries to rediscover. He explains the project from the moulding of the very first mud brick to the philosophy of a concept of life: placing East and West under one single destiny.

Documentary, 1986, colour, France, 16 mm, 18 min.

Director: Jocelyne Saab, DOP: Jérôme Ricardou-Saab, Sound: Marc Julien, Editor: Philippe Gosselet, Production: France 3, Copyright: Nessim Ricardou-Saab.

Les Fantômes d'Alexandrie (The Ghosts of Alexandria)

Alexandria, by turn Hellenistic, Greek, Roman, Copt . . . and then a petit Paris at the end of the 1930s. Inspired by the texts of Cavaffi and the writer Lawrence Durrell, this is a portrait of a city that has long been at the heart of the Arab world.

Documentary, 1986, colour, France, 16 mm, 17 min.

Director: Jocelyne Saab, DOP: Jérôme Ricardou-Saab, Sound: Marc Julien, Editor: Ann-Marie L'Hôte, Production: France 3, Copyright: Nessim Ricardou-Saab.

Les Coptes: La croix des pharaons (Copts: The Cross of the Pharaohs)

A portrait of the Copts, the oldest Christian community in Egypt, of its links to ancient Egypt and, in the face of rising Islamic fundamentalism, its traditions and way of confronting this growing threat to its existence.

Documentary, 1986, colour, France, 16 mm, 16 min.

Director: Jocelyne Saab, DOP: Jérôme Ricardou-Saab, Sound: Marc Julien, Editor: Ann-Marie L'Hôte, Production: France 3, Copyright: Nessim Ricardou-Saab.

L'Amour d'Allah, ou la montée de l'intégrisme
(Love of Allah (Fundamentalism))

Humiliated by the 1967 defeat, the Egyptian people look for ways to rebuild their sense of identity. Religion seems to point the way for them: Jocelyne Saab portrays the success of the Muslim Brotherhood and the increasingly rigid cultural values taking over Cairo at the end of the 1980s.

Documentary, 1986, colour, France, 16 mm, 17 min.
Director: Jocelyne Saab, DOP: Jérôme Ricardou-Saab, Sound: Marc Julien, Editor: Ann-Marie L'Hôte, Production: France 3, Copyright: Nessim Ricardou-Saab.

La Tueuse (The Woman Killer)

Portrait of a woman, Jocelyne Khoueiry, who, in 1976 during the Lebanese civil war, was the muse of the Phalangist militia in Beirut. With her commando group of women she was also responsible for several bloody operations. Fifteen years later, stricken with remorse, she became a nun and founded a religious order.
Documentary, 1988, colour, France, 16 mm, 10 min.
Director: Jocelyne Saab, Editor: Canal+, Production: Canal+, Copyright: Nessim Ricardou-Saab.

Les Almées, danseuses orientales (Al'Alma', Bellydancers)

Curvaceous and always dressed in sequins, the belly dancers – the Alma' – are present at weddings and circumcision parties. They are inspired by the belly dancing stars of the 1940s and 1950s: Samia Gamal, Tahia Carioca, Naaima Aakef, etc. Mainly lower class, they come from every corner of Egypt and dream of becoming the queen of the Cairo dance palaces. Dina, star of the 1980s, made this dream come true . . .
Documentary, 1989, colour, Lebanon, Beta, 26 min.
Director: Jocelyne Saab, DOP: Hassan Naamani, Editor: Philippe Gosselet, Production: Balcon Productions, Copyright: Nessim Ricardou-Saab.

Fécondation in video (Fertilisation in Video)

Using laparoscopic instruments equipped with a camera, Jocelyne Saab films the IVF process as it takes place. Report on implant operations in a hospital.
Documentary, 1991, colour, France, Beta, 26 min.
Director: Jocelyne Saab, Production: Ministry of Research, Ministry of Foreign Affairs, France 2, CNC, Balcon Productions, Copyright: Nessim Ricardou-Saab.

Il était une fois, Beyrouth: Histoire d'une star
(Once Upon a Time, Beirut: Story of a Star)

Celebrating their twentieth birthdays, Yasmine and Leila decide to visit a renowned cinephile and collector, Mr Farouk, to discover a Lebanon that they have never known. Searching for a past, the film archive leads them on a path of memories and the two heroines immerse themselves in the universe of film that has, over forty years, contributed to creating the international image of Beirut as a shining star. In the context of the war that has destroyed this city, the projection of the films (chosen from more than 250) that the two girls set up, returns to the city a taste of its own history, and a bit of hope for the future.

 Docu-fiction, 1994, colour, Lebanon/France, 35 mm, 100 min.

 Director: Jocelyne Saab, Script: Roland-Pierre and Philippe Paringaux, DOP: Roby Breidi, Editor: Dominique Auvray, Actors: Michèle Tyan, Myrna Makaron, Pierre Chamassian, Production: Arte Strasbourg, Hessischer Rundfunk, Balcon Production, Copyright: Nessim Ricardou-Saab.

La Dame de Saïgon (The Lady of Saigon)

Portrait of Dr Hoa, an extraordinary woman who was a minister in the South Vietnamese revolutionary government. Her life is a battle, and that battle is a pleasure. During the war she was at times imprisoned and at times a member of the resistance. She tells Jocelyne Saab about her experiences.

 Documentary, 1998, colour, France, Beta, 60 min.

 Director: Jocelyne Saab, DOP: Patrick Blossier, Sound: Pierre Doussot, Production: ADR Production, Copyright: Nessim Ricardou-Saab.

Dunia (Kiss Me Not on the Eyes)

Dunia (Kiss Me Not on the Eyes) is a meditation on female desire, a notoriously taboo subject in the Arab world, especially in the Egyptian society where the film takes place. Driven by the powerful eroticism of Arab poetry and music, the film talks about love and desire, through the experience of a young woman traditionally and strictly educated. The film leads to the trauma provoked by female genital mutilation.

 Fiction, 2005, colour, Egypt/France, 35 mm, 112 min.

 Director: Jocelyne Saab, Script: Jocelyne Saab, DOP: Jacques Bouquin, Editor: Claude Reznic, Sound: Fawzi Thabet, Music: Jean-Pierre Mas, Patrick Leygonie, Actors: Hanan Turk, Mohamed Mounir, Fathy Abdel Wahab, Sawsan Badr, Youssef Ismail, Ayda Reyad, Khaled El Sawi, Production: Catherine Dussart, Jocelyne Saab, Copyright: Nessim Ricardou-Saab.

What's Going On?

In Beirut, a writer, son of a tailor, cuts and sews his made-to-measure texts on well-known people from around the city. He meets Khouloud, a dancer, who helps him touch the heart of Beirut.

Fiction, 2009, colour, Lebanon, mono-HDTV, 80 min.
Director: Jocelyne Saab, Script: Jocelyne Saab, Joumana Haddad, DOP: Jacques Bouquin, Editor: Catherine Poitevin, Music: Vladimir Kurumilian, Sound: James Galt, Actors: Khouloud Yassine, Nasri Sayegh, Raia Haïdar, Jalal Khoury, Ishtar Yasin Gutierrez, Joumana Haddad, Production: Collection d'Artiste, Copyright: Nessim Ricardou-Saab.

Imaginary Postcard

An imaginary postcard written to the Turkish writer Orhan Pamuk. Jocelyne Saab writes about her illness, about the fragility of her body, and the situation in the Middle East that is ravaged by war.
Art video, 2016, Turkey, digital, 6 min.
Director: Jocelyne Saab, DOP: Meryem Yavuz, Editor: Barbara Doussot, Production: Collection d'Artiste, Copyright: Nessim Ricardou-Saab.

Un dollar par jour (One Dollar a Day)

A silent art video about the life conditions of the Syrian refugees in Lebanon. The video is part of a wider art project, associated with black and white and painted photographs (see below).
Art video, 2016, Lebanon/France, digital, 6 min.
Director: Jocelyne Saab, Text: Etel Adnan, DOP: Meryem Yavuz, Sound: Neset Ufuk Özdemir, Production: Collection d'Artiste, Copyright: Nessim Ricardou-Saab.

My Name is Mei Shigenobu

A delicate portrait of Mei Shigenobu, daughter of the founder of the Japanese Red Army in Beirut, Fusako Shigenobu.
Art video, 2018, Lebanon, digital, 6 min.
Director: Jocelyne Saab, AD: Mathilde Rouxel, DOP: Joe El-Hajj, Léa Najm, Editor: Barbara Doussot, Executive producer: Jad Dani Ali Hassan, Production: Collection d'Artiste, Copyright: Nessim Ricardou-Saab.

ARTWORKS

Sense, Icons and Sensitivity

Series of 100 photographs, 2007. A cycle of photographs arranged around two themes that invite the visitor to decipher the view that Arabs have of themselves, in particular the women and their often sexualised appearance.

Le Revers de l'Orientalisme (The Reverse of Occidentalism)

Taking as a starting point Edward Saïd's reflections on a reversal of Orientalism ('The deformed image that the West has of the Orient in order to better represent, define and dominate it'), Jocelyne Saab interrogates the fractures of meaning between East and West. She photographs Barbie, an icon, to symbolise the cliché of the Western woman, at the heart of an Arab world dominated by religion and traditionalist politics that are dangerous for the freedom of the body.

Architecture molle (Soft Architecture)

A collection of photographs that uses light to expose and interrogate the sensuality of the Orient. Photographing the fragility of Bedouin tents in the desert, Saab reveals a sensuality inherent to Arab culture, although it is often repressed and forgotten.

Strange Games and Bridges

With this 2007 installation, created after renewed bombardments ravaged Beirut in 2006, Jocelyne Saab bears witness to both the recent conflict and the dramatic nature of the renaissance of the war in Lebanon. This came at a time when the country was putting the 1975–90 war behind it, with great difficulty. She also challenges a vision of utopia through the regrowth of a garden in Beirut. She sees the city as her 'childhood garden', a lost Eden, and its destruction questions the possibility of peace and a return to nature. Her installation allows the visitor to wander through an environment heavy with the weight of war, surrounded by archive images of her old documentaries on the war, and images shot in 2006 after the city's bridges had been destroyed by the Israel air bombardments.

Café du Genre (Gender Café)

Produced by MuCEM, Marseille (Musée des civilisations de l'Europe et de la Méditerranée [Museum of European and Mediterranean Civilisations]), France, 2013. Copyright: Nessim Ricardou-Saab.

Six 4-minute short films, each filmed in countries around the Mediterranean, dealing with expressions of gender, the body, sexuality and identity. Six interviews with artists or people talking about these thorny issues create a geographical impression of the suffering body, subject to violence, repression and inhibition.

Café du Genre I: Table du fou vert, avec Walid Aouni (Gender Café I: The Table of Walid Aouni, the Green Mad Man)

Interview with choreographer Walid Aouni in Cairo, digital, 4 min.

Walid Aouni was director of the Egyptian Modern Dance Company at the Cairo Opera House for twenty years. A student of Maurice Béjart, he created within the Opera the first contemporary dance troupe in Egypt. He created engaged shows in Cairo, giving the body all its protesting power, at the heart of performances of flamboyant expressionism. Jocelyne Saab pays homage to his work.

Café du Genre II: Table du Peintre pharaon et ses danseuses (Gender Café II: The Table of the Painter of the Pharaohs and the Dancers)

Interview with painter Adel Siwi in Cairo, digital, 4 min.

Adel Siwi is an Egyptian painter who is worried about the progress of fundamentalism in his country. In the aftermath of the revolution, while in the street, women were abused and their bodies beaten. Jocelyne Saab returns to the work of an artist who painted dancers' bodies, and who believes in art as a tool of resistance.

Café du Genre III: Table de la revue du corps (Gender Café III: The Table of the Magazine on the Body)

Interview with Joumana Haddad in Beirut, digital, 3 min.

Joumana Haddad is a writer committed to the freedom of women to dispose of their bodies as they please, and the freedom of citizens to know and act on their rights. With her magazine *Jasad*, she wanted to give back to the body its aesthetic power, at a time when it was under threat, to once again become a symbol of depravity and dishonour according to a certain conservative morality.

Café du Genre IV: Table de l'Ocra d'Or (Gender Café IV: The Table of the Golden Okra)

Interview with Cuneyt Cebenoyan and Melek Ozman in Istanbul, digital, 5 min.

The competition of the Golden Okra is a feared event in Istanbul: it rewards the films considered to be the most macho of the year. It is organised each year by an association that promotes gender equality in Turkey.

Café du Genre V: Table de la danse et de l'orgueil (Gender Café V: The Table of Dance and Pride)

Interview with Alexandre Paulikevitch in Beirut, digital, 4 min.

The artist and activist Alexandre Paulikevitch is presented by Jocelyne Saab. An innovative dancer, he does not hesitate to use his personal experience of homophobic violence to make his shows vibrate. An activist for the LGBTQI cause, he denounces the legal situation in Lebanon, and the limitations and oppression LGBTQI people are experiencing.

Café du Genre VI: Table de l'exigence (Gender Café VI: The Table of Exigency)

Interview with Wassyla Tamzali in Algiers, digital, 4 min.

Wassyla Tamzali closely followed images of the uprisings that, in 2011, caused a wave of revolutionary movements from Tunisia, and which reached most Arab countries. She witnessed the power of women, ready to use their bodies to express their revolt, and others who experienced immeasurable violence. Feminist activist, former lawyer at the court of Algiers and observer for UNESCO, she offers to Saab her analysis of the situation.

Un dollar par jour (One Dollar a Day)

Series of photographs taken in the Syrian refugee camps of the Beqaa plain, Lebanon, 2015 (untitled photographs) and a video.

Three Flex prints painted with gold and twenty-two black and white prints 60 x 42 cm with and without watercolour; art video, 2016, Lebanon/France, digital, 6 min.

Poetry is everywhere, even in the refugee camps where absolute misery reigns. In front of old plastic posters and billboards, advertising in giant format the big icons of luxury and consumerism, that make up their shelters, refugee children stand like kings. Symbols of life at the heart of war, fragility and death, Jocelyne Saab shows these children as precious notes of hope in the heart of a dehumanised world.

Director: Jocelyne Saab, Text: Etel Adnan, DOP: Meryem Yavuz, Sound: Neset Ufuk Özdemir, Production: Collection d'Artiste, Copyright: Nessim Ricardou-Saab.

Zones de guerre (War Zones)

Book of photographs, 25 x 19.3 cm, 176 pp., December 2018, Editions de l'Oeil, France.

Photographs: Jocelyne Saab, Text: Elias Sanbar, Etel Adnan, Edited by: Nicole Brenez. ISBN: 978 2 35137 255 5.

Jocelyne Saab's photographic oeuvre documents five decades of conflicts in the Third World in general and in the Middle East in particular – a history she captures in the full breadth and diversity of its dimensions, injuries, disappearances and rebirths. Her work provides an exceptional panorama of the recent history (in Lebanon, Libya, Egypt, Iran, Western Sahara, Kurdistan, Vietnam . . .), while revealing the penetrating and loving gaze of a committed artist.

EVENTS

The Lebanese Film Library, 1993

In 1993, at the end of the war, Jocelyne Saab embarked on a vast project to set up a Lebanese Film Library in Beirut. Aware of the necessary work of commemoration to be carried out at the end of conflicts, she believed that cinema, and the images of Beirut that it had recorded since the arrival of the cinematograph in Lebanon, can offer elements of memory. Under the name *Beyrouth, Mille et une images* (*Beirut, a Thousand and One Images*), this project aimed to gather all the films shot in or evoking Beirut since the start of cinema. Through a journey of more than 400 films, the filmmaker was able to go from the first Arab films shot in Lebanon, notably by Egyptian filmmakers or by Frenchmen in the 1930s, to American spy films that depicted Beirut against the backdrop of a Middle East under tension, or to more recent productions made during the war, between 1975 and 1990. This enormous cinephilic archival task, partially funded by the French Ministry of Culture and ARTE France, earned her the award of Officer of the Order of Arts and Letters (Officier de l'Ordre des Arts et des Lettres) following the handing over of about fifteen restored films to the Lebanese Ministry of Culture. The objective of this collection was the foundation, in the long term, of a Lebanese Film Library. The project did not come into being in this form, but screening cycles were organised at the Institut du Monde Arabe (Arab World Institute) in Paris, at the Carthage Film Days in Tunis and at the Casino du Liban in Tabarjah. Over the next decade, these restored films travelled around the world to represent Lebanon on screen, and brought to life a rich filmography freshly unearthed, rethinking the memory of a nation with a fragmented identity.

Cultural Resistance International Film Festival of Lebanon (CRIFFL), 2013, 2014, 2015

In 2013, as violence resumed in Lebanon as a consequence of the outbreak of the Syrian civil war in 2012, Jocelyne Saab tried to find new ways to resist violence. Embarrassed by the absence of Asian films in Lebanese cinemas, she launched the programme of a festival of 'cultural resistance' films, which she sought to screen throughout Lebanon, without distinction of class, community or language. The three editions of the festival have allowed the Lebanese people to see films from all over Asia and the Mediterranean, in places as diverse as Beirut, Zahleh, Sidon, Tripoli and Tyre, in multiplexes as well as in cinemas still undergoing restoration, closed during the war and reopened shortly before the festival.

Lebanese International Biennale for Cinema and the Arts (Biennale Libanaise Internationale pour le Cinéma et les Arts – BLICA), 2017

This event is the second event organised by Jocelyne Saab's 'Cultural Resistance Association'. Initially, Saab aimed to launch this biennale in the Rachid Karame Fair in Tripoli, which had been designed in the 1960s by the famous architect Oscar Niemeyer, but its construction had been interrupted in 1975 because of the civil conflict. The grandeur of the place had inspired Saab's desire to establish a major artistic event that would complete the festival in its next editions. Unfortunately, the negotiations undertaken by Jocelyne Saab with Tripolitan political representatives were never finalised. Interested in holding the Biennale within its walls, the Modern and Contemporary Art Museum (MaCaM) in Alita (Byblos) took care of the competition and launched the first BLICA in 2017, under the patronage of Jocelyne Saab.

UNFINISHED PROJECTS

This list does not claim to be exhaustive. It relates only to the drafts found in Jocelyne Saab's archive. This archive is currently being digitised and organised by the Association of Jocelyne Saab's Friends. At the end of this digitisation and preservation effort, copyright holder Nessim Ricardou-Saab will deposit the original paper archive with the French Cinematheque.

Les Amours contrariés de l'Orient et de l'Occident

[The Thwarted Loves of the East and the West] (undated, late 1970s and early 1980s, in Lebanon). Plans for a documentary series in four episodes retracing the history of the Middle East since the Ottomans.

Documentation, film presentation file. Written by Jocelyne Saab and Jonathan Randal, Directed by Jocelyne Saab.

L'Arrière-quartier

[The Backstreets] (undated, late 1980s). Fiction project on the story of a Christian family living in West Beirut during the Lebanese civil war.

Presentation file, full script. Author: Jocelyne Saab, Screenplay: Jocelyne Saab, Sélim Turquie, Rewritten by Boris Hannoyer, Dialogue: Abido Bacha, Mohamad Kalach, in collaboration with Marc Mourani, Assistant: Shirine Tannous, Thanks to Rafic Boustani and Joseph Tarrab.

Le Temple de la tortue

[The Temple of the Tortoise] (1989). Sci-fi feature film project. In a city at war, victim of deadly radiation for fifteen years, a group of orphaned children hide to protect themselves in the underground of their kingdom. A tsunami is announced. However, the children refuse to leave the city, despite insistent attempts by adults to 'save' them.

Notes, research documents, exchanges of letters with funding institutions, presentation file.

Histoire de Fatehpur Sikri

[Story of Fatehpur Sikri] (undated). Fictional documentary project on the history of Fatehpur Sikri, a city in the Indian state of Uttar Pradesh with multiple religious communities.

Presentation file of the film. Written by Rose Vincent, Directed by Jocelyne Saab.

L'Oeil et le miracle du laser

[The Eye and the Miracle of the Laser] (1994). Documentary project on the same principle as *Fertilisation in Video* on an operation to correct myopia.

Presentation file. Written by Jocelyne Saab, Directed by Jocelyne Saab.

L'Homme de parole

[A Man of His Word] (1996). Presentation file. Adaptation of Nazir Hamad's novel *A Man of his Word*. Written by Jocelyne Saab and Randall Holden, Directed by Jocelyne Saab.

Vietnam, notre amour

[Vietnam, Our Love] (undated, second half of the 1990s). Fiction project telling the story of Dr Hoa and her husband.

Presentation file, research notes. Written by Jocelyne Saab and Philippe Franchini, Directed by Jocelyne Saab, Produced by Catherine Dussart Production.

Portrait d'Hanoï, ou Comment inventer la modernité

[Portrait of Hanoi, or How to Invent Modernity] (undated, second half of the 1990s). Documentary project. Portrait of the city of Hanoi, ravaged by the war that raged in Vietnam for twenty years.

Presentation file of the film. Written and directed by Jocelyne Saab, Produced by Catherine Dussart Production.

Mustafa Kemal

(1997). Documentary project on the Turkish Head of State Mustafa Kemal.

Research notes, documentation, exchange of letters with the production company, script, presentation file. Written by Jocelyne Saab and Delphine Moreau, Directed by Jocelyne Saab, Produced by ADR Production.

Joumana

(1998). Documentary project constructing the unveiling of the amnesia and terrible past of Jocelyne Saab's childhood friend, Joumana, filmed in interaction with four young adults in their twenties who are there to question her. Joumana was the wife of an ambassador who was involved in extreme right-wing militias at the beginning of the Lebanese war. He was assassinated in Spain by a bomb attack on the embassy building where they lived. Joumana's physical memory of the attack is a large scar on her neck.

Notes, interview transcripts, research documents, presentation file. Written by Jocelyne Saab and France Saint-Léger, Directed by Jocelyne Saab, Produced by Catherine Dussart Productions.

Abu Simbel. La Nuit du solstice d'été ou Le Rayon d'amour

[Abu Simbel. The Night of the Summer Solstice or The Ray of Love] (undated, early 2000s). Fiction documentary project on Ramses II and Nefertari.

Paris amoureux

[Paris in Love] (2002). Experimental project in four short films of strolls in the city of Paris.

Presentation file, research notes, edited pilot. Written by Jocelyne Saab and Francis Lacloche, Directed by Jocelyne Saab.

Les Masques

[Masks] (2008). Series of photographic portraits. In southern Egypt, men and women have their faces coated with clay.
Classified and calibrated series.

Le Rouge et le blanc

[The Red and the White] (2009). Fiction project. Love story between two characters, set in a parking lot in Beirut.
Presentation file of the film. Script: Jocelyne Saab and Catherine Arnaud, Director: Jocelyne Saab.

Landscape from Beirut and Cairo to Romeo and Juliet's Town: My Architectural Cities' Love

(2011). Fiction-documentary project on Jocelyne Saab's two favourite cities, Cairo and Beirut. Cairo was to be embodied by a woman called Dunia and Beirut by Ishtar Yasin Gutierrez. The film was to be a tribute to architecture.
Presentation file. Screenplay: Jocelyne Saab and Ishtar Yasin Gutierrez, Director: Jocelyne Saab.

Salwa la Turque

[Salwa the Turk] (2011). Fiction project about the exodus of a Turkish family to Colombia after the dismantling of the Ottoman Empire.
Notes, beginning of screenplay. Written by Jocelyne Saab, Directed by Jocelyne Saab, with Ishtar Yasin Gutierrez as actress.

Untitled

(2011). Biopic project about the destiny of two women in 1930s Egypt: the Egyptian singer Asmahan and the Lebanese Druze university student Nazirah Zeineddine living in Cairo.

La Mère du monde

[The Mother of the World] (undated, early 2010s). Documentary project on oriental dancers.

Être femme en Méditerranée

[Being a Woman in the Mediterranean] (2012). Documentary project on men who dance and teach oriental dance.
    Presentation file of the film. Written by Jocelyne Saab, Directed by Jocelyne Saab.

Untitled

(2013). Film project made with Jocelyne Saab's students in Saint-Joseph University in 2013 about the Egyptian filmmaker Henry Barakat and his films.
    Notes, synopsis, transcripts of interviews, rushes. Production: Institute of Scenic and Audiovisual Studies of the Saint-Joseph University of Beirut.

Cet objet flottant du désir

[This Floating Object of Desire] (2013). Project for an exhibition of Egyptian cinema posters.
    Note of intent, digital files of the posters.

L'Honneur de Faten Hamama

[The Honour of Faten Hamama] (2014). Biopic project on Egyptian film producer Assia Dagher, Lebanese by birth and a woman of excellence in Egypt in the 1930s, as seen through the eyes of actress Faten Hamama.
    Notes, different screenplay versions, variety of documentation, presentation file. Written by Jocelyne Saab, Directed by Jocelyne Saab.

Shigenobu, mère et fille

[Shigenobu: Mother and Daughter] (2018). Hybrid documentary project on the fate of Mei Shigenobu, long-hidden daughter of Fusako Shigenobu, founder of the international branch of the Japanese Red Army who arrived in Lebanon to support the Palestinian struggle.
    Notes, archives, exchange of emails about the film, research documents, several versions of the script, presentation file, filmed archives. Script: Jocelyne Saab with the collaboration of Mathilde Rouxel, Writing consultants: Yomota Inuhiko, Miriam Heard, Direction: Jocelyne Saab, Editor: Barbara Doussot, with the support of Wakamatsu productions.

Index

1967, 32, 63, 104, 129, 269
1975, 2, 4, 5, 20, 22, 23, 37, 38, 40, 41, 49n, 58, 59, 71, 80, 87, 90, 97, 113, 129, 132, 144, 145, 194, 202, 237, 239, 248
1982 bombing of Saab's house, Beirut, 77, 116, 194, 207, 238
2006, 3, 5, 7, 8, 57, 135, 214, 273

A Man of His Word, 76–8
A Suspended Life, 2–4, 12, 14–15, 31, 33, 38, 43–4, 46, 47–8, 161, 175–6, 178, 180–5, 221–4, 226, 229, 232, 235, 236, 238–42, 245
Abandoned Dwellings, Display of Systems (2019 Saab exhibition), 236, 237
Abu Simbel. The Night of the Summer Solstice or the Ray of Love, 72–3
activism, 2, 6, 60, 61, 190, 210
activist, 3, 7, 13, 14, 61, 138, 144–9, 209, 259, 275
Adnan, Etel, 20, 26, 40–1, 62, 65, 67, 88, 161, 202, 214, 252, 257, 258

Akef, Naiemeh, 185
Al-Gazzar, Abdel Hadi, 209
Al'Alma', Bellydancers, 7
Alaouié, Borhane, 6, 39, 48, 88, 107, 243
Alexandria, 72, 247, 252–5
Algeria, 2, 6, 61, 72, 149, 209
amnesia, 76, 105, 117, 134, 139, 279
amnesty, 4, 5, 59, 97, 98, 101, 169
Amnesty International, 169
An-Nahar (newspaper), 252
Aouni, Walid, 33, 61, 72–4, 189–90, 209
Arab Spring (2013), 35, 189, 211, 212
Arafat, Yasser, 19, 21–3, 30–1, 204
Architect of Luxor (The), 6
architecture, 8, 15, 54, 57, 58, 67, 77
archive, 7, 8, 11, 13, 37, 38, 39, 51–7, 58–9, 62, 67, 70–1, 79, 81, 83, 100, 103, 108–10, 114, 116, 133, 138, 181, 225, 238, 247, 253, 271, 273, 277, 281
Artaud, Antonin, 260
Asia, 8, 14, 23, 35, 53, 60, 63, 65, 71, 78, 80–1, 83, 126–8, 131, 133–5, 138–44, 207, 211–12

INDEX 283

Assaf, Roger, 20, 58, 94–5, 202, 243–5, 249, 250, 252, 256, 261
Atlantis, 31

Baghdadi, Maroun, 6, 39, 88, 114, 116, 239–43
Barakat, Henry, 73, 176, 281
Barakat, Saleh, 60, 237
Barthes, Roland, 252
Bassam, Hala, 176
Bedouin, 8–9, 54, 74
Being a Woman in the Mediterranean, 72
Beirut trilogy, 12, 14, 87, 89, 91, 92, 94, 96
Beirut, My City, 2, 4, 20–8, 58, 70, 93–5, 96, 202, 204, 206, 207, 241–5, 248–50, 252, 261
Beirut, Never Again, 2, 20, 25–7, 87–9, 91, 161, 202, 212, 243
Béjart, Maurice, 33, 61, 189
belly dancer / dancing, 7, 71, 115, 162–3, 170, 182, 185–6, 190, 209–10
Beqaa, 3, 34, 194, 212, 257
Borchardt-Hume, Achim, 236
Bourgeoisie, 170, 174, 244
Brenez, Nicole, 11, 63, 67, 113, 174
Butler, Judith, 190

Cairo, 6, 8, 32–3, 53, 54, 61, 72–4, 77, 93, 114, 160, 163, 170, 176, 178, 189, 194, 209
Cannes Film Festival (1985), 175
Carioca, Tahia, 185
Carthage, 175
Cavada, Jean-Marie, 27, 248
Cavafy, Constantine, 252–4
ceasefire, 4, 29, 81
Cebenoyan, Cuneyt, 61, 189, 210
censorship, 8–10, 23, 53, 55, 57, 113, 138, 158, 164, 194, 207, 250

Chahal, Randa, 49, 88, 249
Chamoun, Jean, 88
Char, René, 221, 224, 227
Chariaati, Ali, 156, 202
childhood, 2, 8, 20, 73, 76, 80, 82, 114, 116, 118, 120, 121, 202, 215, 222, 233, 260, 268
Children of War, 2, 5, 10, 20, 26–7, 203, 206
Christian, 1, 5, 71, 75, 80, 89, 90, 91, 95, 113, 116
cinematheque, 7, 11, 25, 38, 62, 63, 113, 139
civil war, 2, 4, 6, 7, 13, 14, 25, 37, 38, 39, 47, 56, 58, 63, 75, 76, 77, 82, 87–91, 95, 98, 102, 108, 129, 132, 133, 134, 145, 160, 176, 185, 193–5, 201, 202, 206, 212, 226, 232, 237, 248, 258
Claro, Andrés, 63
communist, 34, 106, 117, 118
communities, 4, 6, 74, 75, 93, 130, 136, 138
contemporary art, 1, 52–3, 60, 62, 67
Coptics: The Cross of the Pharaohs (The), 7
creation, 4, 13, 51, 52, 56, 58, 59, 60, 63, 70
crossdressing, 190
Cultural Resistance International Film Festival of Lebanon (CRIFFL), 11, 14, 52, 63, 126–7, 133–9, 255

Dagher, Assia, 62, 73–4
Daif wa March (TV programme, France Channel 24), 185
dance, 7, 8, 14, 22, 33, 53, 61, 71–2, 74, 115, 116, 136, 159, 162–6, 168–72, 174–6, 179–83, 185–6, 188–93, 198, 202, 207–11

Daney, Serge, 249
Dante, 257
daughter, 3, 70–3, 81–2, 112–14, 162, 167, 168, 170, 179–83, 205–6, 214, 216
death threats, 5, 10, 33, 171, 205
Dortmund Cologne International Women's Film Festival (2012), 186
Dostoevsky, Fyodor, 252
Druze, 73, 74, 78
duality, 54, 71, 183
Dunia : Kiss me not on the Eyes, 7, 10, 12, 14, 20, 33–5, 53, 56–7, 63, 72–3, 74, 77, 113, 114, 115–16, 159–73, 175, 176, 178–81, 182–6, 202–5, 209, 210
Durrell, Lawrence, 247, 252–3

Egypt, 2, 6, 7, 8, 13, 25, 32–3, 53, 57, 60, 61, 127, 128, 129, 138, 159, 161, 162, 163, 168, 171, 175, 181, 184, 185, 189, 193, 198n, 205, 209, 210
Egypt, the City of the Dead, 6, 32, 70, 72–4, 78, 202–3
El-Aouinet, 6
El-Jazairly, Fouad, 186
Elkoury, Fouad, 237–9, 241
Eye and the Miracle of the Laser (The), 77

Fatah, 22–3
father, 1, 3, 24–5, 74, 78, 80, 81, 82, 83, 95, 104, 114, 117, 118, 120, 130, 176, 180, 239–40, 259
fatwa, 7
Fawzi, Husain, 185
female genital mutilation, 7, 53, 138, 163, 167, 169, 171, 175, 176–80, 182–4, 186, 190
feminism, 174–87, 201
feminist, 14, 61, 143, 153, 174–87, 189, 203, 207, 209–10, 259

Fertilisation in Video, 7, 34, 77, 256
For a Few Lives, 2, 11, 25
forced marriage, 175
Fouad Negm, Ahmed, 32, 202, 267
fundamentalism, 189
fundamentalist, 7, 10, 33, 53, 57, 72, 189

Gaddafi, Muammar, 2, 19, 22, 54, 119, 175
Gaddafi: The Green March, 2
Gamal, Samia, 185–6
Ganz, Bruno, 241
Gender Café, 8, 52, 60–7, 72–3, 188–90, 203, 206, 208–11
Ghosts of Alexandria (The), 7, 72, 247–8, 252–5
Godard, Jean-Luc, 67, 113
Golan, On the Frontline, 2
Gould, Roger, 244
green line, 97, 103
Guéneau, Olivier, 9
guerrilla, 82, 93, 143–58
Guibert, Daniel, 63

Haddad, Joumana, 61, 87, 176, 182–3, 189, 202, 207, 209–10, 259
Hamama, Faten, 62, 73–4
Hamasat / Whispers, 242
Heneiné, Joseph, 236
heritage, 5, 6, 7, 9, 11, 37–8, 48, 56, 63, 81, 103, 110, 134
homophobia, 192, 210
homosexuality, 188, 189, 190–3, 198, 210

identity, 3, 5–10, 15, 45, 54–6, 72, 75, 78, 80, 82, 91, 104, 118, 122, 124, 144, 155, 163, 165–6, 174–5, 181, 190, 202, 205, 213–17, 227–30, 232, 238, 269
Imaginary Postcard, 52, 67, 201, 202, 211

INDEX 285

independence, 2, 4, 8, 27, 70, 79, 117, 127, 114, 145–6, 154–5, 174
India, 24, 80, 81, 114, 127–31, 134–6, 138–9
Indonesia, 114
Institut du Monde Arabe, Paris, 7, 19, 62, 190
internationalism, 14
internationalist, 3, 13, 93, 143, 146–7
Iran, 6, 104, 114, 128–9, 143–58, 160, 161, 192, 204
Iran: Utopia in the Move, 6, 143–4, 146–8, 151–3, 156–8, 160, 191, 202, 204
Iraq, 2, 35, 88, 104, 127–8, 143, 145–9, 154–5, 174
Iraq: War in Kurdistan, 2, 8, 143, 145–9, 154–8
Israeli Army, 29–30, 92, 94–5, 103, 114, 176, 204, 239, 241, 243, 268
Israeli invasion of Lebanon (1982), 5, 7–8, 25, 43, 57, 92–3, 114, 116, 204, 207, 238–9, 241, 243

Japan, 2, 82, 112–13, 118–19, 121, 124, 206, 214–15
Jasad ('The Body', Lebanese feminist magazine), 61, 189, 209
Jordan, 22, 24, 127, 128
journalism, 21–2, 30, 88–9, 109, 143–6, 155, 157, 201
journalist, 1, 2, 6, 22–4, 26–7, 30–1, 35, 40, 80, 87–9, 92–3, 110, 119, 144–6, 149, 152, 154, 160, 174, 201, 232, 237, 241, 248

Kessler, Siegfried, 227
Khan, Mohamed, 205
Khomeini, Ayatollah, 6, 157
Khoueiry, Jocelyne, 4
Kristeva, Julia, 203, 216
Kurds, Kurdistan, 2, 8, 88, 143–9, 153–5, 157, 161, 174

Lacan, Jacques, 190
Lady of Saigon (The), 8, 34, 78, 80
Landscape from Beirut and Cairo to Romeo and Juliet's Town: My Architectural Cities' Love, 77
Laos, 80
Le Monde, 190
Lebanese, Hostages of their City, 2
Lebanese Academy of Fine Arts, 238
Lebanese Association Helem, 192
Lebanese International Biennale for Cinema and the Arts (BLICA), 11, 52, 63, 65–6
Lebanese National Radio, 2, 62, 174
Lebanon in Turmoil, 2, 4, 20, 24–6, 40–1, 87, 144–5, 202, 206
Lebanon: State of Shock, 2
left-wing, 6, 70, 112, 117, 120
leftist, 24, 90
Les Almées, danseuses orientales / Bellydancers, 7, 185
Letter from Beirut, 2, 4, 25–6, 92–3, 125, 161, 202, 215, 248, 250–2, 257
Lewis Carroll, 221–4, 226, 229–32
Libya, 2, 23, 54–5, 119, 127–8, 159, 174–5
Lilith, 61, 115–16, 182, 208–9, 256–7, 259–60
Love of Allah (Fundamentalism), 7
Luxor, 73, 176

Maakaron, Myrna, 176
MaCaM, 63–4, 67
Magazine 52, 119, 143
Mallarmé, Stéphane, 255
Manchevski, Milcho, 161
Mark Anthony, 253
Marsupilamis Have Blue Eyes (The), 2, 62, 174
Martyrs' Square, Beirut, 245
Masks (The), 60, 73
Meltem, 80

Mezher, Marie, 236
Michaux, Henri, 252
militias, 4–5, 25, 31, 42, 46, 76, 93, 95, 103–4, 107, 110, 204, 241, 243, 250
minorities, 7, 23, 61, 130
Morocco, 6, 10, 27–8, 72, 78, 127, 144, 149, 151, 155, 159, 194
Mossad, 118, 122–3, 214
mother, 3, 31, 43, 71–2, 75, 76, 78, 82, 71, 112–14, 162–3, 165–70, 176–83, 205–6, 209, 215–16, 223, 230, 240, 243
Mother of the World (The), 71–2
Mounir, Mohamed, 33, 182
Mubarak, Hosni, 209
MuCEM, 8, 60, 188
Muslim Brotherhood, 189
Mustafa Kemal, 78–9
My Name is Mei Shigenobu, 3–4, 14, 20, 81, 122–5, 206, 214

Naamani, Hassan, 26, 262–70
Naccache, Georges, 240
Nahla, 25
Nakba, 70–1
National Museum of Singapore, 57, 60, 206
neorealist, 162, 163, 168, 224, 232, 233
NETPAC, 63, 135
New Crusader in the Orient, 2
New Lebanese Cinema, 6, 13, 37, 39, 40, 43, 49, 51, 62, 233
New York, 131, 162

occidentalism, 53–6, 205–6
Octavian, 253
October War, 2, 22, 32
Once Upon a Time in Beirut: Story of a Star, 3, 5, 7, 11, 12, 38, 56, 63, 77, 81, 91, 99, 100, 102, 110, 133, 175, 176, 178, 181, 186, 194, 215, 254

One Dollar a Day, 3, 20, 52, 65, 67, 161, 188, 193–8, 203, 206, 212–14
One Thousand and One Nights, 164, 182
orientalism, 54–6
Ottoman Empire, 70, 76–8, 80, 236
Ozman, Melek, 61, 189, 210

Palestine, 2, 22, 70, 112, 113, 118, 145–6, 204
Palestine Liberation Organization, 21–5, 28, 82, 204, 214–15
Palestinian Women, 2, 194
Palestinians Keep Fighting, 2, 194
Pamuk, Orhan, 65, 202, 212
Paris In Love, 78
Paulikevitch, Alexandre, 61, 72, 74, 188–93, 198, 210–11
peace, 5, 63, 92, 93, 102, 104, 114, 139
Peter Pan (J. M. Barrie), 222
Phalangist, 24, 25, 26, 80, 204, 208, 251
poetic, 2, 5, 8, 10, 13, 14, 20, 26, 40, 41, 60, 78, 89, 99, 100, 143, 145, 154, 171, 204, 206, 212, 222, 230, 248, 251, 252, 255, 259
poetry, 7, 8, 14, 83, 88, 114, 115, 118, 136, 143, 145, 149–50, 154, 159, 163–5, 172, 177, 182, 202
politics, 32, 56, 61, 78, 91, 98, 198
pop music, 62, 174
Portrait of Gaddafi, 2
Portrait of Hanoi, or How to Invent Modernity, 80–1
propaganda, 23, 112, 151, 156, 251, 261
protest, 6, 32, 104, 148, 175, 191–2, 211, 244–5

Qasr Heneiné, 235, 236, 239, 240, 242
Qasr Ziadé, 239
Quarantina, 5, 20, 26
Qur'an, 191

Raad, Walid, 251, 36
Ramses II, 72
Rasse, Laurence, 57
reconstruction, 4–5, 35, 49, 58, 62, 67, 77, 81, 91, 97, 207, 240, 245, 249–50, 252–3, 258
refugee camps, 2, 3, 23, 26, 45, 188, 251
refugees, 2, 3, 4, 14, 20, 65–6, 92, 93, 104, 112, 114, 121, 188, 194–8, 201, 204, 212–13, 236, 239
Rejection Front (The), 2
religion, 4, 23, 54, 72, 74–5, 90, 135, 147, 152, 157, 174, 216
reportage, 7, 13, 21, 40, 89, 143–5, 154–5, 157, 175
repression, 7, 32, 155
resistance, 6, 11, 14, 21, 23, 29, 30, 34, 52, 63, 81–2, 93–4, 126, 137–8, 146, 148, 186, 193, 255, 261
Resnais, Alain (*Hiroshima Mon Amour*, 1959), 47, 105, 243
revolution, 3, 6, 15, 32, 61, 70, 78, 82, 88, 119, 143–58, 174, 189, 209–12, 245
revolutionary, 32, 93, 120, 143–5, 157
Reyad, Aida, 205
Riché, Abu, 250
Rimbaud, Arthur, 253
Rivette, Jacques, 249
Robert-Gonçalves, Mickaël, 63
Rossellini, Roberto (*Germany Year Zero*, 1948), 41, 232–3
ruins, 29, 41–2, 44, 45, 47, 48, 56, 58, 70, 77, 89, 94, 98, 99, 108, 194, 231, 242, 249, 251, 255, 260

Sahara, 8–10, 25, 27, 72, 149, 155, 161, 194
Sahara is Not for Sale (The), 6, 10, 27, 72, 143–4, 147, 149, 155, 194, 203
Salem, Yara, 245

Salwa, The Turk, 80
Sandra Bsaibes, 236
Schlöndorff, Volker, 28, 237–9
Schrader, Paul, 161–2
Scorsese, Martin, 161
Sense, Icons & Sensitivity, 10, 52–6, 59–60, 62, 67, 73, 205–6
Sheik Imam, 32
Shigenobu, 3–4, 14, 20, 81–2, 112, 115, 117, 119, 122–3, 125, 206, 214–16
Shigenobu: Mother and Daughter, 3, 82
Ship of Exile (The), 2, 30–1, 204
siege, 3, 4, 21, 25, 29–30, 82, 93–5, 114, 116, 145, 154, 204, 242–4
Siwi, Adel, 61, 73, 189, 209
Soft Architecture, 53–6
Souk Okaz, 208
South Lebanon, 5, 23, 43, 93, 239
South Lebanon, History of a Sieged Village, 2
Stocklin, Jörg, 24
Strange Games and Bridges, 3, 5, 7–8, 52, 57–60, 62, 67, 203, 206–8, 212
subaltern, 203
sufi, 7, 170
Sufism, 113, 163–5, 170, 182, 186
Sundance Film Festival, 53, 159, 175
Sursock Museum, 235, 243
Syria, 2–4, 14, 20, 65–6, 80, 103, 128, 161, 188, 194–8, 212–13, 239

Tabbara, Lina, 25
Tahrir Square protests (2011), 192
Taif Agreement, 4, 97, 98
Tamarind, 185
Taxi Driver, 161
Tel al-Zaatar massacre (1976), 251
television / TV, 1, 2, 13, 22, 25, 26–7, 29, 34, 47, 57, 74–5, 82, 89, 104, 109, 119, 130, 136, 143–7, 149, 154–8, 162, 183, 185, 194, 206, 215, 247

Témoignage, 70, 74–5, 78, 80, 81
Temple of the Tortoise (*The*), 75–6
territory, 27, 63, 127, 129–30, 149, 156, 198, 258
testimony, 1, 4, 8, 23, 40, 51, 61, 70, 91, 107, 121, 144, 248, 252, 261
The Front of Refusal, 22, 43, 194
The Great Love, 176
The Table of Dance and Pride, 188–91, 193, 198, 210
The Table of Exigency, 189, 210
The Table of the Golden Okra, 189, 210
The Table of the Magazine on the Body, 189, 209
The Table of the Painter of the Pharaohs and the Dancers, 189, 209
The Table of Walid Aouni, the Green Mad Man, 189, 209
This Floating Object of Desire, 60, 73
threats, 5, 10, 33, 53, 76, 101, 115, 124, 159
Thwarted Loves of the East and the West (*The*), 75
Tintin (Hergé), 41, 243
Trinh T. Minh-ha, 202–4
Tueni, Nadia, 242
Turk, Hanan, 33, 163, 176
turmoil, 13, 19, 39, 90
Tyan, Michele, 176

Umm Kulthum, 184

Vesoul Asian Film Festival, 60, 74, 135
video installation, 3, 5, 14
Vietnam, 2, 4, 7, 24, 34–5, 80, 161
Vietnam, Our Love, 80
voice-over, 40–1, 87–8, 90, 94–6, 143, 147–8, 153–8, 195, 203, 243, 248, 252, 259

Wahabites, 189
Wakamatsu, Koji, 82, 112, 119, 122
War in the Orient: Egypt, 2
War Zones, 67
Wassyla Tamzali, 61, 63, 189, 210–11
Weber, Jacques, 31, 47
West Beirut, 1, 94–6, 132, 208, 240–1, 244, 250
What's Going On?, 3, 5, 8, 10, 35, 59, 61, 67, 77, 115–16, 175–7, 182–6, 202, 205, 207, 209, 248, 252, 253, 255–60
Woman Killer (*The*), 2
Worringer, Wilhelm, 227, 229

Yassine, Khouloud, 177, 182–3, 185–6, 253, 255–8

EU representative:
Easy Access System Europe
Mustamäe tee 50, 10621 Tallinn, Estonia
Gpsr.requests@easproject.com

www.ingramcontent.com/pod-product-compliance
Lightning Source LLC
Chambersburg PA
CBHW051603230426
43668CB00013B/1960